WORLD ATLAS OF ANIMALS

Alessandro Minelli-Ezio Borella

WORLD ATLAS OF ANIMALS

CRESCENT BOOKS
New York

Contents

Contributors:
Mario Bissoli
Davide Cambi
Maria Pia Mannucci
Luca Tonon

Translated from the Italian by John Gilbert
© 1987 Arnoldo Mondadori Editore S.p.A., Milan
© 1987 Arnoldo Mondadori Editore S.p.A., Milan for the English translation
This 1988 edition published by Crescent Books,
distributed by Crown Publishers, Inc., 225 Park Avenue South, New York, New York 10003
Printed and bound in Spain by Artes Graficas Toledo S.A.
D. L. TO:2124 -1987
ISBN 0-517-65360-5

h g f e d c b a

Introduction

Zoologists have so far provided names for more than one million different species of the animal kingdom, but their task is still not complete; thousands of new names are added each year to the list of animals already described and scientifically classified.

However, very few animals have a geographical distribution extending beyond the bounds of a single continent, and there are not many species which can adapt readily to different surroundings or habitats, ranging, for example, from lowland woods to rocky mountain meadows. Most animal species inhabit precisely defined geographical areas and are seen as symbols of a particular place or environment: the lion, for example, instantly calls to mind the African savanna; the giant panda the bamboo thickets of the Asiatic highlands, and the polar bear conjures up visions of the frozen wastes of the Arctic pack ice.

A few species, because they are particularly well known or representative, may therefore be seen as typifying the animal population or fauna of certain habitats in different parts of the world. This representative element can be identified in the present book, which takes us from the mountains of Europe to the regions of Antarctica and across the world's oceans, covering all the main environments where animal life is to be found.

Short entries of many of the species illustrated provide basic information, including the Latin and common names, classification, physical description and distribution, habitat and behavior. A short descriptive passage and key accompany the color plates.

Living creatures are classified according to their biological similarities and relationships, and their identification combines a number of scientific disciplines. The basis of present-day classification, far from ever being complete since new species are discovered daily, was laid down by the Swedish botanist Carl von Linné (Linnaeus) who, in 1758, introduced the system still used today, of identifying every species by two Latin names. The first refers to the genus to which it belongs, and is written with a capital letter, and the second relates to the actual species (so that the wolf, for example, is known as Canis lupus). *The use of Latin names avoids debate over common names which may differ from one language to another. Zoological classification, which has developed along the lines suggested by Linnaeus, recognizes a series of categories which, from the largest to the smallest, are: kingdom, phylum (type), class, order, family, genus and species. Only when absolutely necessary do scientists use intermediate categories such as superclass, suborder and subspecies. The subspecies, in particular, is indicated by the use of a triple name, the third of which, following the standard names of the genus and species, is that of the actual subspecies; thus the scientific name of the hooded crow is* Corvus corone cornix.

Note: in the entries sections we have not thought it necessary to mention "Phylum: Chordata" in the case of all mammals, birds, reptiles, amphibians, cartilaginous fish (class Chondrichthyes) and bony fish (Osteichthyes). Furthermore, unless otherwise stated, all sizes and colors refer to those of the male animal.

EUROPE

Seen on a large map of the whole of the Earth's surface, Europe, which forms part of the great landmass that also embraces Asia, displays many of the features of the latter continent, jagged in outline and well varied with mountain chains and rivers. Indeed, the natural landscape and the animal and plant populations (fauna and flora) of northern Europe and Asia have many characteristics in common. Broadly speaking, there is the same sequence of habitats, ranging from the frozen tundra, land of the reindeer and the wolf, and the cold forests of conifers known collectively as the taiga, to the broadleaved forests and steppes. Farther south, the vegetation tends to become more varied and complex, and differences are soon evident between the plants of Europe and those of Asia. The flora and fauna of countries bordering the Mediterranean Sea, especially the Iberian peninsula, Italy and their surrounding islands, closely resemble the animal and plant worlds of North Africa.

Cradle of ancient civilizations, and more densely populated than many other parts of the world, Europe's natural landscape shows the clear impact of human presence and activity. Over many centuries agricultural development has brought about the destruction of large tracts of forest. The damage done by the plow has been augmented by the grazing of herds and flocks; and in recent years the rate of devastation has been accelerated by the machines, and, more insidiously, the pollution of industry. Nevertheless, Europe is the home of a large and varied animal population which inhabits every possible place, from mountain meadows and bare rock slopes to coastal dunes and cliffs.

The brown bear is the biggest European land animal; the mammoth, an enormous hairy elephant, migrating herds of which once roamed over much of the continent, became extinct during the Ice Age. But there are also ruminants of considerable size, such as the wisent or European bison (nowadays very rare and confined to a few wildlife reserves in Poland), the elk, the reindeer and the red deer. Felines are rare, being represented only by the lynx and the wildcat; but there are many mustelids, medium-sized carnivores, such as the badger, the otter, the polecat and the stoat. Rodents, too, are abundant, ranging from the tiny harvest mouse to the giant porcupine, and found in the most varied habitats, with the squirrel and the dormouse up in the treetops and the beaver down in the water. The most spectacular of the birds are perhaps the great raptors or birds of prey, flying either by day or by night, and the numerous waders which frequent wet zones, but these are far outnumbered by the smaller passerines. There are very few reptiles and amphibians and only a modest representation of freshwater fish. By contrast, there is an enormous variety of insects and other invertebrates which together comprise at least 100,000 different species.

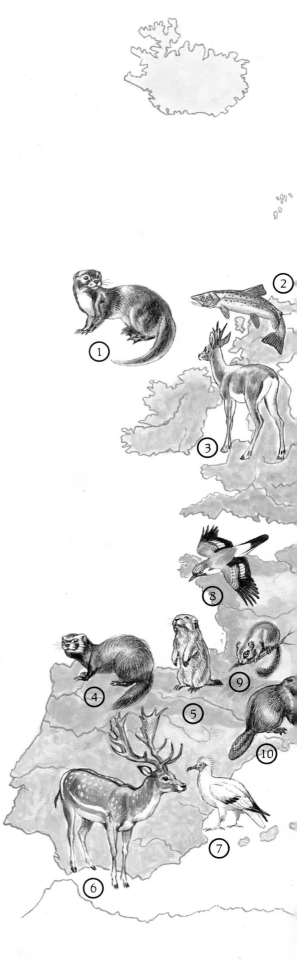

1 otter
2 salmon
3 roe deer
4 polecat
5 marmot
6 fallow deer
7 Egyptian vulture
8 jay
9 edible dormouse
10 beaver
11 greater flamingo
12 kingfisher
13 golden eagle
14 mole
15 gray heron
16 ibex
17 hedgehog
18 viper
19 wild boar
20 porcupine
21 red squirrel
22 weasel
23 griffon vulture
24 green woodpecker
25 wolf
26 pine marten
27 red deer
28 capercaillie
29 white stork
30 badger
31 shrew
32 wildcat
33 eagle owl
34 eel
35 water vole
36 brown bear
37 lynx
38 cuckoo
39 fox

Mountains

ALPINE CHOUGH
CHOUGH
Pyrrhocorax graculus
Pyrrhocorax pyrrhocorax

Classification Class: Aves; Order: Passeriformes; Family: Corvidae

Description The alpine chough is 15 in (38 cm) long, weighs 8 oz (240 g) and is black with a yellow bill and red feet. The chough is 15-16 in (38-40 cm) long, weighs 9 oz (250 g), has shinier plumage and a longer red bill, curved toward the base.

Distribution Southern Europe; the chough is also found in the British Isles. Both are found in Asia and North Africa.

Habitat High mountains and, in the case of the chough, cliffs.

Behavior Exceptional flyers, they use air currents at high altitude for spectacular aerial displays. They nest in colonies, building the nest in rock clefts. The 3-5 eggs are incubated for 17-23 days.

ALPINE IBEX
Capra ibex

Classification Class: Mammalia; Order: Artiodactyla; Family: Bovidae.

Description Total length 45-60 in (115-150 cm), height at shoulder 26-33 in (65-85 cm), weight 88-240 lb (40-110 kg). Reddish-gray above, light gray below. The males, bigger than the females, have a tuft of hair on the chin; their horns, saber-curved, grow to 36 in (90 cm) while those of the females do not exceed 15 in (38 cm).

Distribution The Alps.

Habitat Always above the treeline.

Behavior Vegetarian diet. Fearlessly climbs steep slopes. Males are solitary. During the mating season they fight one another for possession of the female. A single kid is born after a gestation of 160-175 days.

ALPINE LONGHORN
Rosalia alpina

Classification Class: Insecta; Order: Coleoptera; Family: Cerambicidae.

Description Length ½-1½ in (15-38 mm). Gray-blue with black spots.

Distribution Central and southern Europe, southern Scandinavia. Also found in the Middle East.

Habitat Beech woods and mixed woods in hills and mountains.

Behavior Active on sunny days. Feeds on plant sap. The larvae grow in old beeches.

ALPINE MARMOT
Marmota marmota

Classification Class: Mammalia; Order: Rodentia; Family: Sciuridae.

Description Total length 24-36 in (60-90 cm), the tail measuring 5-7 in (13-17 cm), height at shoulder 7 in (18 cm), weight 9-15½ lb (4-7 kg). Reddish-gray. Short feet with strong nails.

Distribution The Alps, Tatras, Pyrenees and Balkans.

Habitat Grasslands at altitudes from 6,500-9,500 ft (2,000-3,000 m).

Behavior Vegetarian diet. Lives in family groups, each occupying an underground burrow into which the animals retire for the winter to hibernate. When threatened, it emits a sharp whistle which alerts the entire colony. The female produces a litter once a year of 4-5 after a gestation of 33-35 days.

ALPINE SHREW
Sorex alpinus

Classification Class: Mammalia; Order: Insectivora; Family: Soricidae.

Description Length of head and body 2½-3 in (6-7.5 cm), tail 2½-3 in (6-7.5 cm), weight ¼-½ oz (6-10 g). Back gray-black, abdomen lighter.

Distribution High mountains.

Habitat Coniferous forests.

Behavior Extremely voracious, it devours daily a quantity of insects, spiders, millipedes, etc. equal to or above its own weight. Unsocial and territorial, it will not tolerate the presence of other shrews on its domain. The female gives birth several times a year to a litter of 5-10 after a gestation of 3-4 weeks.

ALPINE SWIFT
Apus melba

Classification Class: Aves; Order: Apodiformes; Family: Apodidae.

Description Length 8 in (21 cm), weight 3½ oz (100 g). Largest of European swifts. Chestnut above, white below with a dark breast stripe.

Distribution Southern Europe; also Asia Minor and North Africa.

Habitat Rocky places in mountains and along coasts.

Behavior Feeds exclusively on insects captured on the wing, also collecting scraps of straw and feathers with which it builds its nest in a rock cleft or under the eaves of a house. It nests in colonies. Female lays 2-3 eggs, incubating them for 20 days. It winters in tropical Africa.

APOLLO BUTTERFLY
Parnassius apollo

Classification Class: Insecta; Order: Lepidoptera; Family: Papilionidae.

Description The butterfly has whitish wings with black and red spots. Wingspan 2¼-3 in (60-75 mm). Caterpillar black and hairy with lateral red spots.

Distribution The Alps, Apennines, Pyrenees, Carpathians; also Asia.

Habitat Mountain grasslands.

Behavior Slow, heavy flight. The caterpillar lives on different species of evergreens and on stonecrop (*Sedum*).

BLACK GROUSE
Lyrurus tetrix

Classification Class: Aves; Order: Galliformes; Family: Tetraonidae.

Description Also called Blackcock. Length 16-22 in (40-55 cm), weight 2-2¾ lb (900-1,200 g). Male blue-black; female smaller, brown. Characteristic forked tail.

Distribution From the Alps to the Carpathians and north to the Arctic Circle. Also found in Siberia.

Habitat Moors, meadows, forests.

Behavior Feeds on plants and insects. The males perform a characteristic "dance" in the mating season; they gather at dawn in particular areas (leks) and each bird displays his white under-tail feathers to the females, fighting with other males for territory. The female has a single annual clutch of 7-10 eggs, which hatch after 26-27 days' incubation.

BLACK SALAMANDER
Salamandra atra

Classification Class: Amphibia; Order: Urodela; Family: Salamandridae.

Description Also known as the Alpine Salamander. Total length 6¼ in (16 cm). Completely black.

Distribution The Alps, mountains of Yugoslavia and Albania.

Habitat Woods, meadows above the treeline.

Behavior Nocturnal. It hides beneath stones and fallen trees. The female gives birth to two young which look like miniature adults.

BUZZARD
Buteo buteo

Classification Class: Aves; Order: Falconiformes; Family: Accipitridae.

Description Length 21-22 in (53-56 cm), weight 2-2¼ lb (900-1,000 g). Female larger than male. Very variable coloration; upper parts always darker than underparts.

Distribution Throughout Europe. Also found in northern Asia.

Habitat Open places near woods.

Behavior Solitary and territorial. It catches rodents, leverets (young hares) and baby rabbits, birds and reptiles, surprising them while flying at low level or lying in wait on a branch or mound of earth. It surveys its territory by gliding at high altitude. The female lays 2-3 eggs once a year, and these hatch after 33-34 days' incubation.

CAPERCAILLIE
Tetrao urogallus
Classification   Class: Aves; Order: Galliformes; Family: Tetraonidae.
Description   The male is 26-38 in (67-95 cm) long, weighing 4½-11 lb (2-5 kg), and is dark in color, metallic green on breast. The female, half the size, is brown with light and dark streaks. Young are similar.
Distribution   The Alps, Pyrenees, northern and eastern Europe. Also found in northern Asia.
Habitat   Forests with heavy underbrush.
Behavior   Feeds on plants and insects. Heavy, noisy flight. The male has a characteristic courtship position, neck erect, tail spread, wings drooping. It nests in holes in the soil. There is a single annual clutch of 6-10 eggs which hatch after an incubation period by the female alone of 26-29 days.

CHAMOIS
Rupricapra rupricapra
Classification   Class: Mammalia; Order: Artiodactyla; Family: Bovidae.
Description   Length of head and body 41-53 in (103-135 cm), tail 1-1½ in (3-4 cm), height to shoulder 30-34 in (75-85 cm), weight 62-132 lb (28-60 kg). Reddish-brown in summer, almost black in winter. The hooked horns measure about 10½ in (27 cm).
Distribution   The Alps, Balkans, Carpathians, Caucasus. One very closely related species is also found in the Pyrenees and the Apennines.
Habitat   On or near the treeline. In winter it comes down to around 2,700 ft (800 m).
Behavior   Vegetarian. Adult males are solitary, females and young gregarious. In winter, during the mating season, males fight one another to win the females. A single young is born after a gestation of about 6 months.

DIPPER
Cinclus cinclus
Classification   Class: Aves; Order: Passeriformes; Family: Cinclidae.
Description   Length 7 in (18 cm), weight 2 oz (60 g). Gray-brown above and on abdomen; throat and breast white. The short, erect tail is characteristic.
Distribution   Mountain zones throughout Europe. Also found in Asia and North Africa.
Habitat   Clear, fast-running water.

Behavior   It dives to the river bed and walks on it against the current in search of aquatic insects, crustaceans and molluscs. It nests close to streams and rivers in rock clefts and in the soil. There are two annual broods of 5 eggs incubated for 16 days. The chicks learn to swim before they can fly.

EAGLE OWL
Bubo bubo
Classification   Class: Aves; Order: Strigiformes; Family: Strigidae.
Description   Length 28 in (70 cm), weight 4½ lb (2 kg). It is the largest European nocturnal bird of prey. Plumage brown streaked with black above, lighter below. Eyes orange-red. Characteristic feathered "horns" on head.
Distribution   Rare but found almost throughout Europe. Also Asia and North Africa.
Habitat   Woods, steppes, rocky zones.
Behavior   A nocturnal predator, it feeds on mammals and birds up to the size of a hare or a capercaillie. Its call is audible from a great distance. Male and female, having chosen each other, are monogamous and stay together for life. It nests in rock cavities and holes in walls, and takes over the old nests of other raptors. There is one brood a year of 2-3 eggs, incubated for 34-36 days.

GOLDEN EAGLE
Aquila chrysaëtos
Classification   Class: Aves; Order: Falconiformes; Family: Accipitridae.
Description   Length about 33 in (82-84 cm), wingspan about 6½ ft (2 m), weight 8¼-11 lb (3.7-5 kg). One of the largest eagles in the world. Color almost uniform dark brown with golden reflections on head and neck.
Distribution   Iberian peninsula, Scandinavia, Scotland, the Alps, Apennines. Also found in northern Asia, Africa and North America.
Habitat   Rocky slopes, forests.
Behavior   Grasps prey in raking dive. Usual victims include partridges, hares, marmots and baby chamois. Builds a nest on rocks and enlarges it year after year. The female lays 2-3 eggs and incubates them for 43-44 days.

GREEN TIGER BEETLE
Cicindela campestris
Classification   Class: Insecta; Order: Coleoptera; Family: Cicindelidae.
Description   Length about ½ in (12-15 mm). Color grass-green. Exceptionally well-developed jaws. Long legs.
Distribution   Throughout Europe. Also found in Siberia and North Africa.

Habitat   Fields and sandy places.
Behavior   Preys on insects, spiders and millipedes. The larva is also carnivorous and awaits its victims hidden in a hole in the sand, at the bottom of which it also undergoes metamorphosis into an adult.

PTARMIGAN
Lagopus mutus
Classification   Class: Aves; Order: Galliformes; Family: Tetraonidae.
Description   Length 14 in (35 cm), weight 1 lb (450 g). In summer it is gray-brown with large white spots; in winter it is white with a black tail.
Distribution   The Alps, Pyrenees, northern Scandinavia, Scotland, Iceland.
Habitat   Mountain zones above the treeline, tundra.
Behavior   Almost totally vegetarian. Nests in a hollow in the ground hidden by low vegetation. The female lays 6-9 eggs which hatch after 22-23 days' incubation.

RAVEN
Corvus corax
Classification   Class: Aves; Order: Passeriformes; Family: Corvidae.
Description   Length 25 in (64 cm), weight 2¾ lb (1,250 g). It is the largest European crow. Black with metallic tints.
Distribution   Throughout Europe. Also found in northern regions of Asia and Africa.
Habitat   Rocky mountain zones, coasts and steppes.
Behavior   It even attacks hares but will not turn down carrion. Acrobatic flyer. The male and female mate for life. One annual brood of 4-6 eggs incubated for 20-21 days.

RETICULATED GROUND BEETLE
Carabus cancellatus
Classification   Class: Insecta; Order: Coleoptera; Family: Carabidae.
Description   Length ½-1 in (12-27 mm). Copper coloration. Legs long, suitable for running.
Distribution   Throughout Europe except Mediterranean area. Also found in Siberia.
Habitat   Fields and grasslands.
Behavior   Adults and larvae are nocturnal predators; they feed on insects, snails and worms. The female lays eggs in the ground, where metamorphosis into an adult also occurs.

SNOW FINCH
Montifringilla nivalis
Classification   Class: Aves; Order: Passeriformes; Family: Ploceidae.
Description   Length 7 in (18 cm), weight 1½ oz (40 g). Head gray, back chestnut,

Mountains

A succession of vegetational belts leads the climber from the foot of the mountains to the summit: at the bottom are the broadleaved woods, where beech predominates; higher up are the coniferous forests, consisting mainly of fir and, higher still, larch. At even greater heights the vegetational cover is sparse, especially in the rockier zones where rhododendrons bloom and the conifers are represented principally by juniper or dwarf pine. The meadows become narrower and narrower until we reach the highest altitudes where the last vestiges of plant life – the last mosses and lichens – cling to the rock.

1	wall creeper	18	wildcat
2	weasel	19	wolf
3	viviparous lizard	20	capercaillie
4	alpine longhorn	21	varying hare
5	black grouse	22	black salamander
6	millipede	23	alpine shrew
7	reticulated ground beetle	24	dipper
8	golden ground beetle	25	alpine chough
9	centipede	26	golden eagle
10	green tiger beetle	27	alpine ibex
11	eagle owl	28	chamois
12	lynx	29	alpine swift
13	stoat	30	ptarmigan
14	snow vole	31	chough
15	snail	32	apollo butterfly
16	buzzard	33	tiger moth
17	hazel grouse	34	alpine marmot
		35	argus butterfly
		36	*Endrosa* butterfly

edge of wings and tip of tail black, the rest white.
Distribution European mountains. Also lives in Asia.
Habitat Between the treeline and area of perpetual snow.
Behavior Vegetarian. Builds nest in rock clefts but also in roof eaves, like many passerines. One or two broods a year of 4-5 eggs incubated in turn by male and female for 13-14 days.

SNOW VOLE
Microtus nivalis
Classification Class: Mammalia; Order Rodentia; Family: Cricetidae.
Description Length of head and body 4½-5½ in (11-14 cm), tail 2-3 in (5-7.5 cm). Gray-brown above, lighter below.
Distribution The Pyrenees, Alps, Apennines, Tatras.
Habitat Stony zones above the treeline.
Behavior Diurnal and vegetarian.

STOAT
Mustela erminea
Classification Class: Mammalia; Order: Carnivora; Family: Mustelidae.
Description Length of head and body 8-12 in (20-30 cm), tail 2½-5 in (6-12 cm), weight 4½-16 oz (124-450 g). Brown back, white abdomen, tip of tail black in all seasons. In winter (known as ermine) northern and alpine populations turn white.
Distribution Central and northern Europe. Also found in northern parts of Asia and North America.
Habitat Places with sufficient plants.
Behavior Solitary, diurnal hunter. It catches rabbits, hares, rodents and birds. Climbs trees. Mates in summer but the development of the embryos in the mother's body is arrested, so that the young, 5-6 per litter, are born the following spring when food is plentiful.

VARYING HARE
Lepus timidus
Classification Class: Mammalia; Order: Lagomorpha; Family: Leporidae.
Description Also called Alpine Hare. Length of head and body 18-24 in (45-60 cm), tail 2-3 in (5-8 cm), ears 2½-3 in (6-8 cm), weight 6-12 lb (2.5-5.5 kg). In summer it is brown, in winter white with black tips to the ears. The Irish variety remains dark even in winter.
Distribution The Alps, Scotland, Ireland, Scandinavia. Also found in northern Asia and North America.
Habitat Fields and mountain woods.
Behavior Vegetarian; nocturnal, mostly solitary. It digs small burrows. The female gives birth to 1-5 leverets twice a year after 50 days' gestation.

VIVIPAROUS LIZARD
Lacerta vivipara
Classification Class: Reptilia; Order: Squamata; Family: Lacertidae.
Description Also called Common Lizard. Length of body 2½ in (6.5 cm); the tail may be even double this length. Brown, gray or green with stripes above; white, yellow, orange or red with spots below. The young are almost black.
Distribution Throughout Europe except Mediterranean area. In the Alps up to 6,500 ft (3,000 m).
Habitat Grasslands, marshes, outskirts of woods.
Behavior The female does not lay eggs but gives birth to completely formed young.

WALL CREEPER
Tichodroma muraria
Classification Class: Aves; Order: Passeriformes; Family: Sittidae.
Description Length 7 in (17 cm), weight ¾ oz (20 g). Unmistakable thanks to crimson wings with white spots at edges. Thin bill, slightly curved toward base.
Distribution The Alps, Pyrenees, northern Apennines, Carpathians, Balkans. Also found in the Himalayas and China.
Habitat Projecting rock walls.
Behavior It feeds mainly on insects in flight. Climbs rocks, continually opening and closing wings. Builds a nest in rock clefts. Female lays 4-5 eggs once a year, incubating them for 18-19 days.

WEASEL
Mustela nivalis
Classification Class: Mammalia; Order: Carnivora; Family: Mustelidae.
Description Length of head and body 7-9 in (18-23 cm), tail 2-3 in (5-7 cm), weight 1¾-4½ oz (45-130 g). This is the smallest European carnivore. The male is bigger than the female. Brown on back, white on abdomen. Only the northern populations turn white in winter.
Distribution Throughout Europe except Ireland and Iceland. Also found in northern parts of Asia, Africa and North America.
Habitat Wherever there is minimal plant cover.
Behavior Despite its small size it can kill a rabbit. As a rule, however, it catches small rodents, following them into their underground burrows. Litters of 4-6 are produced once or twice a year, after 34-37 days' gestation.

WILDCAT
Felis sylvestris
Classification Class: Mammalia; Order: Carnivora; Family: Felidae.

Description Length of head and body 20-32 in (50-80 cm), tail 11-14 in (28-35 cm), weight 6½-13 lb (3-6 kg). Brown with black stripes. Looks like a large domestic cat, of which it was probably the ancestor, and with which it often cross-breeds.
Distribution Scotland, central, eastern and southern Europe. Also lives in Africa and western Asia.
Habitat Woods and thickets.
Behavior A solitary and nocturnal hunter, it captures its prey by furtively tracking it. It attacks rabbits, rodents, birds, amphibians and fish. Its call resembles that of a domestic cat, but unlike the latter it does not toy with live prey and does not bury its own excrement. The female gives birth to 3-6 kittens after 68 days' gestation.

WOLF
Canis lupus
Classification Class: Mammalia; Order: Carnivora; Family: Canidae.
Description Length of head and body 40-60 in (100-150 cm), tail 12-20 in (31-51 cm), height to shoulder 26-32 in (66-81 cm), weight 25-175 lb (12-80 kg). Males bigger than females. Color varies from black to white according to place. It is the ancestor of the domestic dog.
Distribution Eastern Europe. Small and isolated populations survive in Spain and Italy. It also lives in Asia and North America.
Habitat Forests and tundra.
Behavior Social animal whose efficiency in hunting large herbivores (red deer, elk, caribou, musk ox, etc.) is due to the subdivision of tasks among the members of a pack, within which there is great cohesion. Individuals communicate with each other by means of their characteristic howls. Male and female work together in rearing the 2-3 cubs, which are born after a gestation of 61-63 days.

Woods

ASP VIPER
Vipera aspis

Classification Class: Reptilia; Order: Squamata; Suborder: Ophidia; Family: Viperidae.

Description Length 24-30 in (60-75 cm). There is a characteristic dark zigzag line along the back, the tip of the snout is upturned, the tail is short, the head is flat and triangular, the pupils are vertical. It is poisonous. The fangs, linked to the venom-producing glands, are mobile; the snake raises them when it strikes and then immediately folds them back against the palate.

Distribution Central and western Europe except for almost the whole Iberian peninsula.

Habitat Open, dry slopes.

Behavior It feeds mainly on small mammals, biting them and letting them go; later, thanks to its ability to follow the scent track, the viper finds them dead, killed by the poison. The female does not lay eggs but gives birth to up to 20 live young. In winter it goes into hibernation, often in a group. It is not aggressive to humans but will bite if provoked. The bite is seldom fatal.

BADGER
Meles meles

Classification Class: Mammalia; Order: Carnivora; Family: Mustelidae.

Description Length of head and body 26-32 in (67-80 cm), height to shoulder 12 in (30 cm), weight 22-48 lb (10-22 kg). Gray above, black below; head striped black and white.

Distribution Throughout Europe. Also found in Asia.

Habitat Mountain woods and grasslands.

Behavior It feeds on plants, carrion, worms, snails, insects, rodents and birds. Nocturnal. It lives in a burrow, which may be occupied by more than one individual, comprising a system of underground passages with many openings at the surface. It does not hibernate. The 3-5 cubs are born after a gestation of about 2 months.

BEECH MARTEN
Martes foina

Classification Class: Mammalia; Order: Carnivora; Family: Mustelidae.

Description Length of head and body 16-20 in (40-52 cm), tail 9-11 in (22-28 cm), height to shoulder 5 in (12 cm), weight 3 lb (1.3 kg). Brown with white spot on throat.

Distribution Central and southern Europe. Also found in Asia.

Habitat Mainly forests.

Behavior It captures rodents and birds, often frequenting built-up areas, and ventures into farms and rural smallholdings to hunt mice and poultry. Solitary and nocturnal. One annual litter of 2-4 young after gestation of 8-9 months.

BROWN BEAR
Ursus arctos

Classification Class: Mammalia; Order: Carnivora; Family: Ursidae.

Description Total length 6½-10 ft (2-3 m), height to shoulder 3-4 ft (90-120 cm), weight 330-1,720 lb (150-780 kg). Color variable from brownish-black to light yellow and silver.

Distribution Over much of Europe it is reduced to small, isolated populations; still numerous in Scandinavia and European Russia, the Carpathians and Balkans. Also found in North America (as well as two enormous local species, the Grizzly and the Kodiak) and in northern Asia.

Habitat Woods and tundra.

Behavior It is omnivorous, feeding both on plant and animal substances. In fall, prior to hibernation, it eats vast quantities of berries and acorns; in spring, when it awakes, it also attacks large herbivores, sometimes domestic species. Solitary, territorial and nocturnal. Excellent climber. The 1-3 cubs are born after 6-9 months.

COAL TIT, MARSH TIT, WILLOW TIT, CRESTED TIT
Parus ater, P. palustris, P. montanus, P. cristatus

Classification Class: Aves; Order: Passeriformes; Family: Paridae.

Description Length 4¼-4½ in (10.5-11 cm), weight about ¼ oz (8-11 g). Colors drab, darker above. Characteristic chubby appearance.

Distribution Widespread throughout Europe.

Habitat Woods and thickets.

Behavior They feed on insects and seeds and have a characteristic habit of hanging upside-down from branches. Nest in tree cavities. The female lays 6-7 eggs once or twice a year, which hatch after 13-15 days' incubation.

DARK GREEN RACER
Coluber viridiflavus

Classification Class: Reptilia; Order: Squamata; Suborder: Ophidia; Family: Colubridae.

Description Length 5-7 ft (1.5-2 m). Color basically yellow-green. Round pupils, long tail.

Distribution Southwest Europe except the Iberian peninsula.

Habitat Fringes of forests, sunny slopes, ruins.

Behavior Agile and very swift, it captures lizards, vipers, birds and small mammals. It is highly aggressive and prone to bite, but is in fact quite innocuous. Diurnal, and terrestrial. The female lays between 5-15 eggs.

EDIBLE DORMOUSE
Glis glis

Classification Class: Mammalia; Order: Rodentia; Family: Gliridae.

Description Length of head and body 5-7½ in (13-19 cm), tail 4½-6 in (11-15 cm), weight 3-4 oz (80-120 g). Gray above, darker below.

Distribution Widely found in Europe. Also found in Asia Minor.

Habitat Broadleaved woods with sparse underbrush.

Behavior Vegetarian, arboreal and nocturnal. Hibernates from October to April in a nest made in a tree hollow. The female gives birth to 3-5 young each year after a gestation of 30 days.

GARDEN DORMOUSE
Eliomys quercinus

Classification Class: Mammalia; Order: Rodentia; Family: Gliridae.

Description Length of head and body 4-7 in (10-17 cm), tail 3½-5 in (9-12 cm). Yellowish-brown above, white below; dark spots on head, forelimbs, flanks and tail which ends in a white tuft.

Distribution Throughout Europe except Britain, Iceland, Scandinavia and the Netherlands. Also lives in North Africa.

Habitat Broadleaved and coniferous woods.

Behavior Apart from plants, it feeds on insects, snails, eggs and fledglings, and small rodents. Nocturnal. Frequents trees less than other Gliridae. Hibernates from October to April. Nests in tree cavities, where the female gives birth to 5-6 young sometimes twice a year.

Note The Alpine Dormouse (*Dryomis nitedula*) and the Common or Hazel Dormouse (*Muscardinus avellanarius*) are two Gliridae which live in the same habitat as the Garden Dormouse, which they resemble in size and behavior.

JAY
Garrulus glandarius

Classification Class: Aves; Order: Passeriformes; Family: Corfidae.

Description Length 13½ in (34 cm), weight 6 oz (170 g). Pinkish-brown with

Woods

The woods of Europe boast relatively few species of trees and of those that do exist, one species often tends by far to dominate the others, conferring a typical aspect to the landscape, as happens in woods of fir and beech. As a rule the composition of woods in more southerly regions and at lower altitudes is more varied, dominated in general by oaks, often accompanied by ash, hornbeam, lime and a number of conifers.

1	red squirrel	16	jay
2	badger	17	red deer
3	edible dormouse	18	nutcracker
4	coal tit	19	*Strangalia* beetle
5	brown bear	20	common dormouse
6	asp viper	21	dark green racer
7	red crossbill	22	roe deer
8	crested tit	23	alpine accentor
9	pine marten	24	alpine dormouse
10	willow tit	25	stag beetle
11	marsh tit	26	garden dormouse
12	polecat	27	carpenter's longhorn
13	red ants' nest	28	printer beetle
14	beech marten	29	wood-wasp
15	bullfinch	30	wood-wasp larva

black wings and tail; characteristic tuft of feathers on head and blue spot, streaked with black, on wings.
Distribution Throughout Europe. Also lives in Asia and North Africa.
Habitat Woods and parks.
Behavior It feeds on berries, acorns, nuts, eggs and fledglings of other birds, and insects. Plant food is stored for the winter. Imitates with extraordinary skill the voices of other birds as well as noises of various kinds. In a nest in a tree or a shrub the female lays 5-6 eggs, which hatch after an incubation of 16-17 days.
Note Another member of the Corvidae widely found in mountain and lowland forests is the Nutcracker (*Nucifraga caryocatactes*); it is 12½ in (32 cm) long, weighs 7 oz (200 g) and is dark brown with white specks, feeding mainly on nuts, acorns and pine cones.

PINE MARTEN
Martes martes
Classification Class: Mammalia; Order: Carnivora; Family: Mustelidae.
Description Length of head and body 16½-21 in (42-53 cm), tail 9-10½ in (22-27 cm), height to shoulder 6 in (15 cm), weight 2¼-5½ lb (1-2.5 kg). Brown with yellow spot on throat.
Distribution Almost all of Europe except for extreme southwest and southeast.
Habitat Coniferous, mixed broadleaved woods.
Behavior Fierce hunter of squirrels and dormice, pursuing them with great speed into trees. Solitary at dusk and by night. Usually burrows in a tree hollow or rock cleft. The female gives birth once a year to 3-4 young after a gestation of 8-9 months.

POLECAT
Mustela putorius
Classification Class: Mammalia; Order: Carnivora; Family: Mustelidae.
Description Length of head and body 12-18 in (31-45cm), tail 5-8 in (12-19 cm), weight 1-4½ lb (0.5-2 kg). Dark brown with white areas on head.
Distribution Much of Europe except northern Scandinavia, Iceland and Ireland.
Habitat Woods, river banks and swamps.
Behavior It feeds on rodents, rabbits, birds, amphibians, worms and insects. Solitary and nocturnal. When frightened or when marking territory, certain glands located at the sides of the anal opening secrete a substance which smells strongly of musk; the intensity of this odor distinguishes the polecat from other European mustelids, which possess the same glands. The female gives birth to 4-6 young after a gestation of 6 weeks.

PRINTER BEETLE
Ips typographicus
Classification Class: Insecta; Order: Coleoptera; Family: Ipidae.
Description Length about ¼ in (4.2-5.5 mm). Color dark brown.
Distribution Throughout Europe.
Habitat Coniferous forests.
Behavior It feeds on plant tissues with a preference for fir. As a rule it attacks old trees, digging characteristic tunnels. The larvae also dig, causing considerable damage.
Note The larvae of the Carpenter's Longhorn (*Acanthocinus aedilis*) also dig tunnels; this is a beetle with very long antennae, living in the same habitat.

RED CROSSBILL
Loxia curvirostra
Classification Class: Aves; Order: Passeriformes; Family: Fringillidae.
Description Length 7 in (17 cm), weight about 1½ oz (40-45 g). Adult male brick-red with brown wings, female gray-green. The tips of the two parts of the bill are crossed.
Distribution Throughout Europe but fragmentary. Also found in Asia and North America.
Habitat Woods of Norway spruce.
Behavior It feeds almost exclusively on conifer (pine) seeds which it extracts from the cones with its perfectly adapted bill. When pine seeds are abundant it will nest even in winter. There are two broods a year of 3-4 eggs, incubated for 12-16 days.

RED DEER
Cervus elaphus
Classification Class: Mammalia; Order: Artiodactyla; Family: Cervidae.
Description Length of head and body 8 ft (2.5 m), tail 5-6 in (12-15 cm), height to shoulder 4-5 ft (1.2-1.5 m), weight 220-750 lb (100-340 kg). Reddish-brown in summer, gray-brown in winter. The male is bigger than the female, which has no antlers. The antlers of the adult male are over 3 ft (1 m) long; they branch in characteristic fashion, are shed and regrow each year from March to July.
Distribution Throughout Europe except Iceland and northern Scandinavia. Also found in Asia and North Africa.
Habitat Broadleaved woods, moors and mountain meadows.
Behavior Herbivorous and gregarious. Males and females form separate herds. Only in the fall, the mating season, do the males join the females and fight with one another to gain the most territory and win the greatest possible number of partners. A single fawn is born each year after a gestation of 225-262 days.

RED SQUIRREL
Sciurus vulgaris
Classification Class: Mammalia; Order: Rodentia; Family: Sciuridae.
Description Length of head and body 7-10 in (18-25 cm), tail 5½-8 in (14-20 cm), weight 9-17 oz (250-480 g). Reddish-brown above, white below; in winter it turns darker. Long plumed and hairy tufts on ears.
Distribution Throughout Europe. Also found in Asia.
Habitat Mountain and lowland woods.
Behavior It eats seeds, shoots and fungi, storing food for the winter, when it does not hibernate. It moves through the trees with remarkable agility. In the spherical nest the female gives birth to 2-4 young each year after a gestation of 38 days.

ROE DEER
Capreolus capreolus
Classification Class: Mammalia; Order: Artiodactyla; Family: Cervidae.
Description Length of head and body 4¼ ft (1.3 m), tail about 1 in (2-4 cm), height to shoulder 30 in (75 cm), weight 33-110 lb (15-50 kg). Reddish-brown in summer, grayish in winter. The antlers (only in males) measure up to 9 in (23 cm); they are shed in November-December and regrow the following spring.
Distribution Throughout Europe except for the far north. Also found in Asia.
Habitat Woods with clearings.
Behavior Browses on shrubs and leaves. Solitary in summer, gregarious in winter. Active at dusk and by night. During the mating season, in July-August, the males mark their territory with odorous secretions and scrape the trunks of trees with their antlers. Each year 1-2 fawns are born after a gestation of about 5 months.

STAG BEETLE
Lucanus cervus
Classification Class: Insecta; Order: Coleoptera; Family: Lucanidae.
Description Length of male 3 in (7.5 cm), female about 1½ in (3-4 cm). It is the largest European beetle. The powerful jaws of the male – those of the female are much smaller – are valuable in fights for winning partners.
Distribution Much of Europe.
Habitat Broadleaved woods.
Behavior It feeds on the sap of oaks, where the females lay their eggs. The larvae, equipped with strong mandibles, dig long tunnels in the wood, where metamorphosis occurs. The adult has a very short life: 1-2 months after its appearance in June.

Fields and meadows

ALDER FROGHOPPER
Aphrophora alni
Classification Class: Insecta; Order: Homoptera; Family: Cercopidae.
Description Length ¼-½ in (8-11 mm). Greenish-brown.
Distribution Throughout Europe. Also found in Asia and North Africa.
Habitat Fields, shrubs and trees.
Behavior Agile jumper. The larvae, newly hatched from the egg, produce a foamy secretion (cuckoo-spit) in which they are bathed, thus preventing themselves from drying out and being attacked by enemies.

BARN OWL
Tyto alba
Classification Class: Aves; Order: Strigiformes; Family: Tytonidae.
Description Length 13 in (34 cm), weight 11 oz (300 g). Brown and gray above, white or reddish with dark brown spots below. The heart-shaped facial "mask" is typical.
Distribution Throughout Europe except Iceland, Scandinavia, much of European Russia and extreme southeastern regions. It is found virtually throughout the world.
Habitat Countryside immediately adjoining built-up areas.
Behavior The bird flies more silently than any other. It feeds chiefly on mice and shrews, locating them at night thanks to its exceptionally acute hearing. It nests in tree and rock cavities, on belltowers and in lofts of buildings. The female lays 4-7 eggs, incubating them for 30-34 days.

BUMBLEBEE
Bombus lucorum
Classification Class: Insecta; Order: Hymenoptera; Family: Apidae.
Description Hairy body, black with yellow stripes. The queen, namely the fertile female, is about 1 in (2-2.4 cm) long; the other members of the colony are smaller.
Distribution Throughout Europe. Also found in northern Asia.
Habitat Fields and meadows in lowlands and mountains.
Behavior It is social, living in colonies like honey bees. In the fall members of the community die, except for the fertilized females which, having hibernated, found new colonies in underground nests. It feeds on flower nectar and pollen.

COCKCHAFER
Melolontha melolontha
Classification Class: Insecta; Order: Coleoptera; Family: Scarabeidae.
Description Length about 1 in (2-3 cm). Black with reddish elytra. Males are distinguishable from females by having much bigger, fanlike antennae.
Distribution Widely found in Europe except Spain and southern Italy.
Habitat Fields, woods and gardens.
Behavior Its growth cycle lasts 2-3 years. The larvae live underground, feeding on roots and therefore causing much damage to plants. Their metamorphosis is completed in the fall, but the new adults remain in the ground until spring.

EARTHWORM
Lumbricus terrestris
Classification Class: Clitellata; Subclass: Oligochaeta; Family: Lumbricidae.
Description Length 8-10 in (20-25 cm). Cylindrical, segmented, reddish body.
Distribution Throughout Europe.
Habitat Soil containing plenty of clay.
Behavior Earthworms are enormously important to agriculture. They actually feed on soil, digesting substances of both plant and animal origin and expelling them, via the feces, as minerals. They increase the fertility of the soil by digging tunnels, dragging down dead leaves and enabling air and water to circulate. This stimulates the development of many species of bacteria, whose activities produce the nutritive mineral substances necessary to plants.

EUROPEAN MOLE
Talpa europaea
Classification Class: Mammalia; Order: Insectivora; Family: Talpidae.
Description Length of head and body 4½-7 in (11.5-17 cm), tail about 1 in (2-3.4 cm), weight 2¼-4¼ oz (65-120 g). Dark brown. Ears hidden by hair; very small eyes; very broad, bare forefeet with strong claws.
Distribution Much of Europe. Also found in Asia.
Habitat Fields and broadleaved woods.
Behavior It feeds on earthworms, insect larvae and small vertebrates. It lives almost entirely underground, each individual in its own system of tunnels which is continuously enlarged. The soil removed with the forefeet is from time to time piled up on the surface, forming distinctive molehills. The female produces a litter of 3-4 once a year.

GERMAN WASP
Vespula germanica
Classification Class: Insecta; Order: Hymenoptera; Family: Vespidae.
Description Length about ½ in (1.5 cm), yellow and black striped. Only the female has a sting, which is used for defense.
Distribution Throughout Europe.
Habitat Common practically everywhere, including towns.
Behavior It is a social insect which lives in colonies founded by a fertile female or queen. Using scraps of plant material mixed with saliva, she builds a small nest – in holes in walls, under roofs or attached to a branch – made up of little cells, in each of which she lays an egg. After the eggs hatch, the larvae are fed by the queen until they are mature, and they emerge from the cells as adult insects. The workers have the task of enlarging the nest, building new cells and feeding the larvae. The queen's task will only be to lay the eggs. The adults feed mainly on nectar and ripe fruit.

GREAT GREEN BUSH CRICKET
Tettigonia viridissima
Classification Class: Insecta; Order: Orthoptera; Family: Tettigoniidae.
Description Length 1-1¾ in (2.8-4.2 cm). Completely green. The female has a long swordlike ovipositor.
Distribution Throughout Europe. Also found in Asia Minor, Siberia and North Africa.
Habitat Fields, woods, built-up areas.
Behavior It feeds on insects and plants, being active from July to October, the period when the males give out their loud calls. The eggs, placed in the ground in the fall, hatch in spring.

HOODED CROW
Corvus corone cornix
Classification Class: Aves; Order: Passeriformes; Family: Corvidae.
Description Length 19 in (47 cm), weight 1-1¾ lb (400-800 g). Gray with black head, throat, wings and tail.
Distribution Ireland, Scotland, Scandinavia, Italy, eastern Europe.
Habitat Mountain and lowland woods, farmland, parks.
Behavior It is omnivorous. In the evening the birds assemble in communal "dormitories." It builds its nest in tall trees. The female lays 4-7 eggs, incubating them for 18-20 days. Eastern and Scandinavian populations winter in western Europe.

HOOPOE
Upupa epops
Classification Class: Aves; Order: Coraciiformes; Family: Upupidae.
Description Length 11 in (28 cm), weight 2 oz (60 g). Pinkish-brown with black and white striped wings and tail, and a crest of

Fields and meadows

Most of the plants found in the fields and meadows belong to the Gramineae (family of grasses) which, because of their inconspicuous flowers, tend to go unnoticed. On closer inspection, however, you will find the fields and meadows full, throughout the spring and summer, of various flowering species, so diverse in color. These plants include the Leguminosae, such as clover, the Umbelliferae, such as the wild carrot, and particularly the Compositae, represented by the daisies and the centauries, such as cornflowers.

1	lacewing fly	13	swallow
2	alder froghopper	14	swallowtail butterfly
3	great green bush cricket	15	crested lark
4	seven-spotted ladybird	16	jackdaw
5	aphids	17	German wasp
6	European mole	18	skipper butterfly
7	peacock butterfly	19	earthworm
8	skylark	20	barn owl
9	mole cricket	21	hoopoe
10	hooded crow	22	blue butterfly
11	bumblebee	23	ichneumon fly
12	rook	24	tawny owl
		25	cockchafer

erectile feathers on head. Long, thin bill, slightly curved at base.

Distribution Central and southern Europe. Widely found, too, in Asia and Africa.

Habitat Copses bordering fields and meadows.

Behavior It feeds on insects and their larvae. Nests for preference in tree hollows. The female lays 5-8 eggs which are incubated for 16-18 days. The fledglings defend themselves from predators by spraying on them a foul-smelling substance produced by the uropygial glands.

MOLE CRICKET
Gryllotalpa gryllotalpa

Classification Class: Insecta; Order: Orthoptera; Family: Gryllotalpidae.

Description Length 1½-2 in (3.5-5 cm). The forefeet, sturdy organs for digging, are like those of a mole.

Distribution Throughout Europe. Also found in Asia Minor and North Africa.

Habitat Fields and gardens.

Behavior It feeds on plants, insects and their larvae. From April to October it digs tunnels where the female lays and tends her eggs until the birth of the young insects, which complete their growth cycle in 2 years.

PEACOCK BUTTERFLY
Inachis io

Classification Class: Insecta; Order: Lepidoptera; Family: Nymphalidae.

Description Wingspan 2-2½ in (5-6 cm). Upper side of wings reddish-brown with black dots and a large, multicolored "eyespot" on each wing, underside gray-brown. Caterpillar black with long spines.

Distribution Throughout Euope. Also found in temperate regions of Asia.

Habitat Lowland and mountain meadows.

Behavior It may be seen on flowers from the first warm days of spring. Individuals which have hibernated die around May; their descendants are active from July and hibernate in their turn. The caterpillars feed on nettle leaves, the adults on flower nectar.

ROOK, JACKDAW
Corvus frugilegus, C. monedula

Classification Class: Aves; Order: Passeriformes; Family: Corvidae.

Description Rook: length 18 in (46 cm), weight 12-24 oz (330-670 g); black with violet tints. Jackdaw: length 13 in (33 cm), weight 8 oz (230 g); black with metallic tints and gray nape.

Distribution Rook: British Isles, western, central and eastern Europe; also found in Asia. Jackdaw: throughout Europe except for far north; also found in Asia Minor and North Africa.

Habitat Rook: cultivated land with groups of trees. Jackdaw: open terrain, rock walls, built-up areas.

Behavior Both species feed on animals and plants. They are highly social birds, nesting in colonies: the jackdaw in tree hollows, rock clefts and on tall buildings, the rook in tall trees. Both have one brood a year of 3-9 eggs, incubated for 17-20 days.

SEVEN-SPOTTED LADYBIRD
Coccinella septempunctata

Classification Class: Insecta; Order: Coleoptera; Family: Coccinellidae.

Description Length about ¼ in (5.5-8 mm). Orange with seven black spots.

Distribution Throughout Europe. Also found in Asia and North Africa.

Habitat Sunny places in plains and mountains.

Behavior It feeds mainly on aphids and scale insects, both of which cause much damage to crops and forests. The larvae enjoy the same diet and are thus also useful. The eggs are laid on leaves and the insects hibernate in colonies under stones, tufts of grass and bark.

SKYLARK
Alauda arvensis

Classification Class: Aves; Order: Passeriformes; Family: Alaudidae.

Description Length 7 in (18 cm), weight 1½ oz (40 g). Brown streaked with black above, lighter below with close black lines on breast and flanks. Large, sturdy feet with long claws, suited for running. Small crest on head, not always visible.

Distribution Throughout Europe except for the far north. Also found in central Asia.

Habitat Treeless fields and meadows.

Behavior It eats seeds, shoots and insects. It walks, jumps, and rises vertically into the air, singing almost exclusively when in flight. It builds a nest on the ground, where there may be three broods a year each consisting of 4-5 eggs, incubated for 11-14 days.

Note Similar to the Skylark is the Crested Lark (*Galerida cristata*), which belongs to the same family and lives in the same habitat, with a prominent crest of dark feathers.

SWALLOW or BARN SWALLOW
Hirundo rustica

Classification Class: Aves; Order: Passeriformes; Family: Hirundinidae.

Description Length 7½ in (19 cm), weight ¾ oz (20 g). It is black with metallic tints above, white below; forehead and throat chestnut. The forked tail is characteristic.

Distribution Throughout Europe except for the far north. Found also in Asia, North Africa and North America.

Habitat Countryside, near built-up areas.

Behavior It feeds entirely on flying insects. It builds its nest by cementing mud, straw and feathers with saliva, preferably in cowsheds and stables, barns and haylofts and uses it for many successive years. The female lays 4-7 eggs two to three times a year and incubates them for 14-16 days. It winters in Africa, south of the Sahara, and in northern regions of South America; before setting off the birds assemble in enormous flocks.

SWALLOWTAIL BUTTERFLY
Papilio machaon

Classification Class: Insecta; Order: Lepidoptera; Family: Papilionidae.

Description Wingspan 2-3 in (5-7.5 cm). Sulfur-yellow with black spots. Typical features are the extensions to the hind wings. Caterpillar green with transverse black lines speckled with red dots.

Distribution Throughout Europe except for the far north. Also found in temperate regions of Asia and North America.

Habitat Fields in lowlands and mountains.

Behavior The adult, which lives only 25-30 days, mainly visits herbaceous plants of the family Umbelliferae, on which it lays eggs. The hatched larvae feed on these plants for about 30 days, after which they transform themselves into chrysalids. Fourteen days later or, if it is late in the season, after the winter, they emerge as adults.

TAWNY OWL
Strix aluco

Classification Class: Aves; Order: Strigiformes; Family: Strigidae.

Description Length 15 in (38 cm), weight 1-1¼ lb (450-600 g). Gray or brown streaked with black. Characteristic large, rounded head without ear-tufts, dark eyes.

Distribution Much of Europe. Also found in southern and central Asia and in North America.

Habitat Woods, parks and gardens.

Behavior Nocturnal hunter, capturing small mammals, birds, amphibians and insects. Nests in tree cavities, abandoned nests of other birds, holes in buildings. The female lays 3-5 eggs which hatch after 28-30 days' incubation.

Coastal dunes and Mediterranean scrub

AZURE-WINGED MAGPIE

Cyanopica cyanus

Classification Class: Aves; Order: Passeriformes; Family: Corvidae.

Description Length 13 in (34 cm), weight 2½ oz (70 g). Tail and wings azure, head black, throat white; the rest is gray-brown.

Distribution Iberian peninsula. Also found in eastern Asia.

Habitat Pine woods, olive groves, orchards.

Behavior It feeds on insects and their larvae, olives and berries. Nests in colonies. The female lays 5-6 eggs a year.

BLACK-BELLIED SANDGROUSE

Pterocles orientalis

Classification Class: Aves; Order: Columbiformes; Family: Pteroclidae.

Description Length 14 in (35 cm), weight 13-15 oz (380-420 g). Male larger and more brightly colored than female.

Distribution Spain. Also found in North Africa and Southeast Asia.

Habitat Steppes.

Behavior Vegetarian. Gregarious outside reproductive season, when birds live in pairs. The nest is a hole in the ground, almost without cover, in which are born 2-3 chicks after 22 days' incubation. The male, in order to drink, dips himself in water, soaking his abdominal feathers, and then returns to the nest where the young quench their thirst by sucking the drops of water from his plumage.

COLLARED PRATINCOLE

Glareola pratincola

Classification Class: Aves; Order: Charadriiformes; Family: Glareolidae.

Description Length 9 in (23 cm), weight 2 oz (50 g). Brown above, lighter below; tail forked.

Distribution Southern Europe. Also found in Asia and Africa.

Habitat Steppes and stony terrain.

Behavior It feeds on insects captured on the wing. Nests in colonies. In a hole in the ground, lined with a few twigs, the female lays 2-4 eggs, incubated for 17-18 days.

DUNG BEETLE

Scarabaeus semipunctatus

Classification Class: Insecta; Order: Coleoptera; Family: Scarabaeidae.

Description Length ½-1 in (1.6-2.5 cm). Completely black.

Distribution Throughout Europe, especially in the south.

Habitat Open, sandy places, particularly near the sea.

Behavior It feeds exclusively on excrement, making it available to larvae which feed on it in their turn. The female digs an underground nest where she piles up pear-shaped heaps of dung, in each of which she lays an egg. The newborn larvae thus have a store of food which enables them to complete their growth cycle and transformation to adulthood.

EGYPTIAN VULTURE

Neophron percnopterus

Classification Class: Aves; Order: Falconiformes; Family: Accipitridae.

Description Length about 25 in (62-63 cm), weight 5 lb (2.2 kg). Smallest European vulture. White with black flight feathers. Face and throat naked, light yellow. Crest of long feathers on head. The young are brown.

Distribution Southern Europe. Also found in southern Asia and Africa.

Habitat Rocky zones, open areas close to rivers or lakes.

Behavior It feeds on carrion and waste matter. It is notable (as observed in Africa) for its ability to break open the thick shells of ostrich eggs by dropping stones on them. Nests in rock cavities. The female lays 1-3 eggs, incubated for 42 days. European populations winter in Africa.

EUROPEAN COMMON BEE-EATER

Merops apiaster

Classification Class: Aves; Order: Coraciiformes; Family: Meropidae.

Description Length 11 in (28 cm), weight about 2 oz (50-60 g). Vividly colored azure, red, yellow and green. Bill slightly curved.

Distribution Southern Europe. Also found in Asia Minor, central Asia and North Africa.

Habitat Open sunny countryside with high-banked rivers.

Behavior It feeds on insects and nests in colonies. Male and female dig a tunnel in a river bank, up to about 6 ft (2 m) long, at the end of which is the nest proper where the female lays 4-8 eggs, incubated for 20-23 days. It winters in Africa, south of the Sahara.

EYED LIZARD

Lacerta lepida

Classification Class: Reptilia; Order: Squamata; Suborder: Sauria; Family: Lacertidae.

Description Length of head and body 8 in (20 cm), plus tail which is twice that length. Largest European lizard. Green or brownish above with blue spots on flanks, yellowish below.

Distribution The Iberian peninsula, southern France, northwest Italy. Also found in northwest Africa.

Habitat Dry, bushy terrain.

Behavior It feeds on insects, fledglings, other lizards and small mammals. Excellent climber. Takes shelter in rabbit burrows, piles of stones, etc. The female usually lays 16 eggs.

FALLOW DEER

Cervus dama

Classification Class: Mammalia; Order: Artiodactyla; Family: Cervidae.

Description Length of head and body 4¼-7½ ft (1.3-2.3 m), tail 6-8 in (15-20 cm), height to shoulder 32-42 in (80-105 cm), weight 75-440 lb (32-200 kg). Spotted white in summer, unspotted and more grayish in winter. The antlers, carried only by the males, are flattened at the tips (palmate).

Distribution Originally from Mediterranean region, introduced to many parts of Europe.

Habitat Sparse woodland.

Behavior It feeds principally on the foliage of trees and shrubs. During the rutting season the male gives out his characteristic "belling," a sound between a bark and a roar. A single fawn is born after a gestation of 7-8 months.

GREEN TOAD

Bufo viridis

Classification Class: Amphibia; Order: Anura; Family: Bufonidae.

Description Length up to 4 in (10 cm). Color cream with dense green spots.

Distribution Central and southeast Europe. Also found in North Africa and Asia.

Habitat Dry, sandy places.

Behavior Insectivorous, mainly nocturnal. In built-up areas it often catches insects attracted by electric lights.

GRIFFON VULTURE

Gyps fulvus

Classification Class: Aves; Order: Falconiformes; Family: Accipitridae.

Description Length about 3 ft (1 m), weight 17 lb (7.8 kg). Light brown except for dark flight feathers and tail. Head and neck covered with very short white feathers; white collar.

Distribution Southern Europe. Also found in southern Asia and North Africa.

Habitat Steep rocky zones where it can use rising currents of warm air for support,

Coastal dunes and Mediterranean scrub

The sandy dunes support little vegetation: the loose terrain, poor in mineral substances, allows few plants to grow, but among them is marram grass, with its very long roots. Behind the dunes and the coastal pools lies the maquis, an area of bush and scrub with typical trees and shrubs such as the cork oak and other hard-leaved oaks, junipers, mastic, pistachio, myrtle and the rockrose, with its lovely roselike flowers.

1 gull
2 praying mantis
3 eyed lizard
4 white stork
5 crane
6 oystercatcher
7 Kentish plover
8 Egyptian vulture
9 Montpellier snake
10 green toad
11 dung beetle
12 collared pratincole
13 spoonbill
14 azure-winged
   magpie
15 black-bellied
   sandgrouse
16 bee-eater
17 green tiger beetle
18 griffon vulture
19 wild boar
20 hare
21 ringnecked
   pheasant
22 great bustard
23 wild rabbit
24 roller
25 fallow deer
26 cicada
27 porcupine

enabling it to glide for hours without ever beating its wings.

Behavior It feeds on carrion, searching for it in groups by circling at great heights. It nests, on its own or in colonies, in rock cavities. The female lays one egg, incubated for 47-54 days. The more northerly European populations winter in Africa.

MONTPELLIER SNAKE
Malpolon monspessulanus

Classification Class: Reptilia; Order: Squamata; Suborder: Ophidae; Family: Colubridae.

Description Length up to about 6 ft (2 m). Gray olive-green, reddish brown. Belly yellowish. Characteristic narrow head.

Distribution The Iberian peninsula, Mediterranean coasts of France, parts of Italy, Dalmatia and Greece. Also found in North Africa and Southeast Asia.

Habitat Open, dry and warm areas with shrubs.

Behavior It feeds on lizards and other snakes, small mammals and birds, killing them with a venomous bite. It poses no threat to humans. The female lays 4-12 eggs which hatch after 2 months.

PORCUPINE
Hystrix cristata

Classification Class: Mammalia; Order: Rodentia; Family: Hystricidae.

Description Length of head and body 27 in (70 cm), tail 4½-6 in (12-15 cm), height to shoulder 10 in (25 cm), weight 37-60 lb (17-27 kg). The flanks, hindquarters and tail are protected by stiff spines; the rest of the body is covered with bristles.

Distribution Central and southern Italy, Sicily.

Habitat Woods and thickets.

Behavior It feeds on roots, bulbs and bark. Nocturnal, it spends the daylight hours in underground burrows. The spines, used only for defense can inflict serious wounds. The female gives birth to 2-4 young after a gestation of about 4 months.

PRAYING MANTIS
Mantis religiosa

Classification Class: Insecta; Order: Mantoidea; Family: Mantidae.

Description Length 1½-3 in (4-7.5 cm). The female is bigger than the male. Usually green, it may nevertheless be yellowish-gray. The forelegs are designed for seizing and grasping prey.

Distribution Southern Europe. Also found in Asia and Africa.

Habitat Grassy, sunny places with plenty of bushes.

Behavior Active by day, it feeds on insects, seizing them by striking out swiftly with the forelegs. Its color makes it practically invisible among the vegetation, enabling it to surprise its victim. The eggs survive the winter protected by a case (the ootheca), produced by the female and consisting of a spongy substance.

RINGNECKED PHEASANT
Phasianus colchicus

Classification Class: Aves; Order: Galliformes; Family: Phasianidae.

Description Length 24-32 in (60-80 cm), weight 3 lb (1.4 kg). The male is bigger and more brightly colored than the female, which is gray-brown with dark spots.

Distribution Originally from Asia, introduced to Europe.

Habitat Cultivated areas, copses, reed thickets.

Behavior Feeds on plants, snails, earthworms and insects. During the breeding season each male marks out his territory (lek) into which only the females can enter. In the nest, constructed on the ground in tall grass, are laid 8-12 eggs which hatch after an incubation of 23-24 days.

ROLLER
Coracias garrulus

Classification Class: Aves; Order: Coraciiformes; Family: Coraciidae.

Description Length 12 in (30 cm), weight 5 oz (140 g). Back brown; head, tail and underparts blue.

Distribution Southern and eastern Europe. Also lives in Asia Minor, central Asia and North Africa.

Habitat Warm, dry grasslands studded with groups of trees.

Behavior It feeds on insects, reptiles and small mammals, taken on the ground, usually without perching. It nests in tree hollows or in mounds of clay or sand. There is one brood a year of 6-7 eggs which are incubated for 18-19 days. European populations migrate in winter to the savannas of East Africa.

WHITE STORK
Ciconia ciconia

Classification Class: Aves; Order: Ciconiiformes; Family: Ciconiidae.

Description Length 4 ft (1.2 m), weight 8 lb (3.5 kg). White with black flight feathers; bill and legs coral-red.

Distribution Spain and Portugal, central and eastern Europe. Also found in central and eastern Asia Minor.

Habitat Watery zones.

Behavior It feeds on frogs, fish, reptiles, small mammals and insects. Nesting on its own or in colonies, it builds its enormous nest in trees or on rooftops and uses it for many successive years. The bird has a characteristic manner of clacking the two sections of its beak and at the same time retracting its head so that it rests on its back. One annual brood of 3-7 eggs is incubated for 33-34 days.

WILD BOAR
Sus scrofa

Classification Class: Mammalia; Order: Artiodactyla; Family: Suidae.

Description Length of head and body 6 ft (1.8 m), tail 10-16 in (25-40 cm), height to shoulder 22-44 in (55-110 cm), weight 110-770 lb (50-350 kg). The male is larger than the female and has prominent tusks. Grayish-brown bristly hair. The young have striped coats. It is the ancestor of the domestic pig.

Distribution Large parts of Europe except for England, Ireland, Iceland and Scandinavia. Also found in temperate and tropical Asia and North Africa.

Habitat Deciduous forests, Mediterranean scrubland, swamps.

Behavior Its principal food consists of bulbs, tubers, acorns and beechnuts. Except during the winter breeding season, males and females live apart. Prevalently nocturnal. After a gestation of 4-5 months, the female gives birth to 12 piglets, which are capable of following her about after a few days.

WILD RABBIT
Oryctolagus cuniculus

Classification Class: Mammalia; Order: Lagomorpha; Family: Leporidae.

Description Length of head and body 13-18 in (34-45 cm), tail 1½-3 in (4-8 cm), ears 2½-3 in (7-8 cm), weight 2-4½ lb (1-2 kg). Generally gray with reddish tints on back, lighter below. Smaller than the Hare, with shorter ears and legs.

Distribution Throughout Europe except for eastern and northern regions. Also found in North Africa and has been introduced to Australia, South America and elsewhere.

Habitat Grassy zones with trees and rocks.

Behavior It eats grass, bulbs and bark. Colonial, it digs deep communal burrows. A silent animal, it sounds the alarm by beating the ground with its hind feet. The female has 3-6 litters a year, producing 4-12 young after a gestation of 30-40 days.

Watery regions

ATLANTIC SALMON, EUROPEAN BROWN TROUT, ARCTIC CHAR
Salmo salar, Salmo trutta, Salvelinus alpinus

Classification Class: Osteichthyes; Order: Salmoniformes; Family: Salmonidae.

Description Salmon: length up to 4-5 ft (1.2-1.5 m), weight 45-110 lb (20-50 kg); greenish on back, silver on flanks (pink in breeding season); during the breeding season the male's lower jaw takes on a hooked shape. Trout: length up to 5 ft (1.5 m), weight 110 lb (50 kg); back dark, flanks yellowish with red and black spots. Char: length up to 32 in (80 cm), weight 18-22 lb (8-10 kg); back greenish, flanks silver with bluish reflections and red, yellow or blue spots, belly orange-red. There are three forms of trout, all differing in appearance and behavior: the sea trout, the lake trout and the mountain trout.

Distribution The salmon lives in the Atlantic Ocean, the North Sea, the Baltic Sea and the rivers flowing into these seas, from northern Spain to Scandinavia: it is also found in eastern North America. The sea trout has much the same distribution as the Atlantic salmon, while the lake and mountain trout are widely represented in Europe. The Arctic char is found in the Alps and in northern Europe; it is also found in Siberia, Greenland and North America.

Habitat Clear, cold and well oxygenated fresh-water streams and rivers, large cold lakes, sea.

Behavior The salmon is born in fresh water and remains there for 1-5 years feeding on insect larvae and worms. It then swims down to the sea, where it behaves as a predator, capturing herrings, sardines, etc., and stays there for 1-4 years; it then returns to the same river where it was born in order to breed. Having reproduced, most of these salmon die. The sea trout, lake trout and Arctic char breed in substantially the same manner as the salmon, while the mountain trout and certain nonmigratory varieties of char never leave fresh water.

Note An exclusive fresh-water species is the Grayling *(Thymallus thymallus)*, a member of the salmon family up to 24 in (60 cm) in length, weighing 4½-6½ lb (2-3 kg), which lives in the fresh, clear waters of rivers in central and northern Europe and northern Italy.

AVOCET
Recurvirostra avosetta

Classification Class: Aves; Order: Charadriiformes; Family: Recurvirostridae.

Description Length 18 in (44 cm), weight 12½ oz (350 g). Black and white. Upward-curved bill.

Distribution Very fragmentary around coasts, especially the Mediterranean and northern Adriatic. Also found in Asia and Africa.

Habitat Beaches and river deltas.

Behavior It feeds on crustaceans, molluscs and insects. Nests in colonies. The 3-5 eggs are laid in a hole in the ground among low vegetation. They hatch after 22-25 days' incubation. Northern populations winter in southern Europe.

Note Unmistakable because of its exceptionally long legs, which allow it to feed in relatively deep water, the Blackwinged Stilt *(Himantopus himantopus)*, white with black wings, has much the same distribution as the avocet.

BEARDED TIT
Panurus biarmicus

Classification Class: Aves; Order: Passeriformes; Family: Muscicapidae.

Description Length 6¼ in (16 cm), weight ½ oz (14 g). Reddish-brown above, lighter below. Very long tail; the male has black "mustaches" on cheeks.

Distribution Sporadically throughout Europe. Also found in northern Asia.

Habitat Reedbeds in swamps and lakes.

Behavior It feeds on insects and their larvae, and in winter on the seeds of reeds. It builds a nest on clumps of reeds and the female lays 4-7 eggs which hatch after 12-13 days.

BLUE-GREEN DARNER
Aeschna cyanea

Classification Class: Insecta; Order: Odonata; Family: Aeschnidae.

Description Length 2½-3¼ in (6.5-8 cm), wingspan 3¾-4½ in (9-11 cm). Enormous eyes, membranous wings; abdomen black, the male's with blue and green spots, the female's with reddish-brown spots.

Habitat Throughout Europe except northern regions. Also found in southwest Asia and North Africa.

Behavior The dragonfly is a very swift-flying predator, feeding on insects. It has a life cycle of 2 years.

CADDIS FLY
Phryganea grandis

Classification Class: Insecta; Order: Trichoptera; Family: Phryganeidae.

Description It has long antennae and brownish wings covered with hairs.

Distribution Throughout Europe.

Habitat The adult, which flies, lives near water; the larva develops in water containing plenty of vegetation.

Behavior The female lays her eggs underwater. The larva, using gravel and plant fragments held together by threads of silk which it produces, builds itself a tubular case from which only its head and legs protrude. It abandons the case as soon as it is transformed into an adult.

Note The shape of the case and the material used are different for each species; *Limnephilus flavicornis*, for example, uses the small shells of water molluscs.

CHUB
Leuciscus cephalus

Classification Class: Osteichthyes; Order: Cypriniformes; Family: Cyprinidae.

Description Maximum length 24 in (60 cm), weight about 9 lb (4 kg). Silver-olive with reddish ventral fins and anal fin.

Distribution Throughout Europe. Also found in southwest Asia.

Habitat Rivers and lakes.

Behavior It feeds on insects, worms, molluscs, fish eggs and plants. The female lays 100,000-200,000 eggs, which hatch within a week.

Note Also members of the family Cyprinidae are the Bleak *(Alburnus sp.)*, which lives in slow-flowing waters, and the Gudgeon *(Gobio gobio)*, which is found in clear streams and rivers.

COYPU
Myocastor coypu

Classification Class: Mammalia; Order: Rodentia; Family: Capromyidae.

Description Also known as the Nutria. Length of head and body 17-25 in (43-63 cm), tail 12-16 in (30-40 cm), weight 15½-20 lb (7-9 kg). Coat chestnut-brown on back, brownish-black on underparts. Tail naked and cylindrical. Hind feet palmate.

Distribution Originally from South America, it was introduced into many European countries and bred for the sake of its fur (nutria). In some areas it is almost extinct in the wild.

Habitat Swamps and canals lined with thick vegetation.

Behavior Vegetarian and nocturnal. In a burrow dug in a bank or hidden in the vegetation, the female gives birth to 4-6 young, already covered in fur, after a gestation of 128-132 days.

DIVING BEETLE
Dytiscus marginalis

Classification Class: Insecta; Order: Coleoptera; Family: Dytiscidae.

Description Length 1-1½ in (2.7-3.5 cm). Color dark green. The body and mid-

Watery regions

The banks of rivers and lakes are often lined with alder and willow; closer to the water's edge there is frequently a dense cover of reeds, sedges, cattails and rushes. The enclosed waters of lakes and swamps contain an abundance of aquatic vegetation, some of which, like the water lilies, show above the surface; in running water, however, most of the species are completely submerged, as in the case of eelgrass. Streams are often empty of larger plants.

1	gray heron	25	caddisworm
2	caddis fly	26	blackwinged stilt
3	water measurer	27	Montagu's harrier
4	gray water scorpion	28	Arctic char
5	chub	29	Atlantic salmon
6	greater flamingo	30	trout
7	water rail	31	lamprey
8	whirligig beetle	32	beaver
9	water boatman	33	marsh frog
10	pond snail	34	perch
11	avocet	35	pike
12	great crested grebe	36	crucian carp
13	spined loach	37	bleak
14	bitterling	38	blue-green darner
15	gray heron	39	carp
16	purple heron	40	tench
17	grayling	41	grass snake
18	gudgeon	42	squacco heron
19	eel	43	bearded tit
20	water vole	44	night heron
21	mallard	45	otter
22	shad	46	coypu
23	pondskater	47	kingfisher
24	diving beetle	48	bittern

dle and hind legs, resembling paddles, are remarkably adapted to aquatic life.
Distribution Throughout Europe. Also found in Asia and North America.
Habitat Among underwater plants in stagnant ponds.
Behavior Voracious hunter of larvae, insects, worms and small fish. It lives underwater and breathes by coming to the surface 4-7 times an hour and storing air in a chamber beneath the elytra. The female lays her eggs on water plants; the larvae are also predatory and aquatic. Metamorphosis into an insect occurs on dry land, in a lump of earth.
Note Much smaller is the Whirligig Beetle *(Gyrinus substriatus)*, a swift-swimming surface beetle.

EUROPEAN BEAVER
Castor fiber
Classification Class: Mammalia; Order: Rodentia; Family: Castoridae.
Description Length of head and body 29-51 in (73-130 cm), tail 8½-12 in (21-30 cm), weight 20-70 lb (9-32 kg). The largest European rodent. Brown with black, horizontally flattened tail.
Distribution Scandinavia, European Russia, Poland, basins of the rivers Elba and Rhône. Also found in western Siberia.
Habitat Rivers and lakes surrounded by deciduous woods.
Behavior Vegetarian and largely nocturnal. It constructs dams by stemming the flow of rivers with tree trunks, cut down with its powerful incisor teeth. In these areas of calm water it builds a burrow (lodge) out of heaped branches; in the center is a nesting chamber with a dry floor, with an underwater entrance. The female gives birth to 2 young each year after a gestation of 81-98 days.

GRASS SNAKE
Natrix natrix
Classification Class: Reptilia; Order: Squamata; Suborder: Ophidae; Family: Colubridae.
Description Also called Water Snake. Length up to about 6 ft (2 m). It has a characteristic black-bordered yellow collar.
Distribution Throughout Europe. Also found in Asia and North Africa.
Habitat Wet places near water, along hedges and in meadows.
Behavior It eats frogs and toads, fish, small mammals and nestlings. If threatened it may feign death by turning on its back, tongue hanging out. It is quite harmless to humans.

GRAY HERON
Ardea cinerea
Classification Class: Aves; Order: Ciconiiformes; Family: Ardeidae.
Description Length 36 in (90 cm), weight 3½ lb (1.6 kg). The largest European heron. Gray-white with black markings.
Distribution Throughout Europe. Also found in Asia and Africa.
Habitat Fresh, brackish or salt water provided it is fordable, since the bird obtains much of its food by standing in shallow water.
Behavior It feeds on fish, amphibians, reptiles, small mammals, insects and birds. It nests in colonies on trees or among reeds. The female lays 4-5 eggs, incubating them for 25-26 days. Northern populations winter in southern Europe.
Note Other Ardeidae frequenting wet zones are the Purple Heron *(Ardea purpurea)*, the Night Heron *(Nycticorax nycticorax)*, the Squacco Heron *(Ardeola ralloides)* and the Bittern *(Botaurus stellaris)*. All feed on fish, amphibians, small mammals and nestlings.

GRAY WATER SCORPION
Nepa cinerea
Classification Class: Insecta; Order: Heteroptera; Family: Nepidae.
Description Length ½-¾ in (1.1-2.2 cm). The characteristic thin prolongation of the abdomen, like a tail, floats on the surface and enables the insect to breathe while underwater.
Distribution Much of Europe.
Habitat Stagnant or slow-flowing water with abundant vegetation.
Behavior It feeds on the larvae of flies, mosquitoes, fry, etc., seizing them with the forelegs which are transformed into pincers. Flies at night. The female lays eggs on aquatic plants.

GREAT CRESTED GREBE
Podiceps cristatus
Classification Class: Aves; Order: Podicipediformes; Family: Podicipedidae.
Description Length 23 in (58 cm), weight about 2 lb (0.9-1.1 kg). Characteristic black tufts on head and black-bordered chestnut collar.
Distribution Throughout Europe except for more northerly regions. Also found in Asia, Africa and Australia.
Habitat Lakes, ponds and swamps.
Behavior An extremely agile swimmer and diver, it feeds mainly on fish, captured underwater. The courtship parade is spectacular: male and female draw themselves upright, face each other, dive to collect grass from the bottom, re-emerge, offer each other the grass and then place themselves breast to breast. The 4 eggs hatch

after an incubation of 25-29 days in a floating nest concealed among the reeds on the bank.

GREATER FLAMINGO
Phoenicopterus ruber
Classification Class: Aves; Order: Phoenicopteriformes; Family: Phoenicopteridae.
Description Length 50 in (127 cm), weight 5½-8 lb (2.5-3.5 kg). Pinkish-white with red and black wings. The lower half of the bill is characteristically turned downward, suitable for sieving water and probing the bottom.
Distribution The Guadalquivir delta in Spain and Rhône delta in France. Also found in Asia and Africa.
Habitat Sandy beaches, lagoons and lakes, brackish coastal pools.
Behavior It feeds on minute particles of plant and animal substances, crustaceans, molluscs and insects. The nest consists of a mound of mud and a central depression where the single egg is deposited. The chick is born after 30-32 days' incubation. Adults breed in colonies. Much of the European population winters in North Africa.

KINGFISHER
Alcedo atthis
Classification Class: Aves; Order: Coraciiformes; Family: Alcedinidae.
Description Length 6½ in (16 cm), weight 1¼ oz (35 g). Blue-green with metallic tints above, chestnut below. White spots on throat and sides of neck.
Distribution Throughout Europe except for most northerly regions. Also found in many parts of Asia and North Africa.
Habitat Beside rivers and ponds.
Behavior It feeds on insects, catching them by diving suddenly into the water. The nest consists of a tunnel, dug in a river bank, which ends in a hollow for the eggs. There are two broods annually of 6-7 eggs incubated for 19-21 days.

MALLARD
Anas platyrhynchos
Classification Class: Aves; Order: Anseriformes; Family: Anatidae.
Description Length 23 in (58 cm), weight 2½ lb (1.2 kg). In spring and summer male and female are different colors, in fall and winter they are virtually alike. In courtship livery the male has a green head and white collar, the tail feathers being curled. The female is brown with black markings.
Distribution Throughout Europe. Also found in Asia and Northern America.
Habitat Ponds and lakes.
Behavior Mainly vegetarian, it nests

close to the water. The female lays 7-11 eggs which hatch after an incubation of 24-28 days. The ducklings are able to follow their mother immediately, both on land and in the water.

MARSH FROG
Rana ridibunda
Classification Class: Amphibia; Order: Anura; Family: Ranidae.
Description Length up to 6 in (15 cm). The largest European frog. Olive-green with dark spots above, lighter below.
Distribution Southwestern and eastern Europe.
Habitat Ponds, ditches and streams.
Behavior Insectivorous. Gregarious and very noisy, especially in breeding season whent it croaks day and night. It winters in the water. The female may lay up to 10,000 eggs. The larvae, or tadpoles, breathe oxygen in the water through gills. Only later are the gills replaced by lungs, and the legs appear.

MOORHEN
Gallinula chloropus
Classification Class: Aves; Order: Gruiformes; Family: Rallidae.
Description Length 13 in (33 cm), weight 11 oz (300 g). Gray and black. Bill red with yellow tip, surmounted by a red frontal plaque; wings chestnut, white under tail-coverts, green legs, short tail always in movement.
Distribution Much of Europe. Also found in other continents, but not in Oceania.
Habitat Shore vegetation of rivers, streams and ponds.
Behavior It feeds on aquatic insects, molluscs, dead fish and plants. A mediocre flyer, in order to reach the required speed for takeoff it has to use its legs, beating them against the water surface. It builds a nest in thick vegetation, sometimes on a floating platform of reeds. The 8-10 eggs hatch after an incubation of 19-22 days.
Note Two other important Rallidae have the same distribution and habitat as the Moorhen. They are the Water Rail *(Rallus aquaticus)* and the Coot *(Fulca atra).* The latter has a white frontal plaque and a white bill.

OTTER
Lutra lutra
Classification Class: Mammalia; Order: Carnivora; Family: Mustelidae.
Description Length of head and body 22-33 in (55-83 cm), tail 12-24 in (30-60 cm), weight 11-36 lb (5-16.5 kg). Color dark brown on back, lighter on abdomen and flanks. Tapering body, broad tail, flat head, short legs with palmate feet.
Distribution Throughout Europe. Also found in Asia and North Africa.
Habitat Rivers, lakes and coasts.
Behavior Fish is its favorite food but it also eats frogs, shrimp, birds and small aquatic mammals. Solitary and nocturnal. The female gives birth to 2-3 young after a gestation of about 2 months.

PERCH
Perca fluviatilis
Classification Class: Osteichthyes; Order: Perciformes; Family: Perdicae.
Description Length up to 18 in (45 cm), weight up to 6½ lb (3 kg). Back dark green, flanks greenish with dark vertical stripes which blur toward the belly.
Distribution Throughout Europe except Spain. Also found in Asia Minor and northern Asia.
Habitat Slow-flowing rivers and lakes.
Behavior A voracious predator, it feeds on crustaceans, small fish, amphibians and insect larvae. The female lays up to as many as 300,000 eggs in long gelatinous ribbons, attached to aquatic plants.

PIKE
Esox lucius
Classification Class: Osteichthyes; Order: Salmoniformes; Family: Esocidae.
Description Maximum length 5 ft (1.5 m), weight 77 lb (35 kg). Color dark, with olive spots or stripes on flanks; whitish on belly. Large mouth with teeth that curve inward so that the prey cannot escape.
Distribution Almost all of Europe. Also found in temperate Asia and northern parts of North America.
Habitat Lakes, slow-flowing rivers and brackish water.
Behavior It feeds almost exclusively on fish and can swallow prey up to one-half of its own weight. Throughout its life it is cannibalistic, devouring members of its own species. It hunts from ambush, well hidden among the vegetation. The eggs (15,000-20,000 for each kg of the female's weight) are deposited among the water plants and hatch after 10-15 days.

SPINED LOACH
Cobitis taenia
Classification Class: Osteichthyes; Order: Cypriniformes; Family: Cobitidae.
Description Maximum length 4¾ in (12 cm). Long cylindrical body, brown with dark spots on flanks, whitish on belly. Mouth surrounded by six barbels.
Distribution Much of Europe.
Habitat Bottom of large lakes and swift-flowing riverbeds.

Behavior It feeds on tiny invertebrates. Nocturnal, it spends the day at the bottom of lakes and river beds. The female lays her eggs on stones or on submerged roots.

TENCH, CARP, CRUCIAN CARP
Tinca tinca, Cyprinus carpio, Carassius carassius
Classification Class: Osteichthyes; Order: Cypriniformes; Family: Cyprinidae.
Description Tench: length up to 20 in (50 cm), weight 9-11 lb (4-5 kg); dark green with golden reflections. Carp: length up to 3ft (1 m), weight 65 lb (30 kg); greenish on back, tending to yellow on flanks. Crucian carp: length up to 18 in (45 cm), weight 7½ lb (3.5 kg); olive-green on back and flanks, whitish on belly.
Distribution Throughout Europe.
Habitat Slow or stagnant waters with muddy bottom and abundant vegetation.
Behavior They feed on larvae of flies and mosquitoes, worms, molluscs and plants. They spend the winter close to the bottom of lakes and rivers in a kind of hibernation feeding on little or nothing. The eggs are laid on aquatic plants.

WATER MEASURER
Hydrometra stagnorum
Classification Class: Insecta; Order: Heteroptera; Family: Hydrometridae.
Description Length about ½ in (9-13 mm). Sticklike body, long antennae, slender legs.
Distribution Throughout Europe except for more northerly regions. Also lives in Middle East and North Africa.
Habitat Grassy banks of streams and ponds.
Behavior It feeds on tiny dead animals. It walks or stands still on the water surface without sinking, thanks to its hairy legs.
Note The Pondskater *(Gerris gibbifer)* uses the same system of floating.

WATER VOLE
Arvicola terrestris
Classification Class: Mammalia; Order: Rodentia; Family: Cricetidae.
Description Also called Water Rat. Length of head and body 5½-7½ in (14-19 cm), tail 1½-4 in (4-10 cm). Dark brown above, whitish below.
Distribution Much of Europe except for the Iberian peninsula (excluding the Pyrenees) and southwestern France. Also found in Asia.
Habitat Lakes and slow-flowing rivers.
Behavior Vegetarian, active at dusk. It builds a burrow on the bank, covered with vegetation. The female gives birth to 4-6 young, twice or three times a year, after a gestation of 21 days.

ASIA

It is almost impossible to describe in a few words the characteristic features of the flora and fauna of Asia: this huge continent extends, in fact, from the regions of the extreme north, covered by ice for much of the year, to the hot equatorial zones of the Malacca peninsula and Indonesia, with its dense, luxuriant jungles. What is more, the boundaries of Asia with adjacent continents are not very clearly defined: it is separated from Europe only by the low mountain range of the Urals, and from Africa by the Red Sea, the shores of which are hot and sandy, harboring a fairly uniform population of animals and plants. Finally, stretching east to Australia, it breaks up to form a chain of innumerable archipelagos and islands, some of them large, like Borneo and Sumatra, others small, where the typical Asiatic flora and fauna seem to merge almost imperceptibly with the forms of animal and plant life that characterize the newest of the continents.

To the north of the high peaks of the Himalayan mountain range, however, we find many animals which closely resemble those of Europe, at least in the more westerly sectors where there are wolves and lynxes, along with wild asses and horses and two-humped camels. But farther east and southward the character of the Asiatic fauna becomes more distinctive: in the high valleys of the Himalayas there are many varieties of pheasant, the snow leopard and the extraordinary giant panda; and there are the first representatives, too, of animal species which are found abundantly in the more southerly regions of the continent, notably in India and the countries collectively known as Indochina. Indeed, the most northerly races of the tiger are as well adapted to the harsh climate of Siberia and Manchuria as the more typical southern races are to the humid heat of the jungle.

In southern Asia, therefore, we find a community of large animals which in some ways can bear comparison with that of equatorial and tropical Africa. The leopard, in fact, is found both in Asia and Africa; and in southern Asia there are elephants, rhinoceroses and big apes which are all counterparts of those in Africa; the Asiatic elephant, second largest of all existing land mammals, surpassed only by its African cousin, is joined by three species of rhinoceros, and the orang-utan, from Borneo and Sumatra, belongs to the same family as the gorilla and the chimpanzee.

Large reptiles include the extremely venomous cobra, giant pythons, crocodiles and monitors; and there are some most unlikely creatures, too, such as the flying lizard and the web-footed tree toad which can glide through the warm forest air, living alongside numerous species of every size and zoological class in the jungles of the Sunda Islands. This is a corner of the globe which contains an unusually rich variety of plants and animals, in spite of the deforestation which is proceeding at an alarming rate.

1 two-barred crossbill
2 Siberian wolf
3 snowy owl
4 reindeer
5 lynx
6 saiga
7 hamster
8 blackbuck
9 snow leopard
10 Przewalski's horse
11 Bactrian camel
12 flying squirrel

13 sika deer
14 yak
15 giant panda
16 spectacled cobra
17 gavial
18 Indian rhinoceros
19 tiger
20 golden pheasant
21 Asiatic elephant
22 black panther
23 tarsier
24 flying lemur

25 Rajah Brooke's
    birdwing
26 gibbon
27 orang-utan
28 babirusa
29 flying lizard
30 Komodo dragon

Northern forests, temperate forests, steppes, cold deserts

ASIATIC WILD ASS or KULAN
Equus hemionus
Classification Class: Mammalia; Order: Perissodactyla; Family: Equidae.
Description Length of head and body 5 ft (1.5 m), tail 24 in (60 cm), height to shoulder about 4¼ ft (1.1-1.3 m), weight 570 lb (360 kg). Color sandy above, lighter below. Ears fairly large, shaggy mane, top half of tail hairy.
Distribution Central Asia.
Habitat Steppes and deserts.
Behavior Herbivorous. It lives in small herds led by a stallion. Faster and sturdier than Przewalski's horse, it has suffered less than the latter from human encroachment but has been forced to retreat to parts of the desert which it previously avoided. The female gives birth to one foal every two years, after 12 months' gestation.

BACTRIAN CAMEL
Camelus bactrianus
Classification Class: Mammalia; Order: Artiodactyla; Family: Camelidae.
Description Length of head and body 7-11 ft (2.2-3.4 m), tail 22-30 in (55-75 cm), height (including hump) 6-7½ ft (1.9-2.3 m), weight 1,000-1,430 lb (450-650 kg). Two humps. Short dark brown coat in summer, long and woolly in winter.
Distribution Central Asia. A very small number roam wild in the more inhospitable desert zones but have been replaced almost everywhere by the domesticated camel, of which this is the ancestor and from which it can hardly be distinguished.
Habitat Deserts and steppes both in lowlands and mountains.
Behavior It feeds on grass, branches and leaves, living in small herds made up of females and young led by an adult male. "Bachelor" males live a solitary existence. The female gives birth to one colt after a gestation of 13 months.

BLACK WOODPECKER
Dryocopus martius
Classification Class: Aves; Order: Piciformes; Family: Picidae.
Description Length 18 in (45 cm), weight 10½ oz (300 g). The male is black with a red patch on top of the head; in the female the red is restricted to the nape.
Distribution Temperate Asia. It is also found in central and eastern Europe, the Alps, Pyrenees and Scandinavia.
Habitat Large mixed or coniferous forests.
Behavior In summer it feeds principally on ants, in winter on various insects and larvae which it obtains by ripping open their nests in tree trunks. It excavates its own nest in a tree cavity by repeatedly rapping its strong bill, like a pneumatic drill, against the trunk; once it abandons its nest, this hole is immediately taken over by other birds or small tree mammals. The female lays 4-5 eggs which are incubated for 12-14 days.

BOBAC
Marmota bobak
Classification Class: Mammalia; Order: Rodentia; Family: Sciuridae.
Description Also known as the Steppe Marmot. Length of head and body 19-22 in (49-57 cm), tail 4-5 in (10-13 cm), weight 9-11 lb (4-5 kg). Stocky body, short tail. Reddish-gray on back, darker on head.
Distribution Central and northern Asia. Also found in European part of the Soviet Union.
Habitat Steppes.
Behavior Feeds on herbaceous plants. It digs underground tunnels, up to 65 ft (20 m) long, provided with many entrances in front of which there are characteristic mounds of earth. Each burrow is occupied by a family group. In the fall it hibernates, after carefully barricading the tunnel entrances with stones and other materials. Mating occurs after it awakes and the female, after 40-42 days' gestation, gives birth to a litter of 5-6.

CRANE
Grus grus
Classification Class: Aves; Order: Gruiformes; Family: Gruidae.
Description Length 41-45 in (105-115 cm), weight 10½-12 lb (4.8-5.5 kg). Gray with black and white stripes on head and neck and a red patch on the top of the head.
Distribution Northern Asia. Also found in northeastern Europe.
Habitat Aquatic areas.
Behavior Feeds on plants, small vertebrates and insects, never perching on trees. During migratory flights the flocks often take on a characteristic V-shaped formation, the place in front being occupied in turn by different birds. A continuous chorus of deep trumpeting sounds accompanies these journeys. The complex courtship rituals consist of runs, leaps and bows. The nest is on the ground. The female lays 2 eggs and incubates them for 28-30 days. It winters in southern Asia, Africa and the Mediterranean basin.

DESERT FOX
Vulpes corsac
Classification Class: Mammalia; Order: Carnivora; Family: Canidae.
Description Also known as Corsac. Length of head and body 20-24 in (50-60 cm), tail 9-14 in (22-34 cm). Reddish-gray in summer, grayish-white in winter.
Distribution Central Asia. Also found in European parts of the Soviet Union.
Habitat Steppes.
Behavior Feeds on hares, rodents, reptiles, amphibians and large insects. Moving about incessantly in search of prey, it has no fixed burrow but occasionally uses those of other animals. It is ruthlessly hunted by man for its valuable fur, which in winter becomes extremely soft and thick. The vixen gives birth to 2-11 cubs after a gestation of 49-51 days.

GOOSANDER
Mergus merganser
Classification Class: Aves; Order: Anseriformes; Family: Anatidae.
Description Length 22½-26 in (57-66 cm), weight about 3¼ lb (1.4-1.5 kg). In courtship livery the male is white with a dark green head, black back and red bill and legs. The female is gray with a brown head adorned by a characteristic crest.
Distribution Temperate Asia. It is also found in northern Europe and North America.
Habitat Lakes and rivers.
Behavior Feeds mainly on fish which it seizes with its slender, toothed, sawlike bill. It prefers to nest in tree hollows. The 8-12 eggs hatch after an incubation of 32-35 days. The more northerly populations winter in the Mediterranean area.

GREAT BUSTARD
Otis tarda
Classification Class: Aves; Order: Gruiformes; Family: Otididae.
Description Length 30-40 in (76-102 cm), weight 10-25 lb (4.5-11.5 kg). The male is much larger than the female. Reddish-yellow with black bars above, white below. Head and neck gray. The male has a chestnut band on the breast and long white feathers below the bill.
Distribution Southwest and central Asia. It is also found in the Iberian peninsula and some zones of central and eastern Europe, but in increasingly precarious environmental conditions.
Habitat Wide, open grassy spaces with-

out trees or buildings.

Behavior It feeds on seeds, shoots, insects and small mammals. Despite its bulk, it flies well. Extremely timid, it finds it hard to tolerate any disturbance. During the courtship parade the male rests his head and tail on the back, displaying the white feathers under the tail and on the abdomen, swells his neck and lets his wings hang, so that at the peak of the exhibition he looks like a huge snowball. The nest is a hole dug in the ground, where the female lays 2-3 eggs, incubating them for 21-28 days.

HAZEL GROUSE
Tetrastes bonasia

Classification Class: Aves; Order: Galliformes; Family: Tetraonidae.
Description Length 14 in (36 cm), weight 14 oz (400 g). Plumage brown, blending with the bird's surroundings. The male has a tuft of feathers on the head.
Distribution Northern Asia. Also found in Europe (Scandinavia, Alps, Carpathians and Balkans).
Habitat Mountain slopes with woods that have dense underbrush.
Behavior It feeds on plants. The male courts the female by displaying his half-opened wings, fanlike tail and erect head feathers. The female lays 7-11 eggs once a year in a nest on the ground, incubating them for 22-27 days while perfectly concealed thanks to the color of her plumage.

LYNX
Lynx lynx

Classification Class: Mammalia; Order: Carnivora; Family: Felidae.
Description Also known as the European Lynx, it resembles a large cat. Length of head and body 33-43 in (85-110 cm), tail 5-7 in (12-17 cm), height to shoulder 20-30 in (50-75 cm), weight 11-64 lb (5-29 kg). Light brown with dark spots, tip of tail black, long tufts of black hair on ears. Long legs, feet thickly covered with hair.
Distribution Northern Asia. Also found in Europe (Scandinavia, eastern Europe, Iberian peninsula) and North America.
Habitat Coniferous mountain forests. In Spain it roams the delta of the Guadalquivir.
Behavior Solitary, nocturnal hunter. It often drops on to its prey from a tree. It attacks rabbits, hares, rodents, fawns of red deer and fallow deer, and birds. The female gives birth to 1-5 cubs after a gestation of 60-74 days.

MARBLED POLECAT
Vormela peregusna

Classification Class: Mammalia; Order: Carnivora; Family: Mustelidae.
Description Length of head and body 12-15 in (30-38 cm), tail 6-8 in (15-21 cm). Underparts, legs, head and tip of tail dark brown; upper parts and tail cream with wavy brown streaks; white marks on head and ears.
Distribution Central Asia. Also found in eastern Europe.
Habitat Steppes and semideserts.
Behavior It feeds on rodents, rabbits, birds, amphibians and reptiles. Although capable of digging an underground burrow, it often occupies that of its prey. It defends itself in a manner similar to that of the common polecat, spraying the intruder with a foul-smelling liquid produced by special glands and stored in sacs under the tail. The female gives birth to a litter of 4-8 young after a gestation of about 2 months.

MONGOLIAN GAZELLE
Procapra gutturosa

Classification Class: Mammalia; Order: Artiodactyla; Family: Bovidae.
Description Also called the Zeren. Length of head and body 43-45 in (1.1-1.5 m), tail 2-5 in (5-12 cm), height to shoulder 21-33 in (54-84 cm), weight 44-88 lb (20-40 kg). Color sandy above, whitish below. Horns lyre-shaped, carried only by males. During the breeding season the males develop a characteristic swelling, rather like a goiter, on the throat.
Distribution Mongolia.
Habitat Steppes and semideserts.
Behavior Herbivorous. In summer, outside the breeding season, males and females form separate herds; in winter huge mixed herds migrate to snowfree zones. There are frequent twin births.

MONTAGU'S HARRIER
Circus pygargus

Classification Class: Aves; Order: Falconiformes; Family: Accipitridae.
Description Length 17 in (43 cm), weight 10½ oz (300 g). The male is gray above, whitish striped with brown below; the female is dark brown above and light brown with dark stripes below.
Distribution Temperate Asia. It also lives in Europe and North Africa.
Habitat Dry or swampy plains.
Behavior It feeds on small mammals, birds, amphibians, reptiles and insects. Sometimes it pursues swarms of migratory locusts, of which it is particularly fond. It hunts by swooping low with slow wingbeats, then rapidly diving on its prey and seizing it with its talons. It nests on the ground or in swamp grass and the female lays 3-5 eggs, incubating them for 28-30 days. It winters in the African savannas and on the steppes of southwestern Asia.

NORTHERN THREE-TOED JERBOA
Dipus sagitta

Classification Class: Mammalia; Order: Rodentia; Family: Dipodidae.
Description Length of head and body about 6 in (15 cm), tail 10 in (25 cm), weight 2½-4 oz (70-110 g). Color sandy above, whitish below with a tuft of long black and white hairs at the tip of the tail. It is built for jumping, with hindlegs at least four times as long as forelegs. Tufts of hair on the soles of the feet prevent it from sinking in the sand. The very long tail serves to balance the body during jumps.
Distribution Central Asia.
Habitat Sandy deserts and steppes.
Behavior It feeds chiefly on seeds but also on fresh plants and insects. It does not drink, getting sufficient water from its food. As a rule it moves with slow hops, using the forelegs only for gathering food, but at the first sign of danger it bounds off with leaps up to 10 ft (3 m) in distance. It spends the winter hibernating, in burrows up to 3 ft (1 m) deep, living on fat accumulated in the summer. The female gives birth to 2-6 young after a gestation of 40-42 days.

PRZEWALSKI'S HORSE
Equus przewalskii

Classification Class: Mammalia; Order: Perissodactyla; Family: Equidae.
Description Length of head and body 7-9 ft (2.2-2.8 m), tail 36-43 in (92-111 cm), height to shoulder 4-4½ ft (1.2-1.4 m), weight 440-660 lb (200-300 kg). Reddish-brown above, whitish below; white muzzle, dark mane and tail. The short, hairy mane is characteristic.
Distribution Once abundant throughout central Asia, this wild horse very probably today only survives in zoos, even though some observers claim that it is still to be found in the Gobi Desert in Mongolia. The ease with which it reproduces in captivity leads one to hope that this ancestor of the domestic horse may soon be reintroduced to its natural habitat.
Habitat Steppes.
Behavior Herbivorous. It lives, or lived, in herds of 6-8 that are led by a stallion. It was decimated as a result of being ruthlessly hunted by man.

SABLE
Martes zibellina

Classification Class: Mammalia; Order: Carnivora; Family: Mustelidae.
Description Length of head and body 15-18 in (38-45 cm), tail 5-8 in (12-19 cm), weight 1¾-4 lb (800-1,800 g). Dark brown with lighter mark on throat. Its fur is highly prized.

Northern forests, temperate forests, steppes, cold deserts

Larch, fir, poplar and beech are among the most common trees found in the woodlands of northern Asia. Farther north there is the customary stunted plant growth of the tundra, while to the south, approaching the inhospitable plateaus of central Asia, we find an abundance of bulbous plants, such as iris and tulips, in a great variety of species.

1	sable	10	Siberian wolf
2	Ural owl	11	saiga
3	snowy owl	12	Bactrian camel
4	goosander	13	Przewalski's horse
5	lynx	14	Asiatic wild ass
6	brown bear	15	Siberian chipmunk
7	black woodpecker	16	Siberian tit
8	red squirrel	17	two-barred crossbill
9	hazel grouse	18	Siberian jay

Distribution Northern Asia, from the River Ural to the Pacific Ocean.
Habitat Forests.
Behavior It feeds principally on small mammals. Seldom climbs trees. After a gestation of 250-300 days, 3-4 young are born, in a nest covered with various materials that is usually situated in a tree hollow, a burrow or a shelter abandoned by other animals.

SAIGA
Saiga tatarica
Classification Class: Mammalia; Order: Artiodactyla; Family: Bovidae.
Description Length of head and body 3½-4½ ft (1.1-1.4 m), tail 3-5 in (8-13 cm), height to shoulder 24-32 in (60-80 cm), weight 50-88 lb (23-40 kg). Coat brownish-white in summer, uniformly whitish in winter. Characteristic is the massive head and fleshy nose similar to a small trunk. The horns are carried only by the males.
Distribution Central Asia.
Habitat Steppes.
Behavior Vegetarian. In summer it is active only at sunset, in winter throughout the day. It will eat plants refused by other herbivores as being too tough or toxic. It does not drink, as it normally gets sufficient water from its food. The large herds are continually on the move looking for fresh pastures or, in winter, attempting to escape the snow which, if too deep, can prevent their feeding. The female gives birth once a year to 2 young after a gestation of 145 days.

SIBERIAN CHIPMUNK
Eutamias sibiricus
Classification Class: Mammalia; Order: Rodentia; Family: Sciuridae.
Description Length of head and body 5-6 in (13-15 cm), tail 3¼-4 in (8-10 cm), weight about 3½ oz (100 g). Back gray with five black stripes. Hair thick, especially on tail.
Distribution Central and northern Asia.
Habitat Coniferous forests and grasslands with tree scrub.
Behavior Territorial and diurnal, it feeds on seeds, berries and insects. It hibernates for 5-6 months in its underground burrow comprising chambers, storage places and tunnels, accumulating enormous stocks of food which it eats whenever it wakes briefly from its winter sleep. It carries the food into the burrow in two cheek pouches which can contain a considerable quantity of seeds. It can climb trees. The female gives birth to 3-5 young each year after a gestation of 36-40 days.

SIBERIAN JAY
Perisoreus infaustus
Classification Class: Aves; Order: Passeriformes; Family: Corvidae.
Description Length 12 in (30 cm), weight 5½ oz (155 g). Gray-brown with brown head, flanks and part of wings tawny.
Distribution Northern Asia. Also found in Scandinavia and European part of the Soviet Union.
Habitat Coniferous forests.
Behavior It feeds on plants, insects, eggs and fledglings of other birds, and small mammals. Silent and elusive, especially in the breeding season. The sturdy and carefully built nest is cup-shaped and attached to the trunk of a conifer; in it the female lays 3-4 eggs, incubating them for a period of 18-20 days.

SIBERIAN TIT
Parus cinctus
Classification Class: Aves; Order: Passeriformes; Family: Paridae.
Description Length 5-5½ in (13-14 cm), weight about ½ oz (12-14 g). Upper parts reddish, face and underparts white. Top of head and nape brown, flanks reddish.
Distribution Northern Asia. Also found in Scandinavia and Alaska.
Habitat Birch forests.
Behavior Feeds on small insects and their larvae, spiders and seeds. It nests in holes which it digs in the decaying wood of the birch. The female lays 7-9 eggs, which hatch after 13-16 days' incubation.

SNOWY OWL
Nyctea scandiaca
Classification Class: Aves; Order: Strigiformes; Family: Strigidae.
Description Length 24 in (60 cm), weight 3½-4½ lb (1.5-2 kg). White with black bars. Eyes bright yellow.
Distribution Northern Asia. Also found in Scandinavia, Iceland, Greenland and northern parts of North America.
Habitat Tundra.
Behavior Feeds on small mammals and birds. It hunts both on the wing and from hiding, by night and day. Its most important prey, particularly in the breeding season, is the lemming, whose abundance or scarcity determines the success or failure of reproduction; when lemmings are scarce, the owl does not even mate. Its numbers therefore fluctuate in accordance with those of the lemmings. In good years the number of chicks reared by each pair, which can vary from as few as 4 to as many as 15, fills the gaps brought about in periods of hunger. It nests in a depression in the ground. The incubation of the eggs lasts 32-33 days.

TAWNY EAGLE
Aquila rapax nipalensis
Classification Class: Aves; Order: Falconiformes; Family: Accipitridae.
Description Length 26-30 in (65-77 cm), wingspan 6-7¼ ft (1.8-2.2 m), weight 7½ lb (3.5 kg). Dark brown.
Distribution Central Asia.
Habitat Deserts and steppes.
Behavior It captures small and medium-sized mammals, terrestrial birds, amphibians, reptiles and large insects, but a large part of its diet consists of carrion and waste matter. Sometimes it attacks other raptors to force them to abandon their prey. Lazy by nature, it seldom circles aloft and spends much time on the ground. It nests on the ground, in trees or among rocks; the female lays 1-3 eggs, which hatch after an incubation of 45 days. The northern populations migrate.

TWO-BARRED CROSSBILL
Loxia leucoptera
Classification Class: Aves; Order: Passeriformes; Family: Fringillidae.
Description Length 5¾ in (14.5 cm). It is smaller than the Crossbill and more brightly colored; the male is crimson, the female yellow. In flight the white wing bars show prominently.
Distribution Northern Asia. Also found in Scandinavia and North America.
Habitat Larch forests.
Behavior The crossed bill, weaker than that of the Crossbill, enables it to open only larch cones. Like all its relatives, it often hangs its head upside-down when working on a cone. It usually nests at the top of a tree. The 3-4 eggs hatch after 12-16 days' incubation.

URAL OWL
Strix uralensis
Classification Class: Aves; Order: Strigiformes; Family: Strigidae.
Description Length 24 in (60 cm), weight 1¾-2 lb (800-900 g). The male is smaller than the female. Brownish-gray with dark streaks.
Distribution Temperate Asia. Also found in Scandinavia and eastern Europe.
Habitat Lowland and mountain woods.
Behavior Nocturnal by habit, it feeds on small rodents and birds. After particularly harsh winters the resultant shortage of food prevents it from reproducing. In good years the female lays 2-4 eggs, incubated for 27-29 days. It nests in tree hollows or makes use of a nest abandoned by other birds of prey.

Mountains

BEARDED VULTURE
Gypaëtus barbatus

Classification Class: Aves; Order: Falconiformes; Family: Accipitridae.

Description Also called the Lammergeier. Length 3¼ ft (1.1-1.2 cm), wingspan about 10 ft (3 m), weight 11-15½ lb (5-6.9 kg). Back, wings and tail blackish with white streaks; head and underparts tawny with dark markings on throat and breast. The common name derives from the tuft of feathers, from the eyes to the base of the beak, which forms a kind of beard.

Distribution From the Caucasus to China. It is also found in southern Europe and much of Africa.

Habitat High mountains.

Behavior It feeds on carrion, waste matter of every kind and, above all, bones, which it cracks by dropping them from a height on to rocks below. The female lays 1-2 eggs, incubating them for about 58 days; when two chicks are born, one is immediately killed by the parents.

EARED PHEASANT
Crossoptilon crossoptilon

Classification Class: Aves; Order: Galliformes; Family: Phasianidae.

Description Length 36 in (92 cm). It has two characteristic tufts of white feathers on either side of the head; hence the common name. The two sexes are alike, although the female is smaller, darker and without spurs. The adult male has white upper and lower parts, black head and a bronze tail with metallic reflections.

Distribution Southeastern Tibet, southwestern China.

Habitat Mountain forests and neighboring open spaces.

Behavior Feeds on bulbs and roots which it digs out with its strong bill, and insects. It lives in small flocks which break up only during the breeding season. The female lays 4-7 eggs which hatch after 24 days' incubation.

Note Showy colors are also displayed by the Red-throated Pheasant *(Ithaginis cruentus)*, found from Nepal to northern China, up to the limits of the snowline in summer, at around 15,000 ft (4,500 m), and no lower than 6,000 ft (2,500 m) in winter. It feeds on shoots, seeds, berries and insects, living in small groups except in the breeding season when pairs isolate themselves.

GIANT PANDA
Ailuropoda melanoleuca

Classification Class: Mammalia; Order: Carnivora; Family: Procyonidae.

Description Length of head and body 5½ ft (1.7 m), tail 5 in (12 cm), height to shoulder 28-32 in (70-80 cm), weight 220-330 lb (100-150 kg). The male is larger than the female. It is completely white except for the ears, the surrounds of the eyes, the legs and the shoulders, all of which are black.

Distribution Mountains of southwestern China and Tibetan plateaus.

Habitat Bamboo forests between altitudes of 8,000 and 12,000 ft (2,400-3,600 m).

Behavior It feeds principally on bamboo, supplementing its diet with grass, bulbs and occasional insects and rodents. It eats in a characteristic position, seated with its back leaning against a support, holding its food with the forefeet. Solitary and territorial, it uses secretions from scent glands to mark out its territory. Although strictly protected (it is the emblem of the World Wildlife Fund), it is very rare; estimated figures of surviving animals vary from a maximum of 1,000 to a minimum of 500. A certain number are, however, found in zoos where they have even managed to reproduce. Here it has been observed that the female, although almost always giving birth to 2 young, only looks after one, leaving the other to die. Probably this also happens in the wild. Gestation lasts 125-150 days.

GORAL
Nemorhaedus goral

Classification Class: Mammalia; Order: Artiodactyla; Family: Bovidae.

Description Length of head and body 37-51 in (95-130 cm), tail 2¾-8 in (7-20 cm), height to shoulder 24-28 in (60-70 cm), weight 55-77 lb (25-35 kg). Both sexes have short, pointed horns. Coat gray-brown, very thick.

Distribution Himalayas, China, Korea.

Habitat Mountain zones between 3,300 and 13,000 ft (1,000-4,000 m).

Behavior Herbivorous, grazing in early morning and evening; during the day it rests among the rocks. Females and young live in small groups; males are solitary except in breeding season, September-October. A single young is born after a gestation of 6 months.

HIMALAYAN BEAR
Ursus thibetanus

Classification Class: Mammalia; Order: Carnivora; Family: Ursidae.

Description Also called Asiatic Black or Tibetan Bear. Length of head and body 4½-5 ft (1.3-1.6 m), tail 3-4 in (7.6-10 cm), weight 265 lb (120 kg). Black with a white V-shaped mark on chest like a collar.

Distribution From Iran to Japan.

Habitat Mountain woods.

Behavior Almost exclusively vegetarian. An excellent climber, it spends much time in trees. The female gives birth to 1-2 cubs, which remain with the mother for about 2 years.

LADY AMHERST'S PHEASANT
Chrysolophus amherstiae

Classification Class: Aves; Order: Galliformes; Family: Phasianidae.

Description Length 26-67 in (66-170 cm). Male highly multicolored and bigger than female, which is a modest reddish-brown. The tail may measure up to 3 ft (1 m) long.

Distribution Mountains of southeastern Tibet, southwestern China and northern Burma.

Habitat Rocky slopes between altitudes of 6,500 and 10,000 ft (2,000-3,000 m) covered with bamboo scrub.

Behavior Favorite food consists of bamboo shoots. Only heavy winter snowfalls induce it to come down into valleys, in flocks of 20-30. Like all pheasants, it seldom flies. Little known about its life in the wild; famous as an ornamental bird.

MARKHOR
Capra falconeri

Classification Class: Mammalia; Order: Artiodactyla; Family: Bovidae.

Description Length of head and body 4½-5¼ ft (1.4-1.6 m), height to shoulder up to about 3 ft (1 m), weight 175-220 lb (80-100 kg). The male is larger than the female. Color sandy in summer, gray in winter. Horns spirally twisted, those of the male measuring up to 5¼ ft (1.6 m).

Distribution Himalayas and mountain ranges of central and southwestern Asia.

Habitat Mountain gorges above and below the treeline.

Behavior Vegetarian feeder. Lives at different heights according to the season but even in summer does not ever climb very high. Moves among rocks with remarkable agility. Males fight one another to win females. The female gives birth to 1-2 young after a gestation of 6 months.

MUSK DEER
Moschus moschiferus

Classification Class: Mammalia; Order: Artiodactyla; Family: Cervidae.

Description Length of head and body 32-40 in (80-100 cm), tail about 2 in (4-6 cm), height to shoulder 20-24 in (50-70 cm), weight 15½-37½ lb (7-17 kg). Gray-brown. No antlers. The male has long

Mountains

Hundreds of different species of rhododendron adorn the mountain slopes of central Asia with their beautifully colored flowers. In the woods, conifers and broadleaved trees are mingled, the latter more plentiful on the cooler sides, but there are also thickets of bamboo where these gigantic grasses with their flexible stems grow to the virtual exclusion of other plants.

1 bearded vulture
2 markhor
3 Lady Amherst's
　pheasant
4 snow leopard
5 yak
6 takin
7 snub-nosed monkey
8 Sumatran serow
9 red panda
10 *Parnassus* butterfly
11 giant panda
12 red-throated
　　pheasant
13 eared pheasant

upper canine teeth which protrude from the upper lip, using them for defense; those of the female are not visible.

Distribution Himalayas, eastern Asia, Siberia.

Habitat Forests.

Behavior Unlike the majority of Cervidae, this deer lives alone or in pairs. It feeds on grass, moss, lichens, leaves and shoots. Nocturnal and territorial, it spends the day amid dense vegetation. Fighting one another for possession of the females, the males cause deep wounds with their long canines. The female gives birth to 1-2 fawns after a gestation of 5-6 months.

Note The adult male of this species is notable for his ventral pouch which contains a glandular musk-smelling secretion, which probably serves to attract the female during the breeding period. For centuries Asians have used this secretion (musk) for making perfumes, and continue to do so despite prohibitions. This has led to the animal being hunted so intensively that it is today in danger of extinction.

PALLAS'S CAT
Felis manul

Classification Class: Mammalia; Order: Carnivora; Family: Felidae.

Description Also called the Manul. Length of head and body 20-25 in (50-65 cm), tail 8-12 in (21-30 cm), weight 6½-11 lb (3-5 kg). Stocky build, short legs, flattened head. Hair long, orange-gray above, pale gray below; black and white markings on head.

Distribution From Iran to western China.

Habitat High mountain steppes.

Behavior It feeds principally on rodents. Adapted to withstand very harsh climates. Difficult to detect. The female gives birth to 1-5 kittens.

RED PANDA
Ailurens fulgens

Classification Class: Mammalia; Order: Carnivora; Family: Procyonidae.

Description Also called Lesser Panda. Length of head and body 20-24 in (50-60 cm), tail 12-20 in (30-50 cm), weight 6½-11 lb (3-5 kg). The thick, soft fur is reddish, almost black on legs and underparts. White marks on muzzle and ears, black rings on tail.

Distribution From the Himalayas to mountains of southwestern China.

Habitat Bamboo forests.

Behavior Mainly vegetarian but probably eats insects and small birds as well. An excellent climber, it seems to be active chiefly at night. The presence of glands that secrete an odorous substance which serves to demarcate the bounds of its own domain, induces it to remain solitary and territorial. Precise information about this animal is scant since it is difficult to study it in its natural surroundings. The female gives birth to 1-2 young after a gestation of 90-150 days.

SNOW LEOPARD
Panthera uncia

Classification Class: Mammalia; Order: Carnivora; Family: Felidae.

Description Also called Ounce. Length of head and body 4-5 ft (1.2-1.5 m), tail 3-3¾ ft (90-113 cm), weight 50-90 lb (23-41 kg). Similar to the leopard, but smaller and with longer hair. Pale gray with dark rosettes.

Distribution Altai Mountains, Hindukush and Himalayas.

Habitat Coniferous forests and mountain steppes between altitudes of 6,000 and 16,500 ft (1,800-5,000 m).

Behavior It is the largest predator of the Asiatic mountains, capable of killing even the largest herbivores, such as the markhor, serow, takin, etc. Nocturnal, it lives on its own except in the breeding season, when male and female hunt together. The female gives birth to 1-4 young after a gestation of 98-103 days.

Note Although protected in most countries where it is found, its future is in jeopardy because it is hunted ruthlessly by smugglers profiting from the incessant demand for its splendid fur.

SNUB-NOSED MONKEY
Pygathrix roxellanae

Classification Class: Mammalia; Order: Primates; Family: Colobidae.

Description Length of head and body 26-30 in (66-76 cm), tail 22-28 in (56-72 cm). Upper parts and tail dark brown; underparts, tip of tail and edges of face fairly bright orange. Long, thick hair. Nose flattened and turned up.

Distribution Mountains of southwestern China.

Habitat Conifer and bamboo forests.

Behavior It is rare and hard to observe because it always seems to hide itself in dense vegetation. It is thought to live in large groups, feeding on fruit and bamboo shoots and leaves. Migrates from high summer quarters to winter ones lower down, and vice versa.

SUMATRAN SEROW
Capricornis sumatraensis

Classification Class: Mammalia; Order: Artiodactyla; Family: Bovidae.

Description Length of head and body 4-6 ft (1.2-1.8 m), tail 3-7 in (8-18 cm), height to shoulder 2-3½ ft (70-105 cm), weight 120-310 lb (55-140 kg). The horns measure 6-10 in (15-25 cm) and are present in both sexes. Coat dark brown with a paler mane extending from horns to shoulders.

Distribution Himalayas, Southeast Asia, Sumatra.

Habitat Zones with thick bush beyond the limits of the woods.

Behavior Feeds on acorns and twigs. It withstands humidity better than all other wild goats and this explains its presence even in tropical zones (Sumatra). A creature of unvarying habit, it always takes the same paths and rests in the same places. The female gives birth after a gestation of 7-8 months.

TAKIN
Budorcas taxicolor

Classification Class: Mammalia; Order: Artiodactyla; Family: Bovidae.

Description Length of head and body 5½-7 ft (1.7-2.2 m), height to shoulder 3-4 ft (1-1.3 m), weight 550-770 lb (250-350 kg). The male is larger than the female. Yellowish-brown or blackish. Massive build. Both sexes carry large, backward-turned horns.

Distribution Western China, Bhutan, Burma.

Habitat Bamboo forests at an altitude of around 6,500 ft (2,000 m).

Behavior It feeds on grass and bamboo. In summer it forms large herds, in winter small groups. Adult males are solitary. During the breeding season each male assembles a number of females and defends them furiously against other contenders. The female gives birth to a single young after a gestation of about 8 months.

YAK
Bos mutus

Classification Class: Mammalia; Order: Artiodactyla; Family: Bovidae.

Description This is an animal of truly massive proportions; a wild male may stand as high as 6¾ ft (2.03 m) at the shoulder for every 1,800 lb (821 kg) of weight. The female is noticeably smaller and lighter: about 5¼ ft (1.56 m) for every 670 lb (306 kg). The animal has a large hump on the back and a pair of horns which, in the male, may be as long as 3 ft (90 cm). The hair is long and in winter hangs down halfway over the legs. Wild specimens, nowadays very rare, are dark, almost black, with white around the muzzle; domesticated yaks are reddish-brown or white, speckled black or brown.

Distribution Plateaus of Tibet.

Habitat Tundra and icefields between 13,500 and 20,000 ft (4,000-6,000 m).

Behavior Little is known about its life in the wild. The domesticated female gives birth to a single calf after 258 days.

Tropical forests

ASIATIC ELEPHANT
Elephas maximus
Classification Class: Mammalia; Order: Proboscidea; Family: Elephantidae.
Description Length of head and body 18-21 ft (5.5-6.4 m), tail 4-5 ft (1.2-1.5 m), height to shoulder 8-10 ft (2.5-3 m), weight up to 5 t. Gray, smaller and lighter than the African species, it has shorter tusks (the female often has none), smaller ears and a trunk that terminates in only one prehensile appendage instead of two.
Distribution Southern China, India, Indochina, Malaysia, Indonesia.
Habitat Forests.
Behavior It feeds on grass, leaves, twigs, bark and fruit, requiring about 330 lb (150 kg) of food and 16-20 gal (70-90 l) of water a day. It lives in herds made up of females who are related to one another, each with her own young. The herd is led by the most elderly female. The adult males live on their own except in the mating season. The female, after 22 months' gestation, gives birth to a calf that she suckles for 3 or 4 years, which will reach maturity at 10 years and die at the age of 60. In Southeast Asia the elephant is, even today, an important work animal.

AXIS DEER
Axis axis
Classification Class: Mammalia; Order: Artiodactyla; Family: Cervidae.
Description Also called the Chital. Length of head and body 43-55 in (1.1-1.4 m), tail 8-12 in (20-30 cm), height to shoulder 30-38 in (75-97 cm), weight 165-220 lb (75-100 kg). Coat tawny spotted with white. The antlers, carried only by the male, are branched and lyre-shaped.
Distribution India and Sri Lanka.
Habitat Woods close to rivers.
Behavior It feeds on grass, leaves and shoots. It lives in herds in the vicinity of rivers, where it seeks refuge in case of danger. The males renew their antlers once a year, at no specified season. In the rutting season they fight one another for possession of the largest number of females. These give birth to a single fawn after 210-225 days' gestation.

ENTELLUS MONKEY
Presbytis entellus
Classification Class: Mammalia; Order: Primates; Family: Colobidae.
Description It is also called the Hanu-man. Length of head and body 16-31 in (41-78 cm), tail 27-42 in (69-108 cm), weight 12-52 lb (5.4-23.6 kg). Upper parts gray-brown; underparts and crest of hairs around the face yellowish-white; hands and forearms blackish.
Distribution Southern slopes of Himalayas, India, Sri Lanka.
Habitat Forests, thickets, cultivated fields, villages and towns.
Behavior It eats leaves, flowers and fruit; in the more cultivated regions of India, however, taking advantage of the total protection afforded it by the people, who consider it sacred, it feeds mainly on crops. It lives in packs led by a male; each group has its own territory. Extremely agile both on the ground and in trees, it can easily swing 30 ft (10 m) from branch to branch. All the females in the pack cooperate in rearing the young.

GUAR
Bos gaurus
Classification Class: Mammalia; Order: Artiodactyla; Family: Bovidae.
Description Length of head and body 8½-11 ft (2.6-3.3 m), tail 33 in (85 cm), height to shoulder 5¼-7 ft (1.6-2.1 m), weight 1,550-2,200 lb (700-1,000 kg). The male, much larger than the female, is the largest of all wild cattle. Dark brown or black. Both sexes carry horns.
Distribution India, Indochina, Malaysia.
Habitat Forests.
Behavior It lives in herds of more than twenty. Herbivorous and diurnal, if often associates with other forest animals which, with their sharp senses, help it to identify danger. Its enormous strength usually protects the adult from attacks by tigers, but a good number of calves fall victim to predators. The calves are born after 270-280 days' gestation.

INDIAN COBRA
Naja naja
Classification Class: Reptilia; Order: Squamata; Suborder: Ophidea; Family: Elapidae.
Description Length 5 ft (1.5 m). Color varies from light brown to black. A black and white pattern resembling a pair of spectacles appears on the neck when the snake dilates, and flattens it.
Distribution Central Asia, India, Sri Lanka, southern China, Indonesia.
Habitat Forests and swamps.
Behavior It feeds on rodents, birds, lizards, amphibians and fish. The smallest forms of prey are swallowed at once, the larger ones when they are dead from the venom. Nocturnal and terrestrial. If disturbed it rears up on its body and flattens its neck in a threat position. Its poison is extremely dangerous. The female lays 12-20 eggs which hatch after 50-70 days.

INDIAN GRAY MONGOOSE
Herpestes edwardsi
Classification Class: Mammalia; Order: Carnivora; Family: Viverridae.
Description Length of head and body 17 in (43 cm), tail 15½ in (39 cm), weight 3½ lb (1.5 kg). Silver-gray.
Distribution From Arabia to Nepal, India and Sri Lanka.
Habitat Sparse woodland and thickets.
Behavior It feeds on insects, reptiles, birds and rodents. Diurnal and solitary, it spends the night in burrows abandoned by other animals or dug by itself. In fights against cobras its decisive weapon is its extraordinary agility. The snake is gradually exhausted as the mongoose, with incredibly fast reflexes, avoids its repeated attacks; when the snake's movements are eventually slowed down by fatigue, the mongoose seizes it by the neck, kills it and devours it. The mongoose is not immune to the cobra's venom but a fatal dose is far greater than that required to kill any other mammal of comparable weight. The female gives birth to 2-4 young after about 2 months' gestation.

INDIAN PALM CIVET
Paradoxurus hermaphroditus
Classification Class: Mammalia; Order: Carnivora; Family: Viverridae.
Description Also called the Toddy Cat. Length of head and body 21 in (54 cm), tail 18 in (46 cm), weight 7½ lb (3.4 kg). Woolly coat dark brown with black stripes and spots.
Distribution From India to Indonesia.
Habitat Zones with plenty of palms.
Behavior It eats insects, birds and their eggs, small mammals and fruit. Nocturnal and semiarboreal. It ventures into built-up areas to kill mice, rats and poultry. The female gives birth to 3-4 young in a tree hollow.

INDIAN PYTHON
Python molurus
Classification Class: Reptilia; Order: Squamata; Suborder: Ophidea; Family: Boidae.
Description Length up to 25 ft (8 m), weight 360 lb (115 kg). Color light brown with darker markings on back and flanks. Prehensile tail.
Distribution India, Sri Lanka, Burma.
Habitat Forests and rocky zones.
Behavior It is not poisonous, killing its prey by coiling itself around them and tightening its grip to the point of suffocation. Its usual victims are small and

Tropical forests

In southern and southeastern Asia there are two principal types of forest: the primary forests, the original appearance of which has not been modified, even in the slightest degree, by human activity; and the secondary forests, which have been reestablished wherever primary forests have been cut down but where the terrain has subsequently been left to evolve naturally. All these forests contain a rich variety of tree species, among the most prominent being those belonging to the family Dipterocarpaceae. There is also an abundance of palms, lianas and epiphytic plants.

1 Asiatic elephant
2 Indian rhinoceros
3 Indian python
4 Entellus monkey
5 Axis deer
6 Malayan tapir
7 Indian palm civet
8 tiger
9 peacock
10 collared parakeet
11 Rajah Brooke's birdwing
12 Indian gray mongoose
13 Indian cobra
14 black panther

medium-sized mammals, but it can swallow animals whose diameter is far greater than its own. It does this by "unhooking" the bones of its jaws which, being connected only by elastic ligaments, can open in an enormous gape. It eats infrequently and can fast for long periods. The female lays 8-60 eggs and by curling herself around them "incubates" them for 2 months. Although a reptile, and therefore an animal whose body temperature depends substantially on the outside temperature, she manages to remain a few degrees warmer than her surroundings.

INDIAN RHINOCEROS
Rhinoceros unicornis
Classification Class: Mammalia; Order: Perissodactyla; Family: Rhinocerotidae.
Description Length of head and body 10-12½ ft (3.1-3.8 m), tail 28-32 in (70-80 cm), horn 18 in (45 cm), height to shoulder 4½-6 ft (1.4-1.8 m), weight 1½-2¼ t. The male is bigger than the female. Skin gray, in four large folds almost completely hairless and horny, which makes the animal look as if it were encased in armor. The horn is a projection of skin, without bony support but as hard and solid as that of cattle. It has an extremely sharp sense of smell but poor vision: it would fail to notice a person 100 yards (30 m) away.
Distribution Northeastern India.
Habitat Swamps.
Behavior It feeds on grass and shoots, spending much time submerged in water. Outside the breeding season adult individuals are solitary. If disturbed, it will charge at a speed of up to 20-25 mph (35-40 kmh), revealing itself to be not only powerful but also unexpectedly agile. After a gestation of 16 months, a calf is born weighing about 145 lb (65 kg). It lives for up to 45 years.

LEOPARD
Panthera pardus
Classification Class: Mammalia; Order: Carnivora; Family: Felidae.
Description Length of head and body 3¼-6 ft (1-1.9 m), tail 28-38 in (70-95 cm), height to shoulder 18-32 in (45-80 cm), weight 65-155 lb (30-70 kg). The male is larger than the female. Color light brown with black rosettes. Some are born black but their coat, seen in full light, still shows the typical spotting; these animals, although not a distinct species but simply black leopards, are nevertheless called black panthers.
Distribution Southeast Asia, southern Arabia, Caucasus. Also found in Africa south of the Sahara.
Habitat Tropical forests, savannas and mountains.

Behavior It feeds principally on small and medium-sized mammals and birds, hunting alone, by night. The technique is typically that of the big cats: it creeps up to a few yards from its unsuspecting victim, makes a short but very swift leap and kills the prey with a bite to the throat. An excellent climber, it often hauls its victim up into a tree. Male and female live apart and meet only during the short mating season. The care of the 1-6 cubs, born after a gestation of 90-105 days, is the responsibility of the female alone.
Note Mainly because of the high value of its skin, the leopard is hunted without respite everywhere, so much so that in some areas there are fears for its survival.

MALAYAN TAPIR
Tapirus indicus
Classification Class: Mammalia; Order: Perissodactyla; Family: Tapiridae.
Description Length of head and body 7-8 ft (2.2-2.5 m), tail 2-4 in (5-10 cm), height to shoulder 36-42 in (90-105 cm), weight 550-660 lb (250-300 kg). Head, neck, shoulders, fore and hind legs black, the rest white. The snout extends into a short trunk.
Distribution Burma, Thailand, Malaysia and Sumatra.
Habitat Dense tropical forests.
Behavior It feeds at night on grass, aquatic plants, leaves and shoots. It is solitary and much attached to water, finding refuge there in case of danger and staying submerged for several minutes. The female gives birth to a single young after a gestation of 390-395 days.

NILGAI
Boselaphus tragocamelus
Classification Class: Mammalia; Order: Artiodactyla; Family: Bovidae.
Description Also called the Blue Bull. Length of head and body 6-6½ ft (1.8-2 m), tail 16-22 in (40-55 cm), height to shoulder 4-5 ft (1.2-1.5 m), weight up to 440 lb (200 kg). The male is much larger than the female and is blue-gray, whereas she is brown. The male alone has short, straight horns.
Distribution India.
Habitat Sparse forests and neighboring grassy zones.
Behavior Herbivorous. Females and young live in herds, while the males remain solitary, except in the breeding season. During fights for possession of the females, the males kneel in front of each other, dealing out violent blows with their neck and horns. The strongest males assemble up to 10 females around them, and the boundaries of the territory which they all occupy are marked with the scent of

glandular secretions. The female gives birth to 1-2 calves after a gestation of about 8 months.

PEACOCK
Pavo cristatus
Classification Class: Aves; Order: Galliformes; Family: Phasianidae.
Description Length, including tail, 3-7½ ft (0.9-2.3 m). The male is much larger than the female; his crest, head, neck and underparts are blue, back and tail are green, wings largely tawny. There are numerous eyespots on the tail. The female is brown above, white below, crest and neck green.
Distribution India and Sri Lanka.
Habitat Open spaces near woods, thickets and tall isolated trees.
Behavior It eats plants, insects, reptiles and small mammals, hunting at dawn and dusk, spending the night on a branch. It lives in small groups comprising one male and 2-5 females. During his courtship the male spreads out his tail like a fan, displaying the beautiful eyespots. The female lays 3-5 eggs, which hatch after 28 days' incubation.

TIGER
Panthera tigris
Classification Class: Mammalia; Order: Carnivora; Family: Felidae.
Description Length of head and body 4½-9 ft (1.4-2.8 m), tail 24-38 in (60-95 cm), height to shoulder up to 3 ft (91 cm), weight 220-570 lb (100-260 kg). The male is larger than the female. Color tawny or yellowish with black stripes; underparts white.
Distribution India, Manchuria, China, Indonesia.
Habitat Tropical and monsoon forests, both coniferous and deciduous.
Behavior A solitary predator, whose victims are usually deer and wild boar; but sometimes it will attack very young elephants and rhinoceroses, buffalo and guar. After stalking its prey, the tiger launches a surprise attack, killing the victim with a powerful bite to the throat. Male and female occupy separate territories to which no adult of the same sex is permitted entry. They meet briefly to mate, after which the male takes no interest in the rearing of the 3-4 cubs to which the female gives birth after a gestation of 103 days. The cubs are allowed to remain in the mother's territory until they are 2 years old. The tiger avoids contact with humans; but old or sick animals, lacking the agility to capture their customary prey, may attack a human, swelling the list of victims of these so-called "man-eaters."

Watery regions

ARCHERFISH
Toxotes jaculator
Classification   Class: Osteichthyes; Order: Perciformes; Family: Toxotidae.
Description   Length 9½ in (24 cm). Yellowish-green or brown above, lighter below; 4-6 bands on flanks.
Distribution   Southern Asia, Sunda Islands. Also found in Australia.
Habitat   Mouths of rivers.
Behavior   In the wild it feeds exclusively on insects, which it catches by spitting out at them a stream of water when they alight on a branch above the surface. The insect, once struck, falls into the water and is immediately devoured. In the aquarium, where there are no insects, the fish uses the same technique to catch worms, snails, etc. The stream of water may be expelled to a distance of up to 5 ft (1.5 m).

BIG-HEADED TURTLE
Platysternon megacephalum
Classification   Class: Reptilia; Order: Testudinata; Family: Platysternidae.
Description   Length of carapace (shell) 8 in (20 cm). The large head and exceptionally long tail are protected by horny plates which cannot be completely withdrawn beneath the flat carapace. The structure of the jaws resembles the beak of a parrot. The carapace is dark brown above, yellowish below.
Distribution   Southeast Asia.
Habitat   Mountain streams.
Behavior   It feeds chiefly on molluscs, crushing their hard shells between its beak-like jaws. The long claws and the notable roughness of the tail enable it to negotiate fairly steep slopes and probably even to climb trees. The female lays 2 eggs.

CHINESE ALLIGATOR
Alligator sinensis
Classification   Class: Reptilia; Order: Crocodilia; Family: Alligatoridae.
Description   Length 6½ ft (2 m). Short, broad snout. Color dark olive with yellowish spots.
Distribution   Lower reaches of Yangtze Kiang River in eastern China.
Habitat   Swamps and ponds along river banks.
Behavior   Little is known of its habits. It probably feeds mainly on aquatic turtles but also on fish, frogs and water snails.

The female lays 20-70 eggs in a nest made with plants which, as they rot, produce a temperature inside the nest of around 86°F (30°C), sufficient to allow the eggs to be incubated. The young hatch after 60-70 days and measure 12 in (30 cm).

CORMORANT
Phalacrocorax carbo
Classification   Class: Aves; Order: Pelecaniformes; Family: Phalacrocoracidae.
Description   Length 36 in (92 cm), weight 6 lb (2.7 kg). Dark brown above, black below with metallic blue-green and purple reflections. The nape is adorned with a small tuft.
Distribution   Many parts of Asia. Also found in Europe, Africa and Australia.
Habitat   Rivers, lakes and seashores.
Behavior   Feeds exclusively on fish, which it catches by swimming on the surface or by diving. It nests in colonies on tall trees or cliffs. The female lays 3-4 eggs which hatch after 23-30 days' incubation. Even today the Chinese exploit the fishing ability of the cormorant by training it to capture fish; a narrow ring around the neck prevents the bird from swallowing the prey.

GANGETIC DOLPHIN
Platanista gangetica
Classification   Class: Mammalia; Order: Cetacea; Suborder: Odontoceti; Family: Platanistidae.
Description   Also called the Susu. Length 6½-8 ft (2-2.5 m), weight up to 175 lb (80 kg). Gray above, whitish below. It is practically blind; the small eyes probably help it to determine the direction and intensity of light. In any event, keen eyesight would not be of much use in an environment of cloudy water where visibility is only a few inches. The characteristic long beak is armed with strong teeth. The female is larger than the male.
Distribution   India, Bangladesh, Nepal.
Habitat   Rivers Ganges, Brahmaputra and Meghna.
Behavior   It is thought to eat fish and crustaceans, captured on the seabed after it has located them by means of a complex system of emission and reception of ultrasounds. It lives in small groups. Birth occurs after 10 months' gestation. The dolphin's lifespan is 28 years. Its survival is threatened mainly by dams which, by splitting up the populations, prevent the animals reproducing.

GAVIAL
Gavialis gangeticus
Classification   Class: Reptilia; Order: Crocodilia; Family: Gavialidae.

Description   Length 23 ft (7 m). Yellowish-brown above, lighter below. The principal feature is the long, slender snout, furnished with sharp teeth.
Distribution   India and Indochina.
Habitat   Rivers with deep, fast-flowing water.
Behavior   Because the feeble legs do not allow it to move about easily on dry land, this crocodile spends most of its time in water. Despite its ferocious appearance, it is inoffensive and feeds only on small fish, caught with sideways movements of the snout. The female lays 20-80 eggs in a nest dug on land.

INDIAN WILD BUFFALO
Bubalus arnee
Classification   Class: Mammalia; Order: Artiodactyla; Family: Bovidae.
Description   Length of head and body 8-9 ft (2.4-2.8 m), tail 24-34 in (60-85 cm), height to shoulder 5¼-6 ft (1.6-1.9 m), weight 1,750-2,650 lb (800-1,200 kg). Gray-black with whitish legs to the level of the knee. The horns, present in both sexes, are sickle-shaped and turned backward.
Distribution   The domesticated form is found widely in Asia, South America, Europe and North Africa. The ancestral wild form survives in small numbers in India, Sri Lanka, Nepal, Burma, Indochina and Indonesia.
Habitat   Swamps, areas close to rivers.
Behavior   It is absolutely essential for the animal to remain submerged in water or mud for long periods. Dried mud, in particular, protects it from the sun and from insect bites. It feeds at night on grass and aquatic plants. Lives in herds led by an elderly male. While the leader is sufficiently strong to lead the herd, he will tolerate no other male adults in the group. Once defeated and driven out by a younger male, it leads a solitary life. The female gives birth to one calf after a gestation of 300-340 days.

MUDSKIPPER
Periophthalmus vulgaris
Classification   Class: Osteichthyes; Order: Perciformes; Family: Gobiidae.
Description   Maximum length 6 in (15 cm). Brown or gray above, lighter below. This fish can also breathe out of the water and can lead an amphibious life thanks to pectoral fins which have fleshy bases, capable of supporting the body on dry land. The large eyes are characteristically positioned on the top of the head so that they protrude from the water when its body is still submerged.
Distribution   Southeast Asia. Also found in Africa, Madagascar and Australia.

Watery regions

Many species of the plant family Araceae, with characteristic flowers, grow along the banks of rivers in southern and southeastern Asia. Mangroves, low trees or woody shrubs with roots above ground, so that they look as if they were supported on long stilts buried in the mud, develop in swampy areas near the mouths of rivers. And very abundant, too, are the semiaquatic Graminaceae, such as rice, widely cultivated in this part of the world.

1   painted stork
2   Indian water buffalo
3   purple gallinule
4   mudskipper
5   archerfish
6   Siamese fighting fish
7   cormorant
8   Gangetic dolphin
9   gavial
10 Chinese alligator
11 kissing gourami
12 big-headed turtle
13 red-tailed black shark

Habitat Brackish water at river mouths.
Behavior It hunts insects and small crustaceans in the mud of mangrove swamps. If danger threatens, it flees toward dry land and not in the direction of water. The female lays and guards the eggs in a funnel-shaped nest dug at a point lapped by the water at high tide.

PAINTED STORK
Ibis leucocephalus
Classification Class: Aves; Order: Ciconiiformes; Family: Ciconidae.
Description Length 37 in (93 cm). Large wader, white with wings spotted black and pink; bill yellow-orange, legs pinkish-brown, naked skin on yellowish face.
Distribution Pakistan, India, Sri Lanka, southwestern China, Indochina.
Habitat Flooded fields, swamps, sandy banks of rivers.
Behavior Walking in the water or mire, it catches fish, amphibians, reptiles, crustaceans and insects. Outside the breeding season it lives on its own, in pairs or in small groups; during the period of reproduction it forms colonies consisting of thousands of birds. It builds a large nest of twigs on trees close to the water. The female lays 3-4 eggs. Both parents collaborate in rearing the young.

PHEASANT-TAILED JACANA
Hydrophasianus chirurgus
Classification Class: Aves; Order: Charadriiformes; Family: Jacanidae.
Description No bird anywhere has proportionately longer legs and toes, which cover such a broad surface as to allow the bird to run across floating vegetation without sinking. Both sexes, in courtship garb, have a white head, wings and front of neck; breast, abdomen, back and tail are dark brown; nape and back of neck are golden-yellow. It has a characteristically long pheasant-like tail.
Distribution India, Sri Lanka, China, Afghanistan.
Habitat Rivers and streams with an abundance of vegetation.
Behavior It feeds on insects, molluscs, fish and seeds. In this species it is the female who plays the active role in courtship, surrounding herself with several males who are solely responsible for incubating the eggs for 22-24 days. The chicks, born in a floating nest, are soon able to swim and dive.

PURPLE GALLINULE
Porphyrio porphyrio
Classification Class: Aves; Order: Gruiformes; Family: Rallidae.
Description Length 16-18½ in (40-47 cm), weight 18½-36 oz (520-1,000 g). Blue with red bill, legs and eyes, under-tail feathers white. The bird has a characteristic red forehead plate and extremely long toes which help to distribute the weight of the body over a wide surface, enabling it to walk on waterlilies and other floating plants without sinking.
Distribution Southern Asia, Indonesia, Philippines. Also found in Mediterranean basin, Africa, Madagascar, Australia, New Guinea and New Zealand.
Habitat Swamps.
Behavior It feeds on aquatic plants, insects, molluscs, fish and amphibians. Timid and wary, it never strays far from the dense vegetation where, in spite of its brilliant colors, it is not easily detected. It swims as rarely as it flies. The 2-6 eggs hatch after an incubation of 24-25 days.

RED-TAILED BLACK SHARK
Labeo bicolor
Classification Class: Osteichthyes; Order: Cypriniformes; Family: Cyprinidae.
Description Maximum length 5 in (12 cm). Black with red caudal fin.
Distribution Thailand.
Habitat Streams.
Behavior It feeds mainly on algae covering stones and aquatic plants. Territorial. The male devotes himself to looking after the eggs and fry after chasing away the female. It is a popular aquarium fish.

SARUS CRANE
Grus antigone
Classification Class: Aves; Order: Gruiformes; Family: Gruidae.
Description Length 61½ in (156 cm). Large gray bird with very long neck and legs. The naked skin of the head and the top part of the neck are red, except for a gray area on the top of the head.
Distribution Northern India, Indochina.
Habitat Swamps.
Behavior It eats fish, frogs, lizards, large insects and plants. Male and female mate for life and their link is so close that in India they have become the symbol of conjugal loyalty and for that reason honored. They build a large nest of reeds in a prominent position in the swamp; after a complex courtship ceremony, the female lays 2 eggs, which she incubates for 28 days.

SIAMESE FIGHTING FISH
Betta splendens
Classification Class: Osteichthyes; Order: Perciformes; Family: Anabantidae.
Description Length 2½ in (6 cm). Color variable according to place of origin; red tones predominate in southern varieties, green tints in those from the north. Like all members of the family, it is furnished with a large labyrinth, a supplementary respiratory organ which enables it to breathe out of the water.
Distribution Thailand, Indochina, Malaysia.
Habitat Shallow stagnant waters which are warm and full of vegetation.
Behavior It feeds on small water invertebrates. The aggressive temperament of the males is heightened to such an extent that, in their countries of origin, contests are arranged in which two fish, placed in a small container, fight to the death or until one is exhausted. The male builds a nest of bubbles under the water surface, to which the female anchors the eggs after an elaborate courtship ritual. He alone tends them and, later, the fry.
Note The Kissing Gourami (*Helostoma temmincki*) is another anabantid, measuring a maximum of 12 in (30 cm) and found in Thailand, Malaysia and the Sunda Islands. The common name is derived from the fact that in fights between the males the latter fasten together their fleshy lips, giving the impression of kissing. Like the Siamese Fighting Fish, it is a popular occupant of aquariums all over the world.

SKIMMER
Rhynchops albicollis
Classification Class: Aves; Order: Charadriiformes; Family: Rhynchopidae.
Description Length about 15 in (38 cm). Top of head and rear of neck black, back dark brown, underparts white, bill yellow, the lower mandible being longer than the upper one.
Distribution India.
Habitat Banks of large rivers, sea beaches.
Behavior It feeds by skimming close to the water surface, raking it with the lower mandible of its open bill, while the upper mandible is held above the surface. The moment the submerged part of the bill strikes a fish or a crustacean, the top section clamps down to trap the prey. The bird, without interrupting its flight, folds its head beneath the body, then straightens up and swallows its food. It nests in colonies. The female lays 3-4 eggs in a hole scooped in the sand. At birth the chicks have a normal bill.

Sunda Islands

ANOA
Bubalus depressicornis

Classification   Class: Mammalia; Order: Artiodactyla; Family: Bovidae.
Description   Also known as the Dwarf Buffalo. Length of head and body 5¼ ft (1.6 m), height to shoulder 2-3¼ ft (60-100 cm), weight 330-660 lb (150-300 kg). This is the smallest of wild cattle, with short horns and slender legs which are like those of an antelope. Color dark brown with white markings on throat and chest.
Distribution   Celebes Islands.
Habitat   Marshy woodlands.
Behavior   It feeds on aquatic plants, grass, leaves and fruit. Unlike most cattle, it seems to prefer to spend life on its own or in pairs rather than in a herd. It enjoys bathing and rolling in the mud.
Note Because of the continual shrinking of its habitat, which is converted into farmland, the animal is in danger of extinction.

BABIRUSA
Babirussa babyrussa

Classification   Class: Mammalia; Order: Artiodactyla; Family: Suidae.
Description   Length of head and body 36-42 in (90-110 cm), tail 8-12 in (20-30 cm), height to shoulder 26-32 in (65-80 cm), weight up to 220 lb (100 kg). It is a form of wild boar, characterized by the enormous development of its upper canine teeth which, in adult males, may perforate the skin of the upper part of the snout and bend back in an arc or even circle.
Distribution   Celebes Island.
Habitat   Swampy forests
Behavior   Active mainly at dusk, it eats leaves, fruit and insect larvae. It lives on its own or in small family groups. An excellent swimmer, it will even venture into the sea to reach good grazing land. After 5 months' gestation, the female produces 2 young.

BINTURONG
Arctitis binturong

Classification   Class: Mammalia; Order: Carnivora; Family: Viverridae.
Description   Length of head and body 36-40 in (90-100 cm), tail 32 in (80 cm), weight about 30 lb (14 kg). Long, black, ruffled fur; stocky, massive build, it is the only Old World mammal with a prehensile tail.
Distribution   Eastern India, Indochina, Malaysia, Sunda Islands.

Habitat   Forests.
Behavior   Almost exclusively arboreal. The prehensile tail does not balance the weight of the adult animal, only of the young; but it serves as a useful additional support as it clambers through the branches. It feeds on plants and carrion. The 2-3 young are born after 3 months' gestation.
Note The Banded Linsang *(Prionodon linsang)* is another member of the Viverridae, colored cinnamon with black spots, and as graceful, agile and speedy as the binturong is inelegant, awkward and slow. It is up to 32 in (80 cm) long and weighs a mere 26 oz (750 g). It lives in the forests of Malaysia and the Sunda Islands, where it behaves as a predator both on the ground and in trees.

CLOUDED LEOPARD
Neofelis nebulosa

Classification   Class: Mammalia; Order: Carnivora; Family: Felidae.
Description   Length of head and body 30-42 in (75-105 cm), tail 28-36 in (70-90 cm), weight 31-51 lb (14-23 kg). Yellowish-gray with dark spots. Short, strong legs, claws and upper canines exceptionally long in proportion to the size of the animal.
Distribution   India, Nepal, southern China, Taiwan, Sunda Islands.
Habitat   Forests and swamps.
Behavior   Nocturnal hunter, arboreal. It feeds on birds and small and medium-sized mammals. Extremely agile, it can descend trees head-downward, attached to a branch by the hind legs alone. After 3 months' gestation, the female gives birth to 2-4 cubs.

CRAB-EATING MACAQUE
Macaca irus

Classification   Class: Mammalia; Order: Primates; Family: Cercopithecidae.
Description   Length of head and body 26 in (65 cm), tail 20 in (50 cm). Grayish-brown above, white below; hands, feet, tail and face dark gray.
Distribution   Indochina, Malaysia, Sumatra, Java, Borneo, and the Philippines.
Habitat   Swampy forests.
Behavior   Troops of these monkeys crouch for hours in the branches of half-submerged trees, waiting until low tide uncovers the mud flats; they then come down and find plenty of food in the form of crabs, molluscs and other small animals. There is a strict hierarchy within the troop, which is led by an elderly male, and each group fiercely defends its own hunting territory. The female gives birth to a single young after a gestation of 159-178 days.

EASTERN TARSIER
Tarsius spectrum

Classification   Class: Mammalia; Order: Primates; Suborder: Prosimii; Family: Tarsiidae.
Description   The tarsier is a close relative of the monkey. Length of head and body 6-7 in (15-18 cm), tail 9-10 in (22-25 cm), weight 3½-5¼ oz (100-150 g). Color grayish-brown. Enormous eyes, typical of a nocturnal animal; hind legs extremely well developed, suited for jumping; broad adhesive pads on the tips of the toes assure it of a secure grip.
Distribution   Celebes Islands.
Habitat   Forests.
Behavior   It feeds at night on insects, amphibians, reptiles and birds. A tree dweller, it can jump more than 6 ft (2 m) from branch to branch. It lives alone or in pairs, confined to its own territory. The female produces one young.
Note The Slow Loris *(Nycticebus coucang)* is a prosimian belonging to the family Lorisidae, found in Indochina, Malaysia, Java, Sumatra and Borneo. Nocturnal and arboreal, it moves among the branches very slowly and cautiously, using both hands and feet. It feeds on plants, insects, eggs and fledglings.

FIDDLER CRAB
Uca annulipes

Classification   Class: Crustacea; Order: Decapoda; Family: Ocipodidae.
Description   The chelae (claws) of the male are of very diverse size; one is as big as the body, the other is normal. The large chela, bright orange, moves rhythmically, rather like the arm movements of a violinist, hence its common name. In case of danger, even this chela turns a muddy color like the rest of the body, so that the animal goes unobserved.
Distribution   Southeast Asia and the neighboring islands.
Habitat   Muddy shorelines.
Behavior   It leads an amphibious life, being able to breathe both in water and on dry land. It forms colonies, within which each individual occupies its own territory. The very brightly colored chela of the male, useless for capturing prey or for defense, moves rhythmically as a signal to other males that the territory in question is already occupied and as an indication to females that he is available for coupling.

FISHING CAT
Felis viverrina

Classification   Class: Mammalia; Order: Carnivora; Family: Felidae.
Description   Length of head and body 22½-33 in (57-85 cm), tail 8-12½ in (20-32

Sunda Islands

Over a large area of the Sunda Islands (the largest of which are Sumatra, Java, Borneo and the Celebes) the original vegetation consists of very dense primary forests, full of Dipterocarpaceae, giant figs, palms, Rubiaceae and many other trees; there are numerous lianas, among them several palms, and epiphytes, including many orchids.

1 Smyrna kingfisher
2 orang-utan
3 lar gibbon
4 eastern tarsier
5 flying fox
6 Sumatran rhinoceros
7 proboscis monkey
8 mangrove snake
9 Komodo dragon
10 fishing cat
11 crab-eating macaque
12 anoa
13 babirusa
14 giant hornbill
15 fiddler crab
16 tree shrew

cm). Gray-brown to olive; head and back striped and spotted black.

Distribution   India, Sri Lanka, Indochina, Sumatra and Java.

Habitat   Along river banks and in mangrove swamps on seashores.

Behavior   Although adept at catching fish and fresh-water and marine crustaceans, it seems to prefer large insects, amphibians, birds and medium-sized mammals. An excellent swimmer, it is brave and aggressive. The female, after a gestation of some 2 months, gives birth to 1-4 cubs.

Note   The Flat-headed Cat *(Felis planiceps)* is a strange feline from the forests of Malaysia, Sumatra and Borneo. About 20 in (50 cm) long, including the tail, it is reddish-brown above, white below. Its name is derived from the fact that the top of the head is markedly flattened; this feature, plus the incompletely retractile claws, makes it unique among small wild cats. Terrestrial, if feeds chiefly on crustaceans, fish and amphibians.

FLYING FOX
Pteropus vampyrus

Classification   Class: Mammalia; Order: Chiroptera; Family: Pteropidae.

Description   Length of head and body 16 in (40 cm), wingspan 52 in (140 cm). It is the largest known bat. Color brownish-black.

Distribution   Malaysia, Sunda Islands, Philippines.

Habitat   Forests.

Behavior   It feeds exclusively on fruit. It spends the day hanging upside-down from the highest tree branches, sleeping with wings wrapped round the body. In the evening, forming flocks of hundreds, it flies, often for considerable distances, in search of trees laden with ripe fruit. At dawn it returns to its resting places.

GIANT HORNBILL
Buceros bicornis

Classification   Class: Aves; Order: Coraciiformes; Family: Bucerotidae.

Description   Total length about 5 ft (1.5 m), weight 5½-7¾ lb (2.5-3.5 kg). The male is bigger than the female. Black and white with cinnamon neck, nape, bill and casque. The casque surmounts the large bill; despite their massive appearance, both structures are very light, being empty or containing a network of spongy bone.

Distribution   India, Indochina, Malaysia and Sumatra.

Habitat   Forests.

Behavior   It feeds on fruit, insects, amphibians, eggs and fledglings. The female lays her eggs in the hollow of a tree and walls up the entrance with mud and other materials brought by the male. The latter feeds his companion and, in due course, the young through the narrow opening which remains. This behavior serves as an effective defense against tree predators such as monkeys, snakes and other birds.

KOMODO DRAGON
Varanus komodoensis

Classification   Class: Reptilia; Order: Squamata; Suborder: Sauria; Family: Varanidae.

Description   Total length up to 10 ft (3 m), weight up to 300 lb (135 kg). Grayish-black. It is the largest living lizard.

Distribution   Islands of Komodo, Ringja, Padar and Flores.

Behavior   Weight, build and dentition make this lizard a formidable predator, potentially dangerous to humans. It feeds principally on deer and wild pigs, alive or already dead. There are reckoned to be some 700 to 1,000 surviving individuals whose future, despite protection, is far from secure.

Note The Flying Lizard *(Draco volans)* belongs to the family Agamidae. It lives in the forests of the Sunda Islands, Malaysia and the Philippines, spending its time almost entirely in the trees, feeding on insects. It is able to glide from one tree to another, supported by two folds of skin on either side of the body which function like wings.

LAR GIBBON
Hylobates lar

Classification   Class: Mammalia; Order: Primates; Family: Hylobatidae.

Description   Length of head and body 18-25 in (45-64 cm), weight 11-17½ lb (5-8 kg). Reddish or black with hands, feet and sides of face white. The slim body, short legs in comparison with very long arms, hands which are as efficient as claws, and eyesight keen enough to gauge distances perfectly, make this monkey, like other gibbons, a fantastic forest acrobat, capable of "flying" from tree to tree, barely grazing the branches. Like all the apes, it has no tail.

Distribution   Thailand, Malaysia, Java, Sumatra and Borneo.

Habitat   Forests.

Behavior   It lives in family groups consisting of a male and an adult female with young of various ages. Each group defends its territory against other families by fighting or, more often, by screaming. It eats fruit, insects and small birds, drinking rain water from leaves and flowers. After 200-212 days' gestation, the female gives birth to one young, which becomes independent at the age of around 7 years.

MALAYAN BEAR
Helarctos malayanus

Classification   Class: Mammalia; Order: Carnivora; Family: Ursidae.

Description   Also called the Sun Bear. Length of head and body 55 in (140 cm), height to shoulder 28 in (70 cm), weight 110-143 lb (50-65 kg). Black with a white horseshoe-shaped mark on the chest. Very short fur.

Distribution   Southern China, Indochina, Burma, Malaysia, Sumatra, Borneo.

Habitat   Forests.

Behavior   It feeds mainly on fruit, which it obtains by climbing trees with great agility, spending more of its time there than virtually any other bear. Small vertebrates, insects and honey constitute its diet. The female gives birth to 2 cubs after a gestation of 7 months.

MALAYAN FLYING LEMUR
Cynocephalus variegatus

Classification   Class: Mammalia; Order: Dermoptera; Family: Cynocephalidae.

Description   Also known as the Colugo. Length of head and body 11-16½ in (28-42 cm), tail 8¾-10¾ in (22-27 cm), weight 2¼-3¼ lb (1-1.5 kg). Gray-brown above, reddish below. A large hairy membrane, called the patagium, stretches out to surround almost the whole body and the tail.

Distribution   Indochina, Malaysia, Sunda Islands.

Habitat   Forests.

Behavior   Exclusively vegetarian and aboreal. By day it stays clinging to the tree branches, at night it scampers swiftly along the branches, always keeping a firm grip, or makes powerful jumps from one tree to another. Having clambered to the top of a tree, it launches itself forward by extending the legs and the tail; the patagium opens out and enables the animal to glide, gradually losing height, until it lands on another tree, where it feeds. During the "flight," which may be for a distance of over 100 yards, the tail acts as a rudder. After 2 months' gestation, the female gives birth to one young, which grips its mother's teats during her glides.

MANGROVE SNAKE
Boiga dendrophila

Classification   Class: Reptilia; Order: Squamata; Suborder: Ophidea; Family: Colubridae.

Description   Length 8 ft (2.5 m). Bluish-black with yellow stripes. Poisonous.

Distribution   Malaysia, Sunda Islands, Philippines.

Habitat   Mangrove swamps.

Behavior   A tree dweller, it feeds on birds, amphibians and other reptiles.

Note The Flying Snake *(Chrysopelea ornata)*, yellowish-green with a series of red spots along the back, is a colubrid inhabiting much of Southeast Asia and the neighboring islands. Up to 5 ft (1.5 m) long, it lives in trees and is able to contract its abdominal surface, flattening the ribs and rotating the scales outward so as to form beneath itself a hollow containing a cushion of air which supports it as it glides from tree to tree. During "flight" the snake adjusts direction with sideways movements of the body.

MUNTJAC
Muntiacus muntjak
Classification Class: Mammalia; Order: Artiodactyla; Family: Cervidae.
Description Also known as the Barking Deer. Length of head and body 35-53 in (89-135 cm), tail 5-9 in (13-23 cm), height to shoulder 16-26 in (40-65 cm), weight 33-77 lb (15-35 kg). Color reddish-brown. The back and rump are higher than the front parts. The antlers, found only in the male, are small and set on long hair-covered peduncles. The upper canines of the male are unusally well-developed for a herbivore.
Distribution Southeast Asia and the neighboring islands.
Habitat Lowland and mountain forests, thickets.
Behavior Solitary and wary, it emerges from the vegetation to feed on grass, leaves and shoots only at dawn and dusk. If annoyed, it emits sounds similar to the barks of a dog. Fighting among themselves for possession of the females, the males inflict serious injury on one another with their sharp canine teeth. One young is born after a gestation of about 6 months.

ORANG-UTAN
Pongo pygmaeus
Classification Class: Mammalia; Order: Primates; Family: Pongidae.
Description The native name means "man of the woods." Height 3¾-5 ft (1.15-1.50 m), weight 88-220 lb (40-100 kg). The male is much bigger than the female. It is the second largest ape, after the gorilla. Reddish hair. The legs are short and weak, while the arms, measuring over 6 ft (2 m) across, are very powerful. It has no tail.
Distribution Sumatra and Borneo.
Habitat Forests.
Behavior Almost exclusively arboreal, it feeds on fruit, leaves, bark, eggs and fledglings. Diurnal and solitary, it spends the night sleeping in a nest of branches and leaves, which it often renews daily, situated in a tree between a height of 35-80 ft (10-25 m). After a gestation of 8-9 months, the female produces one infant,

which remains with the mother for 4-5 years, during which time she will bear no other young. Mature at 10 years, it lives for up to 30-40 years.

PROBOSCIS MONKEY
Nasalis larvatus
Classification Class: Mammalia; Order: Primates; Family: Colobidae.
Description Length of head and body 24-30 in (60-76 cm), tail 22-30 in (56-76 cm), weight 15½-50 lb (7-22.5 kg). The male is much bigger than the female. Yellowish-brown above, gray below. The nose of the adult male is a drooping proboscis up to 4 in (10 cm) long, while that of the female and young is pointed and turned upward.
Distribution Borneo.
Habitat Muddy river banks, mangrove swamps.
Behavior It feeds almost exclusively on vegetation, moving calmly and deliberately in groups through the trees. It swims fairly well both on the surface and underwater. The female gives birth to one young.

RAJAH BROOKE'S BIRDWING
Ornithoptera brookiana
Classification Class: Insecta; Order: Lepidoptera; Family: Papilionidae.
Description The female is dark brown with yellow spots, the male black with green spots; her wingspan is up to 7½ in (19 cm), his slightly less.
Distribution Malaysia, Sumatra and Borneo.
Habitat Forests.
Behavior The adult feeds on nectar and the larva on plants. Although it prefers to frequent the upper strata of the forest, it regularly descends to the ground in order to eat and drink. The shape of the wings, their dimensions and the speed of flight give an observer the impression that this is a bird rather than a butterfly.
Note A birdwing butterfly with similar coloration, *Ornithoptera priamus*, inhabits the forests of New Guinea. This is the home, too, of *Ornithoptera alexandrae*, the largest butterfly in the world, with a wingspan of 10 in (25 cm).

SMYRNA KINGFISHER
Halcyon smyrnensis
Classification Class: Aves; Order: Coraciiformes; Family: Alcedinidae.
Description Length 11 in (28 cm). Brown with blue wings, white spot on breast, red legs and bill.
Distribution From Turkey to the Philippines across the whole of southern Asia and the islands.
Habitat Near ponds, rice paddies and seashores.

Behavior Although capable of catching fish, it seems to prefer a diet of insects, amphibians and reptiles. For this reason it may be found some distance from water. It nests in cavities dug in sandy banks.

SUMATRAN RHINOCEROS
Dicerorhinus sumatrensis
Classification Class: Mammalia; Order: Perissodactyla; Family: Rhinocerotidae.
Description Length of head and body 8-9 ft (2.5-2.8 m), height to shoulder 3½-5 ft (1.1-1.5 m). It is the smallest rhinoceros, with a body partially covered with hair. It is the only Asiatic species with two horns, even though the second is a fairly modest protuberance.
Distribution Burma, Thailand, Malaysia, Sumatra and Borneo.
Habitat Forests.
Behavior Almost nothing is known about its life in the wild. From 100-200 individuals survive, and their future is threatened by hunting and the destruction of their habitat.
Note The Javan or Sundra Rhinoceros *(Rhinoceros sondaicus)* is likewise in grave danger of extinction. Its presence has been reported only in Java's Udjung Kulon reserve. This is the only species in which the female has no horn. Similar in appearance to the Indian rhinoceros, it is distinguished from the latter by its smaller size.

TREE SHREW
Tupaia glis
Classification Class: Mammalia; Order: Scandentia; Family: Tupaiidae.
Description Length of head and body 6-8 in (15-21 cm), tail 6-10 in (15-24 cm), weight 3½-7 oz (100-200 g). Black or brown above, whitish below. The tail is similar to that of a squirrel, the snout resembles that of a shrew. With others of the same genus it is considered to be related to the most primitive primates.
Distribution Indochina, Malaysia, Sumatra, Java and Borneo.
Habitat Forests.
Behavior It eats fruit, seeds, eggs, birds and small rodents, being equally at home on the ground or in the trees. From observations carried out with captive specimens, it would appear to be territorial. In a leafy nest built, according to some experts, by the male, the female produces 2 young after a gestation of 45-55 days. Within a month these will leave the nest.

AFRICA

The heart of Africa consists of the dense forests and rolling savannas that extend on either bank of the Congo and Zambezi rivers and around the great lakes (Victoria, Rudolf, Tanganyika and Nyasa). Their courses mark a depression (the Rift Valley) caused by a fracture in the Earth's crust, so that the easternmost part of the continent almost appears to project like a vast island. In these central regions, rich in wildlife, we find the biggest of all existing land animals, the African elephant. Yet its size is hardly an exception, for these central parts of Africa are inhabited by as varied a selection of large animals as can be found anywhere in the world. Among the best known are the hippopotamus, the rhinoceros and the giraffe; here, too, is to be found the largest of all monkeys, the gorilla, and the largest of all birds, the ostrich.

Not all Africa, however, is covered by forests or savannas. Away from the equator – both to the north and to the south – are lands that are increasingly dry, with two enormous areas of desert, the Sahara in the north and the Kalahari (and adjoining regions) in the south. Beyond these desert zones, where animal and plant life is represented by an extremely limited number of species, are two coastal belts with climates that are for the most part temperate or temperate to hot: These are the regions sometimes called Low Africa, facing the Mediterranean Sea, and the Cape region in the extreme south. The former is inhabited by many typical African species, such as the leopard and the striped hyena, but also by animals widely found in Europe, such as the red deer and the wild boar. The Cape region, on the other hand, has very distinctive fauna and flora. In addition to a large contingent of species related to other African animals and plants, we find certain plants related to genera from Australia, and also quite a few genera, or even families, which have no close relatives anywhere else in the world. The huge island of Madagascar (Malagasy) and the various minor island groups (Mauritius, Réunion, Seychelles, etc) deserve separate discussion; they form what is virtually a bridge between East Africa and southern Asia. All these islands, in fact, accommodate some of the most interesting animals and plants, including entire families which are endemic to these particular areas. Madagascar, for example, is the exclusive habitat of all lemurs, distant relatives of the monkeys, with huge eyes and nocturnal habits, and of the tenrecs, insect-eating mammals which are related to both hedgehogs and shrews. Many extremely interesting species from these islands have become extinct in quite recent times as a result of hunting or of changes in the habitat brought about by man. Among these was the legendary elephant bird, the largest bird ever to have lived, which was native to Madagascar, and the dodo, an enormous dove that was unable to fly, which inhabited the island of Mauritius.

1   hyena
2   chimpanzee
3   dromedary
4   fennec
5   giraffe
6   ostrich
7   Egyptian jerboa
8   addax
9   sacred ibis
10 Nile crocodile
11 pelican
12 cheetah
13 lion
14 gorilla
15 African elephant
16 crowned hawk eagle
17 flamingo
18 hippopotamus
19 impala
20 zebra
21 termites
22 rhinoceros
23 oryx
24 hartebeest
25 Malagasy silk moth
26 ringtailed lemur

Deserts

ADDAX
Addax nasomaculatus
Classification Class: Mammalia; Order: Artiodactyla; Family: Bovidae.
Description Length of head and body 5-5½ ft (1.5-1.7 cm), tail 10-14 in (25-35 cm), height to shoulder 38-46 in (95-115 cm), weight 132-275 lb (60-125 kg). White or grayish. Long, spiral-shaped horns, present in both sexes. Large antelope of heavy build and awkward gait.
Distribution Sahara.
Habitat Sandy or stony deserts.
Behavior It lives in herds which are continually on the move in search of places in the desert where a sudden flood has stimulated the growth, within a few hours, of succulent vegetation; the addax seems to have a special sense for detecting such plants. It has no need for water other than that contained in its food. One young is born after a gestation of 10-12 months.

BARBARY SHEEP
Ammotragus lervia
Classification Class: Mammalia: Order: Artiodactyla; Family: Bovidae.
Description Length of head and body 4¼-5¼ ft (1.3-1.6 m), tail 6-10 in (15-25 cm), height to shoulder 30-40 in (75-100 cm), weight 88-308 lb (40-140 kg). Male much larger than female, which has proportionately smaller horns. Reddish-brown above, lighter below. There is a characteristic fringe of long hair on the throat, chest and forelegs.
Distribution Sahara.
Habitat Rocky heights.
Behavior It lives in family groups led by a large male; old males and pregnant females are solitary. It climbs and leaps with great agility over the rocks, and is scarcely visible among them because of the matching color of its coat. It feeds at night on the sparse vegetation. The female gives birth to 1-2 young after a gestation of 154-161 days.

DORCAS GAZELLE
Gazella dorcas
Classification Class: Mammalia; Order: Artiodactyla; Family: Bovidae.
Description Height to shoulder 22-26 in (55-65 cm), weight 44-51 lb (20-23 kg). Pale brown above, white below with a tawny band along flanks. Both sexes carry lyre-shaped horns.
Distribution North Africa.

Habitat Sandy and stony desert and sub-desert zones.
Behavior It lives in herds. Adult males are sometimes solitary while young animals form separate groups. Apparently untroubled by the desert sun, it wanders long distances in search of food and water. In addition to plants, it eats locusts and their larvae. The female generally produces 1-2 young.

DROMEDARY
Camelus dromedarius
Classification Class: Mammalia; Order: Artiodactyla; Family: Camelidae.
Description Length of head and body 7-11 ft (2.2-3.4 m), tail 22-30 in (55-75 cm), height to top of hump 6-7½ ft (1.9-2.3 m), weight 1,000-1,430 lb (450-650 kg). Colors range from fawn or beige to dark brown. Similar to the Bactrian camel, but with only one hump, longer and thinner legs, shorter hair. The hump is an accumulation of fat which represents a stock of food which the dromedary uses when it has nothing else to eat.
Distribution Saharan Africa. Also found in southwestern Asia and India.
Habitat Deserts and subdesert zones.
Behavior Today it lives only as a domestic animal. Its exceptional ability to survive for long periods without water is mainly due to the fact that its blood maintains an almost normal fluid condition even when the body has lost up to a quarter of its weight through dehydration; the blood continues to circulate even through the narrowest surface veins (capillaries) and give off heat. Thanks to this, the animal does not die of heatstroke, as happens to most vertebrates in such conditions, humans included. The female gives birth to one young after a gestation of 365-440 days.

EGYPTIAN JERBOA
Jaculus jaculus
Classification Class: Mammalia; Order: Rodentia; Family: Dipodidae.
Description Length of head and body 4-6 in (10-15 cm), tail 6-10 in (15-25 cm), weight 1¾-2½ oz (50-70 g). Light brown above, whitish below. Looks like a miniature kangaroo because of its hind legs which are much longer and more powerful than the forelegs. The tail, apart from acting as a rudder during jumps (the jerboa's normal method of moving), also serves to support the body when the animal rears on its hind legs.
Distribution North Africa. Also found in Arabia and the Middle East.
Habitat Deserts and steppes.
Behavior Nocturnal, it feeds on plants, seeds and insects, which it seeks after sun-

set. Being highly sensitive to the heat of the day and to cold by night, it digs burrows some 20 in (50 cm) deep, using its forelegs and teeth for this purpose. The female gives birth, two or three times a year, to an average of 3 young after a gestation of 25-30 days.

FENNEC
Vulpes zerda
Classification Class: Mammalia; Order: Carnivora; Family: Canidae.
Description Also known as the Desert Fox. Length of head and body 14-16 in (36-41 cm), tail 7-12 in (18-30 cm), weight up to 3¼ lb (1.5 kg). Hair long and soft, pale brown above, whitish below. It is a small fox with enormous ears and a fairly short muzzle.
Distribution North Africa, Arabia.
Habitat Sandy deserts.
Behavior Lives in small groups of a dozen or so. Nocturnal, it remains burrowed in the sand by day. It eats rodents, birds, lizards, insects and roots. It can survive for long periods without drinking. The female produces 2-5 young in a burrow dug in the sand, after a gestation of about 50 days.

HOUBARA BUSTARD
Chlamydotis undulata
Classification Class: Aves; Order: Gruiformes; Family: Otididae.
Description Length 25 in (64 cm). Upper parts ocher-yellow with dark streaks, underparts white. Tufts of black and white feathers on head and either side of neck.
Distribution North Africa. Also found in southwestern Asia.
Habitat Desert and subdesert zones.
Behavior Although an excellent flyer, it takes wing only in cases of extreme danger, preferring to flee on its strong legs. When it remains quite still on the ground, it blends perfectly with the surroundings, thanks to its mimetic colors. It feeds on plants and insects. The female lays 2-4 eggs.

LANNER FALCON
Falco biarmicus
Classification Class: Aves; Order: Falconiformes; Family: Falconidae.
Description Length 17 in (43 cm). Dark brown or slate-gray above, whitish with dark spots below. Top of head and nape tawny.
Distribution Throughout Africa. Also lives in southwestern Asia and southern Europe.
Habitat Savannas, deserts, open zones in plains and mountains.
Behavior It feeds principally on birds, captured in flight or on the ground. It is a

formidable hunter, with few rivals for speed and dexterity. It builds a nest on rocks and in trees: the 3-4 eggs are incubated in turn by the parents.

LIBYAN ZORILLA
Poecilictis lybica
Classification Class: Mammalia; Order: Carnivora; Family: Mustelidae.
Description Length of head and body 9-11 in (22-28 cm), tail 5-7 in (13-18 cm). Hair long and soft, striped black and white.
Distribution North Africa.
Habitat Desert.
Behavior Nocturnal, it spends the day in burrows abandoned by other animals or dug by itself. It feeds on rodents, birds, reptiles, and insects. It defends itself by turning its back on the enemy and spraying the latter with a foul-smelling liquid produced by special glands. The female gives birth to 2-3 young.

MIGRATORY LOCUST
Locusta migratoria
Classification Class: Insecta; Order: Orthoptera; Family: Acrididae.
Description Length 1¼-2½ in (3.3-6 cm). Chewing mouthparts with very strong jaws. Hind legs (third pair) adapted for jumping. Two pairs of wings, the hind pair being larger.
Distribution Most of Africa. Also found in central-southern Europe, Asia and Madagascar.
Habitat Many and varied.
Behavior The species may appear in either of two distinct phases, characterized by different shapes, colors and habits: the solitary phase, when the animal keeps to itself except in the breeding season; and the gregarious phase, in the course of which the insect gathers in swarms of millions which undertake vast migrations. The transition from the one to the other phase occurs after an intermediate generation. Swarms of locusts in their gregarious phase always represent a plague, periodically affecting many regions of Africa and Asia, devouring virtually any form of plant life.
Note A distant relative of the migratory locust (*Comicus* sp.), wingless, lives in the arid regions of southern Africa.

SAHARA HORNED VIPER
Cerastes cerastes
Classification Class: Reptilia; Order: Squamata; Suborder: Ophidia; Family: Viperidae.
Description Color sandy yellow with brown spots. Above the eyes are two pointed growths similar to horns.
Distribution Sahara.

Habitat Dunes of shifting sand.
Behavior It spends much time buried in the sand; by day, in order to escape the heat, by night, to protect itself from the cold. By rubbing its scales against one another it produces a threatening rattle instead of the hiss of other snakes. It feeds on small mammals and lizards, killing them with its venom. The female is oviparous.

SAND CAT
Felis margarita
Classification Class: Mammalia; Order: Carnivora; Family: Felidae.
Description Length of head and body 16-22 in (40-57 cm), tail 10-14 in (25-35 cm), height to shoulder 10 in (25 cm). Yellowish-gray, lighter on flanks and belly. Small cat with a broad head, large ears and soles of feet covered with long hair.
Distribution Sahara, southwestern Asia.
Habitat Sandy desert.
Behavior A nocturnal hunter, it eats rodents, hares and birds. The burrow is a hole in the sand, underneath a bush; there the female gives birth to a litter of 4.

SAND SKINK
Scincus scincus
Classification Class: Reptilia; Order: Squamata; Suborder: Sauria; Family: Scincidae.
Description Length up to 8¼ in (12 cm), cylindrical body sandy yellow with transverse dark stripes.
Distribution From Senegal to Egypt. Also found in Israel.
Habitat Sandy desert.
Behavior Active at the hottest time of day, it moves very rapidly across the sand, as if it were swimming. It feeds on insects and other small invertebrates. The female does not lay eggs but gives birth to perfectly formed young.

SCIMITAR ORYX
Oryx dammah
Classification Class: Mammalia; Order: Artiodactyla; Family: Bovidae.
Description Height to shoulder 4 ft (1.2 m), weight 440 lb (200 kg). White with reddish-brown neck and chest. Both sexes have long, backward-curving horns.
Distribution Saharan Africa.
Habitat Semidesert zones.
Behavior It lives in herds which are always on the move in search of food. Sometimes old males join other groups of antelopes. It feeds on grass, acacia fruits and succulent plants. Because of excessive hunting, this is the African antelope in greatest danger of extinction. The female gives birth to one young after about 9 months' gestation.

SPINY-TAILED AGAMID
Uromastyx acanthinurus
Classification Class: Reptilia; Order: Squamata; Suborder: Sauria; Family: Agamidae.
Description Length of head and body 10 in (25 cm). The scales of the short tail form a spiny armor casing which is used for defense. Color varies from black with sandy-gray markings to yellowish-brown.
Distribution North Africa.
Habitat Desert.
Behavior Diurnal, it feeds on plants and insects. The burrow is a tunnel up to 8 ft (2.5 m) long, where it spends the night. If a predator tries to get in, the agamid pokes out its tail, waving it about like a whip. It is protected from birds of prey by its mimetic coloration which makes it almost invisible from above.

SPOTTED SANDGROUSE
Pterocles senegallus
Classification Class: Aves; Order: Columbiformes; Family: Pteroclidae.
Description Length 13 in (33 cm). The male is sandy in color with head and throat yellow, neck gray, belly black; the female is densely covered with dark spots. In both sexes the tail is long and forked.
Distribution North and East Africa. Also found in southwestern Asia.
Habitat Steppes and deserts.
Behavior It makes long journeys every day, the round trip being as much as 35 miles (60 km), in search of water. In the breeding season the male, after soaking his breast and belly, returns to the nest where the chicks quench their thirst by sucking the water from his feathers. It nests on the ground.

YELLOW SCORPION
Buthus occitanus
Classification Class: Arachnida; Order: Scorpiones; Family: Scorpionidae.
Description Length 3¼ in (8 cm). Tawny. Four pairs of legs; terminal part of abdomen (tail) furnished with venomous sting; one pair of large clawlike pincers.
Distribution North Africa. Also found in Arabia, Syria, Spain, France.
Habitat Dry, hot zones.
Behavior Strictly nocturnal, it spends the day beneath stones or in underground burrows. It feeds on insects and other invertebrates, seizing them with its pincers and transfixing them with its poisonous sting, killing them immediately. Its venom may be dangerous even to humans. At the time of reproduction, male and female grasp each other with their pincers and perform a sort of courtship dance. The female gives birth to young that are already fully formed.

Deserts

Plants in the desert are few and far between, but despite the lack of variety they do display interesting adaptations to the problems of climate and soil. In the Sahara they grow more densely in areas where ground water reservoirs lie nearest the surface; these spots are known as oases and they are fringed with date palms and certain species of acacia, tamarisk and myrtle. The plants in the southern deserts of Namibia are very different, drawing their moisture requirements from overnight rainfall; they include numerous succulent plants, among them the strange flowering Lithops, known as the "living stone."

1 Barbary sheep
2 horned viper
3 sand skink
4 *Comicus* grasshopper
5 *Stenocara* beetle
6 sand lizard
7 dromedary
8 Egyptian jerboa
9 migratory locust
10 yellow scorpion
11 desert bug
12 addax
13 scimitar oryx
14 spotted sandgrouse
15 fennec

Savannas

AARDVARK
Orycteropus afer

Classification Class: Mammalia; Order: Tubulidentata; Family: Orycteropodidae.
Description Length of head and body 40-60 in (100-150 cm), tail 18-24 in (45-60 cm), height to shoulder 24 in (60 cm), weight 155 lb (70 kg). Gray-brown. Thick skin covered with sparse bristles; head terminating in a snout similar to that of a pig; strong, muscular tail resembling that of a kangaroo; toes furnished with enormous claws for digging.
Distribution Throughout Africa south of the Sahara.
Habitat Open savanna and thin forest.
Behavior It is a remarkable digger, capable of disappearing underground in a few seconds. Solitary and nocturnal, it spends the day below ground in a burrow which is often as complex as a maze. The burrows abandoned by the aardvark serve as places of refuge for many other animals. It feeds exclusively on termites and ants, captured with its long, sticky tongue after it has ripped open the nests with its powerful claws. The female gives birth to one young after a gestation of 7 months.

AFRICAN HUNTING DOG
Lycaon pictus

Classification Class: Mammalia; Order: Carnivora; Family: Canidae.
Description Length of head and body 30-40 in (76-101 cm), tail 12-16 in (30-41 cm), height to shoulder 24-30 in (60-75 cm), weight 35-65 lb (16-30 kg). Coat streaked dark brown, black, yellowish or white. Slender build with carriage of dog; massive head, like that of the hyena; very large, rounded ears.
Distribution Throughout Africa south of the Sahara.
Habitat Open or tree savanna.
Behavior It lives in packs of 6-20, highly organized for pursuing and killing large savanna herbivores. While some of the dogs stalk the prey from close quarters, the rest of the pack follow at a distance, ready to replace their exhausted companions and to keep up the chase. In this way the hunting dog can wear down the resistance of almost any animal. The cubs are born after a gestation of about 2 months and are fed first of all by the mother alone and later by the whole pack as soon as they are capable of taking part in the hunt themselves.

ANUBIS BABOON
Papio anubis

Classification Class: Mammalia; Order: Primates; Family: Cercopithecidae.
Description Length of head and body about 40 in (100 cm), tail 24 in (60 cm), weight 31-73 lb (14-33 kg). Olive-brown. Robust build, head similar to that of a dog, long and pointed canine teeth, especially in the male.
Distribution Western, eastern and central Africa.
Habitat Savanna.
Behavior Terrestrial, gregarious monkey, living in troops of 10-200 that are led by a number of adult males. Each troop, though not avoiding contact with others, will not tolerate intrusions into key places associated with daily routine, such as grazing grounds and drinking spots, or trees where it spends the night or to which it flees in case of danger. It walks on all fours. A vegetarian, it supplements this diet with insects, birds and young antelopes. The female gives birth to one young after a gestation of about 6 months.

BLACKBACKED JACKAL
Canis mesomelas

Classification Class: Mammalia; Order: Carnivora; Family: Canidae.
Description Length of head and body 36 in (90 cm), tail 12-14 in (30-35 cm), height to shoulder 16 in (40 cm), weight 20-30 lb (9-14 kg). Back black streaked with white, flanks and legs reddish-brown, underparts white.
Distribution Eastern and southern Africa.
Habitat Savanna and thin forests.
Behavior As a rule it lives in pairs, but it is not unusual to come across small groups or isolated individuals. It feeds on medium-sized mammals, birds, reptiles and insects. It is particularly drawn to the prey of large carnivores; it keeps its distance while they eat, but as soon as they leave it falls upon the carcass, snatching what it can from rival hyenas and vultures. The female gives birth to up to 6 cubs.

BLACK RHINOCEROS
Diceros bicornis

Classification Class: Mammalia; Order: Perissodactyla; Family: Rhinocerotidae.
Description Length of head and body 10-12 ft (3-3.7 m), tail 28 in (70 cm), height to shoulder 5-5¼ ft (1.5-1.6 m), weight up to 2 t. Skin gray, almost completely hairless; two horns, the front one being much longer: record length 53½ in (1.359 m).
Distribution Central, eastern and southern Africa.
Habitat Arid zones with cover of thorny bush.

Behavior It lives on its own, the only lasting link being that of mother and young, while male and female live together only during the short mating season. It feeds on branches, leaves and bark. Irritable by nature, it is extremely dangerous because, in spite of its bulk, it is agile and speedy; it can charge at up to 30 mph (50 kmh) over a short distance. The single young is born after 17-18 months' gestation.
Note Standing 5¾ ft (1.75 m) high at the shoulder and weighing 2.3-3.6 t. the White Rhinoceros (*Ceratotherium simum*) is, after the elephant, the largest land mammal in the world. It lives in family groups on the savanna in two restricted zones of central and southeastern Africa. It feeds on grass and is less irritable than its black relative.

BRINDLED GNU
Connochaetes taurinus

Classification Class: Mammalia; Order: Artiodactyla; Family: Bovidae.
Description Also known as the Wildebeest. Length of head and body 5½-8 ft (1.7-2.4 m), tail 28-40 in (70-100 cm), height to shoulder 4¼-4½ ft (1.3-1.4 m), weight 350-600 lb (160-270 kg). Slate-gray, with dark stripes on the front of the body. Large antelope with very distinctive features: forelegs of an ox, hindquarters of an antelope, tail of a horse and horns of a buffalo, found in both sexes.
Distribution Eastern and southern Africa.
Habitat Savanna.
Behavior It forms immense herds which, in the breeding season, split into smaller groups comprising 1-3 males (there is no hierarchy among them) and numerous females with young. It often associates with zebras and Thomson's gazelles. A herbivore, it migrates seasonally for long distances in search of fresh grazing and water. A habitual victim of large predators, especially the lion. The female gives birth to one calf.

BURCHELL'S ZEBRA
Equus burchelli

Classification Class: Mammalia; Order: Perissodactyla; Family: Equidae.
Description Length of head and body 6½-8 ft (2-2.4 m), tail 18½-22½ in (47-57 cm), height to shoulder 4-4½ ft (1.2-1.4 m), weight 510-715 lb (230-325 kg). Unmistakable black and white striping. Body of a horse, with mane and tail of an ass.
Distribution Eastern and southern Africa.
Habitat Grassy plains, sparse woodlands.
Behavior It lives in family groups of 5-20, often associating with gnus and other

gregarious antelopes in the enormous mixed herds so typical of the African savanna. The perpetual need for fresh grazing and water compels it to undertake long migrations to escape drought. The breeding season is characterized by fights among the males who employ bites and kicks in their efforts to win the favors of the females. The foals are born after a gestation of 12 months. The zebra is one of the most frequent victims of lions.

CAPE BUFFALO
Syncerus caffer

Classification Class: Mammalia; Order: Artiodactyla; Family: Bovidae.
Description Length of head and body about 8½ ft (2.6 m), tail 30-44 in (75-110 cm), height to shoulder 3-5½ ft (1-1.7 m), weight 700-1,800 lb (320-820 kg), the lower weight that of the forest variety. Black or reddish-brown. Massive open horns measuring up to 5¼ ft (1.62 m).
Distribution Throughout Africa south of the Sahara.
Habitat Savanna and forest, provided there is water.
Behavior It lives in herds, most numerous in an open habitat, dominated by an adult male but led by an elderly female. By day it remains in dense vegetation close to water, coming out to graze only at sunset and during the night. It enjoys rolling in the mud which, as it dries, protects the animal from insect bites. The calf is born after a gestation of 330-340 days.

CHEETAH
Acinonyx jubatus

Classification Class: Mammalia; Order: Carnivora; Family: Felidae.
Description Length of head and body 4½-5 ft (1.4-1.5 m), tail 24-32 in (60-80 cm), height to shoulder 30 in (75 cm), weight 100-145 lb (45-65 kg). Tawny with black spots on the upper parts, whitish on the underparts.
Distribution Western, central-eastern and southern Africa.
Habitat Savanna and semidesert.
Behavior It lives on its own or in small groups. A diurnal predator with very keen eyesight, it hunts in quite a different way from other felines; it does not lie in ambush for its prey but, having crept up as close as possible, launches an attack at top speed, intent on overtaking the victim before its own relative lack of stamina compels it to stop. In the course of the brief chase it may attain a speed of 75 mph (120 km/h), making it the fastest land mammal in the world. Its usual victims are antelopes, hares, warthogs and ground birds. The female gives birth to 2-3 young after a gestation of about 3 months.

ERITREAN DIK-DIK
Madoqua saltiana

Classification Class: Mammalia; Order: Artiodactyla; Family: Bovidae.
Description Length of head and body 20-28 in (50-70 cm), tail 1½-2 in (3.5-5 cm), height to shoulder 14-16 in (35-40 cm), weight 6-7¾ lb (2.7-3.5 kg). Neck and back gray, flanks reddish, underparts white. Tiny antelope with a tuft of erectile hairs on the forehead, hind legs longer than front ones, and tiny horns found only in the males.
Distribution Eritrea, Ethiopia and Somalia.
Habitat Dense, dry undergrowth.
Behavior Lives alone or in pairs, feeding on leaves, shoots, fruit and roots. It can survive without drinking for long periods, deriving enough water from its food. Extremely timid, it moves about only at dawn and dusk. The single young is born after 6 months' gestation.

GERENUK
Litocranius walleri

Classification Class: Mammalia; Order: Artiodactyla; Family: Bovidae.
Description Also called Waller's Gazelle or Giraffe Antelope. Length of head and body 4½-5¼ ft (1.4-1.6 m), tail 10-14 in (25-35 cm), height to shoulder 35-41 in (88-105 cm), weight 80-115 lb (36-53 kg). Upper parts reddish-brown, underparts white. Long neck and legs; horns only in the male.
Distribution Northern Kenya, Somalia, Ethiopia.
Habitat Thorny undergrowth.
Behavior It lives alone or in small groups, feeding on leaves and shoots. Thanks to its long neck and its habit of rearing up on the hind legs while it eats, it manages to feed on high branches which other antelopes of similar size cannot reach. It does not need to drink, deriving enough water from its food. When it runs, it holds its neck stretched forward.

GIRAFFE
Giraffa camelopardalis

Classification Class: Mammalia; Order: Artiodactyla; Family: Giraffidae.
Description Length of head and body 10-13 ft (3-4 m), tail 36-44 in (90-110 cm), height to shoulder 9-11 ft (2.7-3.6 m), height to top of head up to 20 ft (6 m), weight up to 1¾ t. Color chestnut with a network of lighter lines enclosing marks of varying shapes and sizes; underparts light brown. One pair of short horns, rounded at the tip and covered with skin; two other horns on forehead, hardly visible.
Distribution Much of Africa south of the Sahara, but not continuous.

Habitat Savanna and thin forests.
Behavior It lives in herds, except for old males who are solitary. Vegetarian. The long neck enables it to browse on acacia leaves up to 20 ft (6 m) from the ground. In order to bring the head down to the level of water for drinking, the giraffe has to spread its forelegs wide apart. It defends itself against predators by lashing out with the forelegs. The female produces one young after a gestation of 450 days.

GREATER KUDU
Tragelaphus strepsiceros

Classification Class: Mammalia; Order: Artiodactyla; Family: Bovidae.
Description Length of head and body 6-8 ft (1.9-2.4 m), tail 18 in (45 cm), height to shoulder 4-5¼ ft (1.2-1.6 m), weight 400-700 lb (180-320 kg). Bluish-gray or grayish-brown with 6-10 white bands on flanks. The spiral horns, found only in the male, measure up to 4 ft (1-1.1 m).
Distribution Central-eastern and southern Africa.
Habitat Underbrush in hilly zones.
Behavior It lives in small herds of 4-5 from which adult males are often excluded; these, except in the breeding season, lead a solitary life. Prevalently nocturnal, it feeds on leaves, shoots and grass. Gestation lasts about 7 months and there is a single young.

IMPALA
Aepyceros melampus

Classification Class: Mammalia; Order: Artiodactyla; Family: Bovidae.
Description Length of head and body 4¼-6 ft (1.3-1.8 m), tail 10-16½ in (25-42 cm), height to shoulder 30-40 in (75-100 cm), weight 90-200 lb (40-90 kg). Reddish-brown above, white below. Antelope of average size. The female, smaller than the male, has no horns.
Distribution Eastern and southern Africa.
Habitat Savanna.
Behavior Markedly gregarious, it lives in herds of 6-50. In the breeding season each male assembles 15-20 females around himself and there are furious battles among rivals. It browses mainly on acacia leaves. Celebrated for its leaps, which can be as much as 30 ft (9 m) in length and 10 ft (3 m) high. As a rule there is only one young, born after a gestation of about 170 days.

LION
Panthera leo

Classification Class: Mammalia; Order: Carnivora; Family: Felidae.
Description Length of head and body 4½-6 ft (1.4-1.9 m), tail 28-42 in (70-105

Savannas

The savanna is dominated by tall grasses belonging to the family Gramineae, but in zones that are not so dry there are occasional trees, including the acacia, with dense foliage. Another prominent tree of the savanna is the baobab, notable for its enormous, barrel-like trunk.

1 anubis baboon
2 greater kudu
3 Eritrean dik-dik
4 African hunting dog
5 Cape buffalo
6 cheetah
7 lion
8 ostrich
9 warthog
10 Burchell's zebra
11 impala
12 sable antelope
13 black rhinoceros
14 spotted hyena
15 weaverbird
16 giraffe
17 brindled gnu
18 waterbuck
19 gerenuk

cm), height to shoulder up to 3¼ ft (1 m), weight 265-550 lb (120-250 kg). The male is much larger than the female. Grayish-brown above, lighter below. The male has a mane. The tail of both sexes terminates in a tuft of dark hairs.

Distribution   Much of Africa south of the Sahara. The Gir Forest in northwestern India is the home of the last surviving lions of Eurasia, which onced roamed widely from Greece to India.

Habitat   Savanna and semidesert.

Behavior   It lives in family groups consisting of one or more adult males, females and young of various ages. It is active at night, sleeping by day in the shade of trees and bushes. The lion is the only big cat which prefers collective hunting: several animals surprise the prey and drive them toward their hidden companions (generally lionesses) who make a sudden leap on to their backs and kill them with a bite to the throat. This enables the lion to bring down even adult buffaloes and giraffes, but their favorite victims are zebras and antelopes (particularly gnus). The 2-4 cubs are born after a gestation of 105 days.

OSTRICH
Struthio camelus

Classification   Class: Aves; Order: Struthioniformes; Family: Struthionidae.

Description   Length 6½ ft (2 m), height 9 ft (2.75 m), weight 165-330 lb (75-150 kg). It is the largest living bird, incapable of flying. Male black and white, female gray-brown. The neck and the long legs, suited for running, are almost featherless. The feet have only two toes, the longer having a claw that can be used as a weapon.

Distribution   Western, central-eastern and southern Africa.

Habitat   Savannas and subdesert zones.

Behavior   Normally lives in flocks, but in the breeding season it forms family groups made up of an adult male, females and young. It is diurnal and almost wholly vegetarian; in dry zones it can go without water, surviving on the liquid contained in its food. When threatened it runs away at a maximum speed of 35-45 mph (60-70 km/h), which if necessary it can maintain for some time. The male assumes the greater responsibility in the breeding period; he prepares the nest by scooping out a hollow in the ground, incubates the 3-8 eggs laid by the female, and raises the chicks. The eggs weigh over 3 lb (1.5 kg) and hatch after an incubation of 42 days.

SABLE ANTELOPE
Hippotragus niger

Classification   Class: Mammalia; Order: Artiodactyla; Family: Bovidae.

Description   Length of head and body up to 6½ ft (2 m), tail 16 in (40 cm), height to shoulder 3½-4¼ ft (1.1-1.3 m), weight 400-550 lb (180-250 kg). Black above, white below; the same contrasting colors mark the muzzle. The male has very long, backward-curving horns; those of the female are shorter.

Distribution   Southeastern Africa.

Habitat   Savanna with dense tree growth.

Behavior   Herbivorous, it lives in herds consisting of an adult male, numerous females and young of various ages. Very aggressive toward his male companions, he will readily use his fearsome horns against large carnivores. One young is born after a gestation of 270-281 days.

SPOTTED HYENA
Crocuta crocuta

Classification   Class: Mammalia; Order: Carnivora; Family: Hyaenidae.

Description   Length of head and body 5½ ft (1.65 m), tail 13 in (33 cm), height to shoulder 30-36 in (75-90 cm), weight 90-155 lb (40-70 kg). Gray-brown, with irregular black spots.

Distribution   Much of Africa south of the Sahara.

Habitat   Savanna and semidesert.

Behavior   Mainly nocturnal, it spends the day in burrows. It lives alone, in pairs or in small groups, but hunts in packs of 30 or more. Although it often feeds on carrion, it is usually a hunter of large animals, which it captures and kills in the same way as the African Hunting Dog. The prey is devoured completely, even the largest bones crushed by its powerful jaws. The female gives birth to 1-2 cubs after about 110 days' gestation.

THOMSON'S GAZELLE
Gazella thomsoni

Classification   Class: Mammalia; Order: Artiodactyla; Family: Bovidae.

Description   Length of head and body 44 in (110 cm), tail 4¾ in (12 cm), height to shoulder 26 in (65 cm), weight 40-60 lb (18-27 kg). Reddish-brown above, white below; black stripe on flanks. Horns present in both sexes.

Distribution   East Africa.

Habitat   Open savanna.

Behavior   The most common gazelle of East Africa; lives in herds of 5-60 with a single adult male who, when too old to defend his position, separates himself from the group to live alone. During the dry season Thomson's gazelles assemble in herds of thousands and, together with zebras and gnus, migrate to wetter regions. It feeds exclusively on grass. When it flees, it jumps with all four legs held stiffly. Once or twice a year, after a gestation of 5-6 months, the female produces a single young.

WARTHOG
Phacochoerus aethiopicus

Classification   Class: Mammalia; Order: Artiodactyla; Family: Suidae.

Description   Length including tail 4½-6 ft (1.4-1.9 m), height to shoulder 26-34 in (65-85 cm), weight 110-330 lb (50-150 kg). Hair sparse and bristly; skin grayish. A wild boar with an enormous head and covered with warts, very big canine teeth protruding from the lips.

Distribution   Much of Africa south of Sahara.

Habitat   Savanna and semidesert.

Behavior   It lives in family groups; only the older males are solitary. Chiefly diurnal, it rests in burrows abandoned by other animals such as the aardvark. It feeds only on plants. The female gives birth to 3-4 young after 175 days' gestation.

WATERBUCK
Kobus ellipsiprymus

Classification   Class: Mammalia; Order: Artiodactyla; Family: Bovidae.

Description   Length of head and body 6-7¼ ft (1.8-2.2 m), tail 9-18 in (22-45 cm), height to shoulder about 4 ft (1.2-1.3 m), weight 440 lb (200 kg). Brown or gray on back, paler on flank. A white ring encircles the lower part of the rump. The horns, found only in males, are sickle-shaped.

Distribution   Eastern and southern Africa.

Habitat   Thickets close to water.

Behavior   It lives in small herds made up of females, young and a single adult male. It generally stays near water. It feeds on shoots. The female produces one young after a gestation of 7-8 months.

WEAVERBIRD
Quelea quelea

Classification   Class: Aves; Order: Passeriformes; Family: Ploceidae.

Description   Also called Redbilled Quelea. Length 5 in (12 cm). The male in courtship livery is light brown with dark brown bars on back and tail, a black mask and a red bill; the female is drabber in color and has no mask. Outside the breeding season the two sexes look alike.

Distribution   Western, central-eastern and southern Africa.

Habitat   Savanna.

Behavior   It lives in enormous flocks which do not break up even in the breeding season. The nests, made of interwoven blades of grass, are rounded in shape with a side entrance and are generally situated in an acacia tree.

Forests

AFRICAN ELEPHANT
Loxodonta africana

Classification Class: Mammalia; Order: Proboscidea; Family: Elephantidae.

Description Length of head and body, including trunk, 20-25 ft (6-7.5 m), tail 3¼-4¼ ft (1-1.3 m), height to shoulder 10-13 ft (3-4 m), weight 5-7.5 t. The male is bigger than the female, and the forest elephants are smaller than those of the savanna. Gray. Immense fan-like ears, upper incisor teeth developed into tusks.

Distribution Much of Africa south of Sahara.

Habitat Tree savanna, lowland and mountain forests.

Behavior It lives in herds led by an aged female. Old males often become solitary. It communicates with its companions by means of a wide range of sounds, the most impressive of which is a loud trumpeting, emitted when angry or frightened. Normally tolerant, it may sometimes react in an aggressive manner. If it charges, it may work up a speed of 25 mph (40 km/h). It feeds on various types of vegetation and can consume 400-600 lb (180-270 kg) of food daily. It also needs an enormous quantity of water, which it sucks up through the trunk and pours into its mouth. Daily routine entails both wallowing in water and spraying itself with dust. After 22-24 months' gestation the female gives birth to a single young, weighing 265-310 lb (120-140 kg), which becomes adult at 18 months and lives for 60-70 years.

BLACK-CASQUED HORNBILL
Ceratogymna atrata

Classification Class: Aves; Order: Coraciiformes; Family: Bucerotidae.

Description Total length 36 in (90 cm). The male, black with a white tip to the tail, is larger than the female, which is black with reddish-brown head and neck. In both sexes the bill is surmounted by a large, cylindrical, black casque.

Distribution West and central Africa and islands of Fernando Po.

Habitat Forests.

Behavior It lives in pairs. Notable characteristics are the booming call, which can be heard from afar, and the slow, lumbering and very noisy flight. The nest is a tree hollow in which the female spends the entire period of incubation, sealing the entrance with mud. A small opening allows the male to bring her food.

BLACK DUIKER
Cephalophus niger

Classification Class: Mammalia; Order: Artiodactyla; Family: Bovidae.

Description Length of head and body 22-36 in (55-90 cm), height to shoulder 20 in (50 cm), weight 20-35 lb (9-16 kg). Dark brown or gray-black above, lighter below. Forehead, including a tuft of hair, bright chestnut. Forelegs shorter than hind legs, back convex. Short, straight, backward-turned horns found in both sexes.

Distribution West Africa.

Habitat Forests.

Behavior Generally solitary and nocturnal, it spends the day in shelters beneath fallen trees or in dense underbrush. It moves nimbly through the tangled vegetation, sniffing the ground; when threatened it dives into the thickets. Feeds on vegetation, fish, crustaceans and flightless birds. The female gives birth to one young after a gestation of about 120 days.

BONGO
Boocercus euryceros

Classification Class: Mammalia; Order: Artiodactyla; Family: Bovidae.

Description Length of head and body 5½-8 ft (1.7-2.5 m), tail 18-26 in (45-65 cm), height to shoulder 3½-4 ft (1.1-1.2 m), weight up to 485 lb (220 kg). Chestnut to bright red with 12-14 white stripes across shoulders, flanks and haunches. Crest of black and white hairs along the convex back. Massive spiral horns in boths sexes.

Distribution Western, central and eastern Africa.

Habitat Forests.

Behavior It lives in pairs or in small groups, feeding at night on leaves, shoots and lianas. Timid and silent, it leads a retiring life in the dense and tangled forest undergrowth where, having sensed danger thanks to its keen hearing, it will take to its heels with the muzzle pointed forward and horns parallel to the back. The female probably produces more than one young after about 294 days' gestation.

CHIMPANZEE
Pan troglodytes

Classification Class: Mammalia; Order: Primates; Family: Pongidae.

Description Length of head and body 28-37 in (70-93 cm), height to top of head when standing upright 4¼-5½ ft (1.3-1.7 m), weight 88-110 lb (40-50 kg). Very young individuals are black with a pink face; in due course the face becomes dark, the hairs thin out and turn brown and gray, especially on the back. The arms are longer than the legs.

Distribution Western and central Africa.

Habitat Lowland and mountain forests, tree savannas.

Behavior Although spending most of the time on the ground, it climbs trees with great agility. On the ground it walks on all fours, but now and then, for short distances, it will proceed in an upright stance. The only lasting relationships among chimpanzees is between mother and young. Groups and pairs form and dissolve very easily. A diurnal animal, it spends the night in trees, in nests made of bent and interwoven branches. It feeds on plants, eggs, and insects; the savanna populations also hunt other monkeys and small antelopes. The female gives birth to a single young after a gestation of 236 days.

CONGO PEACOCK
Afropavo congensis

Classification Class: Aves; Order: Galliformes; Family: Phasianidae.

Description Total length 24-28 in (60-70 cm). The male is bronze-green with a red mark on the throat and a tuft of white feathers on the head; the female is tawny with a green back.

Distribution Zaire.

Habitat Forests.

Behavior It lives in pairs or in family groups. It is omnivorous. Although diurnal, it always remains in the thick of the forest, sleeping in trees. During courtship the male spreads his tail like the common peacock and the turkey. The female lays 2-3 eggs in a tree cavity and incubates them for 26-29 days.

CROWNED HAWK EAGLE
Stephanoaëtus coronatus

Classification Class: Aves; Order: Falconiformes; Family: Accipitridae.

Description Total length 27-34 in (69-87 cm), weight 6¼-10 lb (2.8-4.6 kg). Upper parts blackish, underparts paler but with close dark bands. Head adorned with a tuft of black and white feathers, short and rounded wings, long tail.

Distribution Africa south of the Sahara.

Habitat Forests.

Behavior It lives in pairs. Capturing most of its prey on the ground, it feeds mainly on small mammals but also on reptiles, including poisonous species. The nest, built in a tall forest tree, is used year after year by a succession of different pairs of birds. The 1-2 eggs hatch after 49 days' incubation.

GABOON VIPER
Bitis gabonica

Classification Class: Reptilia; Order: Squamata; Suborder: Ophidia; Family: Viperidae.

Forests

The equatorial rain forest of central and western Africa is notable for its wealth of trees, epiphytes and other exotic plants. Among the many tree species are some which are of great economic and commercial interest, such as teak, mahogany and ebony; palms are also plentiful.

1 okapi
2 chimpanzee
3 black-casqued hornbill
4 African elephant
5 giant pangolin
6 Congo peacock
7 crowned hawk eagle
8 leopard
9 gorilla

Description The largest viper in the world, its length is up to 6 ft (1.8 m); massive body, broad, flat and triangular head, poison fangs up to 1½ in (4 cm) long. Color reddish-brown brightened with yellow, blue and cinnamon lines.
Distribution Western, central, and eastern Africa.
Habitat Forests.
Behavior It is not aggressive and will bite only if touched. If cornered, it inhales air and swells up to exhale, producing a threatening hiss. It feeds principally on small mammals.

GIANT FOREST HOG
Hylochoerus meinertzhageni
Classification Class: Mammalia; Order: Artiodactyla; Family: Suidae.
Description It is the largest African wild pig. Length of head and body 5-6 ft (1.5-1.8 m), tail 12 in (30 cm), height to shoulder 3½ ft (1.1 m), weight up to 550 lb (250 kg). Blackish. Rump higher than shoulders, large tusks sprouting from lips.
Distribution Western, central, and eastern Africa.
Habitat Forests.
Behavior It lives in small family groups. Old and young males live alone and in separate herds respectively. It feeds on grass, leaves, fruit, and roots. Mainly nocturnal, it always takes the same routes, opening up tunnels through the vegetation. The female gives birth to 2-6 young.

GIANT PANGOLIN
Manis gigantea
Classification Class: Mammalia; Order: Pholidota; Family: Manidae.
Description Length of head and body 28-32 in (70-80 cm), tail 20-26 in (50-65 cm), weight 65 lb (30 kg). Grayish-brown. The body is covered with scales that overlap like the tiles of a roof. It has no teeth. The forelegs are equipped with curving claws which the pangolin uses for tearing open the walls of termites' nests.
Distribution Western and central Africa.
Habitat Forests and savannas.
Behavior It feeds only on ants and termites, which it captures with its very long, sticky tongue. It does not climb trees. Sometimes it walks upright on its hind legs, supported by the tail. Nocturnal by habit, it spends the day in an underground burrow which it has dug.

GOLDEN CAT
Felis aurata
Classification Class: Mammalia; Order: Carnivora; Family: Felidae.
Description Length of head and body 28-38 in (70-95 cm), tail 11-14½ in (28-37 cm), height to shoulder 20 in (50 cm). As a rule reddish-brown, sometimes gray or blackish; dark spots, more or less visible, over whole body but sometimes not on back.
Distribution Western and central Africa.
Habitat Lowland and mountain forests.
Behavior Very little is known about the animal. Although an agile climber, feeds principally on rodents and birds caught mainly on the ground. It takes refuge in tree cavities, among rocks, and in dense bush.

GORILLA
Gorilla gorilla
Classification Class: Mammalia; Order: Primates; Family: Pongidae.
Description The largest and strongest living primate. The male is up to 5¾ ft (1.75 m) tall and weighs about 440 lb (200 kg); the female measures 5 ft (1.5 m) and weighs 265 lb (120 kg). On the rare occasions when the male adopts an upright position he stands 7½ ft (2.3 m) high. Generally black, males over 10 years old have a gray back.
Distribution Western and central Africa.
Habitat Wet lowland and mountain forests.
Behavior It usually stays on the ground, climbing trees only seldom and with great caution. It walks on all fours. Groups consist of an adult male, one or more females and a variable number of young. It employs a varied "vocabulary" and range of gestures. When threatened, the male stands upright on his hind legs and beats his chest, letting out a loud roar. His appearance is then so terrifying as to inspire, quite understandably, superstitious fear among local people. In reality, such fear is scarcely justified because once he has put on this exhibition the gorilla retires, followed by his family. Only if directly attacked will the leader of the group, and he alone, strike back at the enemy. Exclusively diurnal, the gorilla spends the night in a nest built on the ground. It feeds only on vegetation. The female gives birth to one young after a gestation of 251-289 days.

NATAL TERMITE
Bellicositermes natalensis
Classification Class: Insecta; Order: Isoptera; Family: Termitidae.
Description Length ½-1 in (1.2-2.2 cm). Color tawny or blackish. Fertile termites have wings, others (workers and soldiers) are wingless and generally blind. The soldiers have a large head with extremely stong jaws, designed for offensive and defensive purposes.
Distribution West Africa.

Habitat Forests and savannas.
Behavior This insect lives in a family community which is organized according to strict rank and a clear segregation of workers from the other social classes. The colony is composed of a pair of reproductive individuals and their descendants. This pair, having come from a nearby community and shed their wings, which are by now superfluous, go underground and lay their eggs. The larvae that are born are transformed by various stages of growth either into insects capable of reproducing or into sterile workers or soldiers. The colony lives in a pyramid-shaped nest some 6-15 ft (2-5 m) high, with a circumference of about 30-65 ft (10-20 m). Its construction and defense, after the founding pair have provided for the growth of the first workers and soldiers, is entrusted to the latter. The workers are occupied both in distributing food and caring for the larvae. The sole task of the founding pair, from now on, is to continue reproducing. The queen's abdomen swells enormously as she is transformed into a monstrous egg machine capable of producing 30,000-40,000 eggs per day. The colony feeds on soil fungus, constituted of dead wood and green vegetation, which is cultivated in the warm, moist atmosphere of the nest.

OKAPI
Okapia johnstoni
Classification Class: Mammalia; Order: Artiodactyla; Family: Giraffidae.
Description Length of head and body 7 ft (2.1 m), tail 12-16 in (30-40 cm), height to shoulder 5-5½ ft (1.5-1.7 m), weight 550 lb (250 kg). Dark brown with black and white stripes on legs. Body short, back sloping like that of a giraffe, neck long, legs disproportionately long in relation to body. The horns, in the male only, are short and covered with skin.
Distribution Central Africa.
Habitat Forests.
Behavior It leads such a retiring life that at the beginning of the twentieth century the only humans sure of its existence were the pygmies of the equatorial forests of central Africa. It was not described until 1901. Solitary and nocturnal, it hides by day in the dense vegetation. It feeds on leaves, twigs, and fruit, removing this with its long, protractile tongue. While it eats, moving about with extreme caution, it relies mainly on hearing to locate danger. The single young is born after a gestation of 14-15 months.

Rivers and lakes

AFRICAN BUTTERFLY FISH
Pantodon buchholzi

Classification Class: Osteichthyes; Order: Osteoglossiformes; Family: Osteoglossidae.

Description Total length up to 6 in (15 cm). Light brown. Head and back flattened, pectoral fins so big that they seem to be wings. The rays of the ventral fins are tactile organs.

Distribution West Africa.

Habitat Rivers of the Niger or Congo basins.

Behavior It stations itself for long periods just below the surface, among the floating plants, ready to seize any insect that may have fallen into the water or be flying too low. The large pectoral fins make it possible for the fish to leap about 6 ft (2 m) out of the water.

AFRICAN DARTER
Anhinga rufa

Classification Class: Aves; Order: Pelecaniformes; Family: Anhingidae.

Description Total length 36 in (90 cm). Male black with chestnut head and neck, female and young tawny. Straight, pointed bill with finely toothed edges. Very long, snake-like neck.

Distribution Africa south of the Sahara. Also found in southern Asia and its islands, in Australia, and New Guinea.

Habitat Rivers and lakes.

Behavior It feeds principally on fish, swimming underwater and swiftly darting out its head at them. As is the case with the cormorant, its plumage absorbs water and once on dry land again, the feathers have to be dried. This is why the bird exposes itself to the sun, wings spread wide. It nests in colonies. The female lays 3-5 eggs and incubates them for a month.

CAPE CLAWLESS OTTER
Aonyx capensis

Classification Class: Mammalia; Order: Carnivora; Family: Mustelidae.

Description Length of head and body 38-40 in (95-100 cm), tail 22 in (55 cm), weight 31-50 lb (14-23 kg). Dark brown above, lighter below; sides of face, neck and throat white. Feet almost completely unwebbed.

Distribution Western, eastern and southern Africa.

Habitat Broad rivers in open country.

Behavior It lives alone, in pairs or in small family groups, feeding on fish, amphibians, crustaceans, birds and small mammals. The large, strong molar teeth are suitable for cracking the shells of freshwater crabs. Partially diurnal, it enjoys sunning itself on sandbanks alongside rivers. The female gives birth to 2-5 young after a gestation of about 2 months.

CATTLE EGRET
Bubulcus ibis

Classification Class: Aves; Order: Ciconiiformes; Family: Ardeidae.

Description Also called the Buffbacked Heron. Length 20-22 in (50-56 cm). White with yellow bill and dark green legs. During the breeding season both sexes are adorned with long tawny feathers on the head, breast, and back; eyes, bill, and legs take on a deep orange-yellow color.

Distribution Much of Africa, except arid regions. Also found in Spain, Portugal, southern France, India, Indochina, Sunda Islands, Australia, and islands of the Pacific. Its area of distribution is continually expanding.

Habitat Usually frequents open zones, flooded or otherwise. In order to breed it prefers to settle in swamps with plenty of vegetation.

Behavior It has the habit of following herds of grazing herbivores and feeding off any insects they dislodge in their travels. In the breeding season it lives in colonies, often mingling with other herons. The female lays 4-5 eggs, incubating them for 22-26 days.

CROCODILE BIRD
Pluvianus aegyptius

Classification Class: Aves; Order: Charadriiformes; Family: Glareolidae.

Description Length about 8 in (19-20.5 cm). Gray above, tawny below with a contrasting black and white pattern on head, wings and breast.

Distribution Tropical Africa.

Habitat Sandy banks of rivers.

Behavior The female incubates her four eggs in a strange way: she buries them in the sand and crouches over them to prevent them overheating in the sun. When threatened, she even covers the chicks with sand. Until quite recently the bird was thought to venture fearlessly into the mouth of crocodiles in order to clean it of scraps of food, but more detailed observations have failed to confirm that theory. It has been verified, however, that the bird warns the crocodile of imminent danger by flocking and flying away.

ELECTRIC CATFISH
Malapterurus electricus

Classification Class: Osteichthyes; Order: Siluriformes; Family: Malapteruridae.

Description Total length 4 ft (1.2 m), weight about 55 lb (25 kg). Long, cylindrical, flesh-colored body, provided with a powerful electrical apparatus which extends from the head to the attachment of the tail.

Distribution Most of Africa.

Habitat Rivers.

Behavior By continuously giving out light electric shocks, the fish creates around itself an energy shield that functions like a radar system, enabling it to identify prey and possible obstacles in cloudy water. Much stronger shocks prove a terrible and sometimes mortal weapon. It lives near the seabed, feeding on other fish.

HAMMERHEAD
Scopus umbretta

Classification Class: Aves; Order: Ciconiiformes; Family: Scopidae.

Description Total length 20 in (50 cm). Brown with black bill and legs. The common name of this stork is derived from the tuft of feathers on the nape and laterally compressed bill which give the head a vague resemblance to a hammer.

Distribution Africa south of the Sahara. Also found in Madagascar.

Habitat Lakes, rivers, and streams.

Behavior It wades in shallow water, feeding on insects, crabs, small fish, and frogs. The nest is an enormous, almost spherical structure, made of all kinds of vegetation and placed in the fork of a branch, some 40-50 ft (12-15 m) from the ground. The 3-6 eggs are deposited in a small chamber in the center of the nest where male and female incubate them in turn for 30 days.

HIPPOPOTAMUS
Hippopotamus amphibius

Classification Class: Mammalia; Order: Artiodactyla; Family: Hippopotamidae.

Description Length of head and body 13-15 ft (4-4.5 m), height to shoulder 5½ ft (1.65 m), weight up to 3.2 t. Grayish-brown, lighter on underparts; sometimes the body is reddish as a result of secretions from the cutaneous glands. Skin almost completely hairless. Prominent ears, eyes, and nostrils that are visible above surface when the rest of the animal is still submerged. Long, broad teeth.

Distribution Much of Africa south of the Sahara.

Habitat Rivers, lakes and pools surrounded by grassland.

Behavior Herds of females and young are supervised by adult males who assume positions around them, the higher-ranking individuals being closest. The

Rivers and lakes

The banks of many swampy areas in Africa are densely lined with the tall plumes of papyrus or paper reed, together with other reeds, rushes, and marsh plants. On the surface of ponds and lakes, spectacular color is often provided by the purple, red, and white flowers of waterlilies. Invisible but very important, too, are the diatoms and other microscopic algae, which multiply very rapidly in the water, providing food for many fish and also for flamingos.

1 hippopotamus
2 Cape clawless otter
3 cattle egret
4 flamingo
5 sitatunga
6 sacred ibis
7 pinkbacked pelican
8 crocodile bird
9 Nile crocodile
10 African darter
11 shoebill

social order is established after bloody duels that may even end in the death of one of the contenders. Apart from being an excellent swimmer, the hippopotamus can remain underwater for up to 6 minutes and can walk along the riverbed. At dusk, having spent the day in the water or stretched out on a sandbank, it ventures on to dry land to find food. It grazes all night, perhaps wandering some miles from the water. The female gives birth to a single young after a gestation of 233 days.
Note The forests of Liberia are the home of the Pygmy Hippopotamus *(Choeropsis liberiensis),* which differs from its relative only in its smaller size and certain structural details. Total length 5 ft (1.5 m), height to shoulder 30-33 in (77-83 cm), weight 400-570 lb (180-260 kg).

MOZAMBIQUE TILAPIA
Sarotherodon mossambicus
Classification   Class: Osteichthyes; Order: Perciformes; Family: Cichlidae.
Description   Total length up to 16 in (40 cm). Male dark blue with red-bordered dorsal and caudal fins, whitish throat; female gray.
Distribution   Most of Africa.
Habitat   Rivers.
Behavior   It consumes other fish, insects, and vegetation. The species is one of the many so-called mouthbrooders. The male scoops a hole, in the bottom of which mating takes place; immediately after this the female gathers in her mouth the eggs she has just laid and keeps them there until the young are born. Despite the inconvenience, she continues to feed, though in smaller amounts. The newly-hatched fry remain in the mother's mouth until they are able to swim in search of tiny food particles. Even after that, should danger threaten, they take refuge inside her mouth.

NILE CROCODILE
Crocodylus niloticus
Classification   Class: Reptilia; Order: Crocodilia; Family: Crocodilidae.
Description   Total length up to 16½ ft (5 m). Body completely encased in horny plates. In spite of the webbed hind feet, it is the tail, with its sinuous movements, that propels the crocodile when swimming. Color dark green.
Distribution   Africa south of the Sahara.
Habitat   Rivers and lakes.
Behavior   The males, larger than the females, are territorial. Fighting with one another, they win and defend a stretch of bank and the adjacent water. The females have free access to various territories. Crocodiles measuring less than about 6 ft (2 m) feed mainly on fish; only when they

become larger do they begin attacking large mammals while the latter are drinking. Seizing the prey by the muzzle or the leg, they drag it underwater and drown it. The teeth are unsuitable for ripping and chewing flesh, serving only to grasp and drag down the prey; the crocodile is therefore unable to eat its victim immediately, and anchors it beneath the surface for some hours in order to soften it. The female lays the eggs in holes scooped in the sand along the shore. They hatch after 11-14 weeks, during which time the mother tends them and protects them from predators. At birth, the crocodiles measure 10-13½ in (26-34 cm). Following the brief period of maternal care, they live concealed in the grass and the bushes, feeding on insects, crustaceans, amphibians, small birds, and rodents. At this stage of their growth they have to be on their guard as well against adult crocodiles who are likely to eat them.

PINKBACKED PELICAN
Pelecanus rufescens
Classification   Class: Aves; Order: Pelecaniformes; Family: Pelecanidae.
Description   Length 4¼ ft (1.3 m). Light gray; the bill, the legs and a naked patch around the eyes are yellow, and there is a tuft of feathers on the nape. The lower mandible of the huge bill is furnished with a pouch of limp skin which expands enormously when the mouth is wide open.
Distribution   Throughout Africa south of the Sahara.
Habitat   Large rivers, lakes and lagoons.
Behavior   Despite its size, the pelican is light and graceful in flight. It feeds exclusively on fish, locating shoals near the surface and catching them by using the bill as a kind of net. It nests in colonies, mingling with other aquatic birds. The 2-3 eggs hatch after an incubation of 30-42 days.

SACRED IBIS
Threskiornis aethiopica
Classification   Class: Aves; Order: Ciconiiformes; Family: Threskiornithidae.
Description   Length 26-30 in (65-75 cm). White with long blue-black feathers that give off metallic reflections and fall in soft tufts over the closed wings and the tail. The featherless head and neck are black.
Distribution   Most of Africa south of the Sahara. Also found in Madagascar and Iraq.
Habitat   Lakes, rivers, cultivated zones.
Behavior   Eats insects, fish, amphibians, eggs and nestlings, finding its food by wading in shallow water or on dry land provided it is close to water. It builds a nest (a large structure of twigs, lined with grass and leaves) in trees and bushes, on rocks

or directly on the ground. The 2-3 eggs laid by the female hatch after an incubation of 28-29 days.

SHOEBILL
Balaeniceps rex
Classification   Class: Aves; Order: Ciconiiformes; Family: Balaenicipitidae.
Description   Also known as the Whale-headed Stork. Total length 3½-4¼ ft (1.1-1.3 m). Gray. The bill, as broad as it is long, is shaped like a slipper, hence the common name.
Distribution   Central and eastern Africa.
Habitat   Swamps and river banks with dense vegetation.
Behavior   Solitary and nocturnal, it feeds on fish, amphibians and molluscs. An excellent flyer, it often allows itself to be carried upward on spiraling currents of warm air during the heat of the day to glide at high altitude. The nest, situated in thick swamp vegetation, is a simple heap of grass in which the female lays 2-3 eggs.

SITATUNGA
Tragelaphus spekei
Classification   Class: Mammalia; Order: Artiodactyla; Family: Bovidae.
Description   Also known as the Marshbuck. Length of head and body 3½-5½ ft (5.1-5.7 m), height to shoulder 30-50 in (75-125 cm), weight 100-240 lb (45-110 kg). Male dark brown or gray-brown with white spots and stripes. The female, smaller and without horns, is brown or deep chestnut. The hoofs are long, pointed and spread wide, indicating adaptability to waterlogged ground.
Distribution   Western, central and southern Africa.
Habitat   Marshes and flooded forests.
Behavior   It is an amphibious antelope. The spreading hoofs provide a broader supporting surface and so prevent the animal from sinking rapidly into the mud, enabling it to tread lightly and swiftly over wet patches where other antelopes would flounder clumsily. On dry ground, however, it moves with some difficulty. Timid and hard to observe, in dangerous situations it flings itself into the water, where it remains completely submerged apart from the nostrils. It lives alone or in pairs, feeding at night on grass, leaves, twigs, and fruit.

Madagascar

AYE-AYE
Daubentonia madagascariensis
Classification Class: Mammalia; Order: Primates; Suborder: Prosimii; Family: Daubentoniidae.
Description Length of head and body 18 in (45 cm), tail 22 in (55 cm), weight about 4½ lb (2 kg). Long dark brown or black hair. Long, thickly furred tail. The rodent-like incisor teeth emphasize its resemblance to a large squirrel. Long, bony fingers to the hands, especially the middle finger, skeletal and terminating in a curved claw. Only the thumb is furnished with a flat nail which indicates the animal's relationship to the monkeys.
Distribution Northeast and northwest Madagascar.
Habitat Tropical forest.
Behavior The middle finger is a useful and versatile tool, enabling the aye-aye to fish out larvae from rotting wood with the claw, to remove the rind from fruit, to drink by dipping the finger in water and quickly transferring it to the mouth, and to groom its fur. Solitary and nocturnal. The female builds a spherical nest in a tree hollow where she gives birth to a single young.

BROWN MESITE
Mesitornis unicolor
Classification Class: Aves; Order: Gruiformes; Family: Mesitornitidae.
Description Total length 12 in (30 cm). Reddish-brown above, lighter below; long white feathers on sides of neck. Short bill and wings, long and broad tail.
Distribution Eastern Madagascar.
Habitat Tropical forest.
Behavior Almost incapable of flying, moves like a pigeon, bobbing its head in time with its steps. It is rare, with very shy habits, thought to live in pairs or in small groups. It nests very close to the ground so that it can reach eggs and chicks without using its wings.

DWARF LEMUR
Cheirogaleus medius
Classification Class: Mammalia; Order: Primates; Suborder: Prosimii; Family: Lemuridae.
Description Length of head and body 6 in (15 cm), tail about 7 in (17 cm). Gray-brown above, whitish below. Large dark eyes, indicating the lemur's nocturnal habits.

Distribution Western and southern coastal zones of Madagascar.
Habitat Open woodland and tree savanna.
Behavior It feeds mainly on flowers and fruit. During dry periods it falls into a state of torpor, surviving on the stock of fat accumulated in the tail. Solitary but not territorial; by day several lemurs sleep together in the same tree hollow. The female produces 2-3 young after 60-70 days' gestation.

FANALOUC
Eupleres goudotii
Classification Class: Mammalia; Order: Carnivora; Family: Viverridae.
Description Length of head and body 19-22 in (48-56 cm), tail 9-10 in (22-25 cm). Brown above, grayish-white below. Elongated body similar to that of a mongoose; long, slender muzzle, non retractile claws, flattened canine and premolar teeth, unsuitable for tearing flesh.
Distribution Northeast and northwest Madagascar.
Habitat Tropical forest.
Behavior Solitary ground-dwelling animal. The special type of dentition allows it to feed on worms, slugs and insect larvae. It uses its long, sharp claws in self-defense. The single young is born with its eyes open and after a couple of days is able to follow its mother about. This early development, unusual for a carnivore, is not matched by equally rapid growth.

FLYING FROG
Rhacophorus sp.
Classification Class: Amphibia; Order: Anura; Family: Rhacophoridae.
Description Length about 3 in (8 cm). Color orange. At the tips of the toes are small adhesive disks with which the frog manages to attach itself to the surface of leaves.
Distribution Eastern Madagascar. The family is also found in Africa and Southeast Asia.
Habitat Tropical forest.
Behavior A tree-dwelling frog which feeds on insects. Its adaptation to this form of life is shown, among other ways, by the manner in which it reproduces; before laying the eggs, the female ejects a fluid substance, agitating it with her hind legs so as to form a foamy mass. After suspending this to branches or leaves overhanging the water, she deposits the eggs in it, and these are immediately fertilized by the male. From that moment neither sex takes any interest in the foam nest which, when the larvae are sufficiently developed, turns fluid and drops into the water underneath.

FOSSA
Cryptoprocta ferox
Classification Class: Mammalia; Order: Carnivora; Family: Viverridae.
Description Length of head and body 28 in (70 cm), tail 26 in (65 cm), weight 21-44 lb (9.5-20 kg). The coat displays various shades of brown. Head similar to that of a cat, retractile claws. It is a plantigrade animal, walking on the entire sole of the foot, as bears do.
Distribution Eastern Madagascar.
Habitat Tropical forest.
Behavior It is the largest carnivore in Madagascar and the only enemy of the prosimians. A nocturnal, arboreal hunter, its habits in the wild are unknown. Observations on subjects in captivity show that the female gives birth to 2-4 young after a gestation of 10 weeks. These become mature at about 5 years of age, an exceptionally long time for a carnivore, possibly a sign of its primitive nature.

GRAY-HEADED LOVEBIRD
Agapornis cana
Classification Class: Aves; Order: Psittaciformes; Family: Psittacidae.
Description Total length 5½ in (14 cm). The male is green with a light gray head and breast, the female completely green. Short, rounded tail. The pair retain close links.
Distribution Coastal fringe of Madagascar. Also introduced to other islands of the Indian Ocean.
Habitat Open zones with shrubs, edges of forests.
Behavior Usually seen in small flocks of 5-20. It spends most of the day on the ground, eating seeds of herbaceous plants, often together with the Malagasy Weaverbird and other seed-eating birds. It nests in hollow tree trunks. The material intended for the construction of the nest is not carried in the bill but stuck into the feathers of the back. The 3-4 eggs hatch after 23 days' incubation.

GREEN GECKO
Phelsuma madagascariensis
Classification Class: Reptilia; Order: Squamata; Suborder: Sauria; Family: Gekkonidae.
Description Total length 10 in (25 cm). Green with red spots, variable in extent, on back.
Distribution Much of Madagascar.
Habitat Among foliage of trees.
Behavior Diurnal and arboreal, it feeds on insects, nectar and fruit. Although capable of modifying its color to match the surface on which it is resting, when alerted to the presence of a bird of prey it drops to the ground, vanishing among the grass

Madagascar

The island of Madagascar boasts many exclusive species of plants and animals. One of the former is the traveler's tree, its column-like trunk topped by a fan of leaves, the bases of which contain a reservoir of water. There are also many succulent plants which display a surprising similarity to the American cacti.

1   aye-aye
2   lesser mouse lemur
3   dwarf lemur
4   Parson's chameleon
5   Malagasy weaverbird (male)
6   Malagasy weaverbird (female)
7   Malagasy silk-moth
8   tenrec
9   Malagasy blue cuckoo
10 indri
11 ringtailed lemur
12 ruffed lemur
13 Verreaux's sifaka

and fallen leaves. By maneuvering its tail, it can, if necessary, twist in midair so that it always lands on its feet. The female is oviparous.

INDRI
Indri indri

Classification Class: Mammalia; Order: Primates; Suborder: Prosimii; Family: Indridae.

Description Length of head and body 36 in (90 cm), tail 2 in (5 cm), weight 15-22 lb (7-10 kg). It is the largest living prosimian. Long dark brown or black fur, white around ears, on shoulders, arms and underparts. Hind legs markedly longer than front ones. Large yellowish eyes, protected by long lashes.

Distribution Northeast Madagascar.

Habitat Tropical forests.

Behavior It lives in pairs or in small groups on large, isolated trees, feeding on leaves, fruit and seeds. Although diurnal and brightly colored, it is not easy to see because it is very timid and remains hiding in dense foliage. Each group defends its own territory, revealing its presence at dawn and dusk in a chorus of howls that can be heard for some distance. When it runs along the ground, in an upright position, it bears a remarkable resemblance to a human. Little is known about its reproduction, but the female apparently produces one young after a gestation of about 60 days.

LESSER MOUSE LEMUR
Microcebus murinus

Classification Class: Mammalia; Order: Primates; Suborder: Prosimii; Family: Lemuridae.

Description Length of head and body 4½-5 in (11-13 cm), tail 4¾ in (12 cm), weight 1¾ oz (50 g). It is the smallest primate. Brown above, white below. Thick, woolly fur, large eyes of a typical nocturnal animal.

Distribution Widely distributed, except in interior of Madagascar.

Habitat Wet forests, reedbeds, bushy steppes.

Behavior It feeds at night on small birds and nectar. By day it sleeps in a nest similar to that of a bird, and spends the whole dry season here in a state of torpor, living on the fat accumulated in the hind legs and the tail. The female gives birth to 2-3 young after a gestation of 59-62 days.

MALAGASY BLACK PARROT
Coracopsis nigra

Classification Class: Aves; Order: Psittaciformes; Family: Psittacidae.

Description Total length 14 in (35 cm). Brownish-black, speckled with gray on wings and tail. Large whitish bill, yellowish in female.

Distribution Along coastal belt of Madagascar. Also lives in Comoro Islands and the island of Praslin (Seychelles archipelago).

Habitat Forest.

Behavior Often seen in small flocks when feeding off fruit in treetops or when flying high in the forest, uttering loud cries. It is an excellent natural timekeeper, each day leaving and returning to the tree where it spends the night at precisely the same times. It nests in tree trunks.

MALAGASY BLUE CUCKOO
Coua caerulea

Classification Class: Aves: Order: Cuculiformes; Family: Cuculidae.

Description About as big as a pigeon. Color blue. Long, powerful legs with two toes turned forward and two backward. Long tail.

Distribution Eastern Madagascar.

Habitat Tropical forest.

Behavior Essentially a ground bird, it prefers to rely on its legs rather than its wings to escape an enemy. It feeds off fruit and insects. Silent and solitary, except in the breeding season when the male sings and defends his territory. The 2-3 eggs hatch after 10 days' incubation.

MALAGASY CIVET
Fossa fossa

Classification Class: Mammalia; Order: Carnivora; Family: Viverridae.

Description Length of head and body 18½ in (47 cm), tail 4 in (9.5 cm), weight 5 lb (2.2 kg). Brown with darker spots arranged in longitudinal lines.

Distribution Eastern Madagascar.

Habitat Tropical forest.

Behavior Terrestrial and nocturnal, it lives in pairs, unlike the majority of Viverridae, which are solitary. It feeds principally on small mammals, reptiles and amphibians. Although it ventures into trees, it is not a particularly able climber. The single young is born after 3 months' gestation; unusually for a carnivore, its eyes are open at birth and it is able to follow the mother around after a few days.

MALAGASY REAR-FANGED SNAKE
Langaha nasuta

Classification Class: Reptilia; Order: Squamata; Suborder: Ophidia; Family: Colubridae.

Description Total length 40 in (100 cm). Greenish-brown. There is a characteristic fleshy appendage on the snout which, in the female, is leaf-shaped. Thanks to this appendage, when the reptile is hanging from a branch tossed by the wind, it looks just like the tendril of a climbing plant.

Distribution Much of Madagascar.

Habitat Forest.

Behavior Although poisonous, it is not dangerous to humans. It feeds on tree-dwelling amphibians, birds and chameleons.

MALAGASY SILK-MOTH
Argema mittrei

Classification Class: Insecta; Order: Lepidoptera; Family: Saturniidae.

Description Wingspan 6 in (15 cm). Yellow with reddish-brown patterns and red, blue and black eyespots. Hind wings elongated to form a tail.

Distribution Eastern Madagascar.

Habitat Tropical forest.

Behavior The male, active by day, is a good flyer, furnished with enormous antennae. The female flies at night and only to lay eggs. In the course of their brief adult life, neither the male nor the female eats because of inadequately developed mouthparts. The larvae are vegetarian and are transformed into chrysalids inside a silken cocoon from which the adult butterfly emerges.

MALAGASY WEAVERBIRD
Foudia madagascariensis

Classification Class: Aves; Order: Passeriformes; Family: Ploceidae.

Description Total length 5 in (13 cm). The male in courtship livery is red with blackish wings and tail, while the female is brown, lighter on the underparts. Outside the breeding season the two sexes are similar.

Distribution Throughout Madagascar. It also lives on adjacent islands, probably introduced by man.

Habitat Open ground.

Behavior It eats seeds of herbaceous plants, and insects. Outside the breeding season huge flocks of the birds may cause serious damage to rice crops. It builds a nest of elongated shape which is attached to the branch of a tree or to a swamp reed. The female lays 4-6 eggs.

MONGOOSE LEMUR
Lemur mongoz

Classification Class: Mammalia; Order: Primates; Suborder: Prosimii; Family: Lemuridae.

Description Length of head and body 12½-14½ in (32-37 cm), tail 18½-20 in (47-51 cm), weight 4½-5lb (2-2.2 kg). Male gray with light face and reddish cheeks, female brown with dark face and white cheeks.

Distribution Northwest Madagascar. Also found on Comoro Islands.

Habitat Wet, deciduous forests.

Behavior Nocturnal and arboreal. It lives in family groups made up of a male, a female and immature young. Food consists of nectar, flowers, fruit and leaves. Like all members of the family Lemuridae, it takes great care of its thick fur, combing it with the lower incisor teeth (which are turned horizontally forward) and the claw of the second toe. The single young is born after about 4½ months' gestation.

PARSON'S CHAMELEON
Chamaeleo parsonii

Classification Class: Reptilia; Order: Squamata; Suborder: Sauria; Family: Chamaeleonidae.

Description Total length 22½-24 in (57-61 cm). Green. It is distinguished by the two upward-turned growths on the snout and by the nape which is extended to form a kind of helmet. The protruding eyes are independent of each other, so that the chameleon can look in two different directions at the same time. The five toes on the feet are divided into two groups, formed respectively of two and three toes joined to one another; this structure is ideal for grasping branches firmly. Prehensile tail. Very long, extensible tongue terminating in a sticky swelling. Thanks to special epidermic cells, the chameleon is capable of modifying its color to match that of its surroundings, thus going unobserved.

Distribution Eastern Madagascar.

Habitat Tropical forest.

Behavior A typical tree dweller, it moves very slowly along the branches, indicating little agility. It defends personal territory both against its own species and chameleons of different species. It feeds mainly on insects, which it catches by shooting out the tongue from its mouth so swiftly that the prey is hit, stuck fast, and swallowed before it can register any reaction. Very probably it reproduces by laying eggs.

RINGTAILED LEMUR
Lemur catta

Classification Class: Mammalia; Order: Primates; Suborder: Prosimii; Family: Lemuridae.

Description Length of head and body 20 in (50 cm), tail 20 in (50 cm), weight 5-7¾ lb (2.3-3.5 kg). Grayish-brown above, slightly paler below; white face with dark mask around eyes, tip of muzzle black; black and white rings on tail.

Distribution Southwest Madagascar.

Habitat Deciduous forest.

Behavior Highly gregarious, it lives in groups which spend most of the day on the ground, even though it is basically a tree-dwelling animal. The boundaries of each group's territory are marked by secretions from scent glands situated on the forearms and in the anal zone. A characteristic action of this lemur is to rub its tail against the forearm glands: in this way it can produce both visual and olfactory signals, directed toward other members of the species. Fruit appears to be its only food. It spends the night in trees. After a gestation of 4½ months, the female gives birth to one young.

RUFFED LEMUR
Varecia variegata

Classification Class: Mammalia; Order: Primates; Suborder: Prosimii; Family: Lemuridae.

Description Length of head and body about 22 in (54-56 cm), tail 23-26 in (58-65 cm), weight 7¼-10 lb (3.3-4.5 kg). Black and white or black and red; there is a characteristic ruff of white hairs which gives the species its common name.

Distribution Northeast Madagascar.

Habitat Tropical forest.

Behavior Early in the morning, after being active all night, the ruffed lemur basks on branches most exposed to the sun. It feeds on leaves and fruit. This is the only prosimian that does not carry its infant around from birth, but leaves it in the nest. In spite of its bright colors, it is easier to hear than to see.

RUFOUS VANGA
Schetba rufa

Classification Class: Aves; Order: Passeriformes; Family: Vangidae.

Description Total length 7½ in (19 cm). The male has a black head and breast, chestnut back, wings and tail, white underparts; female has grayish underparts.

Distribution Western Madagascar.

Habitat Tree savanna.

Behavior It lives in flocks, often in company with other passerines. Feeding mainly on insects, it builds a cup-shaped nest where the female, taking turns with the male, incubates 3-4 eggs.

Note Belonging to the same family Vangidae, and found only in Madagascar and the Comoros, are the Helmet Bird *(Euryceros prevostii)* and the Sicklebill *(Falculea palliata)*. The former, 10½ in (27 cm) long, has a large, laterally compressed bill surmounted by a kind of helmet; it is black with part of the back and the tail chestnut, and it lives in the forests of eastern Madagascar. The latter measures about 12½ in (32 cm) long, has white head and underparts, a black back and a long, thin sickle-shaped bill. It lives on the tree savannas of western Madagascar.

TENREC
Tenrec ecaudatus

Classification Class: Mammalia; Order: Insectivora; Family: Tenrecidae.

Description Length of head and body 10-15½ in (26-39 cm), tail about ½ in (1-1.6 cm). Shaggy brown hair, mixed with bristles and spines. Long pointed nose.

Distribution Throughout Madagascar.

Habitat Dry, sandy areas, thin lowland, and mountain forests.

Behavior Active at night, it spends the day sleeping in an underground burrow. If frightened, it erects the long spines of the back and hisses. The tenrec feeds on worms, slugs, and other invertebrates which it captures by digging in the ground with the strong claws of its forefeet. It is extraordinarily prolific; the female as a rule gives birth to 12-15 young and litters of more than 20 are not unusual.

VERREAUX'S SIFAKA
Propithecus verreauxi

Classification Class: Mammalia; Order: Primates; Suborder: Prosimii; Family: Indridae.

Description Length of head and body 18 in (45 cm), tail 22 in (55 cm), weight 7¾-9½ lb (3.5-4.3 kg). The thick, bristly coat is variable in color, from pure white to black and white or brown; muzzle, palms of hands and soles of feet are black and hairless. Like all Indridae, the legs are particularly long in proportion to the arms.

Distribution Western and southern Madagascar.

Habitat Deciduous forest.

Behavior It is a formidable jumper, capable of making leaps of some 30 ft (10 m) from branch to branch and of 13 ft (4 m) at ground level. As a rule it moves slowly and carefully, coming down from a tree with arms clasping the trunk, human fashion. It lives in groups composed of various adult males and females. It feeds on leaves, flowers, fruit and bark. The young are born after a gestation of 5 months.

NORTH AMERICA

In certain respects North America has many features in common with Europe and Asia. Covering virtually the same latitudes of the northern hemisphere, it too exhibits the familiar sequence of habitats, from tundra to coniferous forests and broadleaved forests. Furthermore, many animals of North America are very closely related to species which inhabit the northern and central regions of Eurasia, so much so that zoologists consider them simply to be subspecies of the same species. Thus the huge and fearsome gray bear known as the grizzly, which lives in the Rocky Mountains, is nowadays regarded as a subspecies of the brown bear; the same applies to the reindeer, of which there is a single species, in spite of American populations being known by the name of caribou.

As we proceed south, the differences between the Old and New Worlds become more obvious. The American bison, for example, is a species quite distinct from the European bison, and equally different are the various species of marmot, squirrel and wild sheep. Additionally, there are more and more species which can claim no close relationship either in Asia or Europe, such as the raccoon and the pronghorn antelope. These species become increasingly numerous toward the lower latitudes, so that when we reach southern Mexico we find that they have almost entirely replaced the animals in the north. For zoologists, North America extends farther north than it does for geographers: at the latitude of the Mexican city of Acapulco, for instance, the animal community is already more typical of a "southern" world.

There is one important geographical feature which distinguishes North America from Europe and Asia. In these two continents the major mountain ranges more or less follow the lines of latitude, creating barriers to the passage of animals from north to south and vice versa. The Pyrenees, the Alps and the Himalayas, for example, separate regions on either side which vary considerably in terms of climate, vegetation and wildlife. The situation is quite different in North America, where the major mountain chains (the Rocky Mountains in the west and the Appalachians in the east) extend longitudinally, roughly from north to south, and therefore do not constitute important barriers either to animals or plants. This explains why typical South American animals such as opossums, hummingbirds and armadillos are to be found farther north. Certain species left their lands of origin and ventured north, as it were, on reconnaissance; today they are well acclimatized in the United States, and one hummingbird is known to have journeyed as far as southern Alaska.

1   moose
2   grizzly bear
3   Rocky Mountain goat
4   wolverine
5   lemming
6   bald eagle
7   snowshoe rabbit
8   great horned owl
9   black bear
10 timber wolf
11 Canada goose
12 Arctic fox
13 caribou
14 bighorn
15 prairie dog
16 raccoon
17 beaver
18 red squirrel
19 American badger
20 blacktailed jack rabbit
21 pronghorn antelope
22 American bison
23 great blue heron
24 whitetailed deer
25 puma
26 coyote
27 collared peccary
28 alligator
29 roadrunner
30 rattlesnake
31 striped skunk

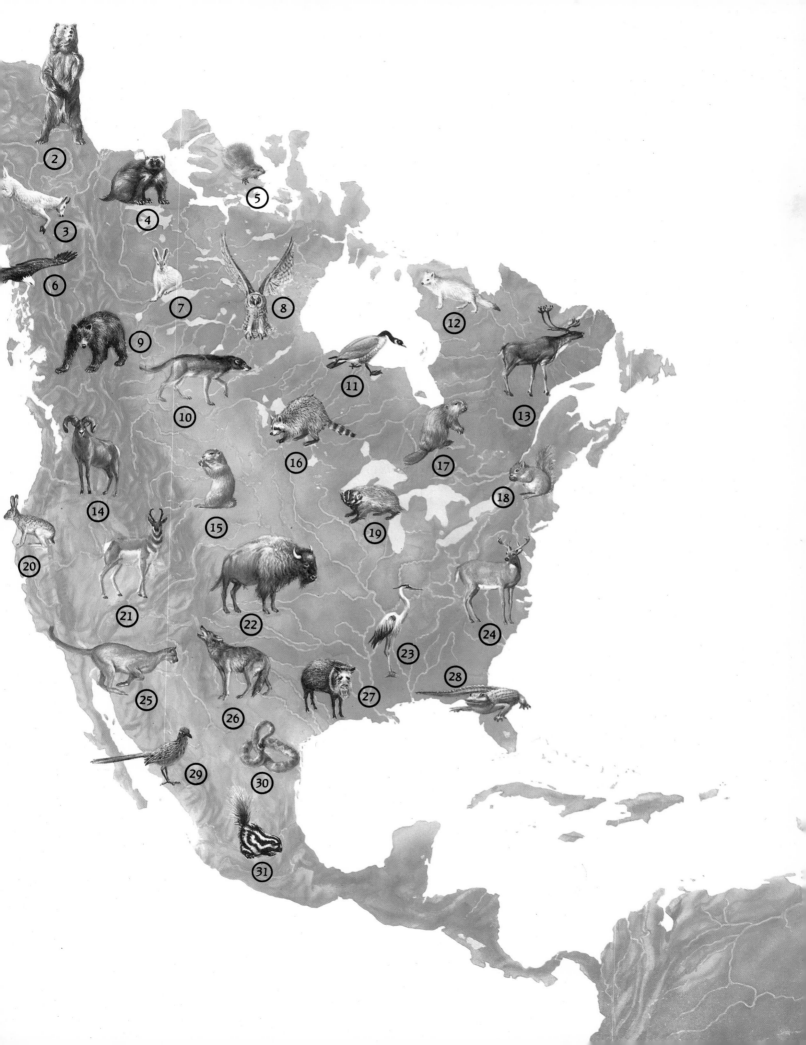

Northern regions

AMERICAN BLACK BEAR
Ursus americanus

Classification   Class: Mammalia; Order: Carnivora; Family: Ursidae.

Description   Length of head and body 4½-5½ ft (1.38-1.68 m), tail 5 in (12 cm), height to shoulder about 3 ft (1 m), weight 265-330 lb (120-150 kg). Color variable: black, reddish-brown, gray-blue, white. It is the smallest and most common North American bear.

Distribution   Most of North America.

Habitat   Lowland and mountain forests.

Behavior   Impervious to human encroachment, which brought about the decline of the Brown Bear, it has even managed to turn the situation to its advantage by changing from a wild woodland inhabitant into a prime tourist attraction in the National Parks of the United States and Canada. Begging for tidbits tossed from car windows, raiding picnic hampers, filching refuse from parking lots – it thrives on them all. In areas removed from the tourist trails its habits are typical of most bears: it feeds on meat, especially on waking from its winter hibernation, honey and vegetation of every kind. Solitary and nocturnal, it is an excellent climber and, if necessary, a good runner. In the interval between hibernations, the female gives birth to 1-2 cubs.

ARCTIC FOX
Alopex lagopus

Classification   Class: Mammalia; Order: Carnivora; Family: Canidae.

Description   Length of head and body 18-27 in (46-68 cm), tail 12-16 in (30-40 cm), height to shoulder up to 12 in (30 cm), weight 5½-20 lb (2.5-9 kg). There are two color phases: blue and white. Both are brownish in summer, but in winter the former is gray-blue and the latter white. Compact body, short muzzle, ears and legs; feet, including the soles, covered with hair, effective against loss of heat.

Distribution   Coldest regions of North America. Also found in Arctic zones of Europe and Asia.

Habitat   Tundra.

Behavior   Active throughout the winter, it shelters in the snow only during the severest storms. To find sufficient food, generally in the form of remains left by polar bears, it is forced to move around continuously, covering vast areas. In summer it feeds on lemmings, fish, sea birds, and their eggs. The six or more cubs are born after a gestation of 51-57 days and are reared by both parents.

ARCTIC GROUND SQUIRREL
Spermophilus parryi

Classification   Class: Mammalia; Order: Rodentia; Family: Sciuridae.

Description   Length of head and body 9-14 in (22-35 cm), tail 3-6 in (7.5-15 cm), weight 2 lb (900 g). Color reddish-brown.

Distribution   Alaska and Canadian Arctic.

Habitat   Tundra.

Distribution   Gregarious by habit, it lives in communal burrows dug in the ground to the point of penetrating the soil of the tundra that is permanently covered by ice (permafrost), at a depth of about 3 ft (1 m). It spends 7 months a year in hibernation, huddled in underground chambers lined with grass, lichen, and caribou hair. In late spring it emerges from a thick cover of snow and begins to reproduce. After little more than a month 5-10 young are born and they complete their growth by the fall. It is basically vegetarian.

BIGHORN
Ovis canadensis

Classification   Class: Mammalia; Order: Artiodactyla; Family: Bovidae.

Description   Length of head and body 5½ ft (1.68 m), height to shoulder about 3 ft (1 m), weight 250-280 lb (113-127 kg). Gray-brown with a large creamy white mark around the tail. Huge horns: in old males they form a complete arc, curving back, outward, and then forward; those of the female are much smaller.

Distribution   Alaska, Rocky Mountains in both the United States and Canada.

Habitat   Steep mountain regions.

Behavior   It lives in small groups of 6-10. Among the males the law governing all wild sheep applies: the larger the horns, the higher their owner's rank. Only males with horns of similar size will confront each other in the exhausting duels which precede mating; the others remain in the flock but behave as subordinates, like the females. The horns of an old male may weigh 30 lb (14 kg), which is as much as its entire skeleton. The crash produced by the horns of two rivals when they come into contact can be heard for a considerable distance. The female gives birth to one lamb after 180 days' gestation.

CARIBOU
Rangifer tarandus

Classification   Class: Mammalia; Order: Artiodactyla; Family: Cervidae.

Description   Length of head and body 6-6½ ft (1.8-2 m), height to shoulder 4 ft (1.2 m), average weight 240 lb (109 kg). Brown with white spots on neck, around tail and above each hoof. More northerly populations are almost white. Broad feet with rounded hoof, semipalmate horns in both sexes. It cannot be distinguished appreciably from the Eurasian reindeer, which zoologists ascribe to the same species.

Distribution   Alaska, Canada, northern United States, Greenland.

Habitat   Coniferous forests, tundra.

Behavior   The tundra caribou migrates in enormous herds twice a year: from the tundra to the conifer forests in fall, from the forests back to the tundra in spring. The distance from one grazing ground to another may be more than 875 miles (1,400 km). The so-called forest caribou, on the other hand, remains at more southerly latitudes throughout the year. It feeds on grass, leaves and reeds, but the favorite food is lichens. To find these in sufficient quantity the caribou is forced to move about continuously in small groups, which join to form huge herds only at the time of migration. The young are born after a gestation of 192-246 days.

FISHER
Martes pennanti

Classification   Class: Mammalia; Order: Carnivora; Family: Mustelidae.

Description   Also known as Pennant's Marten. Length of head and body 28-36 in (70-90 cm), tail 12-20 in (30-50 cm), weight 10-15 lb (4.6-6.8 kg). Fur dark brown.

Distribution   Canada and northern United States.

Habitat   Forests.

Behavior   It feeds on hares, small rodents, birds, carrion and berries. It is one of the few predators, if not the only one, able to catch the porcupine, in spite of its spines; it attacks from the front, inflicting serious wounds to the porcupine's defenseless nose and neck, wears it down, tips it on its back and kills it. In areas where porcupines are particularly numerous, the predatory activities of the fisher are valuable, for by controlling the numbers, it saves the woodlands from the porcupine's insatiable hunger for bark. The 1-5 young are born in spring and become independent by the fall.

GOLDEN PLOVER
Pluvialis dominica

Classification   Class: Aves; Order: Charadriiformes; Family: Charadriidae.

Description   Length 9½-11 in (24-28 cm). In courtship livery the upper parts are golden-brown, densely spotted with black. Face, throat and underparts black. A white line neatly separates the upper from the lower parts. Outside the breeding season it is brown streaked with black.

Distribution It nests in the American Arctic, winters in Oceania and South America. Also breeds in Siberia.

Habitat Tundra in summer, swamps and seacoasts in winter.

Behavior The chicks are fed on insects, worms and berries; in winter it feeds on grass and seeds. A formidable flyer, in the course of migration it is capable of covering some 2,000 miles (over 3,000 km) over open sea without stopping. The female lays 3-5 eggs on the ground, in a small hole lined with grass and lichen. The chicks are born after 27-28 days incubation.

GREAT HORNED OWL
Bubo virginianus

Classification Class: Aves; Order: Strigiformes; Family: Strigidae.

Description Total length about 26 in (65 cm). Brown above, lighter but with dense dark bars below. Prominent white marks around bill and on throat. Characteristic "horns" of feathers on head.

Distribution Throughout North America. Also found in Central and South America.

Habitat From forests to deserts, fields to cliffs.

Behavior Nocturnal and territorial, feeds on rodents, hares and birds, caught mainly at dusk and dawn. It makes a loud and guttural sound. In order to breed it uses nests abandoned by herons or diurnal birds of prey, situated in trees, among rocks or on the ground. The female lays 2-3 eggs, which hatch after 34-36 days' incubation.

MOOSE
Alces alces

Classification Class: Mammalia; Order: Artiodactyla; Family: Cervidae.

Description Also known as the Elk. Length of head and body 8-10 ft (2.4-3.1 m), tail 2-4 in (5-10 cm), height to shoulder 6-7½ ft (1.8-2.3 m), weight 660-1,760 lb (300-800 kg). Dark brown. Unmistakable because of its huge dimensions, the protruding nose, the pendulous dewlap on the throat and the overall ungainly appearance. The male has large palmate antlers.

Distribution Alaska, Canada, northern United States. It is also found in northern Eurasia.

Habitat Forest surrounding shallow bodies of water.

Behavior It leads a solitary life, feeding on twigs, leaves and bark. In summer it also eats aquatic plants, which it tears from the bottom by submerging its head after closing the nostrils. It is an excellent swimmer. During the breeding season fights between males are less ferocious than among other deer. After a gestation of 8 months the female gives birth to 1-2 young which lack the characteristic mimetic spotted coloration frequent in other young deer; this is probably due to the fact that the mother is sufficiently strong and aggressive to protect them from predators, making mimicry unnecessary.

NORTH AMERICAN MINK
Mustela vison

Classification Class: Mammalia; Order: Carnivora; Family: Mustelidae.

Description Length of head and body 14½-16½ in (37-42 cm), tail 7-8 in (17-20 cm), weight about 1¼-3½ lb (500-1,500 g). Dark brown with a small white mark on throat. Semiwebbed feet.

Distribution Most of North America.

Habitat Near lakes and rivers.

Behavior It is an extremely versatile nocturnal hunter, feeding on a wide variety of small animals, captured on the ground, in trees and in water, where it swims with almost as much skill as the otter. As a rule it takes over the burrows of its victims. Outside the brief reproductive season it lives alone. After 39-48 days' gestation the female gives birth to 2-10 cubs, tending them affectionately for a long time.

NORTH AMERICAN PORCUPINE
Erethizon dorsatum

Classification Class: Mammalia; Order: Rodentia; Family: Erethizontidae.

Description Length of head and body about 30 in (76 cm), tail 6 in (15 cm), weight 20 lb (9 kg). Blackish. The body, almost entirely covered with spines, is squat, the legs and the feet equipped with curved claws.

Distribution Most of North America.

Habitat Forests.

Behavior By day it sleeps in rock clefts, under stumps or in trees. At night it goes in search of food, consisting mainly of tree bark. When threatened it raises its spines, turns its hindquarters toward the enemy and begins to wave its spiny tail, stamping its feet and gnashing its teeth. Few predators dare to brave such a defensive system: One of the few is the Fisher (Pennant's Marten), the porcupine's most deadly foe. The female gives birth to a single young after 210-217 days' gestation.

RED FOX
Vulpes vulpes

Classification Class: Mammalia; Order: Carnivora; Family: Canidae.

Description Length of head and body 24-36 in (60-90 cm), tail 14-16 in (35-40 cm), height to shoulder 14-16 in (35-40 cm), average weight 15 lb (7 kg). There are many color variations but the most common is tawny with a white tip to the tail, and black legs and feet.

Distribution Throughout North America. It is also found in Eurasia and Australia, introduced to the latter continent by man.

Habitat Open spaces surrounded by woods.

Behavior Opportunistic and omnivorous, it eats small mammals, birds and their eggs, amphibians, insects, and berries. If driven by hunger it will carry out raids on farmyards for poultry. The cubs, sometimes up to 5 in a litter, are born after a gestation of 53 days and are raised by both parents. In the fall they go off separately in search of their own territory.

ROCKY MOUNTAIN GOAT
Oreamnos americanus

Classification Class: Mammalia; Order: Artiodactyla; Family: Bovidae.

Description Length of head and body 5-5¾ ft (1.5-1.75 m), tail 5-7 in (12-17 cm), height to shoulder 36-42 in (90-105 cm), weight 175-305 lb (80-135 kg). Long yellowish-white hair. Short, black, pointed horns, present in both sexes.

Distribution Alaska, Rocky Mountains of the United States and Canada.

Habitat Slopes near perpetual snowline.

Behavior It is a slow and prudent climber, but so sure-footed that after a downward leap of some 20-25 ft (7-8 m) it will land safely on the narrowest rock ledge. It lives in small groups dominated by females, feeding on the sparse vegetation to be found at high altitude. In the breeding season duels between males are rare, but when they do occur they may end with the death of one or even both contenders. The female gives birth to a single young after 180 days' gestation.

SIBERIAN LEMMING
Lemmus sibiricus

Classification Class: Mammalia; Order: Rodentia; Family: Cricetidae.

Description Total length 5-6½ in (12.7-16.5 cm), weight 2½-4 oz (71-113 g). Gray in summer, brown in winter. Short tail.

Distribution Alaska, Canada and northern United States.

Habitat Tundra.

Behavior All the predators of North America feed, directly or indirectly, on this small vegetarian animal. Its abundance may condition the reproductive activity of some of these predators, to the point of preventing it in years when lemming numbers are low (the snowy owl is a case in point). The numbers of the lemming population decline every 2-5 years,

Northern regions

The vegetation of the frozen regions of the north is made up of grasses, sedges, mosses and many-colored lichens. Southward stretch the forests of conifers, predominantly pines and firs, with dense undergrowth of ferns, brambles and blueberries; and even farther south the conifers gradually give way to broadleaved species, represented principally by oaks, maples, walnuts, chestnuts, hornbeams and limes.

1 Rocky Mountain goat
2 wolverine
3 wolf
4 moose
5 caribou
6 willow ptarmigan
7 great horned owl
8 red fox
9 grizzly bear
10 porcupine
11 bobcat
12 bighorn
13 Arctic fox
14 mink
15 lemming
16 weasel
17 snowshoe rabbit

apparently because of nervous tension brought about by overcrowding, which makes the animal less prolific. Besides, as soon as food begins to run short, the lemming undertakes vast migrations which culminate in mass deaths. It is easy to understand how, in spite of the fact that they are so universally hunted, the rodent community is prone to overpopulation, considering that a female is sexually mature at the age of 2 weeks and that in one year she may have three litters, each of 1-12.

SNOWSHOE RABBIT
Lepus americanus
Classification Class: Mammalia; Order: Lagomorpha; Family: Leporidae.
Description Length of head and body 15-22 in (37-55 cm), tail 1-2 in (3-5 cm), weight 3-4 lb (1.4-1.8 kg). In summer it is brown, in winter white with black tips to the ears; for this reason it is also known as the Varying Hare. The large hind feet are covered with hair which helps it to move more easily over deep snow.
Distribution Alaska, Canada, northwest and northeast United States.
Habitat Lowland and mountain forests.
Behavior It is territorial and habit-bound; its private domains are crisscrossed with a dense network of paths which, being continually trampled, are some inches lower than the surrounding ground. It also makes use of many burrows. It feeds on grass, leaves, shoots and conifer needles. After a gestation of 35-36 days the female produces 2-6 young, twice or three times a year. Like the lemming, and presumably for the same reasons, the Snowshoe Rabbit is subject to periodic fluctuations in population numbers.

STELLER'S JAY
Cyanocitta stelleri
Classification Class: Aves; Order: Passeriformes; Family: Corvidae.
Description Length about 13 in (32 cm). Head, breast and back blackish; abdomen, wings and tail blue. Erectile crest on head.
Distribution Alaska, Canada, western United States. Also found in Central America.
Habitat Coniferous forests.
Behavior Eats acorns, pine nuts, eggs and nestlings of other species. It is a superb imitator of the songs of other birds. The female lays 3-5 eggs in a cupshaped nest situated on a conifer.

TENGMALM'S OWL
Aegolius funereus
Classification Class: Aves; Order: Strigiformes; Family: Strigidae.

Description Also known as the Boreal Owl. Length 10 in (25 cm), weight 4½-5½ oz (130-160 g). Upper parts brown spotted with white, underparts grayish-white with darker tearshaped spots. The young are chestnut. The characteristic large head distinguishes it from the little owl.
Distribution Alaska, Canada, northwest and northeast United States. Also widely distributed in Eurasia.
Habitat Lowland and mountain coniferous forests.
Behavior Strictly nocturnal and territorial, it frequents established forests with plenty of old trees pitted with the holes of woodpeckers, where it can shelter and nest. It feeds principally on voles. The female lays 3-8 eggs in a tree hollow; the chicks are born after 26-28 days' incubation. The male feeds the incubating female who, for three weeks after the eggs hatch, hardly ever leaves the nest.

WAPITI
Cervus elaphus nelsoni
Classification Class: Mammalia; Order: Artiodactyla; Family: Cervidae.
Description Length of head and body 6-8 ft (1.8-2.5 m), height to shoulder 5 ft (1.5 m), weight 1,100 lb (500 kg). The male is much bigger than the female. Reddish-brown, darker on neck; large cream-colored mark around tail. The male has branched antlers which are shed and renewed every year.
Distribution Rocky Mountains in Canada and the United States, Alaska.
Habitat Open forests.
Behavior Outside the breeding season males and females form separate herds. The older males are often solitary. It feeds on grass and leaves. In the mating season adult males expend all their energy, firstly in taking possession of private territory to which as many females as possible can be attracted, and secondly in defending the harem from bachelor male pretenders. Fights are bitter and frequent, so much so that the animals hardly have time to eat enough. At the end, victor and loser are prostrate from fatigue and are liable to fall victim to predators. The female gives birth to a single young after a gestation of 225-262 days.

WHISTLING SWAN
Cygnus columbianus columbianus
Classification Class: Aves; Order: Anseriformes; Family: Anatidae.
Description Length 46-47 in (1.16-1.19 m), weight 11½-14¼ lb (5.2-6.5 kg). White with black, yellow-spotted bill. Upright neck.
Distribution It nests in the American

Arctic and winters in the southwestern United States. It also breeds in Siberia.
Habitat Tundra in summer; lakes, large rivers and bays in winter.
Behavior Markedly territorial. Its size and aggressiveness protect it from attacks by most predators. The long, flexible neck enables it to reach submerged vegetation to a depth of about 3 ft (1 m). It begins breeding at the age of 4-5 years and the links between male and female generally last a lifetime. The 2-3 eggs hatch after an incubation of 29-30 days. The cygnets are able to follow their parents immediately and, contrary to what happens with other Anatidae, help them to find food.

WOLVERINE
Gulo gulo
Classification Class: Mammalia; Order: Carnivora; Family: Mustelidae.
Description Also called the Glutton. Length of head and body 26-34 in (65-87 cm), tail 7-10 in (17-26 cm), weight 44-77 lb (20-35 kg). Dark brown, paler on head; two broad yellow bands run from shoulders to base of tail. Large feet with a membrane between the toes which helps to prevent the animal sinking into snow.
Distribution Northern regions of North America. Also found in northern parts of Europe and Asia.
Habitat Lowland and mountain forests.
Behavior It defends a vast area of private territory, marking the boundaries with a glandular secretion and with excrement. It is a fearsome predator capable of overcoming the largest herbivores and also its dedicated rival, the lynx. Despite this, it will also feed occasionally on carrion and berries. After 9 months' gestation the female gives birth to 2-4 young, which remain with her until they are 2-3 years old.

YELLOW-CHEEKED VOLE
Microtus xanthognathus
Classification Class: Mammalia; Order: Rodentia; Family: Cricetidae.
Description Total length about 9 in (23 cm), weight 4-6 oz (113-170 g). Dark brown with an orange-yellow patch around the nose.
Distribution Alaska and northwest Canada.
Habitat Coniferous forests.
Behavior Population numbers of this rodent peak more or less every 20 years, but even in normal periods they will suddenly and inexplicably appear and vanish in certain zones. The animal lives in colonies, digging burrows in the mossy soil of woods, which is littered with hillocks corresponding to the entry points. After a gestation of 3 weeks the female produces 7-11 young.

Mountains

AMERICAN RED SQUIRREL or CHICKAREE
Tamiasciurus hudsonicus
Classification Class: Mammalia; Order: Rodentia; Family: Sciuridae.
Description Length of head and body 7-8 in (18-20 cm), tail 4-6 in (10-15 cm), weight about 8 oz (230 g). Slightly smaller than the European Red Squirrel, it is reddish-brown above, white below. In winter two characteristic tufts of hair grow on the ears. Bushy tail.
Distribution Northern and central North America.
Habitat Coniferous forests.
Behavior Feeds on a wide range of plants and animals. It will frequently remove the cones of the Norway spruce while they are still green and conceal them in the ground, in cavities or among rocks to enable them to ripen. Its shelter is generally provided by nests abandoned by woodpeckers, where, in spring, the female gives birth to 2-7 young.
Note The broadleaved forests of the eastern United States are inhabited by the Gray Squirrel *(Sciurus carolinensis),* which feeds mainly on acorns that are often hidden in the ground and forgotten, thus helping to disseminate oaks. Introduced in the British Isles, it encroached on the habitat of the indigenous Red Squirrel, much to the latter's detriment.

BALD EAGLE
Haliaëtus leucocephalus
Classification Class: Aves: Order: Falconiformes; Family: Accipitridae.
Description Total length 27-30 in (68-76 cm), wingspan 6-7 ft (1.88-2.1 m), weight 9-13 lb (4.1-5.8 kg). Brown with white head and tail. Immature birds are entirely brown.
Distribution From Alaska to Florida.
Habitat Seacoasts, rivers, and lakes.
Behavior Feeds on fish, birds, and mammals. It often hunts in pairs, in order to land a big fish or catch a sick or injured water bird. Sometimes it behaves piratically, attacking other birds and forcing them to abandon or even regurgitate the prey they have just caught. If need be, it will turn to carrion. Pairs of eagles mate for life and build a nest in a position dominating the surroundings: a tall tree, a rock promontory or a barren islet. The female lays 1-3 eggs and incubates them for about 35 days.

BLACKBURNIAN WARBLER
Dendroica fusca
Classification Class: Aves; Order: Passeriformes; Family: Parulidae.
Description Length 4¼-4¾ in (11.2-12.2 cm). In spring the male is black and white with part of the head, throat and breast brilliant orange; in the female and young these parts are bright yellow. In the fall the colors fade.
Distribution Canada, eastern United States. It winters between Guatemala and Peru.
Habitat Lowland and mountain forests.
Behavior Feeds on insects and their larvae. It has a pleasant song. The nest is built with twigs, lichens and fragments of bark; there are 4 chicks.

BROWN COATI
Nasua narica
Classification Class: Mammalia; Order: Carnivora; Family: Procyonidae.
Description Total length 35-52 in (80-130 cm), of which half is tail, weight 7¼-13¼ lb (3.5-5.6 kg). Gray or brown with tip of snout, throat and abdomen white, feet and rings on tail black. Long and very mobile nose; strong claws on forefeet. It walks on the whole sole of the foot, as bears do.
Distribution Arizona, New Mexico, and Texas. Also lives in Central America, Colombia and Ecuador.
Habitat Wooded highlands, fringes of deserts; in Central and South America it also lives in tropical forests.
Behavior It is the most gregarious of the Procyonidae. The female and young form groups of up to 30. Adult males are solitary. It feeds on small rodents, lizards, insects and plants which it locates with its sensitive nose, scooping them out with its claws. It is an excellent climber, aided by its long tail which helps it to balance. The 2-7 young are born after a gestation of about 74 days.

GOLDEN-MANTLED GROUND SQUIRREL
Spermophilus lateralis
Classification Class: Mammalia; Order: Rodentia; Family: Sciuridae.
Description Length of head and body 6-8 in (15-20 cm), tail 2½-4½ in (6.2-11.7 cm). Head and front part of body copper colored; broad white, black-edged band on each flank; rest of body grayish-brown.
Distribution Western North America.
Habitat Mountain forests of conifers.
Behavior Feeds on seeds, berries, eggs, and insects. It spends the summer collecting food for the winter, transporting it to the burrow in its cheek pouches. These stocks will be consumed during the brief

waking intervals of hibernation. The female gives birth to 2-8 young after a gestation of 1 month.
Note Belonging to the same family are the Hoary Marmot *(Marmota caligata)* and the Yellow-bellied Marmot *(Marmota flaviventris).* Both inhabit the high mountains of western North America, behaving in a similar manner to the Alpine Marmot of Europe.

GRAY FOX
Urocyon cinereoargenteus
Classification Class: Mammalia; Order: Carnivora; Family: Canidae.
Description Length of head and body 21-28½ in (52.5-72.5 cm), tail 11-16 in (27.5-40 cm), weight 7¾-14¼ lb (3.5-6.5 kg). Upper parts silver-gray, underparts bright chestnut-red.
Distribution Southeastern and southwestern United States. Also found in Central America.
Habitat Forests, rocky ground.
Behavior A very unusual fox which barks like a dog and climbs trees with the agility of a cat. This versatile hunter feeds on mammals no larger than a rabbit, birds, reptiles, amphibians, insects, etc. The diet is completed by carrion and vegetation. It shelters in underground burrows abandoned by other animals, in tree cavities or in rocky crevices. Here the female gives birth to 4 cubs after a gestation of about 2 months.

MULE DEER
Odocoileus hemionus
Classification Class: Mammalia; Order: Artiodactyla; Family: Cervidae.
Description Length of head and body 3-6 ft (1-1.9 m), tail 4-10 in (10-25 cm), height to shoulder 36-42 in (90-105 cm), weight 110-475 lb (50-215 kg). Reddish in summer, gray-blue in winter. Very large ears. Males only have branched antlers.
Distribution Canada and western United States.
Habitat Mountain forests, thickets, semidesert zones.
Behavior The long ears, which give rise to the animal's common name, enable it to identify immediately the direction from which danger threatens. It escapes with long leaps, coming down on all four feet simultaneously. For this reason it is also known as the Jumping Deer. It feeds on twigs and leaves. The female usually gives birth to twins.

OSPREY
Pandion haliaëtus
Classification Class: Aves; Order: Falconiformes; Family: Pandionidae.
Description Also known as the Fish

Mountains

The landscape of the mountain regions of North America is in some parts similar to that of Europe, but differs considerably in displaying a richer variety of tree species. Particularly spectacular are the giant redwoods or sequoias, notable both for their size and longevity: some are more than 300 ft (90 m) high and over 2,000 years old. But the most widely distributed and important genera are elm, maple, beech, ash, and oak.

1 golden eagle
2 flying squirrel
3 mule deer
4 puma
5 raccoon
6 whitetailed deer
7 pika
8 red squirrel
9 golden-mantled ground
    squirrel
10 bald eagle
11 gray fox
12 gray marmot

Hawk. Length 22 in (55 cm), wingspan 40 in (102 cm), weight 3¼ lb (1.5 kg). Upper parts dark brown, underparts white; short white crest on nape. Feet covered with horny scales which, on the underside of the toes, are pointed, so that the bird can get a firm grip on the slippery body of its prey.
Distribution It nests in northwestern North America and winters in southwestern North America. Found world-wide.
Habitat Seacoasts, rivers, and lakes.
Behavior It patrols its fishing grounds by flying at a height of 50-100 ft (15-30 m) above the water surface. Having sighted a fish, it hovers momentarily in the air then dives straight down, submerging itself completely and sometimes seizing the victim underwater. Maintaining a tight grip on it with both feet, it settles on a perch to devour the prey. This is the moment when it is often attacked by a Bald Eagle and forced to abandon its victim. In the nest, built with branches and sticks on a high tree, the female lays 2-4 eggs, which hatch after 35-38 days' incubation.

PIKA
Ochotoan princeps
Classification Class: Mammalia; Order: Lagomorpha; Family: Ochotonidae.
Description Also known as the Calling Hare. Total length 8 in (20.3 cm), weight 4 oz (113 g). Gray or brown. Short, rounded ears; tail not visible.
Distribution Western North America.
Habitat High mountains, often above treeline.
Behavior It looks more like a small rodent than a hare. Rather noisy, it accompanies its activities, especially in the daytime, with incessant calls. It is the only American lagomorph to provide for the winter: it lays out grass and other forms of vegetation in the sun to dry, then heaps it all into mounds which it marks with glandular secretions to defend itself against others of its species. After a gestation of about 30 days the female, on average, produces a litter of 3 young, two or three times a year.

PUMA
Felis concolor
Classification Class: Mammalia; Order: Carnivora; Family: Felidae.
Description Also known as the Cougar or Mountain Lion. Length of head and body 3½-5¼ ft (1.05-1.6 m), tail 24-34 in (60-85 cm), weight 145-225 lb (67-103 kg). Tawny or uniformly gray. The cubs are speckled.
Distribution Western North America. Also inhabits much of Central and South America.

Habitat Extremely adaptable, it is equally at home in cold mountain forests, tropical forests, pampas, and fringes of desert.
Behavior The male is only gregarious during the breeding period and lives with the female while the cubs are being reared. At all other times he is solitary and jealously guards his territory. Any animal, from a mouse to a bison, may occasionally be attacked and killed by the Puma, but favorite victims are medium-sized mammals such as deer. After 90 days' gestation the female gives birth to 1-6 cubs in a cave or under a rocky ledge. Like most carnivores, the young pumas, although possessing inborn predatory instincts, only learn to hunt properly after the mother has taught them. This apprenticeship is complete at 18-22 months after which they become fully independent.

RACCOON
Procyon lotor
Classification Class: Mammalia; Order: Carnivora; Family: Procyonidae.
Description Total length 32 in (81 cm), weight 20 lb (9 kg). Gray with black mask, black and white rings on tail. The long, thin toes of the forefeet are highly sensitive, and the raccoon uses them to manipulate its food before putting it in its mouth.
Distribution Central and southern North America. Also found in Central America.
Habitat Everywhere, provided there is water nearby.
Behavior It is nocturnal and solitary, feeding on plants and small aquatic animals and regularly visiting refuse dumps. Individuals in captivity have the habit of washing their food before eating it, something which has never been observed in the wild. Such behavior seems to be due to frustration at not being able to hunt water creatures. In winter it sleeps a lot, but does not hibernate. After a gestation of 64 days the female gives birth to 1-7 young in the hollow of a tree.

RINGTAILED CAT
Bassariscus astutus
Classification Class: Mammalia; Order: Carnivora; Family: Procyonidae.
Description Length of head and body 12-15 in (31-38 cm), tail 12-17 in (31-44 cm), weight 1¾-2½ lb (0.8-1.1 kg). Gray or brown; brown and white rings on tail. Semiretractile claws. Muzzle of a fox, body of a cat.
Distribution Southwestern United States.
Habitat Bushy mountain slopes, dry canyons.
Behavior Strictly nocturnal and very

timid. Feeds on rodents, insects, spiders and plants. It moves nimbly thanks to its flexible body, which can turn back on itself at an angle of almost 180°, and its long tail, which helps it to balance. Arched over the body, the tail also helps to deter predators. The 2-4 young are born after a gestation of about 2 months.

SOUTHERN FLYING SQUIRREL
Glaucomys volans
Classification Class: Mammalia; Order: Rodentia; Family: Sciuridae.
Description Length of head and body 5-6 in (13-15 cm), tail 3½-4½ in (9-11 cm), weight 1¾-2½ oz (50-70 g). Olive-brown above, white below. The skin membrane known as the patagium extends on either side of the body from the front to the back limbs.
Distribution Southeastern United States. Also found in Central America.
Habitat Forests.
Behavior It commences activity at dusk, when other squirrels are retiring to their nests. Perched at the top of a high tree, it launches itself into space, fully extending its limbs. The patagium unfolds and, serving as a parachute, allows the animal to make a soft landing on another tree trunk. It feeds on acorns, seeds, berries, insects and their larvae, and nestlings. During the day it shelters in a tree hollow where it sometimes hangs by the claws of its hind feet, like a bat. The female produces 3-6 young after a gestation of 40 days.

WHITETAILED DEER
Odocoileus virginianus
Classification Class: Mammalia; Order: Artiodactyla; Family: Cervidae.
Description Also called Virginian Deer. Length of head and body 34-81 in (85-205 cm), tail 4-14 in (10-35 cm), height to shoulder 22-44 in (55-110 cm), weight 48-450 lb (22-205 kg). Reddish in summer, gray-blue in winter. Males have branched horns. The lower side of the broad tail is white, and when in flight the deer raises it like a flag, so that members of the group can all keep sight of each other even in dense vegetation.
Distribution Central and southern North America. It also inhabits Central and South America.
Habitat Forests.
Behavior It thrives even in large built-up areas, able to live, quite unobtrusively, in strips of woodland surrounded by fields and farms. For that reason its numbers are still high. It lives alone or in small groups, feeding on twigs, fungi, and shoots. The female gives birth to 1-4 young after a gestation of 196-210 days.

Grasslands

AMERICAN BADGER
Taxidea taxus
Classification Class: Mammalia; Order: Carnivora; Family: Mustelidae.
Description Length of head and body 16½-28½ in (42-72 cm), tail 4-6 in (10-16 cm), weight 7¾-26½ lb (3.5-12 kg). Upper parts gray to reddish, underparts yellowish-brown. A white strip runs from nose to shoulders; cheeks also white. Sturdy build, strong claws for digging, thick fur.
Distribution From southwestern Canada through central and southern United States to Mexico.
Habitat Open plains and mountain zones.
Behavior Nocturnal, solitary, and territorial, with mediocre vision and an excellent sense of smell. It eats rodents, rabbits and hares, invertebrates, carrion, and vegetation. It often ventures into urban areas, roaming parks and private gardens and feeding on refuse, plants, etc. It mates at the end of the summer but, as happens with many mustelids, development of the young in the mother's womb does not begin until the following February, and they are born in April: this avoids the 1-5 cubs being born in the fall and having to survive the winter when food is in short supply.

AMERICAN BISON
Bison bison
Classification Class: Mammalia; Order: Artiodactyla; Family: Bovidae.
Description Also known as the Buffalo. Length of head and body about 10 ft (3 m), height to shoulder 6 ft (1.9 m), weight up to 1 t. The female is much smaller than the male. Color dark brown. Massive head, large hump on shoulders, horns in both sexes.
Distribution Canada and central United States.
Habitat Prairies and forests.
Behavior It lives in large herds made up of females and immature individuals. Adult males wander about alone or in small groups. Food consists of grass and tubers; the subspecies which inhabits woods also eats leaves, shoots and bark. In winter it scoops in the snow to find dry grass, moss and lichen. The bison has the habit of rolling in the dust and rubbing against trees to keep its skin clean and free of parasites. During the breeding season there are frequent and extremely violent fights among the males, but these are seldom fatal. The calf is born in spring after a gestation of about 9 months.

BLACKFOOTED FERRET
Mustela nigripes
Classification Class: Mammalia; Order: Carnivora; Family: Mustelidae.
Description Length of head and body 15-16 in (38-41 cm), tail 4-5 in (11-13 cm), weight about 2 lb (0.9-1 kg).
Distribution Central and western North America.
Habitat Prairies of low grass.
Behavior Rare, little known, and in danger of extinction. It depends on prairie dogs for food and refuge, hunting underground in the mazelike burrows of its victims. Having caught one of these animals, it drags it back to its own lair, which is a tunnel abandoned by the prairie dogs themselves. It has been estimated, in approximate terms, that in order to sustain herself and a litter of four, a female ferret must have access to an underground colony of the rodents covering at least 650,000 sq ft (60,000 sq m) in area. Such requirements, quite apart from the considerable disturbance caused by human activities, help to explain why this species has never been common and abundant. The young are born in spring and disperse in the fall to begin their solitary adult existence.

BLACKTAILED JACK RABBIT
Lepus californicus
Classification Class: Mammalia; Order: Lagomorpha; Family: Leporidae.
Description Also called the California Hare. Total length 24 in (61 cm), weight 5½ lb (2.5 kg). Gray-brown above, whitish below; underside of tail black. Very long ears.
Distribution Western United States. Also inhabits northern Mexico.
Habitat Sagebrush prairies, deserts.
Behavior Like all hares, it relies on speed and mimicry to escape enemies. When danger threatens, it does not run away but flattens itself motionless against the ground, which almost matches the color of its coat; only when the danger is imminent will it scurry off, zigzagging, at more than 35 mph (60 kmh). It eats grass, branches, leaves and cacti. The female produces 2 young, four or more times a year, after 42 days' gestation.

BLACKTAILED PRAIRIE DOG
Cynomys ludovicianus
Classification Class: Mammalia; Order: Rodentia; Family: Sciuridae.
Description Length of head and body 10½-12½ in (27-32 cm), tail 3-4 in (7-10 cm), weight about 2 lb (1 kg). Light brown above, whitish below. Tip of tail black.
Distribution Central United States.
Habitat Prairies of low grass.
Behavior It lives in colonies which dig immense underground towns consisting of a dense network of intercommunicating tunnels. The family groups which make up the colony leave the burrow early in the morning to feed on grass, but do not stray too far. A team of permanent sentries, posted on top of mounds of earth corresponding to the entries to the tunnels, give out sharp alarm whistles at the least hint of danger. Many other animals choose these subterranean burrows as their own homes; some, like the blackfooted ferret and the rattlesnake, prey on the rightful occupants. Reproduction takes place when the animals wake from their winter hibernation; 3-5 young are born after a gestation of 21-28 days.

BURROWING OWL
Speotyto cunicularia
Classification Class: Aves; Order: Strigiformes; Family: Strigidae.
Description Length 8½-10½ in (22-27 cm). Color brown. Round head, long legs, short tail.
Distribution Western and southeastern North America. Also found in many parts of Central and South America.
Habitat Prairies, deserts, embankments.
Behavior It finds shelter and nests in underground burrows abandoned by other animals but, if necessary, it will dig its own. It feeds on insects, amphibians, reptiles, fledglings and small mammals, watching for their movements from a mound or hillock. When disturbed, the owl reacts with a series of jerks and bobs. Should an enemy infiltrate the burrow, both adults and young give out a call which resembles the sound made by a rattlesnake; as a rule this is enough to deter the predator. The female lays 5-9 eggs which hatch after an incubation of 28-29 days.

COYOTE
Canis latrans
Classification Class: Mammalia; Order: Carnivora; Family: Canidae.
Description Also known as the Prairie Wolf. Length of head and body 28-39 in (70-97 cm), tail 12-15 in (30-38 cm), height to shoulder 18-21 in (45-53 cm), weight 25½-33 lb (11.5-15 kg). Mottled tawny-gray; throat and abdomen white.
Distribution Most of North America. Also found in Central America.
Habitat Prairies, lowland and mountain forests.

Grasslands

Agriculture has transformed the immense area of plains lying between the Rocky Mountains and the Alleghenies into vast tracts of corn and cotton. Before man appeared on the scene, however, many of these regions were covered with herbaceous vegetation (particularly grasses), and teemed with herds of buffalo on their periodic migrations.

1   American bison
2   coyote
3   blacktailed prairie dog
4   peccary
5   prairie falcon
6   pronghorn antelope
7   American badger
8   plains pocket gopher
9   rock chipmunk
10   prairie dog
11   sage grouse
12   blacktailed jack rabbit
13   ground squirrel
14   least chipmunk

Behavior It lives in pairs or small groups whose members, though collaborating for food and defense of territory, do not possess the stable social links of wolves. It feeds mainly on mammals, including carrion. Habitual prey are rodents, hares and rabbits, but when hunting in packs it may even kill bighorns, deer and pronghorn antelopes. The characteristic howl is emitted to define and defend territorial boundaries. The female has a single litter a year of 4-6 cubs, born after 63 days' gestation and weaned when they are 5-7 weeks old.

LEAST CHIPMUNK
Eutamias minimus
Classification Class: Mammalia; Order: Rodentia; Family: Sciuridae.
Description Length of head and body about 4 in (9-11 cm), tail 3-4 in (7.5-11 cm), weight 1-1¾ oz (30-50 g). Yellowish with reddish stripes or gray with black stripes.
Distribution Central-northern North America.
Habitat From tundra to prairies.
Behavior Feeds on plants, insects and their larvae, amphibians, reptiles and fledglings. It can cause considerable damage by finding its way into granaries or by unearthing seeds. It hibernates in an underground burrow in which it has collected food during the summer; its sleep is interrupted every now and then, and the animal finds time both to eat and to venture outside. In spring the female gives birth to 5-6 young.

MONARCH BUTTERFLY
Danaus plexippus
Classification Class: Insecta; Order: Lepidoptera; Family: Danaidae.
Description Wingspan 3-3½ in (8-9 cm). Orange wings with dark veins.
Distribution In summer widely distributed in United States and southern Canada; in winter concentrated in its millions in particular zones of California and Mexico.
Habitat Forests. In the course of migrations it rests on the North American prairies.
Behavior The females lay eggs on plants of the family Asclepidaceae (such as milkweed, for example), which grow throughout the United States and southern Canada: the larvae feed on these species. Soon after egg-laying, worn out by a journey of thousands of miles, the adults die. Their offspring, once adult, feed on nectar and reproduce in their turn before the summer is over. With the arrival of the fall, unable to withstand the northern winter, they migrate southward, confidently taking routes they have never

previously traveled. The following spring they mate and return north to repeat the entire cycle.

PRAIRIE FALCON
Falco mexicanus
Classification Class: Aves; Order: Falconiformes; Family: Falconidae.
Description Length 16½-20 in (42-50 cm). Color sandy above, whitish below with darker longitudinal stripes. Long pointed wings, typical of very rapid flyers. Long tail.
Distribution Inland regions of North America. Part of the population winters in Mexico.
Habitat Prairies, canyons, and deserts.
Behavior It eats small rodents and birds captured both on the ground and on the wing. Not even the fastest-flying swallows escape it. An irritable nature causes it to persecute other birds of prey, such as eagles and buzzards, which intrude upon its territory; despite their larger dimensions, they are too slow to resist it and are forced to give way. It nests on the rocks overlooking the plains. The female lays 3-6 eggs which hatch after an incubation of 29-31 days, during which time she is fed by the male.

PRAIRIE RATTLESNAKE
Crotalus viridis
Classification Class: Reptilia; Order: Squamata; Suborder: Ophidia; Family: Crotalidae.
Description Length 32-44 in (80-110 cm). Olive-green with round brown spots arranged in longitudinal rows. Poisonous. The end of the tail is equipped with a rattle, made up of hard, horny rings which fit into one another. When the snake angrily vibrates its tail, these rings produce a loud, chilling sound which can be heard over 100 ft (30 m) away.
Distribution Central-western United States, southern Canada.
Habitat Prairies.
Behavior It eats young prairie dogs, mice and rats, living close to its prey, often in their burrows. It winters in rock clefts above the prairies. The female produces 8-15 perfectly formed young.

PRONGHORN ANTELOPE
Antilocapra americana
Classification Class: Mammalia; Order: Artiodactyla; Family: Bovidae.
Description Total length 4½ ft (1.4 m), height to shoulder 34 in (87 cm), weight 103-154 lb (47-70 kg). The male is larger than the female. Upper parts chestnut; underparts, area around tail, marks on head and neck white. The antlers, found in both sexes, are shed and renewed every

year; those of the male are 17 in (43 cm) long, those of the female only 1¾ in (4.2 cm).
Distribution Canada and western United States. Also found in Mexico.
Habitat Prairies and thickets.
Behavior It is capable of reaching a speed of almost 55 mph (86 km/h) and of maintaining a speed of about 45 mph (70 km/h) for some 4 miles (6 km). Its fascination for moving objects leads it even to approach predators, humans included. It feeds on grass and branches of shrubs. During and some time before the beginning of the breeding season the male defends his own territory, to which only herds of females are granted free access. The young are born after a gestation of 252 days. Within only 48 hours of birth they are able to run faster than a horse but, lacking the stamina to follow the fleeing herd, they remain hidden in the vegetation until they are 21-26 days old.

SAGE GROUSE
Centrocercus urophasianus
Classification Class: Aves; Order: Galliformes; Family: Tetraonidae.
Description Total length 28 in (72 cm), weight about 7½ lb (3.5 kg). The male's upper parts are brown, with minute black and white bars, the breast white, the belly, throat and collar black. There is a bare yellow patch above either eye and there are two air sacs at the sides of the neck; when the latter are inflated, they take on the appearance of little yellow balloons among the sprouting feathers. The female's colors are drabber and there is no black on the throat.
Distribution Central-western United States.
Habitat Prairies and sagebrush.
Behavior It feeds almost exclusively on sagebrush *(Artemisia tridentata)*. Extremely gregarious, it breeds in groups which, in winter, join together to form enormous flocks. During the breeding season the males assemble in particular places and display themselves in characteristic dances: they spread the tail fanwise, lower the wings so that they graze the ground, and inflate and reinflate their air sacs so that these give out sounds that can be heard for hundreds of yards. The females then join them and most of them couple with the dominant male of the group. The nest, constructed on the ground, contains 6-12 eggs which hatch after an incubation of 21 days.
Note The Greater Prairie Chicken *(Tympanuchus cupido)* belongs to the same family, inhabiting the extensive grasslands of the central United States. Its habits are similar to those of the Sage Grouse.

Deserts

ANTELOPE JACK RABBIT
Lepus alleni
Classification   Class: Mammalia; Order: Lagomorpha; Family: Leporidae.
Description   Length of head and body 19-21 in (48-53 cm), ears 6-8 in (15-20 cm), occupying one-quarter of the entire body surface, weight 8 lb (3.6 kg). Brown with whitish flanks and haunches. Very long legs.
Distribution   Extreme southwest of United States.
Habitat   Desert.
Behavior   This hare, the speediest of all American species, can be identified by its exceptionally long ears or by a sudden flash of white amid the desert vegetation. Propelled by its powerful hind legs, it can reach a speed of 40 mph (64 km/h). It feeds on cacti and other succulents which not only satisfy its hunger but also quench its thirst. The female gives birth to 1-2 young after 42 days' gestation.

BOBCAT
Lynx rufus
Classification   Class: Mammalia; Order: Carnivora; Family: Felidae.
Description   Also known as the Bay Lynx. Length of head and body 30 in (75 cm), tail 6 in (15 cm), height to shoulder 24 in (60 cm), weight 26½ lb (12 kg). Brown with gray or white mottling; dark spots over whole body. Characteristic tufts of hair on ears.
Distribution   Most of North America.
Habitat   Deserts, prairies, forests, and suburban zones.
Behavior   Nocturnal predator, solitary and territorial, incredibly strong for its size. Rodents, rabbits and hares are its customary prey, but it can also bring down deer, especially in winter when snow impedes their movements and hunger weakens them. Generally silent, it makes itself heard in the breeding season when it covers long distances in search of a member of the opposite sex. The 2-3 cubs are born after a gestation of 50-60 days.

DESERT TORTOISE
Gopherus polyphemus
Classification   Class: Reptilia; Order: Testudinata; Family: Testudinidae.
Description   Length 14 in (35 cm). Color brown.
Distribution   Southern United States, northern Mexico.

Habitat   Steppes and deserts.
Behavior   It digs deep underground burrows where it spends the hottest hours of the day and the entire winter. It shares this retreat with rodents, reptiles, amphibians and invertebrates which are of no value to it but which do not cause it any disturbance. It feeds principally off cacti, which provide both food and drink. The female covers the eggs with a thin layer of sand, relying on the heat of the sun to incubate them. They hatch after 3-4 months.

GILA MONSTER
Heloderma suspectum
Classification   Class: Reptilia; Order: Squamata; Suborder: Sauria; Family: Helodermatidae.
Description   Length of head and body 14 in (35 cm), tail 6 in (15 cm), weight 2¾ lb (1.3 kg). Yellow or pink on dark ground. Elongated body, large tail and short legs. Poisonous.
Distribution   Southwestern United States, northwestern Mexico.
Habitat   Deserts.
Behavior   Ground-dwelling and mainly nocturnal lizard, hiding in an underground burrow by day. It feeds on small mammals, birds and their eggs. During the long periods of fasting caused by adverse climatic conditions, it survives on the fat stored in its tail. Provided with a primitive poison apparatus, when it bites it does not immediately let go of its prey, as do the majority of venomous snakes, but hangs on for some time, probably to allow time for the poison to penetrate the wound.

GILA WOODPECKER
Centurus uropygialis
Classification   Class: Aves; Order: Piciformes; Family: Picidae.
Description   Length 8-10 in (20-25 cm). Back and tail are striped black and white, underparts and head are gray-brown. The adult male is distinguished from the female by a red spot on the top of the head.
Distribution   Southwestern United States, Mexico.
Habitat   Near sources of water in desert, river banks.
Behavior   It is associated with saguaros, the giant cacti, up to 50 ft (14 m) high that are typical of the southwestern parts of North America. The holes that the bird pecks in them are ideal shelters and nesting places for many desert animals, some of which – snakes, birds of prey, etc – do not even wait for the hole to be abandoned but force out the legitimate occupants. It feeds on insects, cactus fruit and seeds. The female lays 3-5 eggs, which the male helps to incubate.

KANGAROO RAT
Dipodomys deserti
Classification   Class: Mammalia; Order: Rodentia; Family: Heteromyidae.
Description   Length of head and body 5-6½ in (12.5-16.2 cm), tail 7-8½ in (18-21.5 cm), weight 3-5 oz (83-138 g). Yellowish with belly and tip of tail white. Very long hind legs, forelegs correspondingly small.
Distribution   Southwestern United States.
Habitat   Desert.
Behavior   Thanks to its powerful hind legs and the long tail which serves as a rudder, the kangaroo rat, like the marsupial after which it is named, moves by jumping. It leads a nocturnal existence among the sand dunes, feeding on seeds and the green parts of plants. It requires little to drink, deriving sufficient water from its food. Very keen hearing and exceptionally sharp reflexes constitute effective defenses against predators. It finds refuge in enormous underground burrows where it collects large stocks of seeds for the winter. The young are born after a gestation of about 1 month.

KIT FOX
Vulpes macrotis
Classification   Class: Mammalia; Order: Carnivora; Family: Canidae.
Description   Length of head and body 19 in (49 cm), tail 13 in (33 cm), height to shoulder 14 in (35 cm), weight 5½ lb (2.5 kg). Reddish-gray with black tip to tail. Very big ears. Strongly resembles the North African fennec.
Distribution   Southwestern United States, northern Mexico.
Habitat   Deserts.
Behavior   It lives in pairs which apparently stay united for life. Each pair defends its own territory, where a number of burrows are used in rotation. It is a skillful hunter of rodents, hares, rabbits and birds. Every night it patrols its entire territory, systematically exploring all possible hiding places for its prey. The female produces 4-6 young after a gestation of 49-55 days.

MOURNING DOVE
Zenaidura macroura
Classification   Class: Aves; Order: Columbiformes; Family: Columbidae.
Description   Also called the Carolina Dove. Length about 12 in (30 cm), weight 3½ oz (100 g). Upper parts olive, underparts gray-brown. Long wedge-shaped tail.
Distribution   Most of North America. Also found in Central America.
Habitat   Prairies, deserts and towns.
Behavior   It consumes a large variety of

Deserts

Characteristic plants of the deserts of Central and North America include many species belonging to the family Cactaceae: these are typical succulents with small leaves and simple spines, while the stem, having turned green with chlorophyll, also serves as a water reservoir. Growing together with cacti, some of which reach a height of over 30 ft (10 m), are euphorbias, grasses and other plants with leathery or rudimentary leaves.

1 antelope jack rabbit
2 striped skunk
3 diamondback rattlesnake
4 Gila monster
5 grasshopper mouse
6 bicolored grasshopper
7 horned lizard
8 kangaroo rat
9 mourning dove
10 whitefooted mouse
11 roadrunner
12 desert tortoise
13 kit fox

plants. In the desert it nests on cacti or on the ground, elsewhere in trees or shrubs. It is very sensitive to low temperatures: sudden bouts of cold may cause serious lesions on the legs due to freezing.

ROADRUNNER
Geococcyx californianus
Classification Class: Aves; Order Cuculiformes; Family: Cuculidae.
Description Length 25-26 in (63-66 cm). Brown with white spots. Long legs and tail, short wings, erectile crest.
Distribution Southwestern United States, Mexico.
Habitat Stony deserts, dry undergrowth.
Behavior Its pattern of running is extraordinarily versatile; it has both speed (up to 25mph/40 km/h) and stamina, and its characteristic movements include sharp spurts, abrupt changes of direction and sudden stops, the last brought about by rapid flicks of the tail. Only in cases of extreme peril will it take heavily and clumsily to the air. It feeds on invertebrates, reptiles, birds and small mammals. Sometimes it will be seen moving about with part of the body of a snake dangling from its bill: the reptile, too large to be swallowed whole, suffers gradual death as it is slowly digested. The roadrunner has developed no special adaptations to life in the desert, and survives there only by avoiding virtually all activity during the worst heat of the day. The female lays 3-6 eggs which hatch after an incubation of 17-18 days.

SPIDER WASP
Pepsis sp.
Classification Class: Insecta; Order: Hymenoptera; Family: Pompilidae.
Description Wingspan up to 4 in (10 cm). Body bluish, wings rust-colored.
Distribution Southwestern United States. Also found in parts of Central America.
Habitat Steppes and deserts.
Behavior As an adult it feeds on nectar, whereas in the larval stage it is a carnivore. When ready to lay her eggs, the female, after a hard fight, captures a trapdoor spider, fat and hairy with powerful, poisonous chelicerae. The victim is not killed but paralyzed with a liquid which the wasp injects with its sting. Having dragged the prey into a hole, about 10 in (25 cm) deep, which has already been dug, the wasp lays an egg on its victim's abdomen, exits from the hole, seals it with gravel and departs, never to return. The newborn larvae then feed on the tissues of the spider, which is alive but still unable to move.

STRIPED SKUNK
Mephitis mephitis
Classification Class: Mammalia; Order: Carnivora; Family: Mustelidae.
Description Length of head and body 13-18 in (33-45 cm), tail 7-10 in (18-25 cm), weight 3¼-6½ lb (1.5-3 kg). Black with two white stripes from head to tail.
Distribution From Canada to southern United States and Mexico.
Habitat Very varied, including desert.
Behavior Like all mustelids, it possesses anal glands which secrete a foul-smelling substance that is sprayed at intruders and enemies, forcing them to beat a hasty retreat. The substance is an irritant and, if it comes into contact with the eyes, may cause temporary blindness; the smell, furthermore, persists for several days. Solitary and territorial, the skunk eats insects, small mammals, eggs, and vegetation. After a gestation of 62-66 days, the female gives birth to 3-9 young in an underground burrow.
Note The Spotted Skunk (*Spilogale putorius*), smaller, ranges from Canada to Central America. Its habits do not differ substantially from those of the Striped Skunk.

TEXAS HORNED LIZARD
Phrynosoma coronatum
Classification Class: Reptilia; Order: Squamata; Suborder: Sauria; Family: Iguanidae.
Description Also called the Horned Toad. Total length 1½-5 in (4-12 cm). Gray or brown according to its surroundings. The body is covered with spiny scales which, in the neck region, are quite large.
Distribution Southwestern United States.
Habitat Deserts.
Behavior It feeds on insects. Although capable of burrowing into the sand very quickly, when danger threatens it flattens itself against the ground and stays motionless, escaping only when, despite its mimetic colors, it is discovered. Sometimes an unusual phenomenon is seen: the lizard, if persistently harassed, sprays the intruder with a thin jet of blood from the eyes. It reproduces by laying eggs.
Note Two other noted members of the family Iguanidae live in the same surroundings: the Spiny Desert Lizard (*Sceloporus magister*) and the Western Collared Lizard (*Crotaphytus collaris*). The former needs plenty of heat: at an outdoor temperature of 86°F (30°C), it cannot digest captured insects and spiders until its own body registers 99°F (37°C) so it has to spend a great deal of time exposed to the sun. The Western Collared Lizard manages to withstand temperatures that would be fatal to other reptiles by raising

itself on its legs, so that its body is kept as far as possible from ground level. It feeds on insects and other lizards.

WESTERN DIAMONDBACK RATTLESNAKE
Crotalus atrox
Classification Class: Reptilia; Order: Squamata; Suborder: Ophidia; Family: Crotalidae.
Description Length 5-7 ft (1.5-2.2 m). Brown or gray with yellowish or reddish tints. Poisonous.
Distribution Southwestern United States, Mexico.
Habitat Deserts, canyons.
Behavior Along with the Eastern Diamondback Rattlesnake (*Crotalus adamanteus*), found in the southeastern parts of the United States, it is the deadliest snake in North America. The rattle produces a particularly loud, buzzing sound. It feeds on rodents and rabbits. As with all rattlesnakes, the young are born completely formed.
Note The Sidewinder (*Crotalus cerastes*), common in the sandy deserts of the southwestern United States, shares with certain desert vipers of the Old World a particular method of traveling across the sand: instead of using the typical undulating body movement of a snake, it forms its body into two spirals which move alternatively sideways, so that only the two tips of the abdomen touch the sand. By means of this technique it attains a speed of 1-2 mph (3-4 km/h). The snake is nocturnal and eats small mammals and reptiles.

WHITEFOOTED MOUSE
Peromyscus leucopus
Classification Class: Mammalia; Order: Rodentia; Family: Cricetidae.
Description Length of head and body 3-4 in (7-10 cm), tail 2 in (5 cm), weight ½-1 oz (12-31 g). Upper parts reddish-brown, feet and belly white.
Distribution Most of United States. Also inhabits Central America.
Habitat Semidesert zones, broadleaved woods.
Behavior It feeds at night on insects and plants, making its nest among stones, in lofts, in abandoned beehives and in trees. Southern populations reproduce all year round, those in temperate climates only in spring-summer. The average litter numbers 4.
Note Other representatives of the family Cricetidae live on the prairies and in the deserts of the United States; these are the Grasshopper Mouse (genus *Onychomys*), which must resemble those of the genus *Peromyscus*. They feed mainly on insects.

Inland waters

AMERICAN ALLIGATOR
Alligator mississipiensis

Classification Class: Reptilia; Order: Crocodilia; Family: Alligatoridae.

Description Length up to 20 ft (6 m). Greenish-brown above, lighter below. Broad, flat snout.

Distribution Southeastern United States.

Habitat Rivers and swamps.

Behavior When young it eats frogs and small fish; as an adult it catches large fish and small and medium-sized mammals which come to the water to drink. The alligator is considered less dangerous than the crocodile. The female lays 20-70 eggs in a nest, made of vegetation cemented with mud and constructed on the river bank. She immediately covers the eggs with grass and allows the water and the sun, by causing the plant material to decay and ferment, to furnish the necessary heat for their incubation. They hatch after 2 months.

BOWFIN
Amia calva

Classification Class: Osteichthyes; Order: Amiiformes; Family: Amiidae.

Description Length of male 22 in (55 cm), female 34 in (87 cm), weight of latter 15½-16½ lb (7-8 kg). The male is greenish-brown above, lighter below; a black mark bordered with red at the root of the tail distinguishes the male fish from the female.

Distribution United States east of the Rockies.

Habitat Stagnant or very slow-flowing water.

Behavior A nocturnal fish which catches other fish. Only very young individuals feed on aquatic invertebrates. It winters in deep water, in a form of submerged hibernation. In the breeding season the bowfin also becomes active by day. The male supervises the building of the nest, digging a round hole in the muddy bottom, just as deep as is necessary to uncover the roots of water plants on which the female, after an animated courtship, deposits the eggs. These, guarded and tended by the male alone, hatch after 8-10 days; the fry, having spent the first few days of their life in the restricted space of the nest, leave it but continue to be defended and guided by the father until they eventually disperse for good.

BROWN PELICAN
Pelecanus occidentalis

Classification Class: Aves; Order: Pelecaniformes; Family: Pelecanidae.

Description Length 3½-4¼ ft (1.1-1.3 m). Plumage brown with white marks on head and neck.

Distribution Coasts of southern United States. Also lives in Central America and western parts of South America.

Habitat Seacoasts.

Behavior Unlike other pelicans, it does not fish by swimming on the surface but by diving. Sighting a shoal of herring, its favorite food, it nosedives from a height of up to 65 ft (20 m) and vanishes underwater, reappearing soon after with a fish in its broad bill. Along the coasts of Peru the brown pelican is one of the most important producers of guano, a valuable natural fertilizer composed of the droppings and feathers of sea birds. It nests in colonies. The female lays 2-3 eggs that are incubated for 30-42 days. The chicks remain in the nest for 12-15 weeks.

BULLFROG
Rana catesbiana

Classification Class: Amphibia; Order: Anura; Family: Ranidae.

Description Length 3½-6 in (8.7-15.5 cm). Green with dark spots above, whitish below.

Distribution Eastern North America. It has been introduced into Europe.

Habitat Lakes, marshes, ponds.

Behavior It feeds on almost any prey it can catch. Its call, a loud and vibrant succession of low notes, is reinforced by a vocal sac beneath the chin which, as it dilates, acts as a sound box. The male is territorial: The banks of the pond are divided into a series of well-defined "holdings," and any intrusion is immediately punished by an attack. The contenders fight standing upright on their hind legs and striking out with the forelegs. The female lays a large quantity of eggs, surrounded by a gelatinous substance, in the water, and from these the tadpoles are born.

CANADIAN OTTER
Lutra canadensis

Classification Class: Mammalia; Order: Carnivora; Family: Mustelidae.

Description Length of head and body 26-42 in (66-107 cm), tail 12½-18 in (32-46 cm). Dark brown above, grayish below. Long sinuous body, made for fast swimming, waterproof fur, webbed feet. As the animal dives, the ears are closed by special valves.

Distribution Alaska, Canada and the United States.

Habitat Rivers.

Behavior It feeds not only on fish but also on amphibians, crustaceans, water birds, and small mammals; however, it is primarily in underwater fishing that the otter displays its extraordinary adaptation to an amphibious life. Sighting its prey from the bank, it dives down and captures it after a short, swift pursuit. Any small fish is swallowed immediately at the surface, but a larger one is brought back to shore. Fish which are wounded or sick are the first to attract attention and be caught. Fundamentally a solitary animal, it lives in pairs only in the breeding season. The burrow consists of a tunnel with two openings, one underwater and the other concealed in the shore vegetation. Here the female gives birth to 2-3 young after a gestation of 10-12 months (development of the embryos is halted during the winter).

EVERGLADES RAT SNAKE
Elaphe obsoleta rossalleni

Classification Class: Reptilia; Order: Squamata; Suborder: Ophidia; Family: Colubridae.

Description Length 4-6 ft (1.2-1.9 m). Orange with faint gray longitudinal stripes.

Distribution Southern Florida.

Habitat Swamps.

Behavior It consumes mice, rats and birds, suffocating them in its coils. It is an excellent climber, thanks to the particular arrangement of the ventral scales which help it to take a firm grip on the rough surface of trunks and stones. When threatened it seeks refuge in the water, from which it never strays very far, or fights back with the typical aggressiveness of a colubrid; it raises the front part of the body, throws back the head to form an S-shape, hisses in menacing fashion, vibrates the tail rapidly, then attacks and bites. It reproduces by laying eggs.

GREAT BLUE HERON
Ardea herodias

Classification Class: Aves; Order: Ciconiiformes; Family: Ardeidae.

Description Length 38-54 in (98-137 cm). Dark gray with black and white head, adorned with a tuft of black feathers. Yellow bill and greenish-brown legs. The nuptial livery is enlivened with long pale gray feathers on back and neck, reddish eyes and legs.

Distribution Southern United States and Mexico. It winters in Central America and along stretches of the northern coasts of South America.

Habitat Rivers, lakes, freshwater and brackish water swamps, seacoasts.

Behavior It feeds on insects, fish, amphibians, reptiles, birds and mammals. Its

Inland waters

Reeds, cattails and waterlilies are among the many plants familiar to the rivers and marshlands of North America, at least in the temperate parts of Canada and the United States. Farther south these are replaced by a more luxuriant type of tropical vegetation, as can be seen in the Everglades swamps of Florida, full of mangroves, waterlilies and epiphytes.

1 great white egret
2 snowy egret
3 beaver
4 muskrat
5 *Acilius* beetle
6 bowfin
7 Canadian otter
8 salmon
9 tropical gar
10 snakebird
11 double-crested cormorant
12 roseate spoonbill
13 great blue heron
14 American alligator
15 red salamander
16 stone fly
17 bullfrog
18 green heron
19 Everglades rat snake
20 North American manatee

size enables it to capture quite large animals both on dry land and in fairly deep water. It nests in isolated pairs or in colonies. The nest is a platform of twigs more than 3 ft (1 m) wide, built in large trees surrounded by water or on mangrove shrubs. The 3-7 eggs are incubated by both parents for 28 days.

GREAT WHITE EGRET
Egretta alba

Classification Class: Aves; Order: Ciconiiformes; Family: Ardeidae.

Description Length 34-40 in (85-102 cm). White with black legs and feet, yellow bill. In the breeding season the back of the adult birds is adorned with 30-50 long, fringed feathers.

Distribution Southern United States. It is also quite widely distributed in Central and South America, Europe, Africa, Asia, Australia and Oceania.

Habitat All kinds of aquatic environment.

Behavior It feeds, alone or in groups, in shallow water or on dry land, on insects, fish, amphibians, reptiles, fledglings, and small mammals. It nests in solitary pairs or in colonies. Defense of territory and courtship both involve erecting the very beautiful feathers of the back. The nest, generally placed in dense reedbeds, is made of twigs and lined with softer materials. The 2-5 eggs hatch after 25 days' incubation by both parents.

GREEN HERON
Butorides striatus virescens

Classification Class: Aves; Order: Ciconiiformes; Family: Ardeidae.

Description Length about 16 in (40 cm). Upper parts dark green, sides of neck chestnut, throat white, underparts gray. Bill black and legs yellowish-green. In courtship garb the head feathers lengthen to form a crest and the legs turn bright orange.

Distribution Eastern and southern United States. Also found in Central America.

Habitat Dense vegetation around ponds, rivers, and lakes; mangrove swamps along the edges of seacoasts and estuaries.

Behavior It feeds principally on fish and insects, which it hunts from branches overhanging the water or by wading slowly through the shallows. In coastal areas feeding time is regulated by the tides. As a rule it nests in solitary pairs which occasionally turn territorial. The nest, a simple platform of twigs with virtually no lining, is well concealed among shrubs or low trees. The incubation of the 2-4 eggs lasts 21-25 days and is undertaken by both parents.

GREEN TREE FROG
Hyla cinerea

Classification Class: Amphibia; Order: Anura; Family: Hylidae.

Description Length about 2 in (5 cm). Usually it is bright green, but the color varies; it may be yellow when the frog is croaking, blue-gray when it is inactive. A white line runs from snout to flanks.

Distribution Southern United States.

Habitat Swamps, shores of rivers and lakes.

Behavior Like all tree frogs, it is an agile climber of trees and shrubs, thanks to the adhesive pads on the tips of the toes. It feeds chiefly on insects: In zones where these are plentiful it may often be seen on illuminated windowsills in the act of catching victims attracted by the artificial light. Several hours before there is a sudden change in temperature, the frog will settle in a sheltered spot, for which reason it is sometimes known as the Rain Frog. Its call somewhat resembles the tinkling of a bell: During the breeding season hundreds of males make this noise simultaneously, creating a chorus of natural music very characteristic of the subtropical swamplands.

MUSKRAT
Ondatra zibethica

Classification Class: Mammalia; Order: Rodentia; Family: Cricetidae.

Description Also called the Musquash. Length of head and body 12-14 in (30-36 cm), tail 8-10 in (20-25 cm), weight about 1¼-3¼ lb (600-1,500 g). Dark brown above, silver below. Tail flattened from side to side, hind feet partially webbed, internal ear capable of closure by means of a flap of skin (an adaptation for swimming underwater).

Distribution Most of North America. Also found in Europe, where it was introduced at the beginning of the twentieth century.

Habitat Swamps, streams, lakes.

Behavior Despite being one of the most valuable of fur animals, the damage the muskrat does to crops has led some European countries to embark on its extermination. An excellent swimmer and diver, it walks clumsily on land. The muskrat feeds on crops of every kind, aquatic plants and molluscs. Its presence is signaled by the circular lodges, made of scraps of vegetation, reeds, and rushes which it builds underwater but which rises up to 3 ft (90 cm) above the surface; inside is a dry chamber. The animal is very prolific: In southern regions of America it breeds throughout the year, with litters of 7-8 born after a gestation of 28 days.

NORTH AMERICAN MANATEE
Trichecus manatus

Classification Class: Mammalia; Order: Sirenia; Family: Trichechidae.

Description Also known as the Sea Cow. Total length 11-15 ft (3.7-4.6 m), weight 1.6 t. The skin, completely naked, is gray-brown. Lacking hind limbs, the forelegs are transformed into fins as an adaptation to aquatic life. Horizontal, flat tail with rounded edge. The snout is bristly.

Distribution Southeastern United States. Also found in Central and South America.

Habitat Shallow coastal water, estuaries and rivers.

Behavior The exclusively vegetarian diet and an environment with few predators have not endowed the manatee with any degree of speed. With its heavy body, similar to that of a walrus, the animal moves about lazily, feeding on submerged or floating water plants, and only indulges in the occasional burst of speed if danger looms. The reproductive process is likewise extremely slow: The female gives birth to one young every other year, after a gestation of 12 months; care of the young lasts for 12-18 months, and the animal is mature at the age of 5-8 years. The manatee normally leads a solitary life.

PUMPKINSEED
Lepomus gibbosus

Classification Class: Osteichthyes; Order: Perciformes; Family: Centrarchidae.

Description Also called the Sunfish. Length 3-6 in (8-15 cm), rarely 12 in (30 cm). Upper parts greenish with undefined dark bands, underparts silvery with violet tints; sides of head and gill-covers brightly marked with green, yellow, blue and violet.

Distribution Eastern United States. Introduced into Europe around the end of the nineteenth century.

Habitat Lakes and slow-flowing rivers.

Behavior It lives in shallow water rich in vegetation and feeds on insects, crustaceans, and fry. In spring the female, who takes on bright colors while the male becomes drabber, lays her eggs in a hole on the bottom; the male keeps guard nearby until the fry are ready to disperse.

Note Another member of the family is the Large-mouthed Bass (*Micropterus salmoides*), originally from the southeastern and central United States and likewise imported into Europe around the end of the last century. It frequents the same types of water as the Pumpkinseed but swims rather deeper: It is a good deal larger, measuring up to 28 in (70 cm) in length and weighing more than 22 lb (10 kg). It feeds on small fish, frogs and tadpoles, aquatic insects and their larvae, and crustaceans. Unlike the Pumpkinseed, it is the female who keeps guard over both eggs and fry.

RED SALAMANDER
Pseudotriton ruber
Classification Class: Amphibia; Order: Urodela; Family: Plethodontidae.
Description Total length 7 in (18 cm). Young individuals are red with black-spotted upper parts; with age the color darkens until it is reddish-brown, and the dark spots also appear on the underparts.
Distribution Eastern United States.
Habitat Under moss, stones and stumps in or near streams with a sandy or gravelly bed.
Behavior It feeds mainly on insects. It breathes through the skin and the mouth mucus, possessing neither lungs nor, when adult, gills. The female lays eggs in the water, where the larvae, furnished with gills, reach full development. They are transformed into adults in the course of a complete metamorphosis.

ROSEATE SPOONBILL
Platalea ajaja
Classification Class: Aves; Order: Ciconiiformes; Family: Threskionithidae.
Description Length 30-34 in (76-86 cm). Pink with a white neck and broad zones of red on wings. Head greenish, without feathers. Legs and feet red. Spoon-shaped bill brown.
Distribution Southern United States. Also found in Central and South America.
Habitat Seacoasts, lagoons, mangrove swamps.
Behavior It consumes small fish, tadpoles, aquatic insects, and molluscs, which it captures by sifting the water and the muddy bottom with its bill. It lives in flocks, often in company with ibises and herons. Breeding also takes place in mixed colonies, each pair defending against intruders only the space surrounding the nest. The 3-4 eggs are incubated in turn by male and female for about 21 days.

SNAKEBIRD
Anhinga anhinga
Classification Class: Aves; Order: Pelecaniformes; Family: Anhingidae.
Description Also known as the Anhinga or Darter. Length 34 in (85 cm). Blackish with large silvery areas on the front part of the wings. Long, snakelike neck. Straight, pointed bill with finely toothed edges, ideal for striking and grasping the slippery body of a fish.
Distribution Southern United States. Also found in Central and South America.
Habitat Rivers and swamps.

Behavior This underwater swimmer drags large fish to the surface, tosses them into the air and swallows them head first. As in the case of cormorants, its plumage absorbs water and when it has finished swimming it has to dry itself so that the feathers regain their normal consistency and weight. The snakebird is also at home in the air, often soaring to considerable heights on rising currents of warm air, like a vulture. It nests in trees overlooking the water. The eggs are incubated by both parents.
Note The Double-crested Cormorant (*Phalacrocorax auritus*) belongs to the family Phalacrocoracidae, closely related to the Anhingidae. Measuring 30-34 in (75-87 cm) in length, it is black with naked orange-yellow skin on the throat. Distributed over much of North and Central America, it is found not only along the coasts but also on rivers and inland lakes. Its habits are similar to those of the Common Cormorant.

SNOWY EGRET
Egretta thula
Classification Class: Aves; Order: Ciconiiformes; Family: Ardeidae.
Description Length 22-26 in (55-66 cm). Outside the breeding period it is white with black bill and legs, and yellow feet; in nuptial livery some of the feathers of the head, neck and back grow longer and fringed, while the toes turn orange.
Distribution Southern United States. Also found in Central and South America.
Habitat Marshes, seacoasts and mangrove swamps.
Behavior Eats shrimp, small fish, molluscs, aquatic insects, and frogs, which it catches while wading in shallow, open water. It often follows grazing herds of domestic animals with a view to snapping up the many insects which are thus disturbed. It nests with other herons in mixed colonies. The males, spreading their ornamental feathers, defend selected spots where courtship and nest-building take place. The 2-6 eggs are incubated by both parents.

TROPICAL GAR
Lepisosteus tristoechus
Classification Class: Osteichthyes; Order: Lepisosteiformes; Family: Lepisosteidae.
Description Average length 10 ft (3 m), weight 220 lb (100 kg). The streamlined body is covered with a plating of scales which, in contrast to those of other "armored" fish, do not overlap like roof tiles but simply rest against one another. The elongated jaws form a kind of beak, with sharp teeth. Color is olive-green on the back, silver on the abdomen.

Distribution Southern United States. Also found in Mexico and Cuba.
Habitat Rivers.
Behavior As an adult it feeds exclusively on other fish. Its voracity, which sometimes leads it to break fishing nets to devour the contents, has earned it the name of Fresh-water Shark. Like many other predatory fish, it is solitary and not very mobile, preferring to wait for its victims by hiding among the water vegetation. When it sights prey, it approaches imperceptibly and when in range captures it with a swift sideways movement of the head. It winters in deep waters, remaining for months almost motionless on the bottom, without eating, in a state of near-torpor. The eggs, anchored to aquatic plants, hatch after 10-14 days.

WESTERN GREBE
Aechmophorus occidentalis
Classification Class: Aves; Order: Podicipediformes; Family: Podicipedidae.
Description Length 22-29 in (55-73 cm), weight 1¾-4 lb (800-1,800 kg). Black above, white below; yellow bill. Long, slender neck; short legs positioned far back; toes surrounded by lobes of skin which have the same function as the interdigital membrane of geese and ducks.
Distribution Western North America.
Habitat Lakes.
Behavior Like all grebes, it is a strong underwater swimmer with waterproof plumage, capable of staying submerged for more than half a minute and of reaching a depth of over 20 ft (7 m). In contrast, it moves awkwardly on dry land and seldom settles there for long. It feeds on fish. Nesting in large colonies, it builds a floating nest of rotting vegetation, anchoring it to reeds. There are usually 3 eggs, covered every time the incubating bird strays from the nest. The newborn chicks climb on to the parents' back, following them everywhere, even underwater. After a few weeks they learn to dive.

SOUTH AMERICA

The narrow isthmus of Panama links North and South America by way of the region of broken terrain known by geographers as Central America.

Over the last millions of years the isthmus has not always been above sea level, so the connections between the two American continental land masses have alternately been stabilized and interrupted in a manner which has had marked repercussions on the local flora and fauna. During periods when the isthmus of Panama was submerged, in fact, North and South America had the appearance of two immense islands, the inhabitants of which were unable to pass, apart from very exceptional instances, from one to the other. In periods when they were linked, on the other hand, some migrations in both directions were possible, as is the case today. By and large, however, there has been only a modest exchange of species between the two continents, particularly with regard to species from North America pushing southward across Panama. For these reasons the wildlife of South America has very particular features, with many species and entire families which do not exist anywhere else in the world.

And yet, South America does not present just one face to the naturalist. Indeed, at least three distinct areas are clearly recognizable: the tropical and equatorial region, traversed by great rivers such as the Orinoco and, more notably, the Amazon and its tributaries; the southern region, where the grasslands known as the pampas gradually give way to the cold deserts and highlands of Patagonia; and finally the Andes, the lofty mountain chain which extends down the western edge of the entire continent of South America.

The Amazon basin consists mainly of forest. Here in the jungle are many animals adapted to living among the branches, that have developed unusual habits of movement high above the ground in the dense vegetation. Many of the monkey species, for example, are tree dwellers, including the agile spider monkeys; so, too, are the slow-moving sloths, many opossums, a multitude of small carnivores and even one anteater. There are few really big animals, the jaguar and the giant anteater being the largest. There are, however, some extremely colorful birds, especially the parrots and hummingbirds, and a great variety of snakes and other reptiles.

The pampas and the lands farther south boast comparatively few animals. Nevertheless, inhabitants of these regions include flightless running birds such as the rhea, resembling a small ostrich, and mammals similar, though not closely related, to hares and marmots.

The animals of the Andes display characteristic adaptations to life at high altitudes, but they bear only a superficial resemblance to the inhabitants of the Alps or the Himalayas. The llama, the condor and the chinchilla, in fact, belong to exclusively American families.

1 Galapagos giant tortoise
2 collared anteater
3 Haitian solenodon
4 spectacled bear
5 fishing bat
6 nine-banded armadillo
7 sloth
8 capuchin monkey
9 hoatzin
10 spectacled caiman
11 alpaca
12 spider monkey
13 anaconda
14 ocelot
15 toucan
16 jaguar
17 hummingbird
18 giant anteater
19 chinchilla
20 capybara
21 tapir
22 Andean condor
23 rhea
24 viscacha
25 mara

The Andes

ANDEAN CONDOR
Vultur gryphus

Classification Class: Aves; Order: Falconiformes; Family: Cathartidae.

Description Length 3¼-4¼ ft (1-1.3 m), wingspan 10 ft (3 m), weight 22-26 lb (10-12 kg). This is the largest and most majestic diurnal raptor in South America. In the adult male, bigger and heavier than the female, the top of the head is covered with a prominent fleshy crest. Both sexes have glossy black plumage, a large white feathery collar and a broad silvery zone above the wings.

Distribution Entire Andean zone, from western Venezuela to Tierra del Fuego.

Habitat Bare mountains, rocky seacoasts.

Behavior With its exceptional power and prowess in gliding, the condor carries out lengthy patrols of valleys and mountainsides even in the face of strong winds. It feeds mainly on carrion, but occasionally captures injured or sick animals and defenseless young; it also hunts seabirds along the Peruvian coasts. It nests on inaccessible rock ledges. The male courts the female by spreading his wings and erecting his body, curving and inflating the neck. The single egg is incubated by both parents for 54-58 days.

ANDEAN FLICKER
Colaptes rupicola

Classification Class: Aves; Order: Piciformes; Family: Picidae.

Description Length 12½-14¼ in (32-36 cm). Nape and mustache gray, the latter tinted red in the male. Back densely barred black and tawny-yellow. The underparts are yellowish, spotted black on the breast. Pointed and fairly long bill.

Distribution Andes, from Peru to northern Chile.

Habitat Open terrain, including semicultivated zones, from the subtropical belt to that of the paramos.

Behavior It is a ground woodpecker which perches on trees or other supports. As a rule it roams above the treeline, walking or hopping about in search of food where the terrain is uneven. If disturbed, it flies away, skimming the ground until it finds a high perch. It feeds on the larvae of butterflies and beetles, which it stuns on the ground with blows of the beak, even at a depth of some 2 in (5 cm). It usually nests in colonies consisting of 10-

12 pairs. The female lays 2-4 eggs at the end of a long tunnel dug in a bank.

ANDEAN SMOOTH-THROATED IGUANA
Liolaemus multiformis

Classification Class: Reptilia; Order: Squamata; Suborder: Sauria; Family: Iguanidae.

Description Total length about 10 in (26 cm). Color greenish-brown.

Distribution Peru.

Habitat Sunny slopes of the Andes up to about 16,500 ft (5,000 m).

Behavior Like all reptiles, its body temperature depends on that of its surroundings. Its problem therefore is to withstand cold at high altitudes; for this reason it exposes itself to the sun until its body temperature rises to as much as 86°F (30°C) above that of the environment, enabling it to remain active throughout the day. It feeds on a variety of insects, worms and vegetation. The female is ovoviviparous, giving birth to completely formed young.

CHINCHILLA
Chinchilla laniger

Classification Class: Mammalia; Order: Rodentia; Family: Chinchillidae.

Description Length of head and body about 10 in (25-26 cm), tail 3-6 in (7.5-15 cm), weight 18-36 oz (500-1,000 g). Very soft fur; large eyes and ears; long black and white whiskers; short legs with four toes and weak claws. Pearl-gray, brownish hair or bluish above, yellowish-white below. Bushy tail gray with black or brown spots.

Distribution Andes, in northern Chile.

Habitat Rocky zones from 5,000 to 11,500 ft (2,500 to 3,500 m).

Behavior It is an animal of diurnal habits. Very agile, it will rapidly take refuge, if frightened, in rock clefts, living in a burrow scooped out on open ground in contact with the rock face. It obtains necessary water from the plants on which it feeds. The chinchilla lives in fixed pairs, the female courting the male and giving birth to 1-6 young after a gestation of 112 days.

COLPEO FOX
Dusicyon culpaeus

Classification Class: Mammalia; Order: Carnivora; Family: Canidae.

Description Total length 24-28 in (60-70 cm), height to shoulder 12 in (30 cm), weight 13-28½ lb (6-13 kg). Very similar to Azara's Fox, it differs in having a light instead of black margin to the mouth and being larger. Furthermore, the two species have different areas and habitats.

Distribution Andes, from southern Ecuador to Patagonia, and Tierra del Fuego.

Habitat Mountains and woods to more than 15,000 ft (4,500 m), usually in arid surroundings.

Behavior Like Azara's Fox, it is active at night, but unlike the latter it is exclusively a carnivore; its favorite prey are cattle and the European hare, introduced by man around 1915. Once a year, after 58 days' gestation, the female gives birth to 4-5 cubs.

DARWIN'S FROG
Rhinoderma darwini

Classification Class: Amphibia; Order: Anura; Family: Rhinodermatidae.

Description Length 1 in (2.6 cm). The head is triangular with a growth on the tip of its snout. Color of back varies from brown to bright green. Underparts are brightly colored: A zone with white spots separates the rear section, which is almost black, from the front section, which varies from black to ocher-yellow to orange.

Distribution Andes, from Chile to Argentina.

Habitat Rain forests with wet climate and mild temperatures, banks of mountain streams.

Behavior It is mimetic, the back being the color of dead leaves and detritus. After the female has abandoned the eggs in the wet soil, the male swallows them, collecting them in his vocal sac, and it is here that the young develop, emerging only after metamorphosis.

GUANACO
Lama guanicoë

Classification Class: Mammalia; Order: Artiodactyla; Suborder: Tylopoda; Family: Camelidae.

Description Length of head and body 6-7 ft (1.8-2.2 m), tail 6-10 in (15-25 cm), height to shoulder 3-4¼ ft (90-130 cm), weight 130-165 lb (60-75 kg). Short hair on head, legs, abdomen and inside of haunches, long on rest of body; color reddish-brown above, paler below.

Distribution Andes, from southern Peru to Tierra del Fuego.

Habitat Dry and semidesert pastures at high altitude.

Behavior A herbivore, it lives in herds of 20-30 individuals, with a single dominant male; as with the vicuña but not the camels of the Old World, the harem is not seasonal. In the breeding period (November-February) the male becomes violent and territorial, defending his harem from rivals. The female gives birth to a single young after 11 months' gestation.

Note Domestic descendants of the

Guanaco are the Llama (*Lama glama*) and the Alpaca (*Lama pacos*), tamed by the earliest inhabitants of the Andes. From the start the Llama was chosen as a beast of burden; it is therefore strong and sturdy, capable of carrying very heavy loads on its back for long journeys. The Alpaca is smaller and less robust than the Llama; its hair is very thick and long and it is therefore raised only for its wool.

MOUNTAIN CHINCHILLA
Lagidium sp.

Classification Class: Mammalia; Order: Rodentia; Family: Chinchillidae.
Description Also known as the Mountain Viscacha. Length 12½-16 in (32-40 cm), tail 9-12½ in (23-32 cm), weight 2¼-3¼ lb (1-1.5 kg). Similar to the chinchilla, but bigger and with larger ears. Soft, thick fur, varying above from pale beige to dark gray, and grayish, white or yellowish below. Sometimes there are dark stripes on the back. Tip of tail hairy, brown or black.
Distribution Western South America.
Habitat Rocky zones with sparse vegetation, always near water, at heights of 3,000-16,500 ft (900-5,000 m).
Behavior A herbivore, it feeds on moss and lichen, as well as a few superior plants which grow among the rocks. It lives in small groups of 2-5, both male and female, of almost all ages, related or otherwise. Several groups build their burrows and underground lairs in the same place, forming colonies of up to 80 animals.

MOUNTAIN TAPIR
Tapirus pinchaque

Classification Class: Mammalia; Order: Perissodactyla; Family: Tapiridae.
Description Total length up to 6 ft (1.80 m), height to shoulder 30-32 in (75-80 cm), weight 500-620 lb (225-280 kg). Soft, thick hair, brownish-black, longer on abdomen; edge of ears and lips white.
Distribution Andes, from western Venezuela to northern Peru.
Habitat From 6,500-13,000 ft (2,000-4,000 m), up to snowline.
Behavior Active mainly at dusk, it has poor vision but very keen sense of smell and hearing. The upper lip and snout are prolonged into a short trunk with a tactile function, used for exploring the surroundings and for grasping food: Leaves, shoots, green branches and fruit. It lives alone or in pairs. After a gestation of 390-400 days, the female produces a single young, rarely two, which grows rapidly.

PLAIN-CAPPED GROUND TYRANT
Muscisaxicola alpina

Classification Class: Aves; Order: Passeriformes; Family: Tyrannidae.
Description Also called the Alpine Ground Tyrant. Length 7½ in (19 cm). It looks like a thrush, with a slender bill and long legs. The plumage is uniformly brownish-gray above, whitish below, with faint gray markings on the breast. A white eyebrow runs across the sides of the head.
Distribution Andes, from southern Colombia to central regions of Chile and Argentina.
Habitat Partially barren parts of the paramos zones, from 10,000-14,000 ft (3,300-4,200 m).
Behavior Ground Tyrants are typical inhabitants of the high Andes, characterized by a rocky substratum and with few herbaceous plants. Like others of its genus, it feeds on insects and small invertebrates, capturing them after short chases interspersed with sudden halts; sometimes it hops on to a low outcrop in order to survey the ground, flicking its tail. The unlined nest is made of grass and roots, in a rock cavity. The female lays 4 eggs that are white with faint reddish spots.

SPECTACLED BEAR
Tremarctos ornatus

Classification Class: Mammalia; Order: Carnivora; Family: Ursidae.
Description Length of head and body 3½-5¾ ft (1.1-1.75 m), tail 3 in (7 cm), height to shoulder 26-30 in (65-75 cm), weight 130-310 lb (60-140 kg). Black or brownish-black with yellowish-white rings around the eyes; there is often a light mark on the chest.
Distribution Andes, from western Venezuela to northern Peru.
Habitat Hill and mountain regions, from semidesert to jungle at high altitude, from 650-14,000 ft (200-4,200 m).
Behavior Active during the night, it rests by day hidden among the rocks close to streams or rivers. It feeds almost wholly on vegetation, spending much time in trees, where it climbs for fruit and builds temporary nests for sleeping. It lives alone or in pairs. The breeding season is April-June; after 6-8 months' gestation, the female gives birth to 1-3 cubs.

TORRENT DUCK
Merganetta armata

Classification Class: Aves; Order: Anseriformes; Family: Anatidae.
Description Streamlined body, long and slender tail, small spur on fold of wings, the function of which is not known. Color of sexes differs: The female is chestnut below where the top of the head, neck and back are gray; coloration of the male varies according to subspecies, the only constant being the head, which is white with a pattern of black lines.
Distribution Along the entire chain of the Andes.
Habitat Mountain streams to an altitude of 12,000 ft (3,600 m).
Behavior It swims with its head only out of water, with equal ease either with or against the current. It reaches the bank by using its tail as a support, almost as if it were a third leg. It flies seldom, either to move along the stream, from which it never strays far, or to get over a waterfall; to descend the fall it lets itself be carried by the current, hurling itself out when a few feet from the edge in a giddy dive. It feeds on minute animals and plants which live in the pools. A few hours after birth, the ducklings are able to swim rapidly against the current, maneuvering their stiff tail.

VICUÑA
Lama vicugna

Classification Class: Mammalia; Order: Artiodactyla; Suborder: Tylopoda; Family: Camelidae.
Description Length of head and body 4-6 ft (1.25-1.90 m), tail 6-10 in (15-25 cm), height to shoulder 28-44 in (70-110 cm), weight 110 lb (50 kg). Hair longer on chest and throat; head, trunk, neck and haunches reddish-brown, rest of body ocher-yellow. It is the smallest of the Camelidae.
Distribution Andes, from southern Ecuador to northwestern Argentina.
Habitat Pastures with plenty of water, at high altitude, up to 14,000 ft (4,300 m) in summer, in valleys, but never below 10,000 ft (3,000 m), in the dry season.
Behavior It is the most markedly territorial mammal known, forming a harem which lasts all the year round. It feeds on tubers, grass and moss. The breeding season is from April to June; after a gestation of 10 months the female gives birth to a single young. The territorial family group consists of one dominant male and his harem of up to 20 females with young. The territory is marked by piles of dung, visited regularly by all members of the group, which sniff them, tread them down with the forelegs and add more excrement and urine; it is sufficiently extensive to provide enough food for the family group throughout the year. The male watches constantly over the harem, warning of danger with repeated whistles. Herds of males without territory and harem, very variable in numbers (2-100), wander about and continually confront the territorial males in the hope of defeating them and acquiring both the land and the harem.

The Andes

The Andes separate the arid Pacific coast of South America from the hot, humid regions of the Amazon: on the western slopes of the range there is subdesert vegetation, with succulent plants, and in the central highlands there are also giant lupins, and many grasses; on the eastern slopes characteristic trees include araucarias and cecropias.

1 Andean condor
2 llama
3 alpaca
4 ground tyrant
5 guanaco
6 vicuña
7 spectacled bear
8 Andean flicker
9 chinchilla

Pampas

AZARA'S FOX
Dusicyon gymnocercus

Classification Class: Mammalia; Order: Carnivora; Family: Canidae.

Description Total length 24-28 in (60-70 cm), height to shoulder 12 in (30 cm), weight 12¼-17½ lb (6-8 kg). Gray-brown back with transverse black stripes, reddish flanks, light underparts; black margin to mouth; top third and tip of tail black.

Distribution From Strait of Magellan to equator, eastern regions of South America.

Habitat Forests, thickets, and pampas.

Behavior An omnivore, its very varied diet is based principally on small rodents, helping to control their numbers locally. Active at night, it roams its territory, some 2½ miles (4 km) in diameter, in search of food. It often follows the movements of domestic animals as they graze. Once a year, after 58 days' gestation, the female produces 4-5 cubs.

BRAZILIAN CAVY
Cavia aperea

Classification Class: Mammalia; Order: Rodentia; Family: Caviidae.

Description Total length 9-13 in (22.5-33.5 cm), weight 1-1½ lb (450-700 g). Compact body with short legs. Long, rough hair; color uniform, variable from gray to brown.

Distribution Widespread with numerous subspecies in Chile, Colombia, Venezuela, Brazil and northern Argentina.

Habitat Savannas, wet and swampy zones, rocky regions, or regions with grass and shrubs. The exception is the Andean Cavy (*Cavia aperea tschudii*).

Behavior It feeds on plants and bushes, depositing large quantities of excrement always in the same place. Cavies may dig their own burrows or use those abandoned by other animals, either on open ground or beneath rocks. Mainly nocturnal, leaving the burrow at dusk, they always take prearranged paths. The female, after 60 days' gestation, gives birth to 1-4 young; these are ready to procreate at the age of 55-70 days.

Note The Andean Cavy (*Cavia aperea tschudii*) is the ancestor of the various races of the Domestic Cavy or Guineapig (*Cavia aperea porcellus*). Originally from Chile, it lives alone in the mountains, up to 13,000 ft (4,000 m), surviving at such altitudes by virtue of its soft, thick fur.

CARACARA
Polyborus plancus

Classification Class: Aves; Order: Falconiformes; Family: Falconidae.

Description Length 21 in (53 cm). Back, wings and belly dark brown; neck, breast and tail whitish with dense black bars; top of head black with a small tuft on the nape; naked reddish face. Very long legs.

Distribution Throughout South America. Also found in southern United States, Mexico and Central America.

Habitat Open steppes.

Behavior It lives in small groups, feeding on all kinds of tiny animals and carrion. It surveys the ground by flying low or walking, and settles for long periods on isolated trees which afford a broad view of the surroundings. It builds the nest in such a tree. The 2-3 eggs are incubated by both parents.

FAIRY ARMADILLO
Chlamyphorus truncatus

Classification Class: Mammalia; Order: Edentata; Family: Dasypodidae.

Description Length of head and body 5-6 in (12-15 cm), tail about 1 in (2-3 cm), weight 3¼ oz (90 g). Bony armor of very small, pale pink, rectangular plates, situated only on the back. Soft white hair on flanks and belly. The armor-plating, uniquely among armadillos, is connected with the inner skeleton, but there is no thoracic shield; the 23-25 girdles are attached to the body only along the line of the back, remaining free on the sides. It is the smallest of the armadillos.

Distribution Central-western Argentina.

Habitat Sandy or stony regions.

Behavior A very skillful digger, it buries itself quickly if threatened. By day it lives in an underground burrow, emerging at night to look for the ants, larvae and roots which constitute its diet.

MANED WOLF
Chrysocyon brachyurus

Classification Class: Mammalia; Order: Carnivora; Family: Canidae.

Description Total length 40-44 in (100-110 cm), height to shoulder 34-36 in (85-90 cm), weight 40-55 lb (18-25 kg). Long, soft hair reddish-yellow with black patches; black legs; a dark mark on neck and chest, tip of tail white.

Distribution Central and southeastern Brazil, Paraguay, eastern Bolivia, and northern Argentina.

Habitat Open savanna and grassland, also with bushes, close to forests, rivers and swamps.

Behavior It lives alone or in pairs. Omnivorous, it eats cavies, lizards, birds, turtle's eggs, fruit, and berries. A poor runner, it hunts its prey by approaching them silently. The breeding season is June-October; after 2 months' gestation the female gives birth to 2-4 young.

MARA
Dolichotis patagonum

Classification Class: Mammalia; Order: Rodentia; Family: Cavidae.

Description Also called the Patagonian Hare. Total length 16-20 in (40-50 cm), weight 20-35 lb (9-16 kg). Short ears and tail; hind feet with 3 toes, forefeet with 4, all with strong claws. Upper parts gray-brown, flanks cinnamon, underparts white. Black spot inside a white band on tail.

Distribution From Bolivia to Patagonia. Also found in Central America.

Habitat Plains (not desert) with plenty of shrub growth.

Behavior Pairs live in colonies of up to 40, in burrows dug by themselves or as lodgers in those of viscachas. It ventures out only during the coolest part of the day to feed on grass and leaves of shrubs. With keen eyesight and a good turn of speed, it can find refuge from predators with a few long bounds back to its burrow; the 2-3 young are cared for here by the mother until they are 9 months old, when they follow the parents out on to the pampas.

REDWINGED TINAMOU
Rhynchotus rufescens

Classification Class: Aves; Order: Tinamiformes; Family: Tinamidae.

Description Length 15½-17 in (39-43 cm). A huge ground bird, resembling a large quail, with mimetic plumage, streaked reddish and ocher-brown. Black, tawny-edged nape feathers; bright chestnut area on flight feathers, visible only when the bird flaps its wings.

Distribution Southern parts of South America, east of the Andes, from Bolivia and Brazil to the pampas of Argentina.

Habitat Grasslands, but also open zones with shrub growth.

Behavior The two sexes are markedly alike and it falls to the male, like the rhea, to incubate the eggs and care for the young. The female is aggressive and takes the initiative in courtship. Alone or in small groups, it feeds on insects, seeds and berries in the dense grassy vegetation, taking wing only if compelled. In case of alarm, it prefers to crouch low. The female lays a variable number of eggs, with a very glossy shell, in a hole in the ground. The fledglings are able to run and make their first attempt at flying soon after they are born.

Note The Crested Tinamou (*Eudromia*

elegans) is another typical member of the family from the South American pampas. It looks somewhat strange because of the plume of long curved feathers over the back part of the head. It inhabits steppes and dry savanna, soaring to a height of almost 12,000 ft (3,500 m) in the Andes.

PAMPAS DEER
Odocoileus bezoarticus
Classification Class: Mammalia; Order: Artiodactyla; Family: Cervidae.
Description Height to shoulder 24-30 in (60-75 cm). Limbs and upper parts reddish-brown to yellowish-gray, muzzle darker, belly lighter; tail dark brown above, white below.
Distribution Much of South America: Brazil, Uruguay, Paraguay, Argentina, northern Patagonia.
Habitat Desert plains; rarely in woodland regions.
Behavior Grazes alone, in pairs or in herds, consisting of a few individuals in winter, more in spring. The males are solitary for most of the year. During the day the deer rests in shelter, coming out to graze only in the evening. If frightened, it runs off quickly. The female gives birth to one young, which she protects from predators by drawing their attention to herself.

PATAGONIAN WEASEL
Lyncodon patagonicus
Classification Class: Mammalia; Order: Carnivora; Family: Mustelidae.
Description Length of head and body 12-14 in (30-35 cm), tail 2½-3½ in (6-9 cm). Grayish-brown above with streaks of white. The top of the head is white or beige, with a central patch of dark brown, like the throat, chest and legs. The belly is brown to gray.
Distribution Argentina, Chile.
Habitat Typically pampas.
Behavior Little known. A carnivore, it plays an important role in controlling the numbers of rodents, which represent its principal prey.

PLAINS VISCACHA
Lagostomus maximus
Classification Class: Mammalia; Order: Rodentia; Family: Chinchillidae.
Description Length of head and body 19-26 in (47-66 cm), tail 6-8 in (15-20 cm), weight 15½ lb (7 kg). Short forelegs with 4 toes, hind legs twice as long, with 3 toes. Gray-black above, white below; a white stripe runs from nose to cheeks.
Distribution Argentina.
Habitat Arid zones and steppes.
Behavior The animals form quite large colonies, digging communal burrows, the entries to which may be recognized by nearby mounds of earth and also by animal bones and horns, stones and plants which are scattered about the entire territory of the colony. The viscachas emerge from the burrows at dusk to feed on green vegetation and roots. The breeding period is in April; after 5 months' gestation 1-2 young are born. The viscacha burrows are so extensive that they are virtually underground towns; here, without any problems of coexistence, live other animals such as the Mara, the Burrowing Owl, and various lizards and snakes.

RHEA
Rhea americana
Classification Class: Aves; Order Rheiformes; Family: Rheidae.
Description Length 50-55 in (127-140 cm), weight 44-55 lb (20-25 kg). Unlike the ostrich, its thighs, head and neck are covered with feathers. The plumage is soft and drooping, colored gray. The upper part of the neck, nape and breast are blackish.
Distribution South America, east of the Andes, from Brazil to Argentina.
Habitat Open plains, pampas.
Behavior Its social life is notable for marked polygamy. Each male, after fierce fights, gains a harem of 5-6 females, for whom he builds on the ground a nest capable of accommodating up to 60 eggs. Incubation, which lasts 35-40 days, and care of the chicks are tasks carried out exclusively by him. Outside the breeding period the rheas assemble in promiscuous groups of 30 or more, wandering across the plains in search of food. When running, the bird holds one wing raised, rather like a sail, over the back. It feeds on roots, leaves, insects and small ground mammals.
Note Darwin's rhea *(Pteroicnemia pennata)* is the other representative of the Rheidae. Smaller than the rhea, it has white-spotted wings while the body plumage is uniformly dark. It lives in the Andean region, from Peru and Bolivia to Tierra del Fuego, where it frequents wild, uninhabited terrain.

RUFOUS OVENBIRD
Furnarius rufus
Classification Class: Aves; Order: Passeriformes; Family: Furnaridae.
Description Length 8 in (20 cm). Both sexes have identical livery, uniformly reddish-brown, similar to that of a nightingale. The underparts are paler, while the wings and tail are decidedly chestnut.
Distribution From central Brazil and Bolivia to northern Argentina.
Habitat Thickets and plains with trees, often near buildings.
Behavior Individual pairs occupy and defend fixed and independent sites all through the year. The two partners appear side by side, perched in a strategic position, singing together and performing the same body movements. During the rainy season they start work on their large, ovenshaped nest, cementing plant stems with mud and excrement; the heavy structure, 12 in (30 cm) long and 10 in (25 cm) high, leans against a post, a wall or any other visible form of support, and is renewed each year. The 4-5 eggs are laid in an inner chamber with little air but well protected. Food consists in the main of insects and ground invertebrates.

THREE-BANDED ARMADILLO
Tolypeutes sp.
Classification Class: Mammalia; Order: Edentata; Family: Dasipodidae.
Description Length of head and body 16 in (40 cm), tail 3 in (8 cm). Armor-plating gray or brown; projecting beyond the lines of the body, it enables the animal to roll into a ball.
Distribution From Guyana to northern Argentina.
Habitat Open plains and highlands.
Behavior Active by day, it feeds on termites, ants and vegetation. Not being an able digger, it takes over burrows abandoned by other animals. Rolling into a ball is an effective form of defense against large predators such as dogs, foxes and maned wolves. After 6 months' gestation the female gives birth to one young.

TUCO-TUCO
Ctenomys magellanica
Classification Class: Mammalia; Order: Rodentia; Family: Ctenomidae.
Description Length of head and body 7 in (17 cm), tail 2½ in (6 cm), weight 7 oz (200 g). Color brown. It displays striking adaptations to life underground: eyes positioned near the top of the head so as to keep watch on the burrow entrance without exposing itself too much; feet equipped with claws and bearing a fringe of bristly hairs which help to shovel away the excavated soil; and notched incisor teeth for loosening the soil.
Distribution Southwestern South America.
Habitat Pampas.
Behavior A social animal which digs large underground burrows. It feeds exclusively on plants. The name is derived from the alarm cry which carries down into the dark depths of the tunnels. The female gives birth to 1-5 young after a gestation of 103-107 days.

Pampas

The pampas proper is a boundless stretch of rolling terrain with herbaceous vegetation composed mainly of grasses; it merges with the forest to the north, across the Chaco region, where it is studded with palms and trees, and extends south toward the cold lands of Patagonia. Characteristic plants, some having affinities with Australian species, grow in Tierra del Fuego.

1   Brazilian cavy
2   redwinged tinamou
3   Azara's fox
4   rhea
5   maned wolf
6   Patagonian hare
7   rufous ovenbird
8   Darwin's rhea
9   Patagonian weasel
10 viscacha
11 burrowing owl

Galapagos Islands

BLUE-FOOTED BOOBY
Sula nebouxii

Classification   Class: Aves; Order: Pelecaniformes; Family: Sulidae.

Description   Length 33-36 in (83-92 cm), wingspan 5 ft (1.52 m). The plumage is brown on the wings, top of the back and the tail, white on the rump and underparts. The head and neck are delicately striped and spotted. The bright blue feet identify it unmistakably. The chicks have gray feet.

Distribution   Galapagos Islands. It is also found along the west coasts of North, Central and South America, from Mexico to northern Peru.

Habitat   Coasts and rocky islands.

Behavior   It nests in large colonies, close to zones that are regularly fished. It feeds on fish and molluscs near the shore, catching them either by diving from a height or from the surface. When hunting, it alternates winged flight with glides, pointing the bill downward. If food is abundant, the female may lay 2-3 eggs, which are incubated by both parents for about 40 days.

Note   The Red-footed Booby *(Sula sula)* also nests on the Galapagos Islands; its colonies, however, are less common and smaller than those of the blue-footed booby. This one hunts basically out at sea, thus avoiding any direct competition for food with other related species. Each pair raises a single chick.

CRESTED IGUANA
Conolophus subcristatus

Classification   Class: Reptilia; Order: Squamata; Suborder: Sauria; Family: Iguanidae.

Description   Total length up to 44 in (110 cm), half of which consists of tail. Body slightly depressed; low crest along line of spine. Small, uniform scales. Head yellow, upper parts dark brown, underparts lighter.

Distribution   It was once found on all the islands of the Galapagos archipelago; today it lives only on the islands of Narborough, Albemarle, and Seymour.

Habitat   Inland parts of islands, both flat and hilly, even with sparse vegetation.

Behavior   Today the Crested Iguana is in rapid decline because of the rats and cats which, introduced by man, prey on their eggs and young. It digs an underground burrow where it spends the night and from which it emerges during the warmest part of the day to feed on leaves, shoots and berries.

FLIGHTLESS CORMORANT
Nannopterum harrisi

Classification   Class: Aves; Order: Pelecaniformes; Family: Phalacrocoracidae.

Description   Length 34 in (85 cm). Entirely blackish, with a stiff tail and very short wings which are useless for flying; iris blue. The male is considerably larger than the female.

Distribution   Endemic to the islands of Fernandina and Isabela in Galapagos archipelago, where there are now some 800 pairs.

Habitat   Cliffs and surrounding sea.

Behavior   Settlement on a remote archipelago where food is plentiful because of the absence of large predators, led this species to lose its powers of flight. In compensation, the heavy body is an aid to diving: This cormorant feeds on cephalopods and fish caught at depth. After fishing, it hoists itself by its strong legs up on to the cliffs and allows its small wings to dry. The female lays 2-3 eggs in large nests of seaweed, built quite near the water. After the first clutch is laid, the female may couple with a second male and have another brood; despite this, breeding success is fairly low.

GALAPAGOS GIANT TORTOISE
Testudo elephantopus

Classification   Class: Reptilia; Order: Testudinata; Family: Testudinidae.

Description   Total length up to 44 in (110 cm). Heavy, thick carapace; massive build; short, stocky legs with strong claws. There are two principal forms, both represented by many subspecies: The first has a saddle-shaped shell, wider at the front, with long neck and limbs, the second a dome-shaped shell, with short neck and limbs.

Distribution   Galapagos Islands.

Habitat   The saddle-shelled form frequents dry zones with bushes and cacti, with little or no grass; the dome-shelled form is found on the high plateaus, where there is abundant rainfall, with grass and low plants.

Behavior   There are many recognized subspecies, each inhabiting a different island of the archipelago; only on Isabela do five different subspecies live together, although they each occupy different zones around five big volcanos, each of which has different vegetation, separated by detritus and lava flows. All these subspecies therefore vary through isolation, whereas the two saddle-shaped and dome-shaped forms are the result of adaptation to two different environments: The former, thanks to its very long legs and neck, can lift itself up to about 3 ft (1.30 m) from the ground to browse the leaves of shrubs which grow on the more arid islands, while the latter has no feeding problems in zones with plenty of grass and low plants, so that the neck and legs are short.

GALAPAGOS HAWK
Buteo galapagoensis

Classification   Class: Aves; Order: Falconiformes; Family: Accipitridae.

Distribution   Total length 21-23 in (53-58 cm). Plumage brownish-black with faint chestnut markings on flanks and belly. Tail silver-gray, densely barred. Bill blackish, yellow at base.

Distribution   Endemic to Galapagos Islands with about 100-150 pairs.

Habitat   Every available type of environment.

Behavior   It is the only existing diurnal bird of prey in the archipelago and therefore it can enjoy all the various food sources without competition from other raptors. Young marine iguanas provide habitual prey, but the hawk also captures birds of different species, rats, lizards and invertebrates; it also feeds on the carcasses of dead animals. When not hunting, it spends a long time cleaning its plumage or sleeping on habitual roosts (branches of dead trees, rocks, etc). It soars and glides to great heights, descending in a zigzag flight. The female couples with several males, and the latter assume the parental responsibilities. She lays 1-3 eggs in large nests of sticks built on low trees or on rocky outcrops.

GALAPAGOS PENGUIN
Spheniscus mendiculus

Classification   Class: Aves; Order: Sphenisciformes; Family: Spheniscidae.

Description   Length 18-20 in (46-50 cm). In the adults, head, back and flippers are blue-black, underparts white. A dark line runs down either side of the body and across the top of the chest, while a thin white line frames the cheeks. Dark bill with a pink spot near the base.

Distribution   Endemic to the Galapagos Islands, where the total population numbers about 1,000 pairs, along the coasts of Fernandina and Isabela.

Habitat   Coastal waters, rocky islands.

Behavior   It feeds on small fish, chasing and catching them underwater, close to the shore. Feeding and mating usually take place at night. The penguins nest in uncrowded colonies where each pair can be separated, with plenty of available space. The female lays 2-3 eggs in burrows dug beneath the lava. When food is sufficiently plentiful, each pair of birds may reproduce every 6 months; incubation lasts 40 days and the chicks remain in the nest for about 2 months.

MAGNIFICENT FRIGATE BIRD
Fregata magnificens
Classification Class: Aves; Order: Pelecaniformes; Family: Fregatidae.
Description Length 38-42 in (97-107 cm), wingspan 8 ft (2.5 m). The large angular wings and long forked tail give this bird an unmistakable silhouette in flight. The male is black with purple reflections; the female is brownish-black, with a white breast.
Distribution In addition to the Galapagos Islands, it is widely found in the Gulf of Mexico and along the Atlantic coasts of South America.
Habitat Tropical coastal waters, oceanic islands.
Behavior It spends practically the entire day in the air, ever ready to fling itself at other Pelecaniformes and filch the prey they have just caught. These piratical acts intensify while the chicks are being reared; for this reason it nests close to colonies of boobies, cormorants, and other seabirds. The male invites the female to the nest by exhibiting his orange-red throat pouch, inflated like a balloon. A single opaque white egg is laid on a platform of dung and interlaced branches, in trees or shrubs, and incubated by both parents for about 40 days.

MARINE IGUANA
Amblyrhynchus cristatus
Classification Class: Reptilia; Order: Squamata; Suborder: Sauria; Family: Iguanidae.
Description Total length up to 5 ft (1.5 m), of which 32 in (80 cm) is tail, weight up to about 25 lb (12 kg). This is a large lizard, massively built, with a short, wide head, topped by broad, low bony formations, and with very sturdy limbs. There is a high, narrow crest of scales along the line of the spine. The upper parts and the sides are blackish, the underparts grayish or whitish.
Distribution Galapagos Islands.
Habitat Cliffs and rocky shores battered by the waves.
Behavior A herbivore, it lives in enormous colonies, feeding at low tide on algae which grow abundantly in the shallows, and then basking on the rocks in the sun. It spends the night in clefts and cavities of the rocks at sea level. In the breeding season the males engage in ritual fights with rivals to defend their territory. The female lays eggs in holes dug in the soil among the bushes.

SMALL CACTUS FINCH
Geospiza scandens
Classification Class: Aves; Order: Passeriformes; Family: Emberizidae.
Description Length 5 in (13 cm). The male is almost entirely black, except for the lower part of the breast and the under-tail coverts, which are streaked with white. The female is greenish-brown, with close stripes on the front of the body. The bill, although fairly thick as in other species belonging to the same genus, is particularly long, with a curved tip.
Distribution It is found on all the islands of the Galapagos, except Fernandina, where there is a related species which plays the same ecological role.
Habitat Arid terrain colonized by cacti.
Behavior An exclusively vegetarian species, feeding on seeds, fruit, and nectar. It lives mainly among cactus shrubs, eating both the flowers and the pulp of the spiny fruit. The nest, too, is generally situated among these plants.
Note The Large Ground Finch *(Geospiza magnirostris)* is another of the so-called Darwin's finches, typical of the Galapagos Islands. It has an enormous beak, higher than it is long, with which it breaks open even the toughest seeds, collected mostly from the ground.

SWALLOWTAILED GULL
Creagrus furcatus
Classification Class: Aves; Order: Charadriiformes; Family: Laridae.
Description Length 19-20 in (48-51 cm). A medium-large gull with long wings and a deeply forked tail, making it similar to a large tern when in flight. In the breeding season head and neck are dark gray, in contrast to the pearly-gray back and white abdomen. Red orbital ring, dark bill with white tip, reddish legs. The chicks have brown and white bars.
Distribution Endemic to the Galapagos Islands, where there is a total population of 10,000-15,000 pairs. Occasionally strays toward the coasts of Ecuador and Peru.
Habitat Coastal waters, rocky islands.
Behavior It is the only gull in the world with nocturnal habits. It feeds on fish and cephalopod molluscs, hunting them at night near coastal bays and in shallow water. It flies with slow, rhythmical wingbeats, like those of a heron. From time to time it emits a babbling sound which is rather unusual for a gull. It nests in colonies and the female lays a single egg on a pebbly base which hatches after an incubation of 33 days.

VERMILLION FLYCATCHER
Pyrocephalus rubinus
Classification Class: Aves; Order: Passeriformes; Family: Tyrannidae.
Description Length 5½ in (14 cm). The male has blackish upper parts, while the underparts and the top of the head are ruby-red; the female is gray-brown above, whitish with dark stripes below.
Distribution In addition to the Galapagos Islands, it is found in Central and South America and in the southwestern United States.
Habitat Open, arid zones.
Behavior It feeds on insects which it catches by diving from a perch; it seizes the prey on the wing or on the ground, returning to its point of departure to devour it. The female builds a nest among the branches of a shrub and lays 2-3 eggs, which hatch after an incubation of 12 days.

WOODPECKER FINCH
Camarhynchus pallidus
Classification Class: Aves; Order: Passeriformes; Family: Emberizidae.
Description Length 5½ in (14 cm). Both sexes have identical plumage, streaked with brown or olive on the back, whitish or yellowish below. Long and fairly thick beak.
Distribution It is found throughout almost the entire Galapagos archipelago, but is most common on the islands of Santa Cruz, Isabela, San Cristobal, and Fernandina.
Habitat Mountain zones.
Behavior It feeds on large insects which it scoops from under the bark and in rotting wood; sometimes it also eats fruit. It can pick up a cactus thorn in its beak and maneuver it so as to extract larvae from deep crevices; in this respect it is one of the very few birds in the world capable of using tools. Its call consists of a rapid repetition of 7-8 penetrating notes. As is the case among several related species, the male builds or rough-shapes various nests to attract the female. After mating, she completes the chosen nest or provides a new one; the 2-5 eggs are incubated by her alone for some 12 days.
Note The Charles Insectivorous Tree Finch *(Camarhynchus pauper)* is another of the Darwin's finches, found only on the island of Santa Maria in the Galapagos group; its conical beak enables it to feed both on insects and soft seeds.

Galapagos Islands

The flora of the Galapagos Islands has striking affinities with that of South America, but is somewhat impoverished both because of the type of soil and also the remote situation of the archipelago which has made it impossible for many groups of plants (as well as animals) to reach. There are many cacti to be found there, and typical trees belonging to the family Compositae, which grow to a height of some 20 ft (6 m).

1 blue-footed booby
2 Galapagos giant tortoise
3 Darwin's finch
4 marine iguana
5 crested iguana
6 Galapagos penguin
7 flightless cormorant
8 swallowtailed gull
9 woodpecker finch
10 magnificent frigate bird
11 red-footed booby

Forests and rivers

ANACONDA
Eunectes murinus
Classification Class: Reptilia; Order: Squamata; Suborder: Ophidia; Family: Boidae.
Description Length at least 26 ft (8 m), even as much as 36 ft (11 m). Back and flanks from gray to olive green; black streaks on back; black and yellow streaks on flanks; belly yellowish to gray-white, with black spots.
Distribution Brazil, Peru, Ecuador, Colombia, Venezuela, Guyana, Trinidad.
Habitat By streams and rivers, ponds, swamps.
Behavior A carnivore, it preys on birds, rodents, fish and mammals, but also caimans and snakes; it kills its victims by suffocation, crushing them in its coils and then swallowing them whole. Not very active, it spends much time on the banks or in the water, allowing only its snout to protrude. To avoid summer drought it buries itself in mud, going into hibernation. In July-August, after a gestation of 7-8 months, the female produces up to 82 young.

ANGELFISH
Pterophyllum scalare
Classification Class: Osteichthyes; Order: Perciformes; Family: Cichlidae.
Description Length 6 in (15 cm), height about 10 in (25 cm). Flattened, disk-shaped body. Flat head, long fins. Silver-gray with four black transverse stripes.
Distribution Amazon basin.
Habitat Fairly still water with plenty of dense plant growth.
Behavior It feeds on small aquatic organisms which it finds in the dense vegetation, through which, thanks to its laterally compressed body, it moves without difficulty; if in danger, it finds refuge in clefts on the riverbed. Both parents carefully clean a branch or a leaf and here the female attaches the eggs with a sticky secretion. Both the male and the female supervise the eggs until they hatch; then they gather the fry into their mouth as they emerge from the eggs, and reattach them to the branch or leaf; the young break away only when they have become self-sufficient.

ARACARI
Pteroglossus aracari
Classification Class: Aves; Order: Piciformes; Family: Ramphastidae.
Description Length 18-19 in (45-48 cm). The imposing spongy bill, up to 5 in (12 cm) in length, has an ivory-white maxillary (upper part) and a black mandible (lower part). The head and neck are also black, while the breast and belly are bright yellow, separated by a transverse scarlet band.
Distribution Brazil, Venezuela and Guyana.
Habitat Tropical forests, savannas and wooded banks, papaya plantations.
Behavior It lives in small, noisy groups, especially when engaged in feeding. The various individuals proceed in orderly lines, hopping from branch to branch in the middle and upper forest layers. They spend the night in communal dormitories, huddled against one another, inside the same tree hollow. It feeds principally on fruit, but also finds insects appetizing and may even prey on nestlings. Like other toucans, the female lays 2-4 white eggs which are incubated by both parents for about 16 days.

ARAPAIMA
Arapaima gigas
Classification Class: Osteichthyes; Subclass: Actinopterygii; Order: Osteoglossiformes; Family: Osteoglossidae.
Description Length up to 13 ft (4 m), weight up to 400 lb (180 kg). Head covered with bony plates; edged with scarlet scales.
Distribution Amazon basin, Guyana.
Habitat Clean water with plenty of vegetation.
Behavior A carnivore, the fish actively hunts its prey. it is capable of using both dissolved oxygen in water as well as air for breathing. When the water level rises, during the rainy season, the female scoops a circular nest in the riverbed, lined with grass and detritus, and lays up to 50,000 eggs in it. The male looks after them, and even after they are born the young swarm around his head for 2-3 months.

BASILISK
Basiliscus basiliscus
Classification Class: Reptilia; Order: Squamata; Suborder: Sauria; Family: Iguanidae.
Description Length of head and body 12 in (30 cm), tail 20 in (50 cm). There is a characteristic fold of skin on the head, bigger in the male, which also has a crest on back and tail. Color green, with transverse gray-black stripes.
Distribution Northern Colombia. Also found in Panama and Costa Rica.
Habitat Trees beside river banks.
Behavior An omnivore, it feeds on plants and insects. It can climb and scamper about in the trees. If in danger, it runs away on its hind legs, even across the water, thanks to its broad-lobed toes which increase the surface of support. When running it uses the tail as a balance. In spring the female lays up to 12 eggs in a hole dug among the roots of trees, which she then covers.

BLACK CAIMAN
Melanosuchus niger
Classification Class: Reptilia; Order: Crocodilia; Family: Alligatoridae.
Description Maximum length 15 ft (4.5 m). Bony plates on back. Adults black, young black with transverse yellow stripes; light-colored belly.
Distribution Central and northern zones of South America.
Habitat Shallow rivers, lakes and marshes, grassy plains and savannas which are periodically flooded by large rivers.
Behavior It lives in groups that may be quite numerous. Where the climate is drier, it scoops a hole in the mud and remains there until the next rainy season. Not very active by day, it ventures out to feed at dusk, mainly eating capybaras but also birds, fish and other mammals. The female builds a nest of decomposing vegetation.

BOA CONSTRICTOR
Boa constrictor
Classification Class: Reptilia; Order: Squamata; Suborder: Ophidia; Family: Boidae.
Description Length 10-13 ft (3-4 m). Head triangular. Back and sides covered with carinate (keel-like) scales. The color of the back varies from brown to reddish or gray, with dark patterning; the belly is spotted pale gray. A brownish-black longitudinal stripe runs from nose to neck.
Distribution From Mexico to Argentina. Also found in Lesser Antilles.
Habitat Close to water in open woodland or dense thickets.
Behavior By day it stays hidden in hollows of tree trunks, under roots or among rocks, emerging at night to hunt; it lies in wait for its victim (rodents, birds, mammals, and small caimans), then suffocates them in its coils. The female produces up to 60 young.

BRAZILIAN GIANT OTTER
Pteronura brasiliensis
Description Mammalia; Order: Carnivora; Family: Mustelidae.
Description Total length over 6 ft (2 m), weight up to 75 lb (34 kg). Dark brown back, lighter belly. Flattened tail. Toes joined by interdigital membranes.

Distribution Venezuela, Guyana, Brazil, Uruguay, Paraguay, northern Argentina.
Habitat Slow-flowing rivers of the Amazon system, Uruguay, Rio de la Plata and Paranà rivers, lagoons.
Behavior Active by day, it forms small groups and hunts in the water, catching fish, birds, and small mammals on the banks. While hunting it lets out repeated loud whistling cries. It rests close to the bank, among rocks or in vegetation. The female gives birth to 1-2 young once a year.

BUSHDOG
Speothos venaticus
Classification Class: Mammalia; Order: Carnivora; Family: Canidae.
Description Total length 26 in (65 cm), height to shoulder 9 in (23 cm), weight 11-15½ lb (5-7 kg). Short ears, back and flanks reddish-brown, legs and tail dark, head lighter.
Distribution Entire Brazilian region and from Panama to Guyana, also from eastern Peru to Paraguay.
Habitat Dense tropical forest, close to river banks.
Behavior It spends the day in burrows and goes out hunting alone or in small groups at night. A very skillful swimmer, it preys on all rodents including the capybara and the paca, which it chases into the water. Sometimes it even kills a rhea. It uses the abandoned lairs of armadillos but nobody knows whether it can dig its own. In October the female gives birth to 4-6 young after 65 days' gestation. The male helps her to look after the young, hunting for the whole family and defending the territory around the burrow.

CAPUCHIN MONKEY
Cebus capucinus
Classification Class: Mammalia; Order: Primates; Family: Cebidae.
Description Length of head and body 12½-18 in (32-46 cm), tail 16½-20 in (42-50 cm), weight 4¼-8¼ lb (2-3.8 kg). The male is larger than the female. Dark brown except for the hairs surrounding the face and front of the arms, which are white.
Distribution Colombia. Also found in Central America.
Habitat Lowland and mountain forests up to a height of about 6,500 ft (2,000 m); mangrove swamps.
Behavior It lives in groups of 10-24 individuals which often come down from the trees to feed and play. It feeds on various plants, insects, nestlings, etc. The male is polygamous, coupling with more than one female. After 150 days' gestation, each female produces a single young.

CAPYBARA
Hydrochoerus hydrochaeris
Classification Class: Mammalia; Order: Rodentia; Family: Hydrochoeridae.
Description Total length 3¼-4¼ ft (1-1.3 m), weight up to 110 lb (50 kg). Small eyes, positioned at sides of head; small rounded ears; strong legs, toes with swimming membrane and small powerful claws. Hair sparse and bristly, reddish-brown on back, yellowish-brown on belly.
Distribution Most of South America. Also found in a restricted zone of Central America.
Habitat Woods and regions with dense vegetation around lakes, swamps or rivers and streams.
Behavior An excellent swimmer, it spends much of its time in water, where it finds the plants on which it feeds; it rests during the heat of the day in shade, in ground hollows. It lives in groups of 3-30. It does not dig a burrow, but the female prepares a nest in a hole in the ground, lining it with vegetation, and here, after a gestation of 15-18 weeks, she gives birth to 2-8 fully formed young, tending them for a lengthy period.

COLLARED PECCARY
Tayassu tajacu
Classification Class: Mammalia; Order: Artiodactyla; Family: Tayassuidae.
Description Length of head and body 30-40 in (75-100 cm), height to shoulder 16-20 in (40-50 cm), weight 40-55 lb (18-25 kg). Robust body, nose terminating in a snout, very short tail. Coat made up mainly of dark brownish-black bristles with a white collar.
Distribution South America, from northern regions to Argentina. Also found in the southern United States, Mexico and Central America.
Habitat Forests but also dry zones with shrubs.
Behavior It forms herds of 5-50, which remain together for some time, moving about to feed both by night and day: grass, fruit, roots, small animals, and insects. The breeding season is generally in late winter; after 140-150 days' gestation, the female withdraws from the herd to give birth to 1-4 young, normally 2, which are immediately received back into the group.

DOUROUCOULI
Aotes trivirgatus
Classification Class: Mammalia; Order: Primates; Family: Cebidae.
Description Also known as the Night Monkey. Length of head and body 9½-18½ in (24-47 cm), tail 8¾-16½ in (22-42 cm), weight 1¼-3 lb (800-1,300 g). Upper parts gray-brown, underparts orange;

white markings around eyes. It is the only nocturnal monkey in both the Old and New World, as is evident from its enormous reddish eyes, which are capable of vision in almost complete darkness.
Distribution Central-northern South America. Also found in Panama.
Habitat Forests and tree savannas.
Behavior It lives in pairs, each of which occupies a small territory. Active only at night, it spends the day sleeping in tree hollows. It feeds chiefly on insects, fruit and leaves. The single young is born after 133 days' gestation.

DWARF PENCILFISH
Nannostomus marginatus
Classification Class: Osteichthyes; Order: Cypriniformes; Family: Lebiasinidae.
Description Length about 2 in (4-5 cm). Body thin and needle-shaped; fairly undeveloped fins. Small mouth, jaws with tiny teeth. Back olive-green to dark brown; flanks yellowish or whitish; brown longitudinal stripes along the length of the body; large red spots on dorsal, ventral and anal fins.
Distribution Western Guyana, Surinam, Amazon region.
Habitat Middle and upper stretches of rivers.
Behavior It lives in large shoals. An omnivore, its prey consists only of very tiny creatures. Unlike many species of the genus *Nannostomus*, which swim with body inclined and head turned upward, this fish keeps its body horizontal while it swims.

FLAME TETRA
Hyphessobrycon flammeus
Classification Class: Osteichthyes; Order: Cypriniformes; Family: Characinidae.
Description Length maximum 2 in (5 cm). Body laterally compressed. Fins reddish. Back green-gray, flanks greenish with bluish tints, belly white. Rear part reddish.
Distribution Brazil.
Habitat Middle or lower courses of rivers.
Behavior It lives in shoals. It is furnished with sensory mechanisms capable of emitting and receiving high-pitched sounds with which it communicates and perhaps finds its whereabouts. An omnivore, its diet is extremely varied but, lacking all else, it feeds exclusively on vegetation.

FRUIT-EATING BAT
Artibeus sp.
Classification Class: Mammalia; Order: Chiroptera; Family: Phyllostomatidae.
Description The genus *Artibeus* comprises 16 species of bats; the larger mea-

Forests

The rain forest of Amazonia is incomparably the most extensive area of forest in the world, containing at least 4,000 different tree species alone. The tangle of vegetation is made even more impenetrable by lianas and epiphytes, and a single tree may harbor as many as 80 different species. Among the most common and widespread families are the Bromeliaceae (pineapple family), Bignoniaceae and Melastomaceae.

1	spider monkey	14	collared peccary
2	fruit-eating bat	15	hummingbird
3	*Morpho* butterfly	16	ocelot
4	scarlet macaw	17	jaguar
5	golden marmoset	18	giant anteater
6	whitenosed coati	19	jaguarundi
7	prehensile-tailed	20	tamandua
	porcupine	21	giant armadillo
8	hoatzin	22	mouse opossum
9	harpy eagle	23	South American tapir
10	three-toed sloth	24	agouti
11	aracari	25	nine-banded
12	opossum		armadillo
13	boa constrictor		

sure over 4 in (10 cm) in length, the smaller 2 in (5 cm). The teeth are designed for a fruit-eating diet.

Distribution Most of South America. It also inhabits Mexico and Central America.

Habitat Forests.

Behavior Some species frequent caves, taking refuge there in the daytime, and consume small kinds of fruit, which they carry in flight. Other species are typically arboreal and build temporary shelters among the tree branches. These bats, which fly in a straight line for a considerable distance, play a vital role in scattering the seeds of plants whose fruit they eat.

GIANT ANTEATER
Myrmecophaga tridactyla

Classification Class: Mammalia; Order: Edentata; Family: Myrmecophagidae.

Description Length of head and body 40-48 in (100-120 cm), tail 24-36 in (60-90 cm), height to shoulder 24 in (60 cm), weight 66-77 lb (30-35 kg). Long nose, curved downward; tiny mouth and slender, protractile, sticky tongue, up to 3 ft (1 m) long. Small eyes and short, round ears. Tail with thick, bristly hairs up to 16 in (40 cm) in length. Forelegs with strong claws. Grayish, lighter on head and flanks, with two black bands on chest, shoulders and forelegs.

Distribution Most of northern and central South America to Paraguay. Also found in southern Mexico and Central America.

Habitat Rain forests, savannas, and swampy zones.

Behavior Active by day; although it is an excellent climber and swimmer, it is a ground animal, for that is where it finds the nests of the termites and ants on which it feeds, guided to them by its keen sense of smell. It sleeps in holes among the shrubs. After 6 months' gestation, the female gives birth to one young, which she carries on her back for several months.

GIANT ARMADILLO
Priodontes giganteus

Classification Class: Mammalia; Order: Edentata; Family: Dasypodidae.

Description Total length 3 ft (1 m), of which 20 in (50 cm) represents the tail, weight 110-125 lb (50-60 kg). There are 11-13 extremely mobile girdles on the back, 3-4 on the neck. Large ears. Forelegs furnished with very big claws. Dark armor-plating on back, with a light chestnut band on either side.

Distribution South America, in the tropical belt east of the Andes.

Habitat Virgin forest where water is plentiful.

Behavior Active at night, it is continually digging tunnels to find ants, termites and also worms and reptiles.

GOLDEN AGOUTI
Dasyprocta agouti

Classification Class: Mammalia; Order: Rodentia; Family: Dasyproctidae.

Description Length 12-24 in (30-60 cm). Slender, streamlined build, long head and rounded snout; very short tail; legs transformed by running, the hind pair longer than the front ones. Short, smooth hair, longer on hindquarters; brown to yellowish or orange above, white or beige below.

Distribution Brazil. Also found in southern Mexico and Central America.

Habitat Dense grassy or shrubby vegetation in undergrowth; savannas and cultivated fields. Wet climate or dry desert.

Behavior Solitary, it digs a private burrow under rocks, among shrubs or between tree roots. Diurnal by habit, it always follows the same paths in search of the fruit, flowers, and roots on which it feeds. It runs rapidly and is capable of making leaps of up to 20 ft (6 m). After a gestation of 64-100 days, the female produces 2-4 young, which are able to follow their mother to graze after only a few hours.

GOLDEN MARMOSET
Leontideus rosalia

Classification Class: Mammalia; Order: Primates; Family: Callithricidae.

Description Length of head and body 13½-16 in (34-40 cm), tail 10¼-15 in (26-38 cm), weight 22-25 oz (630-710 g). Golden-red with dark and almost bare nose. The long hairs of the head, cheeks and sides of neck form an erectile mane which completely hides the ears.

Distribution Southeastern Brazil.

Habitat Coastal forests.

Behavior It feeds on fruit, flowers, insects, amphibians, and reptiles. The long, slender hands and feet, similar to hooks, enable it to leap from branch to branch with incredible speed and assurance. After a gestation of 128 days the female gives birth to 2 young which, at the age of 4-10 days, are taken into the care of the father, being handed over to the mother only for suckling.

GREENTAILED SYLPH
Aglaiocercus kingi

Classification Class: Aves; Order: Apodiformes; Family: Trochilidae.

Description Length 7 in (18 cm), of which 6 in (15 cm) comprises a caudal train, a male attribute only. The plumage is a glittering bronze-green; the long graduated tail-feathers are violet-blue. The female has a white throat, the breast and center of the abdomen being reddish.

Distribution South America, from Colombia to western Ecuador and northern Bolivia.

Habitat Rain forests, plantations and gardens.

Behavior Alone or in pairs, it frequents both the undergrowth and the uppermost forest canopy. It prefers the edges of woods and may sometimes be seen in company with other hummingbirds on blossoming trees along roads. It sips the nectar by hovering in front of the corollas, inserting its beak or perforating the base of the flower; sometimes it darts off from an exposed position to chase small insects. The female alone builds a large dome-shaped nest lined with moss and fibers, provided with a side entrance; in it she lays 2 eggs, which are incubated for over 2 weeks.

Note The Streamertail (*Trochilus polytmus*) is another hummingbird adorned with long wiry tail-feathers; it may be recognized by its coral-red, black-tipped beak, and black cap. The species is endemic to Jamaica in the West Indies.

HARPY EAGLE
Harpia harpyja

Classification Class: Aves; Order: Falconiformes; Family: Accipitridae.

Description Length 35-40 in (89-102 cm), weight up to 15½ lb (7 kg). A very powerful forest raptor with a two-part erectile crest on the head, big rounded wings and a long black and gray striped tail. Head and neck are gray, upper parts black; underparts white, with a broad black pectoral band and barred legs.

Distribution Widespread from southern Mexico to Brazil and northern Argentina.

Habitat Virgin forest, to heights of not more than about 5,250 ft (1,600 m).

Behavior Its predatory habits place it at the summit of many of the jungle food chains. It almost always conceals itself in the thickest vegetation, skillfully hunting both tree and ground mammals (including monkeys, sloths, and coatis), large birds, and reptiles. It constructs huge nests of sticks in the top of the highest trees, where each pair raises a single chick (rarely 2), generally every other year; incubation lasts 8 weeks and the young bird does not leave the nest for about 5 months.

HOATZIN
Opisthocomus hoazin

Classification Class: Aves; Order: Galliformes; Family: Opisthocomidae.

Description Length 24-26 in (61-66 cm). A strange bird with variegated plumage, bronze-olive and red, and a feathery crest on the head. The small head, naked around the eyes, is set upon a long, slender neck; the tail, too, is quite long, while the wings, although fairly big, are poorly adapted to flying.

Distribution Basins of the Amazon and Orinoco.

Habitat Vegetation along river banks.

Behavior Forming groups that vary in number, up to 50 individuals, it occupies the same territory all year long. It feeds exclusively on the leaves of certain aquatic plants similar to rushes, which it crams in enormous quantities into its large gullet. It nests in colonies on fragile platforms of sticks not far above the water. The 2-5 eggs appear to be incubated in turn by all members of the group. The chicks have strong claws at the tips of their wings with which they clamber through vegetation; they are good swimmers.

JAGUAR
Panthera onca

Classification Class: Mammalia; Order: Carnivora; Family: Felidae.

Description Length of head and body 43-69 in (110-176 cm), tail 13-32 in (33-82 cm), height to shoulder 27-29 in (70-73 cm), weight 73-220 lb (33-100 kg). Coat varies from reddish-yellow to sandy and ocher; pattern of black spots.

Distribution Much of central and northern South America to Uruguay and northern Argentina. It also inhabits the southern United States, Mexico and Central America.

Habitat Forests, but may also venture out on to more open ground.

Behavior Although it is a good climber, because of its bulk it does not often scale trees. An excellent runner and swimmer, it is undeterred by broad rivers. Its victims include animals which live on the banks, such as capybaras, as well as those actually in the water, including fish, turtles, and young caimans. It also hunts peccaries, tapirs, small rodents, birds, and monkeys. It lives alone and will not tolerate intruders on its hunting territory. After 91-111 days' gestation, the female gives birth to 1-4 cubs.

JAGUARUNDI
Felis yagouaroundi

Classification Class: Mammalia; Order: Carnivora; Family: Felidae.

Description Also called the Otter Cat. Length of head and body 22-30 in (56-76 cm), tail 13-24 in (33-61 cm), weight 6-18 lb (2.7-8 kg). Elongated body, long tail, short legs. Color uniform, varying from brown to reddish gray or blackish.

Distribution Most of South America, from northern regions to Argentina.

Habitat Edges of woods, shrubby zones, scrubland and swamps.

Behavior Thanks to its low, long body, it slinks easily through the bushes. Its prey include all kinds of young vertebrates, especially rodents. The female gives birth to 2-4 cubs after about 67 days' gestation.

MATAMATA
Chelys fimbriatus

Classification Class: Reptilia; Order: Testudinata; Family: Chelidae.

Description Length 8-16 in (20-40 cm), weight about 1¼-3¼ lb (600-1,500 g). Flat, triangular head with long, slender snout; small eyes; short tail; short legs with webbed feet. Carapace greenish-brown, plastron yellowish with dark spots. It does not withdraw its neck and head into the shell.

Distribution Venezuela, Guyana, central-northern Brazil.

Habitat Fresh and muddy water.

Behavior By day it stays hidden in the riverbank vegetation; at night it enters the water and hunts actively for fish, larvae of amphibians and invertebrates; it also eats plants. Sometimes it elects to ambush its prey by standing camouflaged on the muddy bed of ponds which contain plenty of rotting vegetation.

MORPHO BUTTERFLY
Morpho sp.

Classification Phylum: Arthropoda; Class: Insecta; Order: Lepidoptera; Family: Nymphalidae.

Description The genus contains some 80 species, most of which exhibit marked sexual dimorphism, the males being brightly colored blue and the females brown. In other species both males and females are brown, or black with blue stripes.

Distribution Much of northern and central South America.

Habitat Forests.

Behavior These are some of the most famous and spectacular inhabitants of the tropical forest. One species, *Morpho diana,* was once collected in the swamps of the Orinoco, but has not been seen there for more than 50 years. The caterpillars of many species feed on plants of the families Lauraceae, Leguminosae, and Myrtaceae.

MOUSE OPOSSUM
Marmosa murina

Classification Class: Mammalia; Order: Marsupialia; Family: Didelphidae.

Description Also called the Murine Opossum. Length of head and body 4-6 in (10-16 cm), weight 25 oz (700 g). Yellowish-gray above, white below; dark "spectacles" around eyes. Ears and tail hairless; the ears are folded during sleep, the tail is scaly and prehensile. The female has no marsupium (pouch).

Distribution Much of South America. Also found in Central America.

Habitat Forests, plantations of fruit trees.

Behavior Strictly arboreal by habit, it feeds on insects, lizards, and fruit, leading a solitary life and sheltering in tree cavities. The female may give birth to up to 18 tiny young, which attach themselves to her nipples between the hind legs.

NINE-BANDED ARMADILLO
Dasypus novemcinctus

Classification Class: Mammalia; Order: Edentata; Family: Dasypodidae

Description Length of head and body 16-20 in (40-50 cm), tail 10-16 in (25-40 cm), weight about 13 lb (6 kg). The whole body, apart from the belly, is covered with black bony plating, which becomes lighter in color with age.

Distribution From Central America to Argentina and Uruguay. It also inhabits the southern United States.

Habitat Woodland and marshland along the banks of rivers.

Behavior Prevalently nocturnal, it digs in the earth for the insects, worms, molluscs, small vertebrates and plants on which it feeds. It excavates a number of burrows among the bushes; while engaged at this, thanks to the dimensions of its lungs and trachea, it can hold its breath for up to 6 minutes. After fertilization, the egg remains quiescent for about 3½ months; it is then implanted in the uterus and divides, creating 4 embryos; after another four months 4 young are born.

OCELOT
Felis pardalis

Classification Class: Mammalia; Order: Carnivora; Family: Felidae.

Description Length of head and body 26-40 in (65-100 cm), tail 12-18 in (30-45 cm), height to shoulder up to 18 in (45 cm), weight 10½-47 lb (4.7-21.7 kg). Color varies from whitish-gray to ocher, with longitudinal rows of dark spots.

Distribution From northern Argentina to southern United States.

Habitat Forest and woodland; never in dry environments.

Behavior A carnivore, it eats medium-sized and small mammals, birds and reptiles, hunting them both on the ground and in the trees. Nocturnal by habit, it spends the day resting in trees. The female gives birth once or twice a year, after a gestation of 70-85 days, to 1-4 cubs.

Rivers

The gallery forest which grows alongside the rivers of the Amazon basin is so called because the tree branches close in together over the water to form veritable tunnels. Among the aquatic plants, waterlilies are particularly widespread. The floating leaves of the giant waterlilies of the genus Victoria may measure more than 6 ft (2 m) in diameter.

1 basilisk
2 capybara
3 anaconda
4 bushdog
5 paca
6 Brazilian giant otter
7 arapaima
8 South American manatee
9 spectacled caiman
10 river dolphin
11 matamata
12 angelfish
13 flame tetra
14 dwarf pencilfish
15 piranha

OPOSSUM
Didelphis marsupialis

Classification Class: Mammalia; Order: Marsupialia; Family: Didelphidae.

Description Length of head and body 12½-20 in (32-50 cm), tail 10-21 in (25-53 cm), weight up to about 11½ lb (5.5 kg). Pointed snout, large ears, long prehensile tail, naked and covered with scales almost to the root. Well-developed marsupium. Thick coat, grayish-white to grayish-black, dark on tail, the point of which is yellowish-white.

Distribution Northern and central South America to Uruguay and Paraguay. It also inhabits Central and North America, to the Great Lakes of southern Canada.

Habitat Extremely varied; plains and hills, steppes, tropical forests, city parks, on ground and in trees.

Behavior An exceptional climber, it has very keen hearing, which it uses to catch prey in the form of small mammals and birds; it also feeds on birds' eggs and plants. By day it sleeps in some hiding place, emerging to look for food at night. To escape predators, if it is impossible to flee, it feigns death. Twice a year, after 12-13 days' gestation, the female gives birth to 8-10 young, which find their way into the pouch. Even though they are independent at 3-4 months, the mother carries them around for some time on her back.

PACA
Agouti paca

Classification Class: Mammalia: Order: Rodentia; Family: Dasyproctidae.

Description Total length up to 28 in (70 cm), weight up to 20 lb (9 kg). Coat light brown to brownish-black, with four longitudinal rows of white spots.

Distribution Most of South America, from northern regions to southern Brazil. It also inhabits Mexico and Central America.

Habitat Areas with woods or dense vegetation along river banks.

Behavior Nocturnal, it sleeps in burrows by day. It lives alone or in pairs. A vegetarian, it eats roots, stems, leaves, and fruit. Although it is a land mammal, it is also a good swimmer and likes to spend time in the water. The female gives birth once a year to 1-2 young.

PIRANHA
Serrasalmus piraya

Classification Class: Osteichthyes; Order: Cypriniformes; Family: Serrasalmidae.

Description Maximum length 12 in (30 cm). Jaws furnished with extremely sharp teeth so arranged as to form a continuous blade. Body laterally compressed. Blue-gray with greenish tints, fins brightly colored, belly lighter.

Distribution River basins of the São Francisco, Orinoco, and Amazon.

Habitat Middle stretches of rivers.

Behavior A carnivore, it feeds principally on other fish. It represents a rare example of group predation in the fish kingdom; this behavior is probably due to its customary overcrowded conditions. The piranha plays an important role in maintaining the equilibrium of wildlife in South American rivers because, by eliminating injured fish, it prevents the spread of epidemics among the populations of its prey. Furthermore, it carries out an important cleaning function, in that it completely strips the carcasses of dead animals.

PREHENSILE-TAILED PORCUPINE
Coëndou prehensilis

Classification Class: Mammalia; Order: Rodentia; Family: Erethizontidae.

Description Length of head and body 12-24 in (30-60 cm), tail 13-18 in (33-45 cm). Body covered with quills, mingled with hairs. Prehensile tail spiny at root, naked toward tip. Point of quills white; coat silver-gray.

Distribution Brazil, Bolivia, Venezuela, and Colombia.

Habitat Forests.

Behavior It uses its prehensile tail for climbing trees, where it spends the greater part of the day, resting in the branches or in a hollow, and eating leaves, shoots and fruit during the night. To get from one tree to another, it often comes down to the ground but remains there for only as long as is necessary before climbing up again. It is preyed upon by the jaguar, and if surprised on the ground defends itself by rolling into a ball.

RED UAKARI
Cacajao rubicundus

Classification Class: Mammalia; Order: Primates; Family: Cebidae.

Description Length of head and body 14-21 in (36-48 cm), tail 5½-7 in (14-18 cm), weight 7¾-9 lb (3.5-4.1 kg). The male is slightly larger than the female. Long, rough chestnut-red hair. Top of head, cheeks and muzzle hairless and brightly colored scarlet; there is a striking resemblance between its head and that of a completely bald man. It belongs to the single genus *Cacajao* comprising short-tailed South American monkeys collectively known as bald-headed monkeys.

Distribution Central-western South America (upper Amazon).

Habitat Forests.

Behavior Diurnal, it feeds principally on fruit, leaves, seeds, and insects, living in groups of 15-30, all lively and continually moving about. Sometimes it runs in an upright position along broad horizontal branches, holding its hands raised to keep its balance. It spends almost its entire life in the treetops without coming down to the ground. The female gives birth to a single young after 6 months' gestation.

RIVER DOLPHIN
Inia geoffrensis

Classification Class: Mammalia; Order: Cetacea; Family: Platanistidae.

Description Also known as the Boutu. Total length 8-10 ft (2.5-3 m). Head prolonged into a long rostrum (beak-like process) furnished with stiff, flat hairs which have a tactile purpose. Small but functional eyes; thoracic fins serving both to direct and propel. Color blue-gray.

Distribution River basins of the Amazon, Orinoco and Rio Negro.

Habitat Main rivers as well as tributaries and secondary streams rising in the rainy season.

Behavior It lives alone, in pairs or in small groups of up to 15 individuals. Being a mammal, it has to come to the surface at intervals in order to breathe. It feeds on fish, molluscs and crustaceans.

Note Another South American dolphin is the Rio de la Plata Dolphin *(Pontoporia blainvillei)*, smaller than the River Dolphin, up to 5¾ ft (1.75 m) in length. It inhabits southern Brazil to the Valdès peninsula in Argentina, the estuary of the Rio de la Plata and the Atlantic coasts. It does not swim upriver.

SCARLET MACAW
Ara macao

Classification Class: Aves; Order: Psittaciformes; Family: Psittacidae.

Description Length 34-36 in (75-80 cm). Large forest parrot with a long tail and pointed wings. The plumage is mostly scarlet, pale blue on the wings, rump and under-tail coverts; the wing coverts are brightly spotted yellow.

Distribution Widely found throughout the Amazon basin to northern Bolivia. It also lives in Central America, northward to southern Mexico.

Habitat Tropical forests, wooded banks of large rivers, tree savannas.

Behavior Markedly gregarious, it flies in single or multiple family groups high above the forest canopy in search of plants bursting with ripe fruit which constitutes its diet. It prefers the oily kernels of fruits with a hard rind, which it can easily rip open with its strong beak. At the end of the day the various groups return to communal dormitories for the night. Social links are also maintained by sharp, chattering cries, emitted especially in dangerous situations. It nests in tree hollows several feet from the ground.

Note The Gold-and-Blue Macaw (*Ara ararauna*) is another of the 14 South American macaws. Its plumage is typically bicolored, blue on the back, yellow underneath. Except in the breeding season it always lives in huge flocks which follow regular patterns in their daily search for food. The female lays 2 white eggs that are incubated mainly by her alone for 24-26 days.

SOUTH AMERICAN MANATEE
Trichecus inunguis
Classification Class: Mammalia; Order: Sirenia; Family: Trichechidae.
Description Length 8-11 ft (2.5-3.3 m), weight up to 660 lb (300 kg). Very thick grayish-brown skin. Front of body massive, with rounded snout. Rounded caudal fin. Limbs reduced to pectoral fins only. Small eyes with nictitating membrane (inner eyelid). Ears, with a diameter of a few millimeters, lack an auricle.
Distribution Amazon basin.
Habitat Shallows of rivers and estuaries.
Behavior Assembling in pairs or in small groups, it consumes vast quantities of aquatic plants, from 55-65 lb (25-30 kg) of vegetation daily. It uses its pectoral fins as hands, both for carrying food to the mouth and, in the case of the female, for holding the young while they suckle.

SOUTH AMERICAN TAPIR
Tapirus terrestris
Classification Class: Mammalia; Order: Perissodactyla; Family: Tapiridae.
Description Total length 6-6¾ ft (1.8-2 m), height to shoulder up to about 3 ft (1 m), weight about 500 lb (225 kg). Massive body, small head, prominent snout; the nose and upper lip are prolonged into a short trunk; small eyes, short ears. Short, sturdy legs colored yellowish to brown. The male has a kind of mane.
Distribution From Colombia and Venezuela to Brazil and Paraguay.
Habitat Dense jungle, close to river banks.
Behavior Solitary and with poor eyesight, it consumes enormous quantities of leaves and fruit. The mane does not seem to have any signaling function but probably serves as protection against the bites of predators on the nape or neck.

SPECTACLED CAIMAN
Caiman crocodylus
Classification Class: Reptilia; Order: Crocodilia; Family: Caimanidae.
Description Total length 9 ft (2.7 m). Color dark olive, with hardly visible transverse black bars.
Distribution Central zones of South America, to northern Uruguay. Also found in Central America and southern Mexico.
Habitat Lakes, ponds and pools, rivers; occasionally brackish lagoons.
Behavior It prefers stagnant water and open zones, where it can bask in the sun. The females build nests close to one another, concealed in the vegetation, heaping up rotting plants in a hollow. After laying 25-40 eggs, they watch over the nests, protecting the eggs from predators. The embryos develop with the heat and humidity furnished by the decaying vegetation.

SPIDER MONKEY
Ateles sp.
Classification Class: Mammalia; Order: Primates; Family: Cebidae.
Description Length of head and body 14-24 in (35-60 cm), tail 20-36 in (50-90 cm), weight up to 13 lb (6 kg). Long limbs, the forelegs longer than the hind pair. Long prehensile tail; the naked tip has a tactile function. Thick hair, longer on the back, flanks and outside of the legs. Naked muzzle. Coat varies from pale gray to black.
Distribution Northern South America. Also found in eastern Mexico and Central America.
Habitat Forests.
Behavior A tree dweller, it moves by clinging tightly to the branches, hands and feet together, helped by the prehensile tail; sometimes it comes down to the ground, walking upright. It lives in small family groups of 2-8, which may join together when looking for food, consisting mainly of fruit but also insects and birds' eggs. The female gives birth away from the group and rears her single young, which initially grasps her belly and is later carried on her back.

TAMANDUA
Tamandua tetradactyla
Classification Class: Mammalia; Order: Edentata; Family: Myrmecophagidae.
Description Also called the Collared Anteater. Length of head and body about 22 in (55 cm), tail the same length, weight 9-15½ lb (4-7 kg). Snout, mouth and tongue are typical of anteaters; small eyes. Feet equipped with claws. Coat thick and hairy, varying from yellowish to brown or blackish, with a broad black stripe on the shoulders and around the neck. Prehensile, almost hairless, tail.
Distribution Most of South America, from northern regions to northern Argentina. It is also found in southern Mexico and Central America.
Habitat Forests, savannas and cultivated zones.
Behavior A tree dweller, mainly nocturnal, it often comes down to the ground, but it hunts for its food in trees, scooping termites, ants or other wood-eating insects from beneath the bark and capturing them with its long, sticky tongue. In spring the female gives birth to one young, which she carries on her back.

THREE-TOED SLOTH
Bradypus sp.
Classification Class: Mammalia; Order: Edentata; Family: Bradypodidae.
Description Length of head and body 20-24 in (50-60 cm), tail 3 in (7 cm), weight 9-11 lb (4-5 kg). Short snout, small ears, eyes directed forward. The 8-10 cervical vertebrae (as against the 7 of other mammals) enable it to revolve its head through 270°. Very long legs, especially the front pair, furnished with long, curved claws. Thick, hairy coat, dark gray to beige, with lighter streaks.
Distribution From Honduras to northern Argentina.
Habitat Forests.
Behavior Exclusively arboreal, it uses its claws for clinging, head-down, to branches; its movements are extremely slow. Nocturnal by habit, it feeds almost wholly on the leaves, flowers, fruit and shoots of *Cecropia*, a tree growing on the fringes of forests and along rivers. Solitary and territorial, the sloth keeps in touch with companions by emitting high-pitched calls. Mating occurs in March-April, and after 6 months' gestation the female produces a single young, which remains clasped to its mother's belly, and is carried about in this manner, given that she does not construct a nest. In this forest environment rainfall is extremely abundant. The hair of the sloth represents an adaptation to its upside-down life, for it is parted on the abdomen and directed from there toward the back: the rainwater thus flows over the animal's coat without soaking through it. The sloth's principal predators are the Ocelot and the Jaguar, but thanks to its very slow movements and to one-celled algae which live in microscopic grooves around each of its piliferous (hair-producing) cells and so give a greenish color to the hair, the animal manages to remain unobserved.

AUSTRALIA

Of all the continents, Australia is perhaps the most distinctive in terms of the animals which live there. The mammals in particular are extremely unusual, being represented by only two very characteristic orders, the Monotremata (monotremes) and Marsupialia (marsupials). The former group, nowadays found only in Australia, Tasmania and New Guinea, are the most primitive of all mammals: although they are covered with hair, like all other members of this class, and given to suckling their young during the first few weeks of life, the monotremes lay eggs, like the ancient prehistoric reptiles from which mammals are derived. The best-known of the monotremes are the platypus, whose bill is similar to that of a duck, and two species of echidna, similar to the hedgehog.

Rather less primitive are the marsupials, virtually the only mammals to be found in Australia today. Because they have no competitors, they have become extremely diversified, giving origin to different families whose manner of life corresponds to that of the ordinary forms of mole, mouse, rabbit, squirrel, wolf and so on. Thus we have a marsupial mole, a marsupial wolf (the thylacine, which may have been extinct for some decades) and a marsupial bear (the koala), etc. The most spectacular marsupials are the kangaroos, vegetarian mammals whose ecological role in an environment with grassy vegetation is akin to that of the antelopes in the Old World.

No less singular than the Australian fauna is that of New Guinea, where the marsupials are also well represented; but the most remarkable aspect of this large island's wildlife is constituted by certain families of birds, such as the birds of paradise and the cassowaries. The latter are powerful birds incapable of flight, similar to ostriches but with a bony helmet on their head which allows them to run at great speed through the tangle of forest vegetation without risk of injury.

Different again, though much less varied, is the fauna of New Zealand, a very ancient land which has felt the effects of long isolation from the rest of the world. On these two islands very many species have become extinct in recent times because of a glacial period and, following that, because of human colonization. With almost no indigenous mammals, New Zealand harbors some exceptionally interesting species of birds, including the kiwi, and one extraordinary reptile, the tuatara, sole survivor of a group which has been virtually extinct for millions of years.

The more remote islands of Oceania (the area of the central and southern Pacific) accomodate highly interesting animals. Particularly remarkable are the creatures of the Hawaiian Islands, such as the Drepanididae (honeycreepers), and thousands of other species, including snails and insects, whose ancestors arrived here after traveling immense distances across the ocean.

126

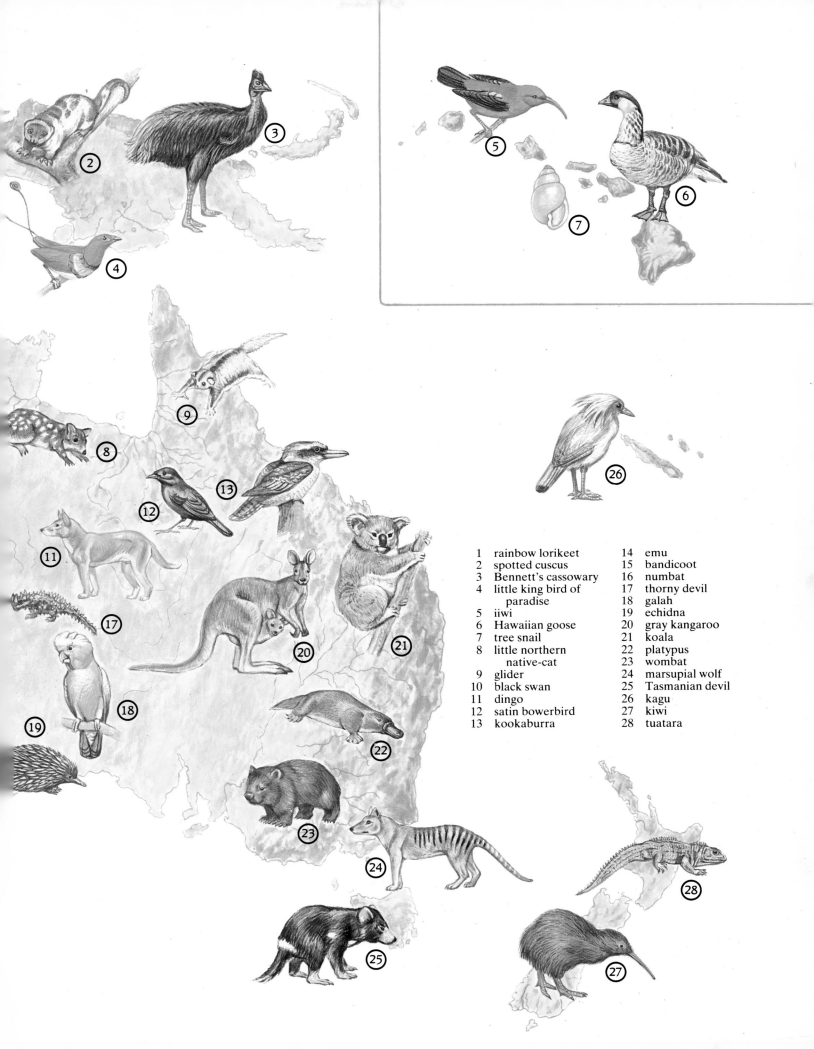

1 rainbow lorikeet
2 spotted cuscus
3 Bennett's cassowary
4 little king bird of
    paradise
5 iiwi
6 Hawaiian goose
7 tree snail
8 little northern
    native-cat
9 glider
10 black swan
11 dingo
12 satin bowerbird
13 kookaburra

14 emu
15 bandicoot
16 numbat
17 thorny devil
18 galah
19 echidna
20 gray kangaroo
21 koala
22 platypus
23 wombat
24 marsupial wolf
25 Tasmanian devil
26 kagu
27 kiwi
28 tuatara

Australia

AUSTRALIAN ECHIDNA
Tachyglossus aculeatus

Classification Class: Mammalia; Order: Monotremata; Family: Tachyglossidae.

Description Length 16-20 in (40-50 cm), weight 5½-13 lb (2.5-6 kg). Body covered with hair and also, on the back and flanks, with long yellow, black-tipped spines, hence the alternative name of Spiny Anteater. The snout is elongated and tube-like, with a narrow mouth opening, through which it protrudes its long, sticky tongue.

Distribution Australia, Tasmania, southern New Guinea.

Habitat Sandy plains, wooded or rocky zones.

Behavior It is solitary and active mainly in the evening. It feeds on ants, termites, worms, and other small invertebrates, capturing them by inserting its snout into clefts and holes. Its eyesight is poor but it is extremely sensitive to any vibration in the ground. The most highly developed sense is that of smell: as soon as it detects prey, it darts out its tongue like lightning and immediately draws it back with the victim stuck to it. When threatened, it rolls itself up into a ball or quickly digs a hole and hides inside. During the breeding season the female lays a single egg, rarely 2 or 3, in the ventral pouch formed for that purpose. After 7-10 days the young Echidna, about ½ in (12 mm) long, emerges from the egg, remaining in the mother's pouch for another couple of months, suckling on the milk from her mammary glands and which flows along the hairs of her abdomen.

BLACK SWAN
Cygnus atratus

Classification Class: Aves; Order: Anseriformes; Family: Anatidae.

Description Length 4-4¼ ft (1.2-1.3 m). Plumage black, mingled with brown, and white tips to the wings. Bill orange or dark red with a white tip.

Distribution Southern and eastern Australia, along the north coasts to Townsville (Queensland); also found in Tasmania.

Habitat Large areas of fresh or brackish water, swamps.

Behavior It feeds in shallow water, submerging the head and sieving the muddy bottom. It lives in groups but pairs establish lasting links. Calls that vary in tone according to sex are important in maintaining contact between partners and between parents and cygnets. Nesting may take place during any month of the year, depending on the progress of the rainy season. Each brood consists of 3-9 eggs, incubated by both parents for 39-43 days. Imported into Europe by the Dutch at the end of the nineteenth century, the bird is now bred in various countries.

DINGO
Canis lupis familiaris

Classification Class: Mammalia; Order: Carnivora; Family: Canidae.

Description Length of head and body up to about 44 in (110 cm), tail 10-16 in (25-40 cm), height to shoulder 20-24 in (50-60 cm), weight 55-77 lb (25-35 kg). It looks like a large dog, uniformly reddish.

Distribution Australia. The Dingo is not a separate species but a dog which has returned to the wild, having arrived with the aborigines between 9,000 and 15,000 years ago.

Habitat Undergrowth and semidesert.

Behavior It generally lives alone or in pairs. Nocturnal by habit, it digs burrows close to water and shelters there by day. It feeds principally on rabbits but also hunts small marsupials. The female gives birth to 4-5 puppies once a year after 63 days' gestation.

EMU
Dromaius novaehollandiae

Classification Class: Aves; Order: Casuariiformes; Family: Dromaidae.

Description Length 5-6 ft (1.5-1.8 m), weight about 120 lb (54 kg). It is the largest living bird after the Ostrich. Coarse plumage with long, cascading dark brown feathers over the whole body. Head and neck are feathered, except for naked bluish zones at the sides of neck and throat.

Distribution Most of Australia.

Habitat Plains and meadows, crop-growing areas, moors, and semidesert.

Behavior It is the only species in its family to have survived colonization, with an inquisitive, sociable disposition which has led to its disappearance in some districts. It is an agile runner and swimmer, feeding both on vegetation and insects. The voice of the male is sharp and guttural, that of the female booming. It is she who initiates courtship, subsequently handing over to the male responsibility for incubating the eggs (5-12, sometimes up to 20) and tending the young. It nests in winter.

FLAT-SKULLED MARSUPIAL MOUSE
Planigale ingrami

Classification Class: Mammalia; Order: Marsupialia; Family: Dasyuridae.

Description Length of head and body about 3 in (8 cm), tail about 2½ in (6 cm), weight under ¼ oz (about 5 g). Gray-brown above, whitish below. Pointed muzzle and flat head.

Distribution Northern Australia.

Habitat Forests.

Behavior It is a voracious eater of insects. Thanks to its singularly flattened skull, it finds refuge in rock clefts, like a lizard. The female gives birth to 12 young at a time.

FRILLED LIZARD
Chlamydosaurus kingi

Classification Class: Reptilia; Order: Squamata; Suborder: Sauria; Family: Agamidae.

Description Length 32 in (80 cm), of which 22 in (55 cm) represents the tail. Body dull brown with a reticulated pattern, covered with small scales. Hind legs markedly longer than front pair. There is a characteristic fold of skin beneath the throat and sides of the neck which inflates when the lizard opens its mouth, forming a collar when the animal is excited or threatened.

Distribution Northern and northwestern Australia, southern New Guinea.

Habitat Savannas and forests with alternating dry and rainy seasons.

Behavior It is mainly arboreal, living on its own, with no hiding places, simply spending the night among the branches. It feeds on spiders, insects, birds' eggs, and small mammals. If disturbed, it assumes a characteristic defensive attitude, mouth gaping wide and collar inflated; at the same time it hisses and lashes its tail like a whip. Should it be unable to frighten the enemy, it suddenly does an about-face and dashes off on its hind legs. The whole elaborate defense strategy is based on surprise and intimidation, a technique which is very widespread in the animal kingdom. All that is known about reproduction is that the female lays eggs.

GOLDEN TREE FROG
Hyla aurea

Classification Class: Amphibia; Order: Anura; Family: Hylidae.

Description Green above, with golden spots arranged in longitudinal rows; whitish below. The tips of the toes expand to form adhesive pads, which enable it to climb with agility.

Distribution Southwestern Australia.

Habitat Swamps.

Behavior It does not behave like a typical tree frog: Although well equipped for climbing, it avoids trees and lives on the banks of swamps like an ordinary frog. It feeds on insects.

GOULD'S MONITOR
Varanus gouldi
Classification Class: Reptilia; Order: Squamata; Suborder: Sauria; Family: Varanidae.
Description Length up to about 4¼ ft (1.3 m). Large lizard, brownish color.
Distribution Australia and southern New Guinea.
Habitat Sandy and steppelike terrain.
Behavior A typical diurnal animal, it becomes active only when the sun is already high. It feeds on insects, fish, crabs, frogs, birds, and small mammals, and is particularly partial to eggs. It is a fast runner, getting a firm grip on the ground with its long claws, and it is also an agile climber. When threatened, it confronts the adversary, hissing angrily and lashing out furiously with its tail.

GRAY KANGAROO
Macropus giganteus
Classification Class: Mammalia; Order: Marsupialia; Family: Macropodidae.
Description Length of head and body 5 ft (1.5 m), tail about 3¼ ft (1 m), weight up to 200 lb (90 kg); in an upright position it is almost 6 ft (2 m) tall. Color gray with a black tip to the tail. Forelegs shorter than hind legs. The female has a pouch.
Distribution Eastern Australia.
Habitat Open forests and undergrowth.
Behavior A herbivore, it feeds at night until the morning; by day it rests in groups under the trees. Its leaps are notably long, in the region of 40 ft (13 m), but not more than 5 ft (1.5 m) or so in height.

KOALA
Phascolarctos cinereus
Classification Class: Mammalia; Order: Marsupialia; Family: Phalangeridae.
Description Length of head and body 24-33 in (60-82 cm), weight up to 35 lb (16 kg). It has no tail. Ash-gray above, whitish below. The female has a pouch.
Distribution East coast of Australia.
Habitat Eucalyptus forests.
Behavior It lives alone or in small groups. Nocturnal and arboreal, it does not build a nest but sleeps in the forks of branches, coming down to the ground only to move from one tree to another. It is exclusively vegetarian, feeding only on the leaves of certain species of eucalyptus (20 or so of about 600 that grow in Australia). It is particularly fussy even in its choice, avoiding the young, soft leaves which contain a high quantity of highly poisonous prussic acid. In order to digest the eucalyptus leaves, which are very tough, the koala has a blind intestine (caecum), 6-8 ft (1.8-2.5 m) long, which is two or three times the length of its whole body. It derives all the water it needs from these same leaves: The name "Koala" is in fact derived from the language of the Australian aborigines, and means "animal which does not drink."

KOOKABURRA
Dacelo gigas
Classification Class: Aves; Order: Coraciiformes; Family: Alcedinidae.
Description Also called the Laughing Jackass. Length 16-18½ in (41-47 cm). It is one of the largest and best-known of kingfishers. Its powerful bill is very long and broad; the big head is whitish, with a dark mark behind the eye. Rump and shoulders are streaked blue, the rest of the plumage is brown. Barred tail.
Distribution Eastern and southern Australia, Tasmania.
Habitat Open woodland, savannas.
Behavior Flocks of birds have the habit of singing in chorus, as it were, at break of day. As it utters its call, which is strikingly similar to a human laugh, the bird raises its tail and stiffens its body vertically. The diet consists less of fish than of reptiles, small mammals, insects and ground arthropods. Although kookaburras form large flocks, individual pairs maintain permanent links. After a brief courtship, the female lays 2-4 eggs in a cavity. These are incubated for 24 days.

NUMBAT
Myrmecobius fasciatus
Classification Class: Mammalia; Order: Marsupialia; Family: Myrmecobiidae.
Description Also called the Banded Anteater. Length of head and body about 9 in (23 cm), tail 7 in (17 cm), weight ½-1 lb (280-450 g). Back reddish-brown with whitish transverse stripes, belly yellowish-white. Long head and pointed snout, bushy tail similar to that of a squirrel. The female has no pouch.
Distribution Southern and southwestern Australia.
Habitat Eucalyptus forests and desert zones.
Behavior It eats termites and ants, capturing them with its long, sticky tongue. It is solitary and, unlike the majority of marsupials, active by day. At night it settles in tree hollows or in other forms of shelter. As a rule the female gives birth to 4 young, one for each of her nipples.

PURPLE-CROWNED LORIKEET
Glossopsitta porphyrocephala
Classification Class: Aves; Order: Psittaciformes; Family: Psittacidae.
Description Length 6-7 in (15-17 cm). Pale green with distinctive coloration on head; forehead orange-yellow, marks of the same color on auriculars, crown dark purple. The upper breast and abdomen are pale blue, the bill black.
Distribution Southern Australia.
Habitat Open woods of eucalyptus, savannas, trees lining roads, rivers, and streams.
Behavior It often flies about in small or large groups from end to end of its territory, normally keeping to the treetops where it finds appetizing flower heads. It feeds mainly on flower nectar, sipping it with the aid of the brush-like tip of its tongue. Several pairs may nest on the same large tree, each in its own cavity. The female alone incubates the 3-4 eggs, being fed periodically by the male.

RAINBOW LORIKEET
Trichoglossus heamatodus
Classification Class: Aves; Order: Psittaciformes; Family: Psittacidae.
Description Length 10-13 in (25-32 cm). Head violet-blue, collar and nape yellow-green, rest of upper parts green. A broad, bright orange band crosses the breast, while the belly is blue. Bill bright red.
Distribution Eastern Australia, Tasmania, New Guinea, and islands adjacent to New Hebrides and New Caledonia.
Habitat Forests and humid woods, plantations, and gardens.
Behavior It feeds principally on nectar and pollen, in addition to fruit, berries, insects and their larvae. It has a special taste for the flowers of eucalyptus, banksia, and other native and introduced plants. In some city parks it has become so tame that it perches on the shoulders and arms of visitors who offer it food. It nests inside hollow branches or trunks. The 2-3 eggs hatch after an incubation of 23 days, the male not participating.

RED KANGAROO
Macropus rufus
Classification Class: Mammalia; Order: Marsupialia; Family: Macropodidae.
Description Length of head and body 4¼-5¼ ft (1.3-1.6 m), tail 32-42 in (80-105 cm), weight 60-155 lb (27-70 kg). Standing upright, it measures more than 6 ft (2 m) tall. Male reddish, female gray-blue and much smaller. Short forelegs, hind legs considerably longer and stronger. The female has a pouch.
Distribution Virtually the whole of Australia.
Habitat Lowland plains.
Behavior It lives in small groups, which often join together to form large troops. A herbivore, it leaves its shady retreats to graze or to drink, usually at sunset, particularly in the hot season. When it needs to move quickly, it makes powerful

Australia

The plant life of Australia is rich and varied, with sharp contrasts in different parts of the continent. The eucalyptus is one of the most characteristic trees, and there are some 100 different species; the acacia, too, grows in many different places and forms. Much of the continent has a dry climate and therefore harbors a variety of thorny plants belonging to diverse families. Other typical shrubs and trees are the banksias, with brightly colored flowers.

1 purple-crowned lorikeet
2 sugar glider
3 koala
4 kookaburra
5 tawny frogmouth
6 galah
7 sulfur-crested cockatoo
8 short-tailed wallaby
9 rainbow lorikeet
10 whiteheaded honeyeater
11 emu
12 red kangaroo
13 black swan
14 gray kangaroo
15 Gould's monitor
16 frilled lizard
17 golden tree frog
18 Australian echidna
19 numbat
20 dingo
21 thorny devil

jumps, propelled by the hind legs alone; these hops may be as much as 45 ft (13 m) long and 10 ft (3 m) high. When at rest or when walking slowly, the tail serves to support the body; when the animal runs or jumps, it acts as a balance. As a rule one young is born, after a gestation of 33 days. The newborn young (joey) finds its way into the marsupium and attaches itself to a nipple, releasing it only when it leaves the pouch, after about 6 months.

SHORT-TAILED WALLABY
Setonix brachyurus

Classification Class: Mammalia; Order: Marsupialia; Family: Macropodidae.
Description Also called the Quokka. Length of head and body 18½-24 in (47-60 cm), tail 10-14 (25-35 cm), weight 4½-11 lb (2-5 kg). It is a small kangaroo, gray-brown, with forelegs shorter than the hind legs. The female has a pouch.
Distribution Western Australia.
Habitat Dense vegetation in marshy zones.
Behavior Unlike medium-sized and large kangaroos, it does not use its tail as support when standing or moving slowly. A herbivore, it feeds at night; by day it remains in the undergrowth, creating a network of veritable tunnels to get from place to place. After a gestation of 27 days the female produces one young, which stays in the pouch for 5 months.

SUGAR GLIDER
Petaurus breviceps

Classification Class: Mammalia; Order: Marsupialia; Family: Phalangeridae.
Description Also called the Shortheaded Glider. Length of head and body 5-7 in (12-17 cm), tail 6-7 in (15-17 cm), weight 2½-3½ oz (70-100 g). Gray with a dark stripe from the tip of the nose to the root of the tail. Broad patagium extending from forelegs to hind legs. Long bushy tail. Female furnished with marsupium.
Distribution East coast of Australia, New Guinea and adjoining islands; introduced into Tasmania.
Habitat Wooded zones.
Behavior It feeds mainly on sugary substances that flow from the bark of certain eucalyptus trees which the animal rips with its powerful incisors; it also eats shoots, fruit, and insects. An arboreal animal, it looks for food by moving from tree to tree, gliding for considerable distances with the aid of the patagium. It lives in small family groups. Nocturnal by habit, it sleeps by day in tree hollows, where it builds a nest of leaves heaped up with its tail. After a gestation of 3 weeks, the female gives birth to 1-3 young, which remain in the pouch for 4 months.

SULFUR-CRESTED COCKATOO
Cacatua galerita

Classification Class: Aves; Order: Psittaciformes; Family: Cacatuidae.
Description Length about 19 in (49 cm). Plumage completely white with a yellow erectile crest on the top of the head. The underside of the wings and the tail feathers are also tinged with yellow. Orbital ring white or faintly tinted blue.
Distribution Much of Australia, Tasmania, New Guinea and Indonesia. It has also been introduced into New Zealand and various island groups in the Pacific Ocean.
Habitat Tropical forests, woods with sclerophyllous plants, cultivated zones; also parks and gardens.
Behavior Although it sometimes lives in close contact with people, it is by nature suspicious and diffident. When feeding on the ground, some individuals remain on guard in the trees, ready to sound the alarm with loud, raucous cries. It feeds at random on seeds, grains, berries, bulbous roots, and insects. The nest is situated in a tree cavity, at some considerable height, or sometimes in rock clefts. The eggs (2, rarely 3) are incubated by both parents for about 30 days.
Note The Galah or Roseate Cockatoo (*Eolophus roseicapillus*) is likewise widely distributed throughout Australia. Endowed with a very beautiful gray and pink livery, it descends in huge flocks on cultivated land, often causing great damage to cereal crops.

TAWNY FROGMOUTH
Podargus strigoides

Classification Class: Aves; Order: Caprimulgiformes; Family: Podargidae.
Description Length 13-18½ in (33-47 cm). Big nocturnal bird with a large bill and a very voluminous mouth cavity. Plumage varies from gray to brown or red, heavily blotched and streaked. Yellow eyes.
Distribution Australia and Tasmania.
Habitat Forests, open woodland, wooded river banks, parks.
Behavior During the day it remains perched on branches, taking up positions that make it almost invisible, thanks to its capacity for puffing up or drooping its feathers almost at will. It takes advantage of shadows to surprise insects and small vertebrates either on the ground or on the branches, grinding them with its powerful beak before swallowing them. Its hunting technique is similar to that of the Kookaburra. The female lays 2 eggs on a flimsy platform of sticks and leaves, placed in a horizontal fork of branches, at a height of about 15-30 ft (5-10 m).

THORNY DEVIL
Moloch horridus

Classification Class: Reptilia; Order: Squamata; Suborder: Sauria; Family: Agamidae.
Description Also known as the Moloch. Total length about 8 in (20 cm). Body and tail covered with large spiny scales; two particularly large spines, like horns, on the head. The color is a mixture of yellow and brown, but this tends to change as the reptile adapts to its surroundings. On the nape there is a raised pad of fatty tissue, likewise furnished with spines.
Distribution Central and southern Australia.
Habitat Steppes and deserts.
Behavior Despite its monstrous appearance, it is absolutely harmless. It feeds exclusively on ants, scooping them up surprisingly rapidly with its fleshy tongue, and consuming as many as 2,000 at a time. It does not need to drink, for it absorbs sufficient ground moisture through its skin; the stored liquid then flows into the mouth and is swallowed. The adipose pad on the nape is an adaptation to the prohibitive conditions of life in the desert; it serves as a store of fats which, as they burn up, enable the animal in times of drought to produce the necessary water to satisfy its fluid requirements.

WHITEHEADED HONEYEATER
Phylidonyris novaehollandiae

Classification Class: Aves; Order: Passeriformes; Family: Meliphagidae.
Description Length 6½-7¼ in (16.5-18.5 cm). Plumage striped black and white, these colors alternating and mingling on the head as well. Margins of wings and tail yellow, eyes white.
Distribution Southern Australia, Tasmania and small islands in the Bass Strait.
Habitat Edges of woods and forests, moors, gardens.
Behavior A restless, gregarious bird which, like all honeyeaters, feeds on flower nectar, particularly that of eucalyptus and banksia. It often interrupts its exploration of the foliage to perch on the top of a tree or shrub, emitting loud calls. Occasionally it launches an attack on larger birds, including raptors. The soft cup-shaped nest is built on a low bush; the 1-3 eggs are incubated for 14-15 days, the chicks being fed with insects and regurgitated nectar.

Tasmania

BLACK CURRAWONG
Strepera fuliginosa

Classification Class: Aves; Order: Passeriformes; Family: Cracticidae.

Description It is one of a group of birds endemic to the Australian region, similar to crows but without hairs at the base of the bill, and with bright yellow eyes. The plumage is completely black, apart from the tip of the tail and a small area on the wings, which are white.

Distribution Tasmania and adjacent small islands.

Habitat Forests; also visits town suburbs and orchards.

Behavior It is notable above all for its characteristically shrill voice which echoes everywhere through mountain woodlands. During the winter it enters built-up areas, searching for food in gardens and orchards; its diet is quite varied and consists of insects and larvae, fruit, eggs, and nestlings of other birds. In flooded and swampy zones it is frequently seen wading in shallow water like a heron. It builds a bulky nest of sticks, usually very high in the treetops, and here the female lays from 2-4 eggs which are streaked red and purple.

CAPE BARREN GOOSE
Cereopsis novaehollandiae

Classification Class: Aves; Order: Anseriformes; Family: Anatidae.

Description Length 30-40 in (75-100 cm). Plumage ash-gray with whitish nape and sparse black spots on shoulders. The short black bill is covered by a yellowish waxy sheath; the legs are dark red, the feet black.

Distribution Tasmania and islands in the Bass Strait; it is also found locally on the coasts of southern Australia and on some of the offshore island groups.

Habitat Open ground, islands with stones and bushes, and edges of lakes and swamps.

Behavior The adults generally live in pairs, which maintain lifelong links; the young assemble in huge wandering flocks. It feeds on grass and vegetable matter, often in company with sheep. Nesting sites are occupied from February onward; defense of the chosen area is entrusted to the male, who is particularly aggressive and hostile to any intruder. The female lays 4-7 eggs in a grassy nest; these hatch after 40 days' incubation.

DUSKY WOOD SWALLOW
Artamus cyanopterus

Classification Class: Aves; Order: Passeriformes; Family: Artamidae.

Description Length 7 in (18 cm). Head and body brown, wings gray-blue edged with white, tail black with white tip, bill blue with black tip.

Distribution Tasmania, southwestern and eastern Australia.

Habitat Open forests.

Behavior It feeds principally on flying insects. Gregarious by habit, it raises its young communally, confronts winged predators in a group to chase them away, and forms large flocks to spend the night in trees. A fairly fragile nest is constructed in the fork of branches. When perched, it flicks its tail from left to right.

EMU WREN
Stipiturus malachurus

Classification Class: Aves; Order: Passeriformes; Family: Maluridae.

Description Length 7-8 in (17.5-20 cm), of which 4 in (10 cm) consists of the tail. Male reddish-brown, with dark bars on upper parts; throat, upper breast and a stripe over the eye are blue-gray. Female and young lack this last color. The tail is made up of only 6 long, fringed feathers, similar in consistency to those of the Emu.

Distribution Southwestern and southeastern Australia, Tasmania.

Habitat Moors and marshes.

Behavior Lives in territorial groups comprising a dominant pair, non-nesting subordinates of either sex, and first-year young. It feeds on insects and seeds. Hopping over the ground or among the branches of shrubs, it keeps its tail straight, almost resting on the back, in a manner typical of a Maluridae. It flies low and feebly. The dome-shaped nest, with a side entrance, is built in the dense undergrowth, and in it the female lays 2-5 eggs. In case of danger, the incubating female draws attention to herself by running with movements resembling those of a small rodent.

GREEN ROSELLA
Platycercus caledonicus

Classification Class: Aves; Order: Psittaciformes; Family: Psittacidae.

Description Length 12½-14 in (32-36 cm). Dark green spotted plumage. Head and underparts lemon-yellow; scarlet patch on throat; cheeks and wing margins cobalt-blue. Male larger than female, with bigger head and bill.

Distribution Tasmania and islands in the Bass Strait.

Habitat Forests and woodlands, from sea level to 5,000 ft (1,500 m).

Behavior It feeds on fruit and tree seeds, preferably early in the morning or evening. It is gregarious even in the breeding season; during courtship the male straightens his body, droops his wings and shakes his feathers, giving out a musical chatter. The female lays 4-5 eggs in the hollow of a trunk; these hatch after an incubation of 20-22 days. The chicks gather in tight groups and remain together until they take on adult plumage and reach sexual maturity, at the age of about 15 months.

PLATYPUS
Ornithorhynchus anatinus

Classification Class: Mammalia; Order: Monotremata; Family: Ornithorhynchidae.

Description Length of head and body 18 in (45 cm), tail 6 in (15 cm), weight up to about 4 lb (2 kg). The body is covered in thick, dark brown fur and rough bristles. On the muzzle is a characteristic broad, flat bill, resembling that of a duck, with two prominent nostrils almost at the tip (the scientific name of the species means "duckbilled"). Instead of teeth, the adult platypus has horny plates capable of grinding food. The tail is like that of a beaver. The legs are very short, with a broad membrane between the toes. The female is not provided with a ventral pouch. The platypus is the only poisonous mammal: On the inside of each hind leg the male is equipped with a spur connected to a venom gland.

Distribution Tasmania, eastern Australia.

Habitat Lowland and mountain rivers, streams, and lakes.

Behavior The platypus is admirably adapted to life in the water, yet it remains there only for a relatively short time; throughout the day it remains in the burrow it has dug along the river bank. The long tunnel leading to the nest chamber sometimes twists so much that the animal can hardly get through; this helps to eliminate any water that has collected in the fur and keeps the burrow dry. It looks awkward on land but is a rapid swimmer, using the forelegs as fins; the hind legs and tail serve as organs of direction. The platypus feeds on crustaceans, aquatic insects and their larvae, worms, fish, etc, found on the riverbed. The female usually lays 2 eggs, which hatch in 10-12 days. The young are born blind and naked, suckling on the mother's milk.

RED-BELLIED PADEMELON
Thylogale billardieri

Classification Class: Mammalia; Order: Marsupialia; Family: Macropodidae.

Tasmania

Tasmania's vegetation is very similar to that of the more temperate and cool regions of the Australian continent, from which the island is separated by a shallow strait. Ferns grow here in abundance; and there are also some genera of plants which can nowadays be found, too, in Patagonia and which in times gone by must have flourished in Antarctica, such as Nothofagus, related to the beech.

1 green rosella
2 marsupial wolf
3 tiger cat
4 red-bellied pademelon
5 Tasmanian devil
6 shortnosed rat kangaroo
7 black currawong
8 platypus
9 Tasmanian barred bandicoot
10 Tasmanian wombat
11 Cape Barren goose

Description Length of head and body 21-30 in (53-77 cm), tail 12½-18½ in (32-47 cm), weight 6½-15½ lb (3-7 kg). Hair gray-brown with olive tints on the back, orange or reddish on the abdomen. Hind legs much longer than forelegs.

Distribution Tasmania, southern Australia.

Habitat Shrub zones, dense forest undergrowth.

Behavior Gregarious and nocturnal, it spends the day in thick vegetation, using paths that take on the guise of tunnels. A herbivore, it also nibbles leaves and shoots. Reproduction is very slow and as a rule only one young is born; for this reason its numbers are rapidly diminishing, and it has almost vanished from Australia.

SHORTNOSED RAT KANGAROO
Bettongia cuniculus

Classification Class: Mammalia; Order: Marsupialia; Family: Macropodidae.

Description Length of head and body 12½ in (32 cm), tail 10-13 in (25-33 cm), weight 3½ lb (1.6 kg). Gray-brown above, lighter below, with white-tipped tail. Forelegs shorter than hind pair, tail partly prehensile with a tuft of stiff comblike hairs at the tip. The female has a pouch.

Distribution Tasmania.

Habitat Grassy plains.

Behavior Nocturnal, it feeds on roots, which it scoops out with strong claws, and on grass. By day it remains hidden in an underground burrow, well camouflaged in the shrubs and bushes, and inside this is a nest of grass, brought in with the tail. When the animal hops around slowly, it uses the tail as support; in the course of longer leaps the tail acts as a balance.

TASMANIAN BARRED BANDICOOT
Perameles gunni

Classification Class: Mammalia; Order: Marsupialia; Family: Peramelidae.

Description Length of head and body 8-17 in (20-42 cm), tail 3-7 in (7.5-17 cm), weight up to about 1¼ lb (550 g). Back brown with dark stripes across rear part, underparts lighter. Long pointed snout, pointed ears, toes with sharp claws suitable for digging. Forelegs very short, hind legs long. The female's marsupium opens backward, this being characteristic of the majority of excavating marsupials.

Distribution Tasmania.

Habitat Open plains.

Behavior It is terrestrial and nocturnal, digging in the earth for insects, worms and sometimes roots, or to build a nest which it lines with grass. Although it has the legs of a kangaroo, it does not hop but runs on all fours. The female gives birth to 1-5 young, which remain in the pouch for 2 months.

TASMANIAN DEVIL
Sarcophilus harrisii

Classification Class: Mammalia; Order: Marsupialia; Family: Dasyuridae.

Description Length of head and body 20 in (50 cm), tail 8-12 in (20-30 cm), weight 13-20 lb (6-9 kg). Looks like a small bear. Black with a white mark on the chest, shoulders and root of tail. Short muzzle, transparent ears, stocky tail, forelegs with strong claws. The female has a marsupium.

Distribution Tasmania.

Habitat Eucalyptus forests.

Behavior The largest existing carnivorous marsupial, it is extremely voracious, its prey consists mainly of small and medium-sized kangaroos, but also smaller animals and even those that are dead. All these are devoured completely, including the bones, which are crushed with the strong teeth, notably the canines and fearsome molars. It is active at night, spending the day concealed in dense undergrowth, occasionally emerging to curl up in the sun. Extremely aggressive, the animal looks truly ferocious when confronting an enemy, making its common name seem well justified. The female gives birth to 2 young, which remain in the completely closed pouch for 15 weeks.

Note The Thylacine or Marsupial Wolf (*Thylacinus cynocephalus*), another dasyurid, also came originally from Tasmania, but has probably been extinct for some decades. Nocturnal by habit, this animal resembled a wolf and bore a series of characteristic black stripes on the back; the female was furnished with a marsupium.

TASMANIAN WOMBAT
Vombatus ursinus

Classification Class: Mammalia; Order: Marsupialia; Family: Vombatidae.

Description Length of head and body 28-42 in (70-105 cm), tail 2 in (5 cm), height to shoulder 8-10 in (20-25 cm), weight 55-77 lb (25-35 kg). Stocky body, short legs. Hair short and bristly, sandy gray to dark gray on back, lighter on abdomen. The female has a marsupium which opens backward.

Distribution Tasmania, southeastern Australia.

Habitat Broadleaved forests, rocky zones, and seacoasts with dense shrub growth.

Behavior A skillful digger, it lives as a rule in colonies, in a vast network of tunnels, some of which are up to 100 ft (30 m) in length and 1-2 ft (30-60 cm) below ground, terminating in the living quarters. It is mainly nocturnal, feeding on grass, roots, bark, and fungi. The female produces one young at a time, which remains in the pouch for 8-9 months.

TIGER CAT
Dasyrus maculatus

Classification Class: Mammalia; Order: Marsupialia; Family: Dasyuridae.

Description Also known as the Large Spotted-tailed Native Cat. Length of head and body 26-30 in (65-75 cm), tail 10-12 in (25-35 cm), weight 2½ lb (1.1 kg). Fur dark with white spots. The female has a pouch.

Distribution Tasmania, eastern and southeastern Australia.

Habitat Wooded terrain.

Behavior Prevalently arboreal and nocturnal, it eats birds, reptiles, and small mammals, and when hunting is very skilled in following a trail. It sometimes raids chicken runs, and for this reason has been almost totally exterminated. This solution has proved unwise, for the tiger cat could have continued to play a very important role in eliminating pests such as mice, rats, and wild rabbits. The female produces up to 24 young at a time, but most of them die because the mother has only 6 nipples in the marsupium, to which the survivors cling for about 2 months.

TIGER SNAKE
Notechis scutatus

Classification Class: Reptilia; Order: Squamata; Suborder: Ophidia; Family: Elapidae.

Description Maximum length 6 ft (1.8 m). Upper parts tawny with transverse black stripes, underparts yellow with small dark spots.

Distribution Exclusive to Australia and Tasmania.

Habitat Arid zones with sparse shrub growth.

Behavior Feeds on lizards and small marsupial mammals. It is the most venomous snake on the continent. If threatened, it attacks immediately and its poison, if not properly deactivated by specific antidotes, can kill a large dog in 20 minutes or a human within an hour. Notably prolific, the female produces up to about 50 young, already fully formed, each year.

New Guinea

COMMON CASSOWARY
Casuarius casuarius

Classification Class: Aves; Order: Struthioniformes; Family: Casuaridae.
Description Length 5-6½ ft (1.5-2 m), weight up to about 130 lb (60 kg). Plumage glossy black with hard, drooping feathers. Head naked, blue-green, topped by a bony casque; showy caruncles hang from the sides of the neck. The female is larger and more brightly colored than the male.
Distribution New Guinea, Aru and Ceram islands, northeastern Australia.
Habitat Swampy rain forests.
Behavior Difficult to observe in the wild, the cassowary is by nature evasive and quarrelsome. It feeds on fallen fruit and seeds, sometimes on dead animals as well. Thanks to the protection afforded by its casque, it can easily break its way through the thickest undergrowth; if necessary it resorts to swimming. The female assumes the dominant roles, inducing the male to copulate and giving him the task of incubation. A shallow platform of stems and leaves accommodates the 3-6 eggs (generally 4), their shell bright green. Both parents rear the chicks.

GREATER BIRD OF PARADISE
Paradisaea apoda

Classification Class: Aves; Order: Passeriformes; Family: Paradiseidae.
Description Length 13-18 in (33-45 cm). In the male a group of long, filmy yellow or orange feathers grows on the sides of the breast and can be raised above the back; these feathers may measure up to 5 ft (1.5 m) in length. Top of head golden yellow, chin emerald green; a cushion of brown feathers forms a kind of collar beneath the throat. The female's plumage is more drab, uniformly brown.
Distribution New Guinea, Aru islands. Recently the bird has been introduced successfully into Tobago, in the West Indies.
Habitat Rain forests.
Behavior It performs collective parades in remote parts of the forest, where up to 20 males may assemble. The display includes hops on to high branches, the emission of nasal sounds that grow in intensity, and strutting postures in the presence of the females, with wings outspread and ornamental feathers puffed up over the bent back. It feeds on fruit and probably insects as well. The female lays only 2 eggs.

GREEN TREE PYTHON
Chondropython viridis

Classification Class: Reptilia; Order: Squamata; Suborder: Ophidia; Family: Boidae.
Description Length about 6 ft (2 m). Color green with white spots on the back of the adult, yellow on that of the young.
Distribution New Guinea, Solomon and Aru islands, northern Australia.
Habitat Tropical rain forests.
Behavior It lives in trees, hanging from branches by its prehensile tail. It is active mainly at night, feeding on birds, frogs, and small tree mammals which it grasps firmly with its long front teeth. The female lays eggs, which she then incubates.

LITTLE KING BIRD OF PARADISE
Cicinnurus regius

Classification Class: Aves; Order: Passeriformes; Family: Paradiseidae.
Description It is the smallest member of the family. The head and back of the male are ruby red, the belly white. Two wire-like feathers protrude from the tail region and terminate in a disk of green feathers. The female has inconspicuously colored, barred plumage. Legs blue.
Distribution New Guinea and neighboring islands: Aru, Misool, Salawati, and Yapen.
Habitat Lowland and mountain tropical forests.
Behavior It settles in the treetops, feeding on arthropods and fruit. The males are polygamous, displaying and singing continuously to attract the females while perched in a tangle of branches some 50-65 ft (15-20 m) from the ground. After coupling with the favored male, each female devotes herself to incubating her 2 eggs for about 17 days. As far as is known, it is the only bird of paradise which nests in tree hollows.

LONG-BEAKED ECHIDNA
Zaglossus bruijni

Classification Class: Mammalia; Order: Monotremata; Family: Tachyglossidae.
Description Length of head and body 18-36 in (45-90 cm), weight 11-22 lb (5-10 kg). Color brown or black. The spines, buried in the thick hair, are hardly visible except on the flanks. Very long tube-like snout, curved downward.
Distribution New Guinea and smaller neighboring islands.
Habitat Mountains.
Behavior It feeds on ants, termites, and other insects, caught with the worm-like tongue. Lacking teeth, it grinds food against the horny covering of the palate. In case of danger, it buries itself very rapidly. The female lays the eggs in a ven-tral pouch where they hatch after 7-10 days. The young feed on the milk flowing from the mammary glands inside the pouch.

MATSCHIE'S TREE KANGAROO
Dendrolagus matschiei

Classification Class: Mammalia; Order: Marsupialia; Family: Macropodidae.
Description Length of head and body 21-32 in (52-81 cm), tail 17-37 in (42-93 cm), weight 17½-26½ lb (8-12 kg). Back reddish, muzzle, underparts and tail yellow. The tail does not serve as a support and the forelegs, provided with strong claws, are almost as long as the hind legs. The female has a pouch.
Distribution New Guinea.
Habitat Wooded zones.
Behavior The species of the genus *Dendrolagus* are the only tree kangaroos, moving with some dexterity among the branches, using the tail as a balance when jumping, and feeding on leaves and fruit. It is active at dusk and during the night. The female generally gives birth to a single young.

PALM COCKATOO
Probosciger aterrimus

Classification Class: Aves; Order: Psittaciformes; Family: Cacatuidae.
Description Also called the Great Black Cockatoo. Length 20-25 in (51-64 cm). A large parrot, its plumage entirely dark gray, with an exceptional erectile crest on the head. Naked crimson patches in front of the eyes; forehead and lores black.
Distribution In addition to New Guinea and adjacent islands, it is found locally on the Cape York peninsula in northern Australia.
Habitat Rain forests and wooded savannas up to an altitude of 4,200 ft (1,300 m).
Behavior It lives alone, in pairs or in small bands made up of 5-6. It can crack the hardest seeds, including palm kernels, with its very strong beak. It also feeds on fruit, berries, and leaf shoots. Very noisy, it often perches on a dead tree overlooking the forest and utters a powerful two-syllabled cry. It nests in a tree cavity, lining it with broken twigs. The female lays 1 egg.

PARADISE KINGFISHER
Tanysiptera galatea

Classification Class: Aves; Order: Coraciiformes; Family: Alcedinidae.
Description Length 13-17 in (33-43 cm). Blue-black on back and sides of head, with bright blue nape; underparts and rump silver-white. The long tail feathers form a bluish-white train, completely white in some races. Bill coral-red.

New Guinea

Although still incompletely explored, the flora of New Guinea is one of the richest in the world. Orchids alone total some 2,600 different species. Bilberries and rhododendrons, growing mainly in the mountains of the interior, have affinities with the plants found in Asia; and there are many species of nutmeg, clove, pepper and other spice-producing genera.

1 palm cockatoo
2 little king bird of paradise
3 pied imperial pigeon
4 paradise kingfisher
5 greater bird of paradise
6 Prince Rudolph's blue bird
   of paradise
7 tree kangaroo
8 striped opossum
9 Victoria crowned pigeon
10 New Guinea birdwing
11 long-beaked echidna
12 Vogelkop gardener bowerbird
13 Macleay's wallaby
14 green tree python
15 common cassowary
16 spotted cuscus

Distribution New Guinea and islands extending to Moluccas.

Habitat Tropical forests.

Behavior It watches for its prey from a well-concealed perch in the undergrowth; these consist mainly of insects caught as a result of sudden swoops either in flight or on the ground. When at rest, it flicks its tail nervously. In spite of the showy plumage, the bird is not easily discovered, but its presence is revealed by its characteristic musical trills, uttered in rapid succession when excited. It leads a solitary life, displaying aggressive, territorial behavior. It nests in a tree cavity or in termite nests in a tree; the brood consists of 5 eggs.

PIED IMPERIAL PIGEON
Ducula bicolor

Classification Class: Aves; Order: Columbiformes; Family: Columbidae.

Description Length 16-18 in (39-45 cm). Plumage entirely white, tinged here and there with yellow. Flight feathers and stripe on tip of tail black; the under-tail feathers may also be spotted black. Bill gray with yellow tip.

Distribution In addition to New Guinea, it is found throughout the Malay Archipelago and on the coasts of northern Australia.

Habitat Wooded zones, marshes and mangrove swamps.

Behavior It feeds on various types of fruit and berries, including wild figs and nutmegs. In order to find food it embarks on daily flights and seasonal migrations throughout its range. It alternates normal flight with sharp downward glides. When singing, it stretches and lowers the neck in characteristic manner. It nests among mangroves; the female lays one shiny white egg on a platform of sticks placed on a tree or shrub. Incubation lasts 21 days.

PRINCE RUDOLPH'S BLUE BIRD OF PARADISE
Paradisaea rudolphi

Classification Class: Aves; Order: Passeriformes; Family: Paradiseidae.

Description Length 12-14 in (30-35 cm). The male's body is blackish, the wings pale blue, and there is a cascade of blue feathers in the tail region; the two central tail feathers are wire-like and very long. Other notable features are the white bill and an interrupted orbital ring. The female has no ornamental feathers and the underparts are barred chestnut.

Distribution Southeastern New Guinea.

Habitat Mid-mountain tropical forests.

Behavior It leads a solitary life and does not display itself like others of its genus. The male sings from an exposed perch in the morning; when courting the female he perches with head upward, showing his feathers and uttering a series of vibrating calls. It eats fruit and arthropods, found in the treetops. In some areas it shows great confidence and is sometimes seen in gardens and on the edges of forests. Its population density varies greatly from one zone to another.

SPOTTED CUSCUS
Phalanger maculatus

Classification Class: Mammalia; Order: Marsupialia; Family: Phalangeridae.

Description Length of head and body 11-26 in (27-65 cm), tail 10-24 in (24-60 cm), weight up to 13 lb (6 kg). Thick fur, the color ranging from gray in the female to rust-red with light spots in the male. Rough scales cover the lower half of the naked tail, which is prehensile. The eyes are very large, typical of a nocturnal animal. The female has a marsupium.

Distribution New Guinea, Cape York peninsula in Queensland, Solomon Islands, Bismarck Archipelago.

Habitat Forests.

Behavior It is arboreal and nocturnal, resting by day in dense foliage or in a tree hollow, and climbing about very slowly at night in search of leaves and fruit; it also eats birds and small reptiles. When disturbed it gives out a penetrating and repellent odor. As a rule the female produces 1-2 young. The natives of New Guinea hunt it for its fur and for its flesh, which is considered something of a delicacy. Among its natural enemies are monitors and pythons.

STRIPED OPOSSUM
Dactylopsila trivirgata

Classification Class: Mammalia; Order: Marsupialia; Family: Phalangeridae.

Description Length of head and body 7-13 in (17-32 cm), tail 10-16 in (24-40 cm), weight 6 oz (170 g). Hair white with three black stripes running longitudinally down the body; the central stripe extends to the tail. The female has a marsupium.

Distribution New Guinea, Cape York peninsula in Queensland.

Habitat Tropical forests.

Behavior Strictly arboreal, it sleeps during the day in tree cavities, in nests of leaves, and ventures out at night for food which comprises leaves, fruit, and, above all, insects and their larvae; the last are rooted from under the dry bark of branches with the sharp incisor teeth or scooped out of holes in trees with the long and very thin fourth finger of the forefeet. When threatened, it gives out a characteristic foul odor, which serves as a means of defense.

VICTORIA CROWNED PIGEON
Goura victoria

Classification Class: Aves; Order: Columbiformes; Family: Columbidae.

Description Length 26-33 in (66-83 cm). It is one of the largest living pigeons, with blue-gray plumage and a lacy fan of feathers on the head. Breast dark purple-red; pale blue spot, outlined in purple, on wing. Iris, legs and feet red. Male and female have identical livery.

Distribution Northern New Guinea and small offshore islands; replaced by two related species in southern and eastern sectors.

Habitat Rain forests.

Behavior It spends most of its time on the ground, where it finds fallen fruit. When alarmed, it seeks refuge in trees, perching on broad horizontal branches. A deep, resonant cooing call signals its presence and maintains contact between partners or members of the same flock. The male invites the female to mate by raising and twisting his tail, while bending his head rapidly forward. The female is believed to lay a single egg.

VOLGELKOP GARDENER BOWERBIRD
Amblyornis inornatus

Classification Class: Aves; Order: Passeriformes; Family: Ptilonorhynchidae.

Description Length 9-10 in (22-25 cm). Both sexes have uniformly olive-brown plumage, without special markings. The bill is blackish and thinner than that of several related species; the head, however, is larger.

Distribution New Guinea, limited to certain mountains in the Vogelkop region (Amfak, Tamrau, Vandammen), from about 3,000-6,500 ft (1,000-2,000 m) high.

Habitat Rain forests.

Behavior During the breeding season the male attracts the female and mates with her in a bower, constructed on the ground. This has a circular roof of interwoven twigs attached to the main stem of a shrub; in front of the bower the male collects brightly colored shells, pebbles, flowers, and berries, which are purely ornamental. The bower is quite separate from the nest, which is built in a tree, probably by the female alone. Food is presumed to consist of fruit and insects.

New Zealand

ARCHEY'S FROG
Leiopelma archeyi

Classification Class: Amphibia; Order: Anura; Family: Leiopelmidae.

Description Length up to 2 in (5 cm). Color greenish to golden brown. It has no vocal sacs and therefore only emits calls of moderate volume.

Distribution New Zealand.

Habitat Mountain zones far away from water.

Behavior It feeds on insects and other invertebrates, caught by swiftly darting out its sticky tongue. The reproductive habits of this and other species of the genus *Leiopelmus*, all from New Zealand, are interesting. The female lays 2-8 large white eggs, not in water but under pebbles and fragments of wood scattered over the ground. After 6 weeks a completely formed young frog is hatched.

KAKAPO
Strigops habroptilus

Classification Class: Aves; Order: Psittaciformes; Family: Psittacidae.

Description Also known as the Owl Parrot. Length 24-25 in (60-64 cm). Large forest parrot with many primitive features. The form of the head is like that of an owl, with bristles at the base of the bill, and facial disks. Plumage green and yellowish, with wavy markings; barred tail.

Distribution One of the rarest New Zealand birds; the only known surviving populations live in the Milford district of the South Island and on adjacent Stewart Island.

Habitat Established forests and moors, in mountain zones.

Behavior Virtually incapable of flying, it is confined to the ground, moving by means of hops or short glides. By day it remains hidden inside a fissure or in a burrow dug for the purpose. The bird feeds on moss, ferns, fungi, and various plants; sometimes it catches lizards. The female lays 2-4 eggs at the bottom of a hole lined with slivers of wood and feathers. Incubation is probably the responsibility of the female alone.

KEA
Nestor notabilis

Classification Class: Aves; Order: Psittaciformes; Family: Psittacidae.

Description Length 18-19 in (45-48 cm). Large parrot with greenish brown plum-age, bordered with black; the feathers of the rump and back have an orange-red base. The square tail is blue-green with a dark band near the tip; wing margin blue. The bill is sharply hooked.

Distribution South Island of New Zealand.

Habitat Meadows and mountain moors, edges of forests.

Behavior It normally lives beyond the upper limit of the treeline. In addition to shoots, leaves, and wild fruit, it feeds on insects and, in winter, on animal carrion. At one time it was thought to attack and kill grazing lambs, which caused it to be locally persecuted. It nests on the ground, in a rock cleft or sometimes in a hollow tree stump. The 2-4 eggs are incubated for 21-28 days mainly by the female. The chicks leave the nest after 13-14 weeks.

KIWI
Apteryx australis

Classification Class: Aves; Order: Apterigiformes; Family: Apterigidae.

Description Length 26-28 in (66-71 cm). The body is covered with coarse, drooping brown feathers. The long bill is slightly curved, with prominent bristles at the base, varying in color from ivory white to pink. The legs are flesh-colored or dark brown.

Distribution Stewart Island and North Island of New Zealand.

Habitat Forests and moors.

Behavior Unable to fly, it spends the day in complex burrows dug beneath the roots of trees, emerging during the night to look for food in the form of worms and insects, locating them by touch with the sensitive facial hairs and by its keen sense of smell. It nests in underground burrows. The female lays one large egg which is incubated by the male; this takes 75-80 days, after which period the female may lay a second egg before tending to her chick. On North Island the kiwi has even settled in areas modified by human activity.

RIFLEMAN
Acanthisitta chloris

Classification Class: Aves; Order: Passeriformes; Family: Acanthisittidae.

Description Length 3 in (8 cm). Tiny forest bird similar to a wren, with greenish back and white underparts. Distinguishing marks are a yellow wing band and a long white eyebrow. The tail is very short and the tip of the slender, pointed bill is turned up. The female has brown, striped plumage.

Distribution New Zealand and adjacent small islands.

Habitat Forests, plantations, and zones with trees.

Behavior It clambers nimbly up and down tree trunks, probing fissures of wood and the moss and lichen growing on bark for the insects and spiders which constitute its diet. It nests at varying heights, up to 60 ft (18 m) from the ground, in the protection of a large branch. The nest is lined with feathers and has a side entrance; both parents incubate the 2-4 eggs for 20-21 days annually; the nestlings of the first brood generally assist the parents in feeding those of the second. Polygamy is frequent.

SOOTY SHEARWATER
Puffinus griseus

Classification Class: Aves; Order: Procellariiformes; Family: Procellariidae.

Description Length 16-20 in (41-51 cm). Pelagic bird with wholly dark plumage; in flight it is possible to glimpse some silvery feathers beneath the wings. After the seasonal molt the upper parts are gray-black, the underparts gray; then the plumage turns brown.

Distribution New Zealand and adjacent islands, also small islands off the shores of Tasmania and coasts of southeastern Australia; it also nests on the Falkland Islands and on some islands belonging to Chile.

Habitat Open ocean, cliffs, and rocky islets.

Behavior It takes off from the surface of the water by skittering a short distance. As a rule it alternates flapping flight with brief sideslips, but in a strong wind it indulges in long glides. It feeds on oily refuse, crustaceans, and small fish. A single egg is laid in a burrow scooped in the shelter of plants, and the chick remains there for about 97 days. Around the nest both parents give out raucous cries composed of rhythmical notes in which air is alternately indrawn and expelled.

TAKAHE
Notornis mantelli

Classification Class: Aves; Order: Gruiformes; Family: Rallidae.

Description Length about 26 in (63-65 cm). Dimensions of a turkey. Showy green and bright blue plumage, heavy bill and frontal plaque both red. Large legs of same color. The wings are rudimentary so that the bird is incapable of flight.

Distribution New Zealand. Extinct on North Island, in 1948 a small group was found surviving in a small valley on South Island.

Habitat Dense grassy vegetation and forests near Lake Te Anau, at altitudes of about 2,000-3,300 ft (600-1,000 m).

Behavior It is extremely retiring and only a few details are known about it. Apparently members of each pair keep in

New Zealand

The flora of New Zealand is somewhat poor in species, little more than 1,700 in all. Some genera, such as the ranunculi and gentians, show a striking resemblance to these flowers in Eurasia, but there are also many, like the evergreen Pittosporum, which have obvious affinities with Australian plants. Particularly curious and spectacular, too, are the tree ferns which grow prolifically in the forests.

1 kea
2 red fox
3 yellowhead
4 tui
5 wattled crow
6 sooty shearwater
7 tuatara
8 kiwi
9 weta
10 Archey's frog
11 weka
12 kakapo
13 rifleman
14 takahe

contact with each other by means of characteristic melodious duets. The nest is a well-protected, small construction in the grass. The female normally lays 1-3 eggs (but sometimes up to 4), creamy white with brown and mauve spots. The chicks have black plumage and a white mark in the wing region.

TUATARA
Sphenodon punctatus
Classification Class: Reptilia; Order: Rhynchocephalia; Suborder: Sphenodontoidea; Family: Sphenodontidae.
Description Length up to 26 in (65 cm), weight up to about 2 lb (1 kg). Resembles a large lizard with an enormous head, a strong tail and a long crest of mobile plates down the length of the back to the tip of the tail. Brown or grayish with yellowish spots.
Distribution Island of Karewa and another 20 small islands in the New Zealand archipelago.
Habitat Shrubs and dense vegetation of ferns.
Behavior The Tuatara is the sole survivor of the entire order of Rhynchocephalia. It is some 200 million years old yet during that time it has changed little from its ancestors, so that it is regarded as a "living fossil." Active at night, it normally feeds on worms, snails, insects, lizards, and birds' eggs. It avoids the sun by day, sheltering in ground cavities, showing a marked preference for burrows excavated by Shearwaters, living alongside them in perfect harmony. It is unique among reptiles (cold-blooded animals which need heat in order to become active) in that it is active even when the weather is cold. The female lays 2-15 eggs in a burrow, covering them with earth and vegetation, and then taking no further care of them; the eggs hatch after 13-15 months.

TUI
Prosthemadera novaeseelandiae
Classification Class: Aves; Order: Passeriformes; Family: Meliphagidae.
Description Length about 12 in (29-31 cm). Plumage metallic green with purple and bronze tints; back and scapulars brown. Two tufts of white feathers, curving over the throat like a clerical collar, have caused it to be known locally as the Parson Bird.
Distribution New Zealand and neighboring islands: Stewart, Auckland, Chatham, and Kermadec.
Habitat Forests, parks, and gardens.
Behavior It has learned, better than other native species, how to adapt to modified natural habitats, living alongside hu-

mans in some places. On Auckland Island it nests in pines and other exotic trees growing in built-up areas. It is an excellent singer; the calls vary from zone to zone and include imitated notes. It feeds on insects, fruit, and nectar. At varying heights from the ground it builds a massive cup-shaped nest, lined with grass and moss, where the female lays 2-4 eggs. While she incubates, the male continues singing from a nearby tree.

WATTLED CROW
Callaeus cinerea
Classification Class: Aves; Order: Passeriformes; Family: Callaeidae.
Description Length 15-18 in (38-45 cm). Large blue-gray bird resembling a magpie; wings and tail brown; velvety black stripes at base of bill and around eyes. Two big, fleshy wattles hang from either side of the beak.
Distribution New Zealand; on North Island the local race has blue wattles, on South Island, much rarer, is a race with orange wattles.
Habitat Mountain forests.
Behavior It flies seldom and only for a short distance. Much more typically, it advances over the ground with long, vigorous hops. Food consists basically of vegetable matter, leaves, flowers, and fruit sometimes collected with the foot, like a parrot. Pairs remain united throughout the year, building a rough open nest of interwoven twigs, moss and bark. The 2-3 eggs hatch after the female alone has incubated them for about 25 days. The nestlings are fed with a mixture of chopped fruit and leaves.

WEKA
Gallirallus australis
Classification Class: Aves; Order: Gruiformes; Family: Rallidae.
Description Also known as the Wood Rail. Length 20-21 in (50-53 cm). The size of a chicken, it has a sturdy beak and long legs suitable for running and digging, a compensation for the fact that it is flightless; the wings are rudimentary. Brown and black plumage, the color varying somewhat from one race to another.
Distribution New Zealand. Introduced successfully in 1872 also to Stewart and Macquarie Islands, where today it is numerous.
Habitat Coastal vegetation, swamps.
Behavior Active around dusk, but inquisitive by nature, it often emerges from the thickets and looks for food in the open. In addition to invertebrates and small fish, it feeds on refuse and preys on rodents, eggs, and fledglings of sea birds, digging into burrows with its strong feet.

The various pairs live separately and build a cup-shaped nest of grass and leaves in the undergrowth. The 3-6 eggs, with brown and purple spots, are incubated by both parents for 20-27 days.

WRYBILL
Anarhynchus frontalis
Classification Class: Aves; Order: Charadriiformes; Family: Charadriidae.
Description Length 8 in (20 cm). Gray above, white below; in the breeding season there is a dark pectoral band. The bill is unique in the bird world, the tip being curved toward the right.
Distribution New Zealand; nests in South Island, winters in North Island.
Habitat Riverbeds in summer, seacoasts in winter.
Behavior The shape of the bill enables it to probe under stones for small invertebrates. It nests on the gravel shores of rivers. Occasionally it moves in characteristic fashion by hopping on one leg. The 2-3 pear-shaped eggs hatch after 30 days' incubation.

YELLOWHEAD
Mohoua ochrocephala
Classification Class: Aves; Order: Passeriformes; Family: Sylviidae.
Description Length 6 in (15 cm). Small forest bird with bright yellow colors on the head and on the underparts; wings and back are yellowish-brown. The tips of the tail feathers look threadbare, with the barbless rachises (shafts) protruding.
Distribution South Island of New Zealand; its presence on neighboring Stewart Island is nowadays doubtful.
Habitat Forests.
Behavior It spends a lot of time in treetops where it is notable chiefly for its varied and musical song, rather like that of a canary. It hunts insects and larvae by exploring leaves, branches, and the highest part of trunks, rummaging in particular through heaps of fallen detritus in the forks of branches. Digging with one foot, it anchors itself to the bark with the aid of its spiny tail. The nest of moss and spiders' webs is built in a tree hollow. The 3-4 eggs laid there by the female are incubated by her for about 21 days. Many males are polygamous.

Islands of Oceania

AKIALOA
Hemignathus obscurus

Classification Class: Aves; Order: Passeriformes; Family: Drepanididae.

Description Length 7 in (17 cm). One of the group of so-called Hawaiian honeycreepers. Upper parts brilliant green, underparts more opaque; wings and tail brown. It has a characteristic sickle-shaped bill, about 2 in (5-6 cm) long.

Distribution Today it survives for certain only on the islands of Kauai and Hawaii, where it is still in grave danger of extinction.

Habitat Tropical mountain forests.

Behavior It spends most of its time exploring tree bark, as the particular structure of the bill enables it to probe the deepest clefts to extract insects and larvae. Occasionally it sips flower nectar. Only one nest of this species has been observed and described; this was built in a fork at the tip of a branch in a tall tree and contained one nestling.

Note The Pseudonestor or Maui Parrotbill (*Pseudonestor xanthophrys*) is another green-plumaged honeycreeper, with a very broad bill which is hooked like that of a parrot. It hangs from branches and slices through the bark in order to reach the holes harboring insect larvae, on which it feeds exclusively. It has been found only in the mountain forests of the island of Maui.

BLACK-FOOTED ALBATROSS
Diomedea nigripes

Classification Class: Aves; Order: Procellariiformes; Family: Diomedeidae.

Description Length 28-36 in (71-91 cm), wingspan about 6½ ft (2 m). Sooty brown with white areas at base of bill, on flight feathers and sometimes on the underside of the tail. Bill and legs are black. In the young the upper side of the tail is white.

Distribution It nests on the Hawaiian Islands. It is found over the Central and North Pacific from latitudes 20° to 55°N

Habitat Ocean and sandy shores of islands.

Behavior It follows in the wake of large ships, waiting to swoop on refuse, and is a familiar traveling companion of Hawaiian sailors. It also feeds on fish and molluscs. When settling on the waves, it holds its wings half-open for some time, in an attitude generally used for courtship. It nests in October, in colonies, on sandy beaches. Amid a constant uproar of cries, the female of each pair lays a single egg in a conical nest of sand and mud. The chick does not join the adults in the sea until August.

BLUE LORY
Vini peruviana

Classification Class: Aves; Order: Psittaciformes; Family: Psittacidae.

Description Length 7 in (18 cm). Dark blue-mauve, with auriculars, throat and upper breast white, in striking contrast. Bill and legs orange-yellow.

Distribution Today it is restricted to the Society Islands, and the Tuamotu and Cook Islands, in the South Pacific.

Habitat Tropical forests, palm plantations, gardens.

Behavior Given its rarity, the species has been little studied in the wild. It is believed that the cutting down of forests and the introduction of predatory species have led to its disappearance on most of the Society Islands. On Tuamotu and Bora Bora it frequents palm plantations and shrubberies near the coast, while on Aitutaki it has been seen in gardens and plantations and on wooded hills. Very active in its search for food, it clambers through the foliage and flies fairly rapidly from tree to tree, making a typical rustling sound with its wings. It feeds on the nectar of flowers and of coconut palms. It may nest either in a tree cavity or out in the open, in nests abandoned by other birds. The 2 eggs are incubated by both parents for 21 days.

Note Kuhl's Lory (*Vini kuhli*) is another small member of the Psittacidae endemic to the South Pacific. Its showy plumage is green and red, and it inhabits some of the Line Islands as well as Rimatara (Austral Ridge), where it enjoys special protection and is known as the Queen's Parakeet.

BLUE-TAILED SKINK
Emoia cyanura

Classification Class: Reptilia; Order: Squamata; Suborder: Sauria; Family: Scincidae.

Description Dark brown with lighter longitudinal stripes and a bluish tail.

Distribution Along the Indopacific island belt.

Habitat Coastal zones.

Behavior It is one of the smallest reptiles ever to have reached the islands of the Pacific and Indian Oceans, presumably traveling on pieces of floating wood. It is able to climb and also to dive and swim in the sea to catch crabs; it also feeds on small fish left in pools along the beach at low tide. It breeds throughout the year, the female laying 2 eggs each time.

FAIRY TERN
Gygis alba

Classification Class: Aves; Order: Charadriiformes; Family: Sternidae.

Description Length 11-13 in (27-33 cm). A seagull which is unmistakable with its completely snow-white plumage and black orbital rings, like spectacles. The bill is black, bluish at the base; the feet have yellowish webbing.

Distribution Widely found on the islands of the South Pacific. It also inhabits the equatorial belts of the Atlantic and Indian Oceans.

Habitat Seas, coastal lagoons and coral islands.

Behavior It flies gracefully some 50-65 ft (15-20 m) above the surface of the sea, diving in now and then to catch small fish, cephalopods, and also insects. When fishing it often emits a long, high-pitched cry. The female lays and incubates one egg on a bare, slender branch of a tree; incubation lasts 36 days. The newborn chick remains for a few days in the tree, then falls or jumps to the ground.

GRAY-BREASTED SILVER-EYE
Zosterops lateralis

Classification Class: Aves; Order: Passeriformes; Family: Zosteropidae.

Description Length 4½ in (11 cm). Olive-green, underparts gray and yellow. A distinctive mark is a prominent ring of white feathers around the eye.

Distribution Throughout Oceania, from Australia and New Zealand to the islands of central Polynesia.

Habitat Zones with trees and shrubs, open forests, plantations and parks.

Behavior It is commonly found in many environments, including cultivated areas. It forms small groups around trees and bushes, hunting insects or looking for flowers and fruit. The tubular tongue, with its brush, is ideal for collecting nectar, while the pointed beak perforates the skin of ripe fruit to get at the pulp. It builds a tiny nest attached to a vertical stem; this is quite a work of art, consisting of blades of grass interwoven with hairs and spiders' webs. The female lays 2-4 turquoise eggs, which are incubated for 12-14 days.

GREAT FRIGATE BIRD
Fregata minor

Classification Class: Aves; Order: Pelecaniformes; Family: Fregatidae.

Description Length 34-40 in (86-101 cm), wingspan up to 7½ ft (2.3 m). Large seabird with wings folded at an angle, forked tail and hooked bill. Male's plumage almost entirely black, female's throat and breast white. During the breeding

Islands of Oceania

Alongside New Caledonia, with its luxuriant flora which includes many characteristic local forms, we find innumerable remote oceanic islands with comparatively little plant growth, mainly consisting of palms, screw-pines and a few herbaceous species. Seeds tend to be carried from one island to another by birds rather than by the wind or the waves. Breadfruit and eucalyptus trees also grow freely. The Hawaiian Islands, too, boast a rich variety of plants, with about 1,200 different species.

1 iiwi
2 Hawaiian goose
3 Hawaiian hawk
4 fairy tern
5 black-footed albatross
6 Kuhl's lory
7 blue lory
8 apapane
9 akialoa
10 rainbow dove
11 kamehameha
12 blue-tailed skink
13 apapane
14 pseudonestor

season the male's throat pouch turns bright red and can be inflated.

Distribution Coasts and tropical islands of central and western Pacific; it is found locally, too, in the Indian and Atlantic Oceans.

Habitat Oceans and coastal waters, beaches, wooded cliffs.

Behavior Because the plumage is permeable, it cannot dive or remain too long in the water. A tireless flyer, it is able to accelerate very suddenly and perform a variety of acrobatics, pursuing and attacking boobies and other seabirds, and forcing them to let go of their food, seizing it on the wing. It nests in treetops and bushes, where the male puts on a varied display to attract the female. The single egg and the chick that hatches from it are cared for by both parents; incubation lasts about 6 weeks.

HAWAIIAN GOOSE
Branta sandvicensis

Classification Class: Aves; Order: Anseriformes; Family: Anatidae.

Description Length 23-26½ in (58-67 cm), weight 4½-6½ lb (2-3 kg). It is the largest bird native to the Hawaiian Islands, known locally as the Nene. Face and top of head are black, sides of neck reddish, with prominent wrinkles. Back and breast variously shaded brown, abdomen white.

Distribution Frequently reported on the verge of extinction, a small population survives today on Hawaii and on the volcanic terrain of Mauna Kea and Mauna Loa.

Habitat Semiarid highlands.

Behavior It feeds at ground level on grass and small fruits. In the rainy season it comes down to lava valleys where the grass is more tender and here it raises its young. Because of its unusual habits, the interdigital membranes have atrophied and the feet have become correspondingly stronger. It builds a nest in a depression on the ground; the female lays 3-8 eggs and incubates them for 30 days.

HAWAIIAN HAWK
Buteo solitarius

Classification Class: Aves; Order: Falconiformes; Family: Accipitridae.

Description Length 15-18 in (39-46 cm). The plumage, somewhat variable, may be blackish-brown (dark phase), tawny (intermediate phase) or whitish with dark spots on the underparts (light phase).

Distribution It is found only on the island of Hawaii, but in considerable numbers.

Habitat Forests and their edges, at altitudes of 2,000-5,000 ft (600-1,500 m).

Behavior It catches rats and other rodents by swooping from low perches. Sometimes it manages to catch a Common Mynah *(Acridotheres tristis),* a member of the starling family (Sturnidae) which feeds at ground level, but its predatory activities are negligible compared with those of the indigenous forest birds. It performs aerial displays, flying in broad circles at a great height. It builds a bulky nest of branches and sticks in a tree, not very far from the ground.

IIWI
Vestiaria coccinea

Classification Class: Aves; Order: Passeriformes; Family: Drepanididae.

Description Length 5-6 in (12-15 cm). Body bright scarlet, with black wings and tail. Long pink bill, strongly curved in a very individual manner. The chicks have greenish-yellow plumage with black spots.

Distribution Widespread throughout the Hawaiian archipelago.

Habitat Tropical forests.

Behavior This honeycreeper feeds on the nectar of flowers which are inaccessible to other species, with a long tubular corolla. It supplements this diet with insects. It lives in small flocks, but defends its nesting territory primarily by singing, showing no hesitation in chasing away rivals. During courtship it emits strident, dissonant calls. It nests in trees, the female laying 1-3 eggs and incubating them for 14 days.

Note The Apapane *(Himatione sanguinea)* is another honeycreeper with red and black plumage, still fairly numerous in the Hawaiian Islands. It varies from the Iiwi in having white under-tail coverts and a different bill. Highly gregarious, it feeds principally on caterpillars and insects. When it flies the wings produce a typical buzzing sound. It nests in low bushes.

KAGU
Rhynochetos jubatus

Classification Class: Aves; Order: Gruiformes; Family: Rhynochetidae.

Description Length 22-24 in (55-60 cm). It looks like a heron, but is not a close relative. Ash-gray, it is adorned with a long erectile tuft. Conspicuous brown and white bars on the flight feathers. Bill and legs are orange-red.

Distribution Exclusive to New Caledonia, where only a very small population survives and is in danger of extinction.

Habitat Mountain forests.

Behavior It uses its short rounded wings more for purposes of display than for flying. Nocturnal by habit, it walks and runs nimbly, always touching the ground. It eats worms, insects and snails, breaking

open the shell with its strong bill. The call, rather like a roar, can be heard mainly at night. During courtship the partners face each other and dance in an upright position, raising their crests and displaying the spectacular barring on the outspread wings. Both parents incubate the single egg for 36 days.

KAMEHAMEHA
Pyrameis tammeamea

Classification Class: Insecta; Order: Lepidoptera; Family: Nymphalidae.

Description Wingspan about 4 in (10 cm). Orange, wingtips black with white spots. It is very closely related to the Painted Lady *(Vanessa cardui),* found in Europe and in many other parts of the world.

Distribution Exclusive to the Hawaiian archipelago.

Habitat Forests.

Behavior When settled, it keeps its wings vertical; in this position the drab colors and the toothed wing margins give it the appearance of a dead leaf, hardly recognizable to an insect-eating bird which relies on vision to identify prey.

PHILIPPINES RAIL
Rallus philippensis

Classification Class: Aves; Order: Gruiformes; Family: Rallidae.

Description Length 10 in (25 cm). Brown, speckled with white, on back; underparts closely barred blackish and white, throat uniformly gray. A chestnut band crosses the eye and nape, in contrast to the prominent white eyebrow.

Distribution Tropical islands of central Pacific, Indonesia, New Guinea, Australia and New Zealand.

Habitat Open grassy zones, fresh-water and brackish water swamps, gardens.

Behavior It is active by day and less shy than other members of its family. It is often to be seen scurrying rapidly from one tuft of plants to another. Reluctant to fly, it will cover only short distances, legs dangling. It feeds on insects and larvae, molluscs, crustaceans and vegetable matter. When walking, it flicks its tail rhythmically. Once or twice a year the female lays 4-7 eggs in a well concealed nest, and these are incubated by both parents for 19-25 days; the chicks are covered in thick black down.

POLYNESIAN STARLING
Aplonis tabuensis

Classification Class: Aves; Order: Passeriformes; Family: Sturnidae.

Description Length 8 in (19 cm). Stocky gray-brown bird with very dark upper parts; underparts have faint light stripes, throat and lower abdomen slightly tawny. Color of bill varies from brown to yellow, according to geographical distribution.

Distribution Central Polynesia, from Santa Cruz to Fiji, Tonga and Samoa.

Habitat Forests and inhabited areas.

Behavior Arboreal and strictly linked to the forest on the larger Polynesian islands, but found almost anywhere, including villages and suburbs, on smaller islands. It settles in modest flocks in the higher parts of trees, feeding on small fruits, berries and insects. Its vocal repertory comprises a wide range of calls, including a characteristic whistling trill. It makes its nest in a tree hollow or in rotting wood, the female normally laying 2 eggs with a dark-streaked bluish shell.

PRITCHARD'S SCRUB FOWL
Megapodius pritchardii

Classification Class: Aves; Order: Galliformes; Family: Megapodidae.

Description Length 15 in (38 cm). Large ground bird with dark ash-gray plumage and a lighter nape; rump and wings reddish-brown. A small grayish cap contrasts with the sturdy yellow bill; legs orange-red.

Distribution It is found exclusively on the island of Niuafo'ou in central Polynesia, but has recently been introduced as well to the island of Tofahi.

Habitat Semiwooded volcanic zones.

Behavior It obtains food by raking through fallen foliage, seeking small invertebrates, fruit and plant detritus. It resorts to flight only if compelled to do so. The female lays her eggs in holes scooped in the volcanic soil, at a depth of 3-6 ft (1-2 m); she then covers them with earth and abandons them, letting the heat of the sun incubate them effectively. The eggs hatch after at least 26 days; as soon as they emerge into the open air, the chicks are immediately independent and even capable of flying.

RAINBOW DOVE
Ptilinopus perousii

Classification Class: Aves; Order: Columbiformes; Family: Columbidae.

Description Length 9 in (23 cm). Small fruit-eating, tree-dwelling dove with brightly colored plumage, different in either sex. In the wild the male appears to be creamy yellow, with the rear parts of the body darker. Seen close up, the purple colors of the nape, under-tail coverts and a broad band across the back stand out. The breast is delicately speckled pink. Female and young are more opaque and greenish.

Distribution Pacific islands: Samoa, Fiji, Tonga and smaller islands.

Habitat Tropical forests.

Behavior It is fairly well camouflaged in the play of light and shade so typical of the jungle. It forms flocks in the treetops, where it adopts a dominant, aggressive attitude toward other competing species. It feeds on berries and wild fruit. The call consists of a repeated single note which is alternatively speeded up and slowed down. It nests on a fragile platform built very high up in the foliage. The female lays 1-2 eggs.

RED-TAILED TROPIC BIRD
Phaethon rubricauda

Classification Class: Aves; Order: Pelecaniformes; Family: Phaethontidae.

Description Also known as the Phaethon. Length 36-40 in (91-100 cm). Plumage mostly white with a large, slightly curved coral-red bill and two extremely long red tail feathers which protrude far beyond the tip of the tail, like a train. The younger birds lack these tail feathers and have barred plumage and a black bill.

Distribution Tropical and subtropical zones of the Pacific and Indian Oceans.

Habitat Oceans, beaches and rocky islands.

Behavior It flies with very powerful wingbeats over the sea and dives from a height into the water to catch its prey, which includes fish and cephalopod molluscs. When swimming, it keeps the long tail feathers raised. It nests alone or in colonies of varying numbers, ranging from a few dozen to several thousand. On atolls it settles on low beaches with scrub growth, and on volcanic islands it occupies cliffs. The female lays 1-2 eggs on the ground, these being fiercely defended by both parents during the 28-day incubation.

RED-HEADED PARROT FINCH
Erythrura cyaneovirens

Classification Class: Aves; Order: Passeriformes; Family: Estrildidae.

Description Length 4 in (10 cm). Small seed-eating bird, bright green with scarlet rump and tail. The forehead is red, while throat and breast have lovely bluish tints.

Distribution Islands of Fiji, Samoa and New Hebrides.

Habitat Forest edges, plantations, grassy zones, ricefields, and gardens.

Behavior It flies in a characteristically uneven, fluttering manner, with very rapid wingbeats. It feeds mainly on the seeds of certain grasses, both wild and cultivated, but also insects scooped from under the bark of large trees; it causes much damage to rice crops. The big cup-shaped nest, with a side entrance, is built in a thick bush; the 3-4 spherical eggs have a white shell.

SILKTAIL
Lamprolia victoriae

Classification Class: Aves; Order: Passeriformes; Family: Sylviidae.

Description Length 5 in (12 cm). It is considered by some to be related to the birds of paradise. The silky plumage is black and metallic blue, the rump and much of the tail velvety white.

Distribution Fiji.

Habitat Mountain forests.

Behavior The bird is always on the move, making short darting flights through the lower layers of the forest, suddenly swooping on small insects in the foliage or on the ground; it feeds on termites and cockroaches. The bird seldom frequents the treetops. It builds a solid nest of vegetable fibers, spiders' webs and pieces of bark, artistically interwoven with feathers and green leaves. The single egg is pale pink, with faint or purple speckles.

TOOTHBILLED PIGEON
Didunculus strigirostris

Classification Class: Aves; Order: Columbiformes; Family: Columbidae.

Description Length 13-19 in (32-48 cm). Various details of structure and behavior make this bird a real ornithological puzzle. Its extraordinary orange-red bill, hooked and sawlike on the inner edge, links it directly to the celebrated dodo of Mauritius, which became extinct between the seventeenth and eighteenth century. The plumage is black with green reflections, the rump and underwings chestnut, the legs and feet red.

Distribution Found exclusively on the Samoan islands.

Habitat Tropical mountain forests.

Behavior It feeds on fruit and berries belonging to certain native trees that only grow in mature forest, apparently employing techniques normally adopted by parrots, tearing off the food with its bill and using one foot to carry it to the ground. It spends part of the day on the ground and part in trees. The flight pattern is heavy and cumbersome. It is not yet known for certain whether it nests on the ground or in a tree.

ARCTIC

The North Pole and the surrounding Arctic regions do not constitute a continental land mass. They consist of the northernmost outposts of Europe, Asia and North America, the islands encircling them and, above all, the huge Arctic Ocean, the surface of which consists mainly of floating ice.

The boundaries between land and sea are therefore not clearly demarcated in these polar regions. The common denominators are the expanses of ice and the extremely low temperatures, to which living organisms must adapt. Many species in fact lead a kind of amphibious existence, such as seals and walruses among the mammals, and gulls, gannets and auks among the birds. For all these animals food comes from the sea in the form of fish, molluscs and crustaceans. But a few find sustenance on land, such as herbivorous lemmings and reindeer, and that giant of carnivores, the polar bear.

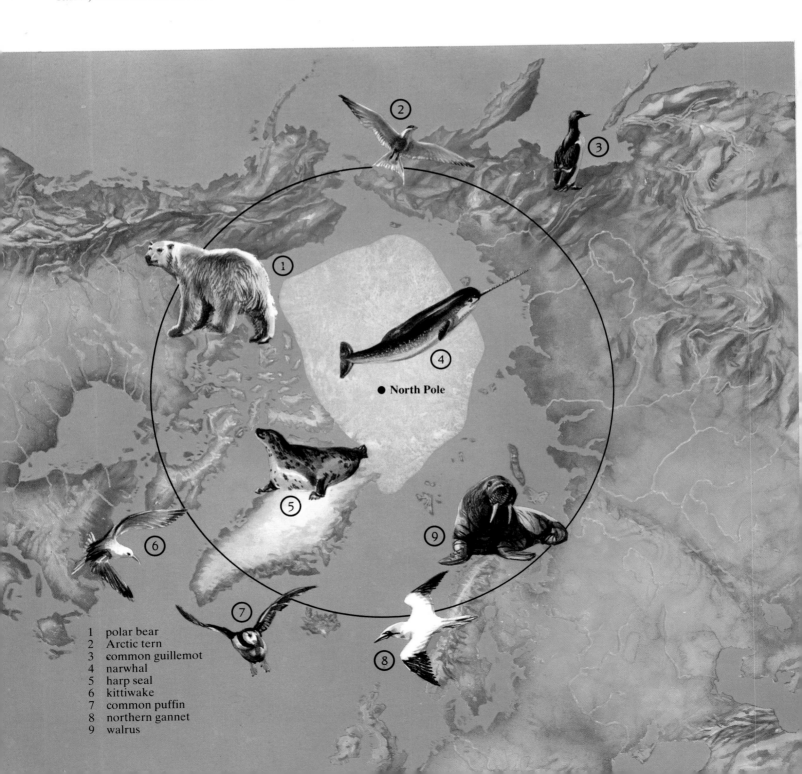

1 polar bear
2 Arctic tern
3 common guillemot
4 narwhal
5 harp seal
6 kittiwake
7 common puffin
8 northern gannet
9 walrus

ANTARCTIC

The map of the southern hemisphere shows a greater area occupied by sea than by land masses, but in the extreme south, around the Pole, there is an actual continent. This is Antarctica, completely covered by a thick layer of ice, which makes it completely uninhabitable for plant and animal species. Only at the extreme edges, where the ice merges with the waters of the ocean, have a few rare plants managed to establish themselves, and several animal species found living conditions bearable.

The surrounding seas, however, teem with life, providing sufficient food for many species which come in to shore regularly at certain times of year, mainly in order to breed. Among these animals are certain species of seal and, particularly, penguins.

Conditions on some remote southern islands, such as Kerguelen, Crozet and Macquarie, are less extreme than in Antarctica, and here there is a richer variety of plant and animal life.

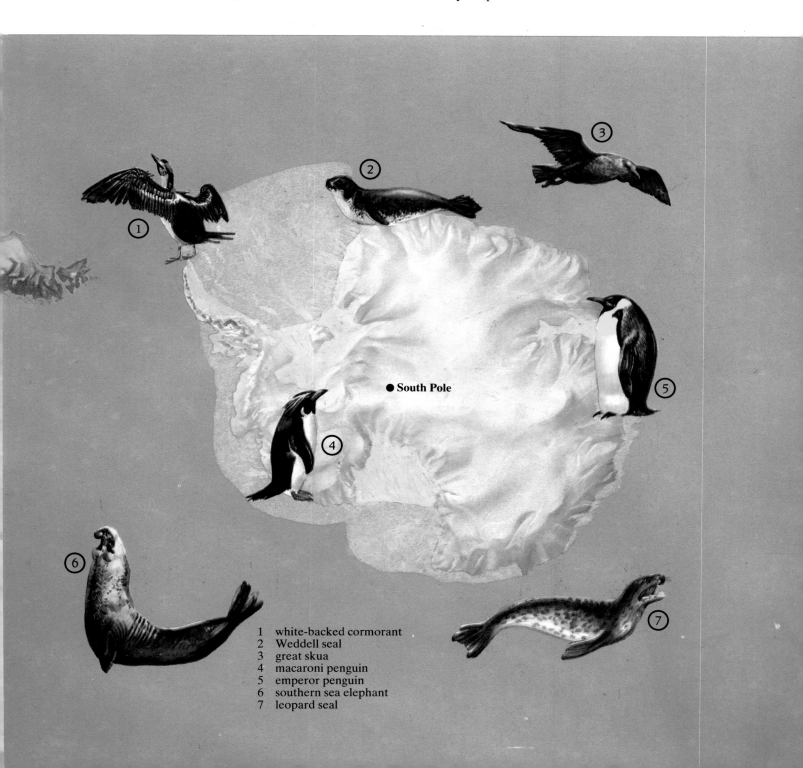

1   white-backed cormorant
2   Weddell seal
3   great skua
4   macaroni penguin
5   emperor penguin
6   southern sea elephant
7   leopard seal

Tundra

ARCTIC HARE
Lepus arcticus

Classification Class: Mammalia; Order: Lagomorpha; Family: Leporidae.

Description Also known as the Polar Hare. Total length 27 in (69 cm), weight about 12 lb (5.4 kg). Gray or brown with white tail in summer, white with black ear-tips in winter. In the extreme north of its range it stays white for the whole year.

Distribution Northern Canada and Greenland.

Habitat Tundra.

Behavior In winter it digs in the frozen snow to get at moss and lichen, scraping them from rocks with its incisor teeth. It also eats meat; attracted to the bait set in traps for foxes, it often gets caught in them. In summer groups of over one hundred feed, sleep and bathe together in the sun. The female gives birth to up to 8 leverets after a gestation of about 50 days.

BRENT GOOSE
Branta bernicla

Classification Class: Aves; Order: Anseriformes; Family: Anatidae.

Description Length 22-23 in (56-59 cm), weight 2½-3½ lb (1.2-1.6 kg). The male is bigger than the female. Upper parts gray-brown, belly gray; head, neck and breast black, hindquarters white, two characteristic white spots at sides of neck.

Distribution Siberia, Canada and Greenland. It winters along the northern shores of the Atlantic and Pacific Oceans.

Habitat Rocky tundra, seacoasts.

Behavior It feeds on vegetation and small molluscs. Gregarious, it assembles in enormous flocks which do not break up even in the breeding season. The nest, situated in low vegetation or among rocks, consists of a shallow depression in the tundra soil, lined with feathers, moss and lichen. The 2-8 eggs are incubated by the female alone for 24-26 days. The goslings, often raised communally by different couples joining together, remain in the family circle until the next brood.

GRAY PHALAROPE
Phalaropus fulicarius

Classification Class: Aves; Order: Charadriiformes; Family: Phalaropididae.

Description Length about 8 in (20 cm). In summer the female, slightly bigger than the male, has brighter colors than her companion, but in winter the two sexes look alike. Upper parts brown, with blackish spots and stripes, underparts reddish; top of head black, cheeks white.

Distribution It nests in the Arctic regions and winters at sea, ranging to the southern hemisphere.

Habitat Tundra in summer; open sea, bays, estuaries and coasts in winter.

Behavior It eats crustaceans, molluscs, insect larvae, algae, moss and small fish. In the sea it catches crustaceans and jellyfish, often in the wake of whales. Graceful and confident, it is both an excellent swimmer and a rapid flyer. The female, completely reversing normal roles, couples with several males, taking the initiative in courtship. The 3-4 eggs hatch after an incubation of 23-24 days. The male alone builds the nest, incubates the eggs and raises the young.

Note The Northern Phalarope *(Phalaropus lobatus)* is smaller than the Gray Phalarope, measuring 7 in (18 cm) in length, and has a wider range over the Arctic zones of Eurasia and North America. Habitat and behavior of the two species do not differ substantially.

HUDSON'S COLLARED LEMMING
Dicrostonyx hudsonius

Classification Class: Mammalia; Order: Rodentia; Family: Cricetidae.

Description Total length 4-7 in (10.2-17.8 cm), weight 2 oz (57 g). Grayish brown with a black stripe along the back; in winter completely white. The third and fourth toes of the forefeet have a double claw which grows in fall and is shed in spring. This unique feature among mammals is believed to be an adaptation to facilitate intensive digging activity in frozen snow, which the animal is obliged to undertake in winter to keep open its underground burrows. Like all lemmings, it has no auricles and the ear can be sealed with a tuft of hair to prevent soil getting inside.

Distribution Eastern Canada, to the east of Hudson's Bay (especially in the Labrador peninsula).

Habitat Tundra.

Behavior It does not tend to embark on mass migrations like other lemmings; it will do so only if compelled by the large-scale invasions of vegetarian animals (such as migratory birds) which rob it of food. In winter it does not go into hibernation. The female gives birth twice a year to 3-4 young after a gestation of about 3 weeks.

LONGTAILED DUCK
Clangula hyemalis

Classification Class: Aves; Order: Anseriformes; Family: Anatidae.

Description Total length of male 31 in (79 cm), of which 9 in (23 cm) represents the tail; female 19 in (47.5 cm). The male, uniquely among ducks, has three liveries a year: winter, spring and late fall. The most spectacular plumage is in midwinter when the birds pair off: head, neck, belly and part of the back are white; cheeks, breast, remainder of the back, wings and tail are chocolate brown. The female is no less colorful than her partner. It is the only duck in the northern hemisphere which changes its livery after breeding. In fall the two sexes look alike.

Distribution Arctic regions of North America and Eurasia. It winters in the United States and in northern regions of Europe and Asia.

Habitat Fresh water in tundra during the summer, seas and large lakes during the winter.

Behavior It feeds on insect larvae, crustaceans and molluscs, obtaining the last from the seabed, diving to a depth of up to 120 ft (55 m). The nest consists of a depression, lined with a thick layer of feathers, in the shore vegetation. The 4-11 eggs are incubated by the female alone for 24-25 days.

MERLIN
Falco columbarius

Classification Class: Aves; Order: Falconiformes; Family: Falconidae.

Description Length 10¼-12½ in (26-32 cm). The male is slate-gray above, cream with reddish stripes below; the upper parts of the female are dark brown.

Distribution Northern regions of Eurasia and North America.

Habitat Tundra, open hilly terrain, cliffs.

Behavior In physical characteristics and behavior it is a miniature gyrfalcon. It feeds almost entirely on birds as big as a turtledove, wearing down its victim's stamina by pursuing it, directly from behind, at high speed. The diet is supplemented with lemmings and other small rodents. It takes over an old nest abandoned by another bird, either on the ground or on a bare rock ledge. The 4-6 eggs hatch after an incubation of about one month. In fall it migrates to the Mediterranean regions, following the birds on which it feeds, and returns north in March.

MUSK OX
Ovibos moschatus

Classification Class: Mammalia; Order: Artiodactyla; Family: Bovidae.

Description Total length 6-8 ft (1.8-2.4 m),

height to shoulder 3½-4½ ft (1.1-1.4 m), weight 770 lb (350 kg). The male is bigger than the female. The long, thick brown hair hangs down to the feet. Both sexes have horns.

Distribution Northern Canada and Greenland.

Habitat Tundra.

Behavior Females and young form herds separately from those of adult males, who may even lead a solitary life. In the breeding season the groups merge and the males engage in violent duels for possession of the females. In summer the musk ox visits the banks of rivers and lakes, as well as marshy meadows, where it feeds on willows and swamp grass; in winter, however, it climbs hillsides where the incessant winds sweep the vegetation clear of snow. The amount of fodder it needs for survival is roughly one-sixth of that necessary for a domestic herbivore of equivalent size. When threatened, especially by wolves, the adults in the herd arrange themselves in a circle, protecting the young in the middle with their heavy bodies and sharp horns pointed toward the enemy. Now and then a member of the group will briefly leave the ranks to charge, head lowered, at the adversary.

POMARINE SKUA
Stercorarius pomarinus

Classification Class: Aves; Order: Charadriiformes; Family: Stercorariidae.

Description Total length 26-31 in (65-78 cm). Blackish-brown above, yellowish-white below. Dark band on breast, top of head black. Some have uniformly dark coloration. The two central tail feathers are 7-8 in (17-20 cm) longer than the others and are blunt at the tip.

Distribution Arctic regions. It winters as far as the southern hemisphere.

Habitat Tundra in summer, open sea, straits and bays in winter.

Behavior In flight, the straight, angled and pointed wings give it a similarity to a falcon. Swift and aggressive, it behaves like a pirate, attacking gulls and terns repeatedly and forcing them to release or regurgitate the prey they have just caught. It also follows ships and fishing boats to snatch up refuse and scraps of fish. In the tundra, which it visits in summer for nesting, it eats the eggs and fledglings of other birds, but particularly lemmings, the numbers of which have a direct bearing on its breeding success. In years when these small rodents are scarce, many birds fail to reproduce. The female lays 2 eggs in a hollow lined with grass on the ground.

Note Another member of the family is the Longtailed Skua *(Stercorarius longicaudus)*, which is smaller than the Pomarine Skua, measuring 20-23 in (50-58 cm) in length, differing also in certain color details, and with the two central tail feathers ending in a point. Distribution, habitat and behavior are, by and large, the same as for the Pomarine Skua.

RED-BACKED SANDPIPER
Erolia alpina

Classification Class: Aves; Order: Charadriiformes; Family: Scolopacidae.

Description Also called the Dunlin. Length 7 in (18 cm), weight 1½ oz (40 g). In summer the upper parts are rust-colored with dark spots, the underparts whitish with a black mark on the lower breast. In winter it is grayer and there is no abdominal spot. The bill is slightly curved downward.

Distribution It nests in the Eurasian and North American Arctic regions, wintering along shores at lower latitudes.

Habitat Marshy tundra in summer, muddy and swampy seacoasts in winter.

Behavior It feeds on insects, worms, crustaceans, molluscs and vegetation. In winter flocks of several thousand seek food on beaches. If a winged predator appears, the sandpipers all take off together and present the enemy with a wall of bodies; the predator does not dare come close for fear of being unbalanced by the air currents produced by thousands of flapping wings. The nest is bowl-shaped, lined with moss and lichen. The 3-5 eggs, incubated by both parents, hatch after 21-22 days.

ROUGHLEGGED BUZZARD
Buteo lagopus

Classification Class: Aves; Order: Falconiformes; Family: Accipitridae.

Description Length 24 in (60 cm), weight 2¼ lb (1 kg). Upper parts and belly brown; breast and head cream with dark bars; underside of wings and tail white with blackish borders. It derives its common name from the whitish feathers which grow down to the base of the toes.

Distribution Northern regions of Eurasia and North America.

Habitat Tundra and open spaces.

Behavior It eats fieldmice, leverets and lemmings, diving on its prey after sighting it from on high or from a mound on which it has been lying in wait motionless. It nests on the ground or among rocks. The 2-7 eggs hatch after an incubation of 28-31 days. It winters in Europe and the central-southern United States.

SNOW BUNTING
Plectrophenax nivalis

Classification Class: Aves; Order: Passeriformes; Family: Emberizidae.

Description Length 6½ in (16.5 cm), weight about 1 oz (31 g). In spring the male has a white back, with part of the wings and tail black. The female and young resemble him but black parts are brown. In winter the white of the male loses its brilliance and black areas turn brownish.

Distribution Northern regions of Eurasia and North America.

Habitat Rocky tundra, coasts and mountain zones.

Behavior It feeds on seeds and shoots, but in the breeding period it consumes large quantities of insects, on which it feeds its young. The flight is undulating. When large flocks alight on the ground, they look like falling snowflakes. The nest, built among rocks, is a cup made of dry stems, feathers, moss and lichen. The 4-8 eggs are incubated for 10-15 days. It winters along the coasts of northern seas.

Note Another member of the family is the Lapland Longspur *(Calcarius lapponicus)*, nesting in the arctic and subarctic zones of Eurasia and North America. It does not range as far north as the Snow Bunting and frequents tundra with low vegetation rather than bare rocky ground. The male in nuptial garb has upper parts which are tawny with dark brown streaks, underparts whitish. Head, throat, breast and flanks are black; nape chestnut-orange, and a white stripe extending from eye to sides of neck.

WILLOW PTARMIGAN
Lagopus lagopus

Classification Class: Aves; Order: Galliformes; Family: Tetraonidae.

Description Also known as the Willow Grouse. Length 15-16 in (38-40 cm), weight about 1 lb (450-470 g). During the summer it is reddish-brown with wavy dark streaks, white wings and black tail. In winter it is entirely white with a black tail. There are red caruncles over the eyes.

Distribution Northern regions of Eurasia and North America.

Habitat Tundra, moors.

Behavior It has a preference for scrubland with willows, birches and rushes, where it feeds on shoots, leaves and berries. In winter it digs holes in the snow to find food and shelter from the cold. Like the majority of Galliformes, it flies fast but not for long, alternating rapid wingbeats with long glides. It lives in pairs or in family groups. The nest consists of a shallow depression in the ground, in the shelter of shrubs. The 4-17 eggs are incubated by the female alone for 20-26 days.

Tundra

In the most northerly parts of Europe, Asia and North America the ground is covered with snow and ice for most of the year, and the areas just under the surface stay permanently frozen. In such conditions plant growth is sparse and stunted, even though the tundra is dotted with brightly colored flowers during the brief warm season. In addition to mosses and lichens, the plant cover consists mainly of grasses, sedges, blueberries and dwarf willows.

1   Arctic fox
2   lemming
3   snowy owl
4   Arctic hare
5   pomarine skua
6   caribou
7   longtailed duck
8   Alaskan wolf
9   willow ptarmigan
10 Arctic ground squirrel
11 musk ox
12 gray phalarope
13 longtailed skua

ATLANTIC WALRUS
Odobenus rosmarus

Classification Class: Mammalia; Order: Carnivora; Family: Odobenidae.

Description Total length of male 12-12½ ft (3.6-3.8 m), weight up to 3,300 lb (1,500 kg). The female is much smaller. Heavy, massive body covered with brown fur, which is later lost. The most remarkable feature is the pair of tusks, which are transformed upper canines, measuring up to 3 ft (90 cm) long. The mouth is surrounded by strong whiskers, tactile bristles which help the animal to identify molluscs and crustaceans on the seabed.

Distribution Arctic regions.

Habitat Shallow coastal waters in areas of pack ice.

Behavior It is gregarious, forming large herds which sleep during the day on the ice or on dry land. The male lives in separate groups from the females and calves. It feeds principally on molluscs, which it obtains by raking the seabed with its tusks. The latter are indispensable tools of survival; the walrus uses them for procuring food, for clambering out of the water on to an ice floe, for digging a lair, for piercing holes in the ice to be able to breathe, and for repelling predators. The female gives birth to one calf every other year, after 10-11 months' gestation.

BLACK-BROWED ALBATROSS
Diomedea melanophrys

Classification Class: Aves; Order: Procellariiformes; Family: Diomedeidae.

Description Length 30-38 in (76-95 cm), wingspan 7½ ft (2.3 m). It is distinguished from other albatrosses by its particularly large yellow bill, and a prominent dark stripe across the eye. Back, wings and tail are blackish, remaining parts white.

Distribution Southern oceans, from latitudes 30°-60°S, and islands, including the Falklands, Kerguelen and Macquarie.

Habitat Oceans; nests on rocky islets.

Behavior It spends most of its time gliding over the waves, feeding on squid, fish and crustaceans caught near the surface. Sometimes it follows ships for long distances, swooping on any refuse thrown out from the galleys into the sea. It builds a conical nest of grass cemented with mud on rock ledges or cliffs. The single egg weighs about 9 oz (260 g) and is incubated for more than 50 days.

CAPE PIGEON
Daption capense

Classification Class: Aves; Order: Procellariiformes; Family: Procellariidae.

Description Also called the Pintado Petrel. Length 14-16 in (35-41 cm). Black and white plumage with checkered back and rump. Two large white marks on wings; rounded tail with broad black tip. The head is sooty, in contrast to the white underparts.

Distribution Antarctic and subantarctic islands.

Habitat Open sea, rocky shores.

Behavior It has very rapid wingbeats, and is very noisy both on land, and close to its nest, and when hunting at sea. It feeds on crustaceans, fish and molluscs, but will also eat refuse and carrion. It nests in colonies that vary in numbers from 10 to more than 2,000 pairs. The female lays a single egg. When the breeding season is over, it embarks on large-scale migrations to the north, sometimes above the equator.

COMMON GUILLEMOT
Uria aalge

Classification Class: Aves; Order: Charadriiformes; Family: Alcidae.

Description Length 17-19 in (45-47 cm), weight 17-45 oz (490-1,280 g). Upper parts and cap chocolate or brownish-black, breast and belly white. In summer the throat and front of the neck also turn brown. Long, straight, pointed bill. Some guillemots have white lores, which look like spectacles.

Distribution North Atlantic, North Pacific and adjacent Arctic sea; in winter it reaches the Straits of Gibraltar, California and Japan.

Habitat Open sea, rocky islets, coastal cliffs.

Behavior It eats fish and marine invertebrates caught beneath the surface during long submerged periods; it uses its wings for propulsion, in what is genuine underwater flight. It does not build a nest, the female laying a single egg on bare rock; long and pearshaped, it is unlikely to roll off. The egg hatches after 28-31 days' incubation, both parents helping to rear the chick.

COMMON PUFFIN
Fratercula arctica

Classification Class: Aves; Order: Charadriiformes; Family: Alcidae.

Description Length 11-14 in (28-36 cm), weight ½-1 lb (250-450 g). Black above, white below; sides of head white. Bill triangular, flattened from side to side, crossed by brightly colored orange-red and yellow bands. Legs orange.

Distribution North Atlantic and adjacent Arctic seas; in winter part of the population ranges as far as Gibraltar and Massachusetts in the United States.

Habitat Open seas, coastal waters, rocky shores.

Behavior It feeds mainly on small species of fish, herrings, sardines and bluefish, and these constitute the diet of the single chick born annually to each pair. From the end of April onward both parents scoop a nest in the soil with their beak or use an existing cavity where the female lays her egg; she alone incubates it for more than 40 days.

EMPEROR PENGUIN
Aptenodytes forsteri

Classification Class: Aves; Order: Sphenisciformes; Family: Spheniscidae.

Description Length 40-48 in (100-122 cm). It is the largest living penguin, with head and upper parts dark gray, sides of neck orange-yellow. A large black band runs down the top of either side of the body. Bill curved at tip, with red mandible at base.

Distribution Widely found on coasts of Antarctica.

Habitat Coasts and open sea.

Behavior It feeds on fish, molluscs and crustaceans, caught below the surface. It is the only penguin to lay its single egg at the beginning of the southern winter; incubation, lasting 8 weeks, is entrusted solely to the male, who stands upright, holding it between the toe membranes, which are covered by a fold of skin. The female spends this period in the sea, returning when the egg is about to hatch, then helping to rear the chick. The young are capable of reaching the sea and feeding themselves at the age of about 4 months.

Note The Adélie Penguin (*Pygoscelis adeliae*) is likewise found throughout the Antarctic, living and breeding on certain subantarctic islands. During the courtship ceremony the male gives the female pebbles with which a rudimentary nest is then prepared. Year after year, each pair returns unerringly to the same breeding site, sometimes after long tramps through the snow.

FULMAR
Fulmarus glacialis

Classification Class: Aves; Order: Procellariiformes; Family: Procellariidae.

Description Length 18-20 in (46-51 cm), weight 19-33 oz (535-1,000 g). Similar to a large gull, but with a stockier outline. Plumage variable, either entirely gray or with whitish head and underparts.

Distribution Arctic zones of North Atlantic and North Pacific.

Habitat Oceans and open seas; islets, cliffs and coasts during the breeding season.

Behavior It skims the surface of the sea with characteristic glides and circling flights, feeding mainly on refuse, floating oily substances and carcasses of marine mammals and fish. Nesting occurs in large colonies from May onward. The female lays a single egg on the ground, in a depression scooped out with movements of the breast and feet; it hatches after an incubation of 52-53 days.

GIANT PETREL
Macronectes giganteus

Classification Class: Aves; Order: Procellariiformes; Family: Procellariidae.

Description Length 36-40 in (80-100 cm), wingspan over 6 ft (2 m). Plumage variable in color, generally dark brown with whitish head and neck, sometimes almost entirely white. Large bill yellow to greenish-gray.

Distribution Subantarctic islands: South Orkneys, South Georgia, the Falklands, Macquarie, Kerguelen, Auckland, Campbell and other minor islands.

Habitat Open sea, coasts in breeding season.

Behavior On the high seas it feeds on fish, molluscs and crustaceans; in summer, along the coasts, it looks for animal carcasses and filches eggs and nestlings of penguins and other seabirds. If threatened, it vomits its stomach contents at the aggressor and emits foul-smelling oily substances. The female lays one egg, weighing over 7 oz (200 g), which is incubated for 55-65 days.

GREAT SKUA
Catharacta skua

Classification Class: Aves; Order: Charadriiformes; Family: Stercoraridae.

Description Length 21-35 in (53-63 cm), weight about 2½-3½ lb (1.2-1.6 kg). Robust body; dark plumage with large white patch at the base of the primary flight feathers which shows up in flight. Large hooked bill.

Distribution Southern oceans and Antarctic seas. Also found in the North Atlantic.

Habitat Open sea and coasts.

Behavior Like most other skuas, it attacks and preys on various seabirds, sometimes forcing them to abandon or regurgitate their food. It also feeds on carrion and animal leftovers. The Antarctic form often preys on penguins' eggs and chicks which have been left temporarily unguarded. It defends its own nesting site fiercely against any intruders, humans included. Both sexes help to incubate the 2 eggs, which hatch after 28-30 days.

Note Many subantarctic islands are also inhabited by the Antarctic Tern *(Sterna vittata)*, whose nesting colonies are often found among those of gulls.

HARP SEAL
Pagophilus groenlandicus

Classification Class: Mammalia; Order: Carnivora; Family: Phocidae.

Description Total length up to 6 ft (1.8 m), weight up to 400 lb (180 kg). Gray with dark spots which grow bigger with age and eventually merge into a single saddleshaped patch on the back and along the sides.

Distribution Arctic shores of the Atlantic Ocean.

Habitat Coastal waters and pack ice.

Behavior This is a colonial, migratory species which in summer moves northward and in winter returns south to breed. It feeds on crustaceans and fish. After 11 months' gestation a single pup is born. The young are completely white and remain so for about two weeks before turning gray; it is during this period that they are killed for their fur.

ICELAND GULL
Larus glaucoides

Classification Class: Aves; Order: Charadriiformes; Family: Laridae.

Description Length 21-24 in (52-60 cm), weight about 26-30 oz (730-860 g). Plumage entirely white, with mantle and wings pale gray; bill yellow with red tip; legs pink.

Distribution Rocky arctic and subarctic coasts of North America and Greenland; ranges to Iceland and shores of Central and South America in fall and winter.

Habitat Rocky coasts.

Behavior It feeds mainly on fish, catching them both by diving from a height and by ducking partially below the surface of the water. Along the shore it will sometimes eat dead animals and will prey on the eggs and nestlings of other seabirds. It nests on high cliffs. The female lays 2-3 mottled eggs in a bulky heap of grass and moss. Both parents rear the young.

Note Related to gulls and with a widespread distribution in arctic and subarctic zones is the Arctic Tern *(Sterna paradisaea)*, notable for its long forked tail. After breeding, which occurs in crowded colonies on coasts or on rocky, sandy islets, it flies to the Antarctic polar circle, final destination of a remarkably long and spectacular migration across the oceans.

KILLER WHALE
Orcinus orca

Classification Class: Mammalia; Order: Cetacea; Family: Delphinidae.

Description Also called the Grampus. Length over 30 ft (9.5 m) and weight up to 8 t in males. Distinctive coloration: back and flanks black, ventral parts white, two deep white grooves along the flanks toward the rear of the body. The dorsal fin, about 5½ ft (1.7 m) long, is a key feature for identification.

Distribution It inhabits all the world's oceans but is most common in those of the Arctic and Antarctic.

Habitat Coastal waters.

Behavior This is the most formidable of all marine predators, attacking virtually any animal that can be eaten, including penguins, seals, fish, other whales and dolphins. It hunts large prey in packs. A rapid swimmer (up to 30 knots per hour), it often leaps high out of the water, and can remain beneath the surface for over 20 minutes, diving to below 3,000 ft (1,000 m). As a rule they assemble in groups of 10-15. The female gives birth every other year to one young, after a gestation of 13 months or more.

KITTIWAKE
Rissa tridactyla

Classification Class: Aves; Order: Charadriiformes; Family: Laridae.

Description Length 14-18 in (36-46 cm), weight about 10-18 oz (300-500 g). Uniformly dark gray above with black wingtips; rest of plumage white. Bill greenish-yellow, legs black.

Distribution Throughout arctic and subarctic zones of North America and Eurasia.

Habitat Open sea, cliffs.

Behavior It feeds on fish and marine invertebrates which it finds during winter on the high seas. It submerges and dives with agility, frequently following in the wake of ships and fishing vessels. It nests in colonies that are sometimes very numerous on inaccessible rocks and cliffs; occasionally it will also nest on buildings.

LEOPARD SEAL
Hydrurga leptonyx

Classification Class: Mammalia; Order: Carnivora; Family: Phocidae.

Description Length of female up to 13 ft (4 m), weight up to 840 lb (360 kg); the male is slightly smaller. Dark gray coat

Arctic regions

Southern islands

1	harp seal	15	kittiwake
2	hooded seal	16	swift
3	polar bear	17	white-tailed sea eagle
4	Arctic tern	18	common guillemot
5	Iceland gull	19	northern gannet
6	narwhal	20	Wilson's petrel
7	Atlantic walrus	21	lesser sheathbill
8	fulmar	22	giant petrel
9	white whale	23	Cape pigeon
10	peregrine falcon	24	black-footed albatross
11	common puffin	25	southern sea elephant
12	shag	26	white-backed cormorant
13	razorbill	27	macaroni penguin
14	wild pigeon	28	Magellan penguin

Cliffs

Antarctic regions

29 Antarctic tern
30 great skua
31 emperor penguin
32 Ross seal
33 killer whale
34 leopard seal
35 Adélie penguin
36 Weddell seal
37 crabeating seal

with bluish tints on back, lighter with gray or black spots on underparts.

Distribution Antarctic coasts, occasionally along the shores of Australia, New Zealand, South Africa and South America.

Habitat Coastal and open waters.

Behavior It is solitary and in winter embarks on long migrations toward the coasts of Antarctic islands. The particularly wide distribution of this species is reflected in its varied diet, which consists of krill, fish, other seals and, mainly, penguins. These are pursued and killed underwater, then the floating body is smashed violently against the surface of the water so that it becomes dismembered and can then be eaten. The breeding season is unknown, but presumably the female gives birth to a single pup between November and January.

Note The seals of Antarctica are represented by three other species, all found around the Pole, and with individual feeding habits: the Crabeater Seal *(Lobodon carcinophagus)* feeds principally on krill, the Weddell Seal *(Leptonychotes weddelli)* on fish, and the Ross Seal *(Ommatophoca rossi)* on algae.

LESSER SHEATHBILL
Chionis minor

Classification Class: Aves; Order: Charadriiformes; Family: Chionidae.

Description Length 15-16 in (38-41 cm). Plumage entirely white; bill and caruncles close to the eye black. Legs dark or pinkish-white. In flight it looks like a pigeon.

Distribution Certain islands in the southern Indian Ocean: Prince Edward, Marion, Crozet, Kerguelen, Heard.

Habitat Coastal zones.

Behavior Although a good swimmer, it prefers to live on dry land. It feeds on animal and plant detritus, carrion, eggs, nestlings and small invertebrates. It lives in small groups but nests in sparse couples, almost always near colonies of penguins and cormorants, from which it filches food. The 1-3 chicks are reared in nests situated in crevices and animal burrows.

MAGELLAN PENGUIN
Spheniscus magellanicus

Classification Class: Aves; Order: Sphenisciformes; Family: Spheniscidae.

Description Length 26-28 in (65-71 cm). Back, feathers and cheeks blackish. A white band frames the face and extends down to the throat; double gray barring on the upper breast; remainder of underparts pure white.

Distribution Southern coasts of Chile, island of Juan Fernandez, Tierra del Fuego and the Falkland Islands.

Habitat Open waters and seacoasts.

Behavior Along with three other species this is a "shortailed penguin," of average build and a particularly agile and speedy underwater swimmer. It feeds on small fish, molluscs and crustaceans. As a rule it nests in colonies, from October to December; the female lays 2 eggs in a nest scooped in the ground, and these are incubated for 22-24 days. When breeding is over, part of the population migrates northward as far as the coasts of Uruguay.

Note The Macaroni Penguin *(Eudyptes chrysolophus)* is one of the so-called "crested penguins," because of the two golden yellow tufts on either side of the head. It feeds basically on crustaceans and cephalopod molluscs, living and breeding on many subantarctic islands.

NARWHAL
Monodon monoceros

Classification Class: Mammalia; Order: Cetacea; Family: Monodontidae.

Description Length up to 20 ft (6 m), weight up to about 1 t. Color varies according to age: blue-gray at birth, it gradually turns black or blue-black; the adult is dark gray above, whitish below. The distinctive tusk, usually present only in the male, is merely one of the two upper incisors which has broken through the gums and grown enormously to a length of about 10 ft (3 m).

Distribution Arctic Ocean.

Habitat Deep waters.

Behavior It is gregarious, living in groups of twenty, of the same sex or of both sexes. A slow swimmer, it usually settles at the edge of the ice, especially in winter, while in summer it approaches the coasts. The Narwhal feeds mainly on fish, squid and crustaceans. In order to breathe it comes to the surface and pokes its head out of the water. As a rule one young is born after a gestation of 14 months.

Note Related to the Narwhal, belonging to the same family, is the Beluga or White Whale *(Delphinapterus leucas),* only found in shallow Arctic coastal waters. In summer it swims up major rivers. It measures 18 ft (5.5 m), weighs about 2 t, and is whitish in color. It feeds on fish and molluscs.

NORTHERN GANNET
Sula bassana

Classification Class: Aves; Order: Pelecaniformes; Family: Sulidae.

Description Length 35-40 in (87-100 cm), weight 5½-7¾ lb (2.5-3.5 kg). Body tapered with thick and largely milky-white plumage; head and upper neck tinted tawny-yellow. Narrow, angular wings with black flight feathers; pointed tail. Feet blackish, completely webbed. Bill gray-blue with dark grooves.

Distribution Northern regions of Europe and North America.

Habitat Coastal waters, cliffs and rocky islands.

Behavior It feeds on fish caught as a result of spectacular nosedives from a height of about 30-50 ft (10-15 m); at the moment of impact with the water, the wings close and the bird plunges down like a torpedo. It breeds on small islands in crowded colonies, the nests placed close to one another. The female lays a single egg, incubated by both parents for 44 days, held between the interdigital membranes.

Note The Shag or Green Cormorant *(Phalacrocorax aristotelis)* is another member of the Pelecaniformes, found not only in the North Atlantic but also in the Mediterranean, the Black Sea and North Africa. It is so named because of the characteristic curly tuft of feathers on the nape. It always lives near seacoasts.

PEREGRINE FALCON
Falco peregrinus

Classification Class: Aves; Order: Falconiformes; Family: Falconidae.

Description Length 15-20 in (38-50 cm), weight 14-46 oz (390-1,300 g). Distinctive sequence of fine bars on abdomen and large black mustaches at sides of head. Top of head black; back, wings and tail slate-gray. Populations living at more northerly latitudes are larger, have paler colors and smaller mustaches than their southern counterparts.

Distribution Cliffs, but also seen in towns.

Habitat It inhabits a wide variety of environments in addition to rocky zones and cliffs.

Behavior Expert at capturing birds on the wing, it dives from great heights and seizes its prey with extraordinary speed. Victims include doves, gulls, ducks and other medium and small birds. The courtship displays also entail spectacular aerial acrobatics. The eggs (average 3-4) are laid directly on bare rock, on the ground or in an old nest. The chicks are fed mainly by the female.

Note The Gyrfalcon *(Falco rusticolus)* is another large member of the family. Color of plumage is variable, and there is one phase when it is almost completely white. Its distribution is restricted to the arctic and subarctic zones of Eurasia and North America; it favors rocky surroundings and tundra.

POLAR BEAR
Ursus maritimus

Classification Class: Mammalia; Order: Carnivora; Family: Ursidae.

Description Also known as the White

Bear. Length of head and body 4-5 ft (1.2-1.5 m), tail 3-5 in (8-12 cm), height to shoulder 4-4½ ft (1.2-1.4 m), weight 330-1,100 lb (150-500 kg). It is the largest land carnivore. Long, shaggy, yellowish-white fur. Forelegs shorter than hind legs.

Distribution Throughout Arctic regions.

Habitat Ice floes.

Behavior Mainly carnivorous, it feeds on fish, but its favorite prey is the Ringed Seal *(Pusa hispida)*, which it catches, sometimes after many hours of waiting, around the breathing holes which the seals pierce in the ice. It is an excellent swimmer, slow but with immense stamina, using the forelegs for propulsion, and can remain in the water for hours or even days at a time. It is active by day and solitary, forming pairs only for the few days needed for mating, in April-May. In late fall the Polar Bear digs a shelter in a snow-covered slope on dry land, and the cubs (generally two) are born in December-January. An adult will wander about continuously on floating ice but will not let itself drift along passively, even if heading toward its habitual hunting grounds.

RAZORBILL
Alca torda

Classification Class: Aves; Order: Charadriiformes; Family: Alcidae.

Description Length 16-18 in (39-46 cm), weight 1¼-2 lb (545-920 g). Upper parts, head and neck brownish-black, underparts pure white; sides of neck turn white in summer. Sturdy, high beak, laterally compressed, black with a transverse white stripe. A narrow white band also hems the secondary flight feathers.

Distribution Northeastern America, western Greenland, northern Europe.

Habitat Open sea, rocky coasts.

Behavior When swimming, it holds the pointed tail raised. It dives with agility, propelling itself underwater with its wings in pursuit of the small fish and molluscs which make up its diet. On land it walks awkwardly and prefers to stand in a semi-upright position, like penguins. It nests in colonies on cliffs, often alongside other seabirds. Each pair rears a single chick, which stays in the nest for about two weeks before taking to the water.

Note The Little Auk *(Plautus alle)* is another member of the Alcidae, found at very high latitudes between the pack ice and the cliffs of Arctic seas. It measures only 8 in (20 cm) in length, and is one of the smallest diving seabirds, feeding mainly on planktonic crustaceans.

SOUTHERN SEA ELEPHANT
Mirounga leonina

Classification Class: Mammalia; Order: Carnivora; Family: Phocidae.

Description This is the largest pinniped (representative of the suborder Pinnipeda, including seals and walruses), the male measuring up to 21 ft (6.5 m) and weighing up to approximately 3½ t. The female is much smaller. Coat dark gray in males, brown in females. The animal has a kind of trunk, which accounts for the common name.

Distribution Islands and archipelagos of Antarctic seas and coasts of Tierra del Fuego.

Habitat Rocky coasts.

Behavior It is active mainly at night, feeding on fish and cephalopods. It lives almost permanently in the water, but emerges in order to breed (from September to November) and to molt. The males reach the beaches first and fight for territory; the pregnant females, having conceived the previous year, then arrive and form harems of 10-12. Each gives birth about a week later to a single calf, and about three weeks later the adults mate. Within a month of arrival at the breeding grounds, they all return to the sea; but they come back to dry land a month later to molt.

WHITE-BACKED CORMORANT
Phalacrocorax atriceps

Classification Class: Aves; Order: Pelecaniformes; Family: Phalacrocoracidae.

Description Length 27-30 in (68-76 cm). Upper parts black with a distinctive white mark high on the back. Dark cap, white face and underparts. Two bright orange-yellow caruncles adorn the upper root of the bill; pink legs.

Distribution Southern coasts of Chile and Argentina, antarctic and subantarctic islands.

Habitat Coastal waters, cliffs.

Behavior It lives in small groups, generally of 20-40 pairs. Colonies inhabiting Antarctica take advantage of the period of thawing ice to feed excessively on fish and build up considerable reserves of fat for the long southern winter. It builds a nest by collecting algae and bones, cementing them with guano. There are 2-3 chicks.

WHITE-TAILED SEA EAGLE
Haliaëtus albicilla

Classification Class: Aves; Order: Falconiformes; Family: Accipitridae.

Description Length 34-40 in (86-100 cm), weight 6½-15½ lb (3-7 kg). Plumage brown; short wedgeshaped tail, white in the adults, dark in the young. Tarsi largely naked.

Distribution Greenland, Iceland, coasts of Scandinavia, central and eastern Europe, Asia Minor, central and northern Asia.

Habitat Coasts and rocky islands, shores of large lakes and wooded rivers, estuaries, extensive swamps.

Behavior It feeds on fish, mammals, birds, carrion and animal carcasses. It glides slowly over the water, immersing its powerful talons to catch fish; occasionally it dives. It builds bulky nests on rock ledges, in trees or on the ground, using them and renovating them for many years. The female normally lays 2 eggs.

WILSON'S PETREL
Oceanites oceanicus

Classification Class: Aves; Order: Procellariiformes; Family: Hydrobatidae.

Description Length 6-8 in (15-19 cm). Dusky brown with white rump; light band across wings. Long legs, with yellowish webbing on feet.

Distribution Antarctic coasts and adjacent subantarctic islands: South Shetlands, South Orkneys, Sandwich, South Georgia, Falklands, Kerguelen and others.

Habitat Open sea; rocky islands in breeding season.

Behavior It flutters above the water and skims the surface with outspread wings. On land it lies down on its folded legs. It feeds on floating oil and animal fats and on planktonic crustaceans. Long wandering journeys over the high seas bring it to the North Atlantic in winter. It visits dry land only to breed, courtship rituals taking place at night. The female lays one white egg in a crevice or in a hole scooped out for the purpose; incubation lasts about 40 days.

OCEANS

The area occupied on the face of the Earth by seas and oceans is much greater than that covered by dry land; but if we simply draw up a list of all known living species, we find that land organisms are far more numerous than marine organisms. The difference in proportion is due mainly to the immense variety of flowering plants and insects on land, whereas these groups are virtually nonexistent in the sea.

However, where marine animals are concerned, the diversity is incomparably greater than might be suggested in the above general comparison. There are, for example, representatives in the sea of all groups of organisms living on land and in inland waters; furthermore, there are many zoological groups exclusive to the marine environment, such as echinoderms (starfish, sea lilies, sea urchins and sea cucumbers), tunicates (ascidians and salpas), anthozoans (corals, madrepores and sea anemones) and cephalopods (cuttlefish, squid and octopuses).

The sea also differs from land in having an important third dimension, that of depth. The average depth of the sea is about 12,000 ft (3,700 m), and it is remarkable to think that every stratum is inhabited, from the surface to the seabed. The deepest abyssal trenches lie more than 30,000 ft (10,000 m) below the surface. Naturally, the fauna varies strikingly according to the depth, as it does according to the distance from the coast and from the bottom.

The inhabitants of the high seas have certain features in common, so that whales, dolphins, tuna, sunfish, sharks and the like are to be found in virtually all the world's oceans. The animals living in the depths and along the coasts are much more varied, however, because they are more affected by differences in temperature, light, direction of current and the nature of the substratum. There is a world of difference, for example, between a Pacific coral reef, a muddy river estuary and a cliff that slopes steeply into the freezing waters of a northern sea. The sea is also the home of the largest animal ever seen, the blue whale, which may measure up to 110 ft (33 m) in length.

The sea, furthermore, is the kingdom of a myriad of tiny organisms which measure less than a millimeter in length, living either in the depths among grains of sand or in open water where they drift with the movements of waves and currents. These organisms collectively constitute what is known as plankton.

A large number of marine creatures develop indirectly, hatching from an egg in the form of a larva and then undergoing a metamorphosis whereby they eventually assume their definitive form, sometimes very different from the initial form. These larvae, which are as a rule tiny and transparent, represent an extremely large proportion of the planktonic population of all the world's seas and oceans.

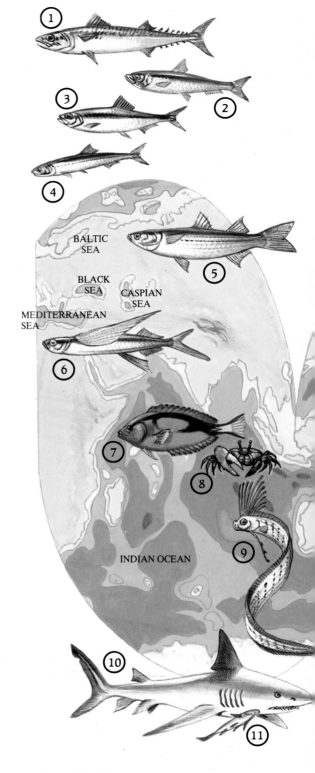

1	mackerel		
2	herring	10	great white shark
3	sardine	11	remora
4	anchovy	12	Greenland right
5	gray mullet		whale
6	Rondelet's	13	killer whale
	flying fish	14	tuna
7	yellowtailed	15	common dolphin
	surgeonfish	16	sea anemone
8	fiddler crab	17	stony coral
9	giant oarfish	18	ocean sunfish

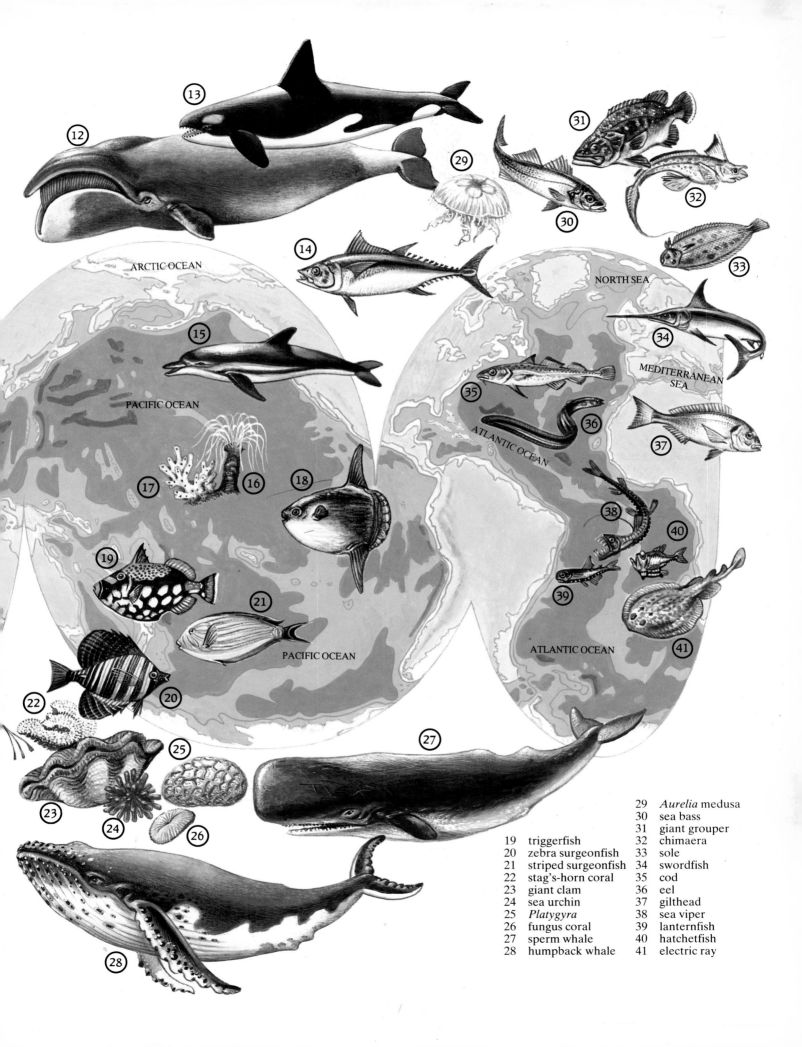

ARCTIC OCEAN

PACIFIC OCEAN

NORTH SEA

MEDITERRANEAN SEA

ATLANTIC OCEAN

PACIFIC OCEAN

ATLANTIC OCEAN

19 triggerfish
20 zebra surgeonfish
21 striped surgeonfish
22 stag's-horn coral
23 giant clam
24 sea urchin
25 *Platygyra*
26 fungus coral
27 sperm whale
28 humpback whale

29 *Aurelia* medusa
30 sea bass
31 giant grouper
32 chimaera
33 sole
34 swordfish
35 cod
36 eel
37 gilthead
38 sea viper
39 lanternfish
40 hatchetfish
41 electric ray

The open sea

ATLANTIC MANTA
Manta birostris

Classification Class: Chondrichthyes; Order: Rajiformes; Family: Mobulidae.

Description Flattened body, up to 23 ft (7 m) wide, weight up to 15 t. Two small fins, similar to horns, protrude from the head. Upper jaw lacks teeth, whereas lower jaw contains a very large number, arranged in some 200 transverse series. Color of back brown, reddish or even black, underparts white, often spotted gray or black.

Distribution Warm oceans.

Habitat Shallow waters, often near coasts.

Behavior Unlike the majority of rays, it spends a good deal of its time some distance from the seabed; it feeds on plankton, filtering it with its numerous teeth. The female gives birth to one young at a time, which at birth measures 5 ft (1.5 m) in length.

AURELIA MEDUSA or MOON JELLYFISH
Aurelia aurita

Classification Phylum Coelenterata; Class: Scyphozoa; Order: Semeostoma; Family: Ulmaridae.

Description Diameter up to 8 in (20 cm). Typical jellyfish with flat, transparent bell or umbrella, whitish or yellowish, in which the four reddish masses of the gonads can be seen through the transparent gelatinous body. Four long, fleshy tentacles surround the mouth.

Distribution In many temperate seas.

Habitat Surface waters, sometimes close to coasts.

Behavior The mature jellyfish releases its tiny larvae (planulae) in the water and these sink to the bottom, where they are transformed into minute polyps (scyphistomae); from these, by means of a nonsexual process of reproduction, tiny jellyfish (ephyrae) are detached, and these in their turn create an adult. Jellyfish are predators.

BLUE WHALE
Balaenoptera musculus

Classification Class: Mammalia; Order: Cetacea; Family: Balaenopteridae.

Description With a length of up to 110 ft (33 m), and a weight up to 130 t, this is the largest animal in the world. Body gray-blue, throat and underside of fins almost white. The mouth contains over 700 baleen plates, short and broad at the base, which serve as filters, and retain food.

Distribution Oceans and seas at all latitudes.

Habitat Surface waters.

Behavior Like all whales that do not possess teeth, the Baleen, Rorqual and Humpback Whales, it feeds on plankton, especially crustaceans belonging to the order Euphausiacea. It is a swift swimmer, capable of reaching speeds of over 25 mph (40 kmh). The female gives birth to one calf at a time, which she suckles for 6-7 months. Growth is extremely rapid; at 2 years of age a Blue Whale has already reached a length of about 75 ft (22-23 m) and is capable of reproducing.

BY-THE-WIND SAILOR
Velella velella

Classification Phylum: Coelenterata; Class: Hydrozoa; Order: Hydroida; Family: Velellidae.

Description Colonial organism consisting of a kind of flat disk, up to 3 in (8 cm) long, on which is set a triangular sail; hanging down from the lower surface of the disk are numerous structures (zooids), each representing a small polyp or highly modified medusa. In appearance and jelly-like consistency, in fact, this hydroid resembles a medusa or jellyfish.

Distribution Subtropical and tropical seas.

Habitat Surface waters.

Behavior The hydroids often swarm in large groups, driven by the wind. They feed on plankton. The complex growth cycle includes a phase of single medusa, moving independently in the water.

COD
Gadus morhua

Classification Class: Osteichthyes; Order: Gadiformes; Family: Gadidae.

Description Length up to 5 ft (1.5 m), weight up to 90 lb (40 kg). Back olive-green, with a few darker spots; underparts yellowish. There is a barbel on the lower lip.

Distribution Northern parts of the Atlantic and Pacific Oceans.

Habitat Cold surface waters.

Behavior An extremely voracious predator, it feeds on other fish, molluscs and crustaceans. It is one of the most fertile species, a single female being capable of laying as many as 15 million eggs. These float and hatch into small larvae which feed on plankton.

COMMON DOLPHIN
Delphinus delphis

Classification Class: Mammalia; Order: Cetacea; Family: Delphinidae.

Description Length up to 8½ ft (2.6 m). Color of back mostly blue-black, sometimes tending to dark brown or greenish; underparts almost white; yellow, gray and white lines run longitudinally along sides. Steamlined build, with a backward-curving dorsal fin. Each jaw has almost 100 teeth.

Distribution Temperate and warm seas throughout the world.

Habitat Shallow waters, especially away from coasts.

Behavior Gregarious animal which lives in schools of up to 100. A very fast swimmer, it can reach speeds of over 20 mph (35 km/h). It feeds on fish, molluscs and crustaceans. At the beginning of the summer the female gives birth to a single young, which at birth measures 20-24 in (50-60 cm). It is reared by both parents.

COMMON SEA SNAIL
Janthina janthina

Classification Phylum: Mollusca; Class: Gasteropoda; Order: Mesogasteropoda; Family: Janthinidae.

Description Almost spherical shell, about ¾ in (20 mm) in diameter, densely ribbed and very light in weight.

Distribution Temperate and warm seas.

Habitat Surface waters.

Behavior To facilitate floating, the snail produces a kind of raft, consisting of air bubbles encased in mucus; it remains attached to this structure for its entire life, and at the time of reproduction also attaches the eggs to it. It feeds on planktonic organisms, with a preference for siphonophores – colonial coelenterates with sting cells which do not cause it any harm.

COMMON SQUID
Loligo vulgaris

Classification Phylum: Mollusca; Class: Cephalopoda; Order: Decapoda; Family: Loliginidae.

Description Length 20 in (50 cm). Body reddish above with small dark, white-bordered spots; whitish below. Body elongated, supported by a distinctive "pen" (gladius), which is a feather-shaped, bony internal shell; two broad fins on either side of the body; eight short tentacles and two longer tentacles, with suckers.

Distribution Atlantic Ocean and Mediterranean Sea.

Habitat Shallow waters, especially in the open sea, occasionally near coasts.

Behavior Very fast and efficient swimmer, feeding on fish. The female produces relatively large eggs, from which hatch young already similar in appearance to the adult squid.

FISH DOLPHIN
Coryphaena hippurus
Classification Class: Osteichthyes; Order: Perciformes; Family: Coryphaenidae.
Description Also called the Dorado. Length maximum 6½ ft (2 m). Body much elongated and brighly colored: back blue or blue-green, underparts yellow or white; sides often speckled black or blue; tail yellow. Very large dorsal fin.
Distribution All tropical and subtropical seas.
Habitat Shallow waters, far from coasts.
Behavior Very swift swimmer, often forming shoals. It feeds on other fish, with a preference for flying fish.

FOUR-WINGED FLYINGFISH
Cypselurus heterurus
Classification Class: Osteichthyes; Order: Atheriniformes; Family: Exocoetidae.
Description Length up to 12-14 in (30-35 cm). Body fairly long, with two enormous pectoral fins resembling wings, and two smaller pectoral fins. The adult has a bluish back and silver sides; the young have prominent dark spots on the fins.
Distribution Atlantic Ocean and Mediterranean Sea.
Habitat Open waters, especially near surface.
Behavior Flyingfish are so called because of the very long gliding flights which they make out of the water, rising to some 15-20 ft (5-6 m) above the sea surface, reaching speeds of 45 mph (70 km/h) and covering distances of up to 1,000 ft (300 m). The females lay floating strings of eggs 2 mm in diameter. The young differ greatly from the adults in the proportionate size of wings to body.

GREAT WHITE SHARK
Carcharodon carcharias
Classification Class: Chondrichthyes; Order: Squaliformes; Family: Isuridae.
Description Length up to 33 ft (10 m), weight over 3 t. Lead-gray above, white below.
Distribution Warm and temperate seas world-wide.
Habitat Open sea, at some depth; occasionally near coasts.
Behavior Extremely voracious, it eats prey of any size, including tuna, turtles and seals. The female is ovoviviparous.
Note Another distinctive representative of the family is the Six-gilled Shark (*Hexanchus griseus*), over 10 ft (3 m) long, and differing from other sharks by having six instead of five gill slits. This species is ovoviviparous too, and is found in practically all warm and temperate seas.

GREENLAND RIGHT WHALE
Balaena mysticetus
Classification Class: Mammalia; Order: Cetacea; Family: Balaenidae.
Description Length up to 60 ft (18 m), weight 40-50 t. Body dark gray, with lighter patches at the base of fins and tail. Enormous head; mouth contains no teeth, but instead a row of about 300 baleen plates.
Distribution Arctic seas.
Habitat Surface waters.
Behavior Feeds on small planktonic crustaceans and small fish, which it filters in seawater through the baleen plates in its mouth. The female gives birth to a single calf at a time.

HAMMERHEAD SHARK
Sphyrna zygaena
Classification Class: Chondrychthyes; Order: Squaliformes; Family: Sphyrnidae.
Description Length up to 13 ft (4 m), weight up to about 1,500 lb (700 kg). The body is typically that of a shark, but there is a marked difference in the shape of the head, which is expanded sideways to form the distinctive "hammer" from which the common name is derived; the eyes are situated at the tip of the head's 2 lateral extensions.
Distribution In all warm and temperate seas.
Habitat Open sea, not in very shallow water, sometimes even near coasts.
Behavior Although a strong swimmer, it seeks its food in the depths. The female gives birth to 10-40 young, which at birth are approximately 20 in (50 cm) long.

HERRING
Clupea harengus
Classification Class: Osteichthyes; Order: Clupeiformes; Family: Clupeidae.
Description Length up to 18 in (45 cm). Greenish-gray back, silver sides and belly.
Distribution Northern parts of the Atlantic and Pacific Oceans.
Habitat Cold and temperate waters; closer to coasts in breeding season.
Behavior The female lays eggs 1-2 mm in diameter. Like those of almost all bony sea fish, they do not float, but being a little heavier than water, sink to the bottom. Larval development takes 4-6 months, at the end of which the young herring make for open water where they feed on small crustaceans and other plankton.

LOGGERHEAD TURTLE
Caretta caretta
Classification Class: Reptilia; Order: Chelonia; Family: Cheloniidae.
Description Length up to 44 in (110 cm).

Back protected by a strong carapace, reddish-brown with darker stripes in young. Flattened legs transformed into sturdy fins.
Distribution All oceans, including Mediterranean and Black Seas.
Habitat Open waters; comes to shore to lay eggs.
Behavior Not very active, it feeds mainly on marine invertebrates, but also on algae and fish. The female lays her eggs in a hole 20 in (50 cm) deep, which she digs in the sand. After 6-8 weeks the eggs hatch, and the young, about 2 in (4-5 cm) long, make for the sea immediately; many fall victim to predators, especially sea birds.

NEEDLEFISH
Belone belone
Classification Class: Osteichthyes; Order: Atheriniformes; Family: Belonidae.
Description Length maximum 3 ft (1 m), but only 28 in (70 cm) in Mediterranean specimens. Body very elongated but not snakelike; the fairly long jaws are pushed forward to form a characteristic rostrum and are equipped with large numbers of sharp little teeth. The dorsal fin is situated very far to the rear. Greenish back with a darker median line, belly silver. The greenish color of the bones, due to the presence of a biliary pigment, is very distinctive.
Distribution Atlantic Ocean, Mediterranean and Black Seas.
Habitat Open sea; in fall it approaches the coasts.
Behavior The predatory needlefish feeds mainly on small fish. A powerful swimmer, it can make jumps out of the water. The female lays relatively large eggs (about 3 mm in diameter), which are covered with long threads that link them together and provide an attachment to underwater vegetation. The newborn larvae, which measure just under ½ in (1 cm) long, have an almost normal head with jaws that hardly jut forward; the mandible or lower part soon begins to grow longer, whereas the maxilla or upper section only starts to extend later.

OCEAN SUNFISH
Mola mola
Classification Class: Osteichthyes; Order: Tetraodontiformes; Family: Molidae.
Description Variously known as the Mola or Moonfish. Length over 10 ft (3 m), weight 2 t. Body markedly compressed and truncated, very distinctive in form; it is, in fact, shaped like a disk, slightly oval lengthways, with two long, unpaired dorsal and anal fins. The caudal fin is reduced to a large rim which borders the rear section of the disk. The pectoral

The open sea

In the open sea there is little scope for large forms of vegetation, with the exception of the sargasso or gulfweed, which is so abundant in places that it has given its name to the Sargasso Sea. Plant life does exist however, wherever the water is best illuminated, namely near the surface. It takes the form of innumerable algae (seaweed), almost all single-celled, and it constitutes, in terms of weight, the largest mass of plankton in all oceans and seas. These unicellular algae represent the starting point of a food chain which starts from tiny crustaceans and small fish larvae up to the whales, sharks and other giants of the sea.

1	by-the-wind-sailor	16	common dolphin
2	common sea snail	17	Atlantic manta
3	plankton	18	gull
	(much enlarged)	19	paper nautilus
4	herring	20	flathead
5	ocean sunfish	21	great white shark
6	hammerhead shark	22	remora
7	common squid	23	porbeagle shark
8	sperm whale	24	loggerhead turtle
9	*Aurelia* medusa	25	tuna
10	football jellyfish	26	blue whale
11	cod	27	Greenland
12	swordfish		right whale
13	golden sword	28	fish dolphin
14	sailfish	29	four-winged
15	storm petrel		flyingfish

fins are comparatively small, in the form of a blade, and there are no ventral fins.

Distribution   In all seas.

Habitat   At the water surface and near the seabed, although not at very great depths.

Behavior   Gregarious, especially early in life, it embarks on irregular migrations, possibly linked to the mass movement of plankton on which it feeds. It is indolent by nature and tends to stay in one place, almost immobile. The female lays tiny eggs from which emerge larvae less than 2 mm long; these undergo complex processes of metamorphosis before attaining their definitive appearance.

PAPER NAUTILUS
Argonauta argo

Classification   Phylum: Mollusca; Class: Cephalopoda; Order: Octopoda; Family: Argonautidae.

Description   Female 8-12 in (20-30 cm), male only about 1 in (2.5 cm) long. The pronounced sexual dimorphism of this species is not restricted to length. Although she looks much like an octopus, with tentacles that are each furnished with two rows of suckers, the female, in fact, constructs a kind of shell in which she lays and incubates the eggs; this shell, transparent and pink or violet in color, is produced by two of the tentacles. The male is incapable of creating shells; furthermore, seven of his tentacles are short, while the eighth is very long, with a tip that at the moment of copulation becomes detached in order to fertilize the female.

Distribution   Atlantic   Ocean   and Mediterranean Sea.

Habitat   Shallow open water; the empty shell may be carried enormous distances by the waves.

Behavior   A predator, like all cephalopods, the Paper Nautilus reproduces from May to October.

PORBEAGLE SHARK
Lamna nasus

Classification   Class: Chondrichthyes; Order: Squaliformes; Family: Isuridae.

Description   Length up to 10-13 ft (3-4 m). Gray-blue back, whitish belly. Typical shark shape; tail with two almost equal lobes.

Distribution   Northern   Atlantic   and Mediterranean Sea.

Habitat   Open sea, even fairly deep water.

Behavior   An active swimmer, it hunts fish and squid, frequenting shallow water in winter. The female gives birth to up to 5 young, which already measure 24 in (60 cm) at birth.

REMORA or SHARKSUCKER
Remora remora

Classification   Class: Osteichthyes; Order: Perciformes; Family: Echeneidae.

Description   Maximum length 28 in (70 cm). Color gray, brown or blackish. On the head is an adhesive disk containing 17-19 pairs of plates.

Distribution   World-wide.

Habitat   Open waters, generally far from shore.

Behavior   By means of the adhesive disk, it attaches itself to large fish or cetaceans, turtles or even boats, using them for transport, although it is also a good swimmer. It feeds mainly on plankton, on the remains of its host's food or on parasites attached to the latter's skin.

SPERM WHALE
Physeter catodon

Classification   Class: Mammalia; Order: Cetacea; Family: Physeteridae.

Description   Length of male 40-60 ft (12-18 m), but specimens as long as 80 ft (24 m) have been reported. The female is somewhat smaller. The head is enormous, but its volume is not completely accounted for by the skull; in the forehead, in fact, is the huge spermaceti organ, containing up to 5 t of colorless oil. The upper jaw lacks teeth, but there are 38-48 teeth in the lower jaw. The caudal fin is large, measuring up to 14½ ft (4.5 m).

Distribution   In all seas, especially those that are warm or temperate.

Habitat   Mainly in the open sea, but occasionally close to shore, where from time to time they are found stranded. Apparently it can dive to a depth of more than 3,000 ft (1,000 m).

Behavior   A fairly sociable creature, it feeds almost exclusively on cephalopod molluscs, including giant squid, which it hunts in deep water. After a gestation of about one year, the female gives birth to a single calf, rarely two.

SWORDFISH
Xiphias gladius

Classification   Class: Osteichthyes; Order: Perciformes; Family: Xiphiidae.

Description   Total length up to 13 ft (4 m), of which about one-third is taken up by the sword, weight 1,100 lb (500 kg). Elongated, streamlined body, rather like that of the Tuna, but slightly longer and characterized particularly by the long sword which extends horizontally from the upper jaw.

Distribution   All warm and temperate seas.

Habitat   Shallow water, far from coast; it may occasionally dive to a depth of up to

about 2,500 ft (800 m).

Behavior   A solitary animal, regarded as one of the fastest-swimming sea creatures, it often leaps from the water. It feeds on fish and, above all, cephalopod molluscs. At the beginning of the summer the female lays transparent, floating eggs, from which, within 2-3 days, larvae hatch measuring 4-4.5 mm long, and without a sword.

Note A relative of the Swordfish is the Sailfish (*Istiophorus* spp.), which has an enormous dorsal fin resembling a long sail; it is frequently found in the Atlantic Ocean. It often swims on the surface, with the sail above the water.

TUNA or BLUEFIN TUNA
Thunnus thynnus

Classification   Class: Osteichthyes; Order: Perciformes; Family: Scombridae.

Description   Maximum length 10 ft (3 m), weight up to about 900 lb (400 kg), the record being 1,600 lb (725 kg). Very solid but streamlined body; distinctive series of finlets behind the second dorsal and anal fins. The back is dark blue, sometimes almost black; the sides are silver, the fins gray, the finlets yellow.

Distribution   All oceans, including the Mediterranean and Black Seas.

Habitat   Open water, not very deep.

Behavior   A tireless and very fast swimmer, it can also leap out of the water, despite its size. The young feed on plankton then, later on fish, squid and large crustaceans. The eggs, 1-1.2 mm in diameter, float in the water, and hatch within 2 days. Within a year the 3 mm newborn larva develops into a young fish of 24-28 in (60-70 cm), already weighing 6½-11 lb (3-5 kg). Gregarious in the breeding season, the Tuna leads a solitary life for much of the year.

The depths

COMMON OCTOPUS
Octopus vulgaris

Classification Phylum: Mollusca; Class: Cephalopoda; Order: Octopoda; Family: Octopodidae.

Description Length of body up to 6 in (15 cm), length of tentacles up to 36 in (90 cm). Body in the form of a sac, with eight long tentacles each with two rows of suckers. Color may vary to match that of the substratum.

Distribution Mediterranean Sea and Atlantic, Pacific and Indian Oceans.

Habitat Rocky seabeds with clefts affording shelter.

Behavior A predatory animal, feeding mainly on crabs, paralyzing them with its venomous bite.

Note Related to the Octopus is the Musk Octopus (*Eledone moschata*), about 16 in (40 cm) long, with a single line of suckers along the tentacles. It is distinctive for the odor of musk that it emits.

COMMON SEA URCHIN
Paracentrotus lividus

Classification Phylum: Echinodermata; Class: Echinoidea; Order: Diadematoida; Family: Echinidae.

Description Diameter 2½ in (6 cm), plus spines which measure up to ¾ in (2 cm). Color violet-black or dark green. It is spherical in shape, as outlined by the strong calcareous dermaskeleton beneath the skin.

Distribution Northeastern Atlantic Ocean and Mediterranean Sea.

Habitat Rocky shores, up to a depth of 270 ft (80 m).

Behavior Feeds on algae and detritus which it scrapes with its teeth from rock surfaces. The first stage of development is a planktonic larva known as the pluteus. The sea urchin moves slowly on the seabed by means of innumerable pedicels which are furnished with an adhesive disk at the tip and set in motion by a hydraulic system.

Note Another common sea urchin found in the Mediterranean is the Dark Violet Sea Urchin (*Sphaerechinus granularis*), furnished with short, densely packed spines which are violet with a white tip.

DALMATIAN SPONGE
Spongia officinalis

Classification Phylum: Porifera; Class: Demospongiae; Order: Dictioceratida; Family: Spongiidae.

Description Diameter up to 12 in (30 cm). Shapeless blackish-brown mass, supported by a corneous, flexible skeleton. The body contains many very tiny pores through which water enters, and a small number of larger pores through which it is driven out, having provided the sponge with oxygen and suspended food particles.

Distribution Mediterranean Sea.

Habitat Littoral zones, up to about 35-130 ft (10-40 m) in depth.

Behavior It lives by filtering water, from which it obtains food particles.

ELECTRIC RAY
Torpedo torpedo

Classification Class: Chondrichthyes; Order: Rajiformes; Family: Torpedinidae.

Description Also called the Torpedo. Length up to 24 in (60 cm). Flat body, back chestnut with black-edged blue spots; underside white. Sturdy tail with a well-developed caudal fin.

Distribution Mediterranean Sea and western Atlantic Ocean.

Habitat It generally lives on sandy seabeds, at no great depth, but may also be found deeper down in mud.

Behavior The female is viviparous, giving birth to some 20 young. The ray is equipped with two large electric organs, which represent a kind of cell or battery, made up of over 100,000 overlapping disks; these produce electric shocks which stun the fish on which it feeds.

EUROPEAN SPINY LOBSTER
Palinurus elephas

Classification Phylum: Arthropoda; Class: Crustacea; Order: Decapoda; Family: Palinuridae.

Description Also known as the Rock Lobster. Length up to 16 in (40 cm). Head and thorax covered by a spiny carapace; forelegs lack chelae (claws). Body terminates in characteristic fanshaped tail. Colored reddish-violet with yellow spots.

Distribution Mediterranean Sea and European Atlantic coasts.

Habitat Rocky seabeds, but not at great depths.

Behavior The female lays eggs from which hatches a distinctive larva, known as a phyllosoma; it has a flattened body with four 4 pairs of long thoracic appendages, and molts 10-20 times before becoming an adult.

GIANT GROUPER
Epinephelus guaza

Classification Class: Osteichthyes; Order: Perciformes; Family: Serranidae.

Description Length up to about 3 ft (1 m), weight up to 130 lb (60 kg). Color light brown with whitish spots.

Distribution Atlantic Ocean and Mediterranean Sea.

Habitat Rocky seabeds.

Behavior A voracious predator, it has a particular preference for cephalopods. As a rule groupers are hermaphrodite; thus the same fish changes sex with age, the female phase preceding the male phase.

MEDITERRANEAN FEATHER STAR
Antedon mediterranea

Classification Phylum: Echinodermata; Class: Crinoidea; Order: Comatulida; Family: Antedonidae.

Description Overall diameter up to 8 in (20 cm). The principal body mass is made up of ten long arms, yellowish in color, which radiate from a cup; this is attached to the seabed by a tuft of slender appendages known as cirri.

Distribution Mediterranean Sea.

Habitat Coastal rocks covered with algae and posidonias; exceptionally it will descend to a depth of up to about 650 ft (200 m).

Behavior Feeds on plankton, collecting it by means of the mucous material contained in grooves on the arms; thus enveloped, the food particles are conveyed to the mouth by the movements of tiny hairs (cilia). A barrel-shaped larva hatches from the egg, and this swims freely, eventually becoming metamorphosed into the typical adult feather star.

MUSSEL
Mytilus sp.

Classification Phylum: Mollusca; Class: Bivalves; Order: Anisomyaria; Family: Mytilidae.

Description Length of shell 2½-3 in (6-8 cm). The shell is dark violet or blackish, with a pointed tip.

Distribution Black Sea, Mediterranean Sea, Atlantic Ocean.

Habitat Rocks and cliffs near coasts; frequently found on port installations.

Behavior After a larval life as part of the plankton, it attaches itself to the substratum by means of filaments known as byssi, made of protein material secreted by a special gland.

PRIDEAUX'S HERMIT CRAB
Pagurus prideauxi

Classification Phylum: Arthropoda; Class: Crustacea; Order: Decapoda; Family: Paguridae.

Description Length about 1½ in (3.5-4 cm). A characteristic feature of the hermit crab is the abdomen, which is protected inside an empty snail shell.

Distribution Mediterranean Sea.

Habitat Rocks, at no great depth.

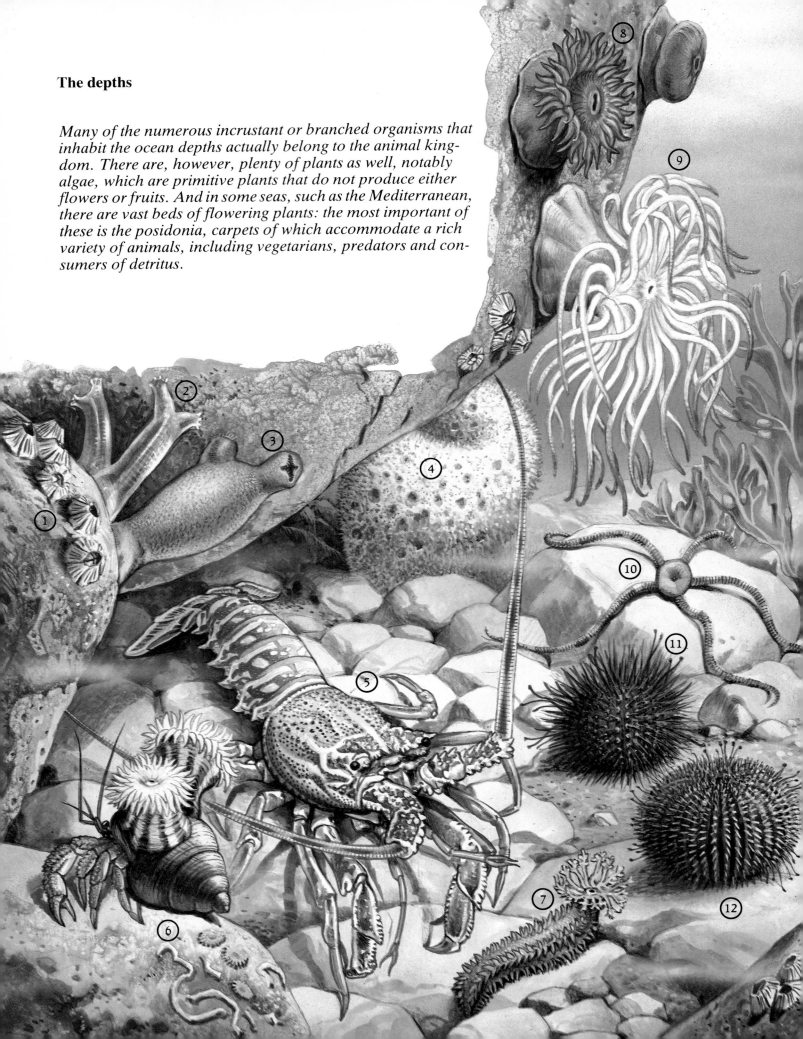

The depths

Many of the numerous incrustant or branched organisms that inhabit the ocean depths actually belong to the animal kingdom. There are, however, plenty of plants as well, notably algae, which are primitive plants that do not produce either flowers or fruits. And in some seas, such as the Mediterranean, there are vast beds of flowering plants: the most important of these is the posidonia, carpets of which accommodate a rich variety of animals, including vegetarians, predators and consumers of detritus.

1 rock barnacle
2 sea squirt
3 sea squirt
4 Dalmatian sponge
5 European spiny lobster
6 Prideaux's hermit crab with
    sea anemone
7 sea cucumber
8 sea anemone
9 sea anemone
10 serpent star
11 common sea urchin
12 dark violet sea urchin
13 rainbow wrasse
14 giant grouper
15 electric ray
16 musk octopus
17 sabellid worm
18 sole
19 warty crab
20 Mediterranean feather star
21 yellow gorgonid
22 bream
23 mussel
24 red starfish
25 octopus

Behavior As it grows, the Hermit Crab has to change its abode; it abandons the shell in which it has lived so far, transferring to a bigger one, moving in with a small sea anemone (*Adamsia pallaiata*); it thus enters into a symbiotic relationship, from which both derive advantage.

RAINBOW WRASSE
Coris julis

Classification Class: Osteichthyes; Order: Perciformes; Family: Labridae.

Description Length up to 10 in (25 cm). Elongated body, with long, broad dorsal and anal fins. All wrasse up to about 5½ in (12-14 cm) long exhibit primary coloration: the upper parts are red or brown, and there is a yellow or brown stripe on the sides, with white lines beneath; the underparts are white, with a greenish tail. These, as a rule, are females which are later transformed into males: the latter then change their livery, which becomes much more brilliant; the back is often blue or green, and a red or orange band along the sides has blue lines underneath; the color of the fins is also brighter.

Distribution Northeastern Atlantic Ocean and Mediterranean Sea.

Habitat It lives among rocks, among posidonias, and on gravelly seabeds.

Behavior A carnivorous fish, it is active only by day. The young are gregarious, but older wrasse become solitary and territorial.

ROCK BARNACLE
Balanus sp.

Classification Phylum: Arthropoda; Class: Crustacea; Subclass: Cirripedia; Order: Thoracica; Family: Balanidae.

Description Also known as Acorn Barnacles or Acorn Shells. Diameter ½-¾ in (1-2 cm). They have a very strong exoskeleton, consisting of six whitish, calcareous plates, joined together to form a conical trunk, the upper opening of which is closed by two mobile valves. These can be opened or closed, and when the barnacle is not disturbed it extends a tuft of cirri, the fine hairs of which perform sweeping motions, allowing water to be exchanged and suspended food particles to be collected.

Distribution Rocky coasts of all seas.

Habitat Prefers intertidal zones.

Behavior The barnacle is hermaphrodite. The larvae are typically crustacean in appearance and swim freely for some time before attaching themselves to rocks.

SABELLID WORM
Spirographis spallanzanii

Classification Phylum: Annelida; Class: Polychaeta; Order: Sabelliformes; Family: Sabellidae.

Description Length 12 in (30 cm). Elongated body, almost cylindrical, segmented, protected by a parchment-like tube; front end of body has a crown of yellow-brown feathered tentacles.

Distribution Mediterranean Sea.

Habitat Soft seabeds.

Behavior Feeds on plankton, which it collects with the long feathery appendages that surround the mouth and which also help it to breathe. At the least sign of danger the worm withdraws into its tube. It develops indirectly, with a planktonic larva.

SEA CUCUMBER
Cucumaria planci

Classification Phylum: Echinodermata; Class: Holothuroidea; Order: Apoda; Family: Cucumariidae.

Description Length 4-6 in (10-15 cm). Body sac-shaped; rough teguments, with a few calcareous elements inside, reddish-brown color. The mouth is surrounded by a crown of ten branched tentacles; there are five rows of ambulacral pedicels (foot-like parts) along the body.

Distribution Atlantic Ocean and Mediterranean Sea.

Habitat Sandy beds.

Behavior Feeds on plankton, gathering this with the tentacles around the mouth. If disturbed, it may expel sticky, irritant filaments from the anus, which force the aggressor to withdraw. These filaments are then regenerated.

SEA SQUIRT
Halocynthia papillosa

Classification Phylum: Chordata; Class: Ascidiacea; Order: Pleurogona; Family: Pyuridae.

Description Length up to 4 in (10 cm). Body shaped like a barrel, coral-red, with an inhalant siphon at the tip and an exhalant siphon on the sides.

Distribution Mediterranean Sea and Atlantic Ocean.

Habitat Rocky seabeds.

Behavior Hermaphrodite. The larva leads a free-swimming life for some time. The adult feeds on microorganisms in the water, which enter through the inhalant siphon and find their way into the gill chamber.

SOLE
Solea solea

Classification Class: Osteichthyes; Order: Pleuronectiformes; Family: Soleidae.

Description Length up to 20 in (50 cm). Color gray-brown, with darker spots; black patch on the pectoral fin. Flat asymmetrical body: it lies on the seabed on its left side, which is whitish; the left eye moves round, in the course of development, to the right side, next to the other eye. The body is almost completely encircled by two long unpaired fins, dorsal and anal.

Distribution Mediterranean Sea and northeastern Atlantic Ocean.

Habitat Soft seabeds at average depths.

Behavior Active at night, it feeds on invertebrates and small fish. By day it remains buried in the mud. The female lays eggs in winter and spring. The larva is at first symmetrical, as in all fish species.

STARFISH
Echinaster sepositus

Classification Phylum: Echinodermata; Class: Asteroidea; Order: Spinulosa; Family: Echinasteridae.

Description Diameter up to 8 in (20 cm). Color bright red. The central disk merges imperceptibly into the five long and sturdy arms, the lower sides of which are equipped with a large number of pink or yellowish pedicels, terminating in a red sucker.

Distribution Eastern Atlantic Ocean and western Mediterranean Sea.

Habitat Sandy seabeds, but especially rocks, up to a depth of 850 ft (250 m).

Behavior An extremely voracious predator of bivalve molluscs, it pulls apart the valves and enfolds them in its stomach which projects out of the mouth; in this way the digestive juices are poured over the prey. The stomach is then retracted, with its contents already totally digested.

Note The Serpent Star (*Ophioderma longicauda*) is a sea star which has long, slender arms set in a central disk, about 1 in (2-3 cm) in diameter, and which is more clearly identifiable than in most ordinary sea stars. It lives on sandy and muddy seabeds at no great depth.

WARTY CRAB
Eriphia verrucosa

Classification Phylum: Arthropoda; Class: Crustacea; Order: Decapoda; Family: Xanthidae.

Description Length up to 4 in (10 cm). Massive body with trapezoid carapace, greenish-yellow; forelegs dark brown, furnished with strong chelae.

Distribution Mediterranean Sea and Atlantic Ocean.

Habitat Rocks and pebbly shores.

Behavior A predator, this crab usually hides among algae after its hunting forays. The female lays a large number of very small eggs. Development is indirect, and it feeds on planktonic larvae.

Inland seas and lagoons

ANCHOVY
Engraulis encrasicholus
Classification Class: Osteichthyes; Order: Clupeiformes; Family: Engraulidae.
Description Length up to 7 in (18 cm). Back blue-green, sides and belly silver; a longitudinal blue line runs along each side.
Distribution Northeastern Atlantic Ocean, Mediterranean Sea, Black Sea.
Habitat Near coasts during larval stage and breeding season; in more open waters at other times.
Behavior Feeds principally during the daytime on tiny crustaceans and the larvae of other fish and invertebrates. A gregarious animal, it breeds mainly in summer, the female laying up to 40,000 eggs; after 2-3 days the larvae hatch, little more than 2 mm long.

ATLANTIC MACKEREL
Scomber scombrus
Classification Class: Osteichthyes; Order: Perciformes; Family: Scombridae.
Description Length maximum 20 in (50 cm). Back metallic blue-green with black bands; sides silvery or whitish.
Distribution Mediterranean Sea, Black Sea, northern Atlantic Ocean.
Habitat Coastal waters during breeding season; open waters at all other times.
Behavior It forms large shoals, feeding on fish and small crustaceans. In the Mediterranean it spawns in winter and early spring.

COCKLE
Cerastoderma edule
Classification Phylum: Mollusca; Class: Bivalves; Order: Eulamellibranchia; Family: Cardiidae.
Description Diameter of shell up to about 1½ in (4 cm). The shell is fairly thick, with radial ribs; the foot is large and muscular.
Habitat Soft beds in shallow water, even brackish.
Behavior It can make leaps on the seabed, thanks to rapid foot movements.
Note Another bivalve is the Sea Scallop (*Pecten varius*), which moves by jet propulsion, closing its valves to force out a powerful jet of water.

COMMON SAND FLEA
Talitrus saltator
Classification Phylum: Arthropoda; Class: Crustacea; Order: Amphipoda; Family: Talitridae.
Description Also called the Sandhopper. Length about ½ in (1.5 cm). Yellowish-gray compressed body; two pairs of antennae, the second fairly long.
Distribution European coasts.
Habitat Among beach detritus in tidal zones.
Behavior Feeds on vegetable substances and decomposing animals. It is capable of making long jumps over wet sand. The female has a ventral incubating pouch in which the eggs are kept until they hatch; there are no larval stages.

COMMON SHRIMP
Crangon crangon
Classification Phylum: Arthropoda; Class: Crustacea; Order: Decapoda; Family: Crangonidae.
Description Length up to about 2 in (4.5 cm). Color variable, matching the sand where the animal lives. Head and thorax covered by a carapace provided with three spines. The second pair of thoracic legs terminates in a tiny chela.
Distribution European seas.
Habitat Sandy seabeds, sometimes mixed with mud, mainly at depths of about 30-165 ft (10-50 m).
Behavior Agile in its movements, this shrimp reproduces twice a year, in winter and summer; the female carries the eggs for some time between the appendages of the abdomen.

CROAKER
Umbrina cirrosa
Classification Class: Osteichthyes; Order: Perciformes; Family: Sciaenidae.
Description Length up to about 3 ft (1 m), weight up to 26 lb (12 kg). Color silver with many oblique golden stripes on its sides.
Distribution Mediterranean Sea, Black Sea, Atlantic Ocean from Bay of Biscay to Senegal.
Habitat Sandy seabeds.
Behavior It lives on its own or in small groups near the coasts, sometimes in brackish water. Carnivorous, it eats invertebrates. At the beginning of summer the female lays many eggs containing a drop of oil which enables them to float.

EUROPEAN EEL
Anguilla anguilla
Classification Class: Osteichthyes; Order: Anguilliformes; Family: Anguillidae.
Description Length up to about 4½ ft (1.4 m), weight up to 13 lb (6 kg). Body almost cylindrical and snakelike, with small head. The rear two-thirds of the body are surrounded by a single unpaired fin which begins on the back, passes over the tail and folds back over the abdomen to form an anal fin.
Distribution Coasts of Europe, Asia Minor, Middle East and West Africa, and tributary river basins of these seas.
Habitat A migratory animal which spawns at sea, but when young swims up rivers, remaining in fresh water until the breeding season approaches.
Behavior The spawning habits of eels living in Mediterranean river tributaries are still not sufficiently known; eels of European rivers which flow into the Atlantic breed in the Sargasso Sea. The larvae, known as leptocephali, hatch from tiny eggs; they are transparent, with a flattened body. As they approach European shores the body becomes cylindrical and they are subsequently known as elvers. The eel probably remains in fresh water for up to fifty years.

FLOUNDER
Platichthys flesus
Classification Class: Osteichthyes; Order: Pleuronectiformes; Family: Pleuronectidae.
Description Maximum length 16 in (40 cm). Asymmetrical, flat body, resting on the seabed on its left side, which is whitish, while the right side is olive-brown or greenish-black, usually spotted.
Distribution European coasts from the White Sea to the Black Sea.
Habitat Sandy and muddy seabeds, at no great depth.
Behavior It spends much time buried in the muddy bottom. Feeds on crustaceans, molluscs and other small animals. Metamorphosis into a fish with a flat body occurs at two months.

GILTHEAD
Sparus auratus
Classification Class: Osteichthyes; Order: Perciformes; Family: Sparidae.
Description Maximum length 28 in (70 cm), weight 11 lb (5 kg). Back blue-gray, sides silver; there is a distinctive double bar, gold and black, between the eyes.
Distribution Mediterranean Sea, Black Sea, northeastern Atlantic Ocean.
Habitat Coastal waters at depths of about 15-100 ft (5-30 m).
Behavior It can tolerate marked variations in salinity and is thus often found in brackish water, where it finds plenty of food. It changes sex with age: The young are male and then become female. At this stage they lay their eggs.

Inland seas and lagoons

In shallow coastal waters the vegetation is almost always plentiful and varied, especially in lagoons where the influx of fresh water enables even certain flowering plants to grow. Nevertheless, algae predominate, represented by species that differ according to whether the substratum is muddy, sandy or rocky, the amount of water movement and, above all, the depth. In the upper layers of water, where there is more light, green algae tend to be most abundant, while with the progressive increase of depth, brown and red algae gradually replace the green forms.

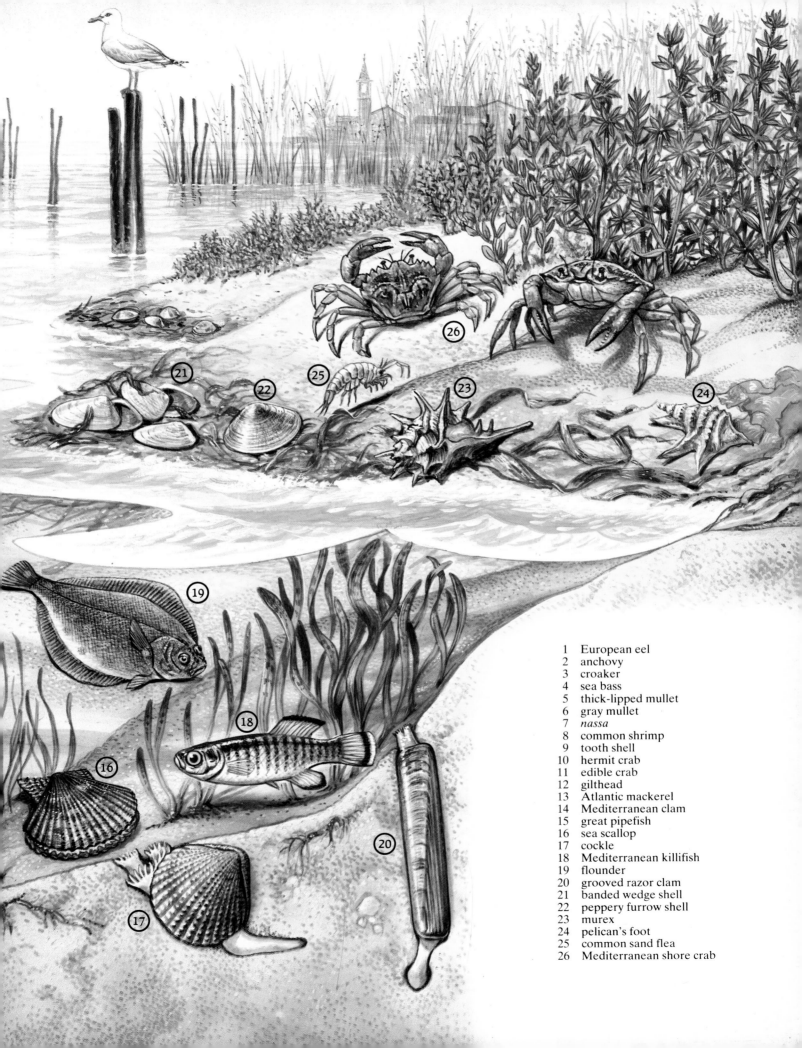

1 European eel
2 anchovy
3 croaker
4 sea bass
5 thick-lipped mullet
6 gray mullet
7 *nassa*
8 common shrimp
9 tooth shell
10 hermit crab
11 edible crab
12 gilthead
13 Atlantic mackerel
14 Mediterranean clam
15 great pipefish
16 sea scallop
17 cockle
18 Mediterranean killifish
19 flounder
20 grooved razor clam
21 banded wedge shell
22 peppery furrow shell
23 murex
24 pelican's foot
25 common sand flea
26 Mediterranean shore crab

GRAY MULLET
Mugil cephalus

Classification Class: Osteichthyes; Order: Perciformes; Family: Mugilidae.
Description Length up to 28 in (70 cm), weight up to about 18 lb (8 kg). Back dark green, blue or black; sides silver-gray.
Distribution All oceans, including Mediterranean Sea.
Habitat Coastal waters, even brackish. It tolerates salinity equivalent to barely one-tenth that of seawater.
Behavior Often gregarious, it can leap out of the water. It feeds on algae, small invertebrates and various kinds of detritus found in mud. It spawns in the fall.
Note A relative is the Thick-lipped Mullet *(Chelon labrosus)*, which is vegetarian.

GREAT PIPEFISH
Syngnathus acus

Classification Class: Osteichthyes; Order: Gasterosteiformes; Family: Syngnathidae.
Description Length up to 18 in (45 cm). Color variable: reddish, greenish, brown or gray, generally with alternating light and dark spots. Very long body, distinctive in outline, with an elongated head that looks like a thin tubular snout. The male has a ventral incubating pouch.
Distribution Along European coasts, represented by different races.
Habitat Seabeds covered with algae and posidonias.
Behavior The female lays eggs in the male's incubating pouch, where they remain until they hatch. These orange-red eggs, 300-400 in number, measure 2 mm across. The newborn fry measure about 1 in (2.4-2.8 cm) long and have a bent head.
Note In the Seahorse *(Hippocampus hippocampus)*, related to the Pipefish, it is likewise the male who cares for the young.

GROOVED RAZOR CLAM
Solen marginatus

Classification Phylum: Mollusca; Class: Bivalves; Order: Eulamellibranchia; Family: Solenidae.
Description Also known as the Razor Shell. Length up to 5 in (13 cm). Elongated shell, almost rectangular. The animal holds itself vertically in the sand; the two siphons for breathing and feeding are thus situated near the top, while the feet, at the opposite end, enable the clam to bury itself rapidly in the sand.
Distribution European coasts.
Habitat Sandy seabeds.
Behavior Feeds on food particles borne by the currents, the inhalant siphon passing them into the gill chamber. It reproduces in spring, laying numerous eggs from which emerge tiny planktonic larvae.

MEDITERRANEAN CLAM
Chamelea gallina

Classification Phylum: Mollusca; Class: Bivalves; Order: Eulamellibranchia; Family: Veneridae.
Description Shell of about 1 in (2-2.5 cm), with close concentric bands, white with brown patterns that are very variable. The hinge which holds the two valves in the correct position is made up of three notches.
Distribution Mediterranean Sea, Black Sea.
Habitat Shallow sandy seabeds.
Behavior It lives buried in the sand, with only the two siphons protruding, so that there is a continual exchange of water: the water passes through the gills, releasing oxygen and food particles.
Note Other bivalve species widely found on sandy seabeds include the Banded Wedge Shell *(Donax trunculus)* and the Peppery Furrow Shell *(Scrobicularia plana)*, with a flat shell.

MEDITERRANEAN KILLIFISH
Aphanius fasciatus

Classification Class: Osteichthyes; Order: Cyprinodontiformes; Family: Cyprinodontidae.
Description Length up to 2½ in (6 cm). Color varies according to sex: The male has a brown or bluish back, and the sides have ten white stripes alternating with others which are the same color as the back. The female is lighter, with 10-14 white stripes on the sides.
Distribution Mediterranean Sea.
Habitat Brackish water.
Behavior It tolerates considerable variations in salinity and can also live in fresh water. Feeds on tiny animals.

MEDITERRANEAN SHORE CRAB
Carcinus mediterraneus

Classification Phylum: Arthropoda; Class: Crustacea; Order: Decapoda; Family: Portunidae.
Description Length of carapace 1½ in (4 cm), width 3 in (8 cm). Back greenish-brown, underparts yellowish. Pedunculate (stalked) eyes. Lower limbs provided with fairly strong chelae.
Distribution Mediterranean Sea.
Habitat Sandy seabeds.
Behavior An animal of the seabed, it is nevertheless able to swim. The female carries many small eggs in a ventral incubating pouch beneath the folded abdomen.

MUREX
Phyllonotus trunculus

Classification Phylum: Mollusca; Class: Gastropoda; Order: Neogastropoda; Family: Muricidae.

Description Length of shell up to about 3 in (7 cm). The foot of the mollusc is provided with an operculum (gill cover) which closes the opening of the shell when the animal withdraws inside it.
Distribution Mediterranean Sea, northeastern Atlantic Ocean.
Habitat Any type of hard substratum.
Behavior A predator, it also feeds on dead animals. The female lays eggs in enormous gelatinous masses.
Note Another distinctive gastropod is the Pelican's Foot *(Aporrhais pespelecani)*, in which the mouth of the shell is expanded to form appendages similar to the toes of a bird.

SEA BASS
Dicentrarchus labrax

Classification Class: Osteichthyes; Order: Perciformes; Family: Serranidae.
Description Length up to about 3 ft (1 m), weight up to 26 lb (12 kg). Color silver, tending to green on upper parts. The young are slightly spotted.
Distribution Northeastern Atlantic Ocean, Mediterranean Sea, Black Sea.
Habitat Varied types of seabed, lagoons.
Behavior A predator which feeds mainly on other fish. It spawns from January to March.

TOOTH SHELL
Dentalium entalius

Classification Phylum: Mollusca; Class: Scaphopoda; Order: Dentaliiformes; Family: Dentaliidae.
Description Also called the Elephant's Tusk Shell. Up to 2½ in (6 cm) long, whitish, shaped like a slender tusk and slightly curved; the surface is lined with thin ribs. The shell is open at both ends, allowing water to flow in and out.
Distribution European coasts.
Habitat Soft seabeds, in which it lives buried.
Behavior Only the rear tip of the shell habitually protrudes from the sand. There are separate sexes and development is indirect, with planktonic larvae.

The abyss

ABYSSAL BRACHIOPOD
Abyssothyris sp.

Classification Phylum: Brachiopoda; Class: Articulata; Family: Terebratulidae.

Description Length 1 in (2 cm). Sedentary animal furnished with a shell which gives it the outward appearance of a bivalve mollusc; in the brachiopod, however, the two valves of the shell are dorsal and ventral respectively, not left and right. The mouth opening is surrounded by two fringed arms, the appendages of which create a current of water essential for breathing and feeding.

Distribution Seas of the southern hemisphere.

Habitat Abyssal depths.

Behavior Not known. Like Brachiopods of shallower waters, it is probably a filter-feeder. Feeding on tiny animal particles conveyed to the mouth by the two fringed arms.

ABYSSAL OCTOPUS
Cirrothauma murrayi

Classification Phylum: Mollusca; Class: Cephalopoda; Order: Octopoda; Family: Cirroteuthoidae.

Description Overall length up to 8 in (20 cm). It is the only cephalopod which has become blind as one of the adaptations to life in the abyss. Its tentacles are provided with special structures, derived from the transformation of the customary suckers, which are believed to be luminescent, probably used by the octopus to ensnare prey.

Distribution Northern Atlantic Ocean.

Habitat At depths of about 6,500-10,000 ft (2,000-3,000 m).

Behavior Abyssal waters are also the home of giant squid belonging to the family Architeuthidae. The largest specimen so far observed (off the coast of Newfoundland) measured about 72 ft (22 m) overall, including body and arms. Giant squid are the habitual prey of sperm whales, and fierce fights take place between these species in the depths of the ocean.

BARRELEYE
Opisthoproctus soleatus

Classification Class: Osteichthyes; Order: Salmoniformes; Family: Opisthoproctidae.

Description Length about 4 in (10 cm). Massive body, with a flattened ventral plate projecting slightly forward, similar to a sole, hence the specific name. Very small mouth with weak, toothless jaws. Telescopic eyes, turned upward. Brownish-black color heightened by silvery luminescence, especially on the sides and in the eye region.

Distribution Pacific and Indian Oceans.

Habitat Abyssal depths, from about 3,000-10,000 ft (1,000-3,000 m).

Behavior It probably consumes small, soft food particles.

BLACK SWALLOWER
Chiasmodon niger

Classification Class: Osteichthyes; Order: Perciformes; Family: Chiasmodontidae.

Description Length 2 in (5 cm). Body fairly long and compressed, almost without scales. Very prominent lower jaw with two rows of long teeth.

Distribution Warmest part of the Atlantic, Pacific and Indian Oceans.

Habitat Abyssal depths.

Behavior A highly voracious predator, it is capable of swallowing quite large prey thanks to its stomach, which can be enormously expanded.

CHIMAERA
Chimaera monstrosa

Classification Class: Chondrichthyes; Subclass: Holocephali; Order: Chimaeriformes; Family: Chimaeridae.

Description Length up to 3-5 ft (1-1.5 m). Body laterally compressed, with a large head which has fairly big eyes and a mouth positioned low down, like that of a shark; the body becomes progressively thinner toward the rear, culminating in a very long tail. Large pectoral and ventral fins. Color silvery, usually variegated with brown; dorsal and anal fins black-bordered. On his forehead the male has a curious appendage covered with spines.

Distribution Mediterranean Sea and eastern coasts of Atlantic Ocean.

Habitat Fairly deep water, even below 3,000 ft (1,000 m).

Behavior Feeds on small fish and varied invertebrates. The female lays large eggs, especially in summer, with a parchment-like shell, up to 6 in (16 cm) long.

COMMON LANTERNFISH
Myctophum punctatum

Classification Class: Osteichthyes; Order: Myctophiformes; Family: Myctophidae.

Description Length up to 4 in (10 cm). Grayish in color with numerous visible photopores (light-producing organs) arranged principally in long lines on the lower part of the sides. The fairly big eyes are reddish.

Distribution Mediterranean Sea and northern Atlantic Ocean.

Habitat At depths of around 1,650 ft (500 m).

Behavior Feeds on plankton. Every day it travels considerable distances vertically, spending the night in surface waters. The larvae have characteristic stalked eyes, acquiring their definitive appearance when they measure about 1 in (2 cm) in length.

Note Another member of the family is Risso's Lanternfish (*Electrona rissoi*), 3 in (8 cm) long and distributed in the Mediterranean Sea, the Atlantic and Indian Oceans and beyond, to the Tasman Sea.

DEEPSEA ANGLER
Linophryne arborifer

Classification Class: Osteichthyes; Order: Lophiiformes; Suborder: Ceratioidea; Family: Linophrynidae.

Description Length up to 8 in (20 cm). Blackish body, apart from the tree-like structure on the chin, which is reddish. The shape of the body is very distinctive: The head is hardly separated from the trunk, so that together they form a single globular mass which is extended behind into a short tail. The mouth is enormous and provided with long teeth; the eyes are small, the operculum which covers the gills is armed with long spines. On the head, in front of the eyes, is a long appendage which serves as a bait for trapping the fish on which it feeds; in the darkness of the abyss this bait becomes luminous. However, the fish possesses a second luminescent system in the form of the branching appendage on the chin; the light from this is due to a chemical process controlled by the fish itself.

Distribution All three major oceans.

Habitat Abyssal depths, usually below about 6,500 ft (2,000 m).

Behavior A predatory creature, it feeds mainly on other fish. The males, which are much smaller than their partners, lead a free-swimming existence for a short time, then attach themselves to the body of the female, becoming, in a sense, their parasites.

GIANT OARFISH
Regalecus glesne

Classification Class: Osteichthyes; Order: Lampridiformes; Family: Regalecidae.

Description Also known as King-of-the-Herrings. Length 16-20 ft (5-6 m), perhaps up to 33 ft (10 m). The body is very elongated and tapered, and laterally compressed, the length being about twenty times the height, which is virtually constant from the head to most of the trunk and tail. The dorsal fin is furnished with 300-400 rays, the first of which are much longer than the rest and form a distinctive tuft. The ventral fins are each reduced to

The abyss

The great ocean depths represent one of the few habitats where life consists entirely of animal forms. Plants are unable to survive in the deepest strata of water because there is no light in the abyss; and plants must have light for the formation of chlorophyll. Even the remains of dead or decaying plants that grow in surface water barely reach abyssal depths; as they drift down, in fact, they are inevitably snapped up by a fish or other sea creature, ever on the lookout for sources of food such as these, which become increasingly scarce with depth.

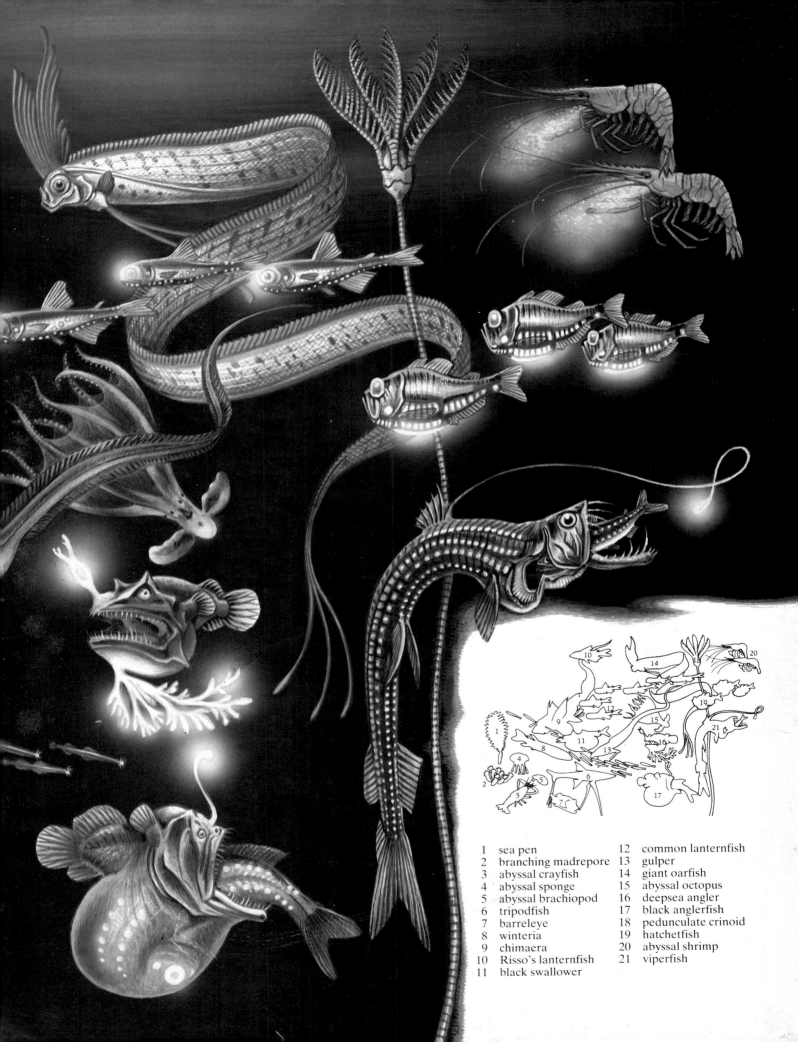

a simple long ray. The skin is naked, without scales. The mouth contains no teeth. The color is silver, with numerous little brown spots arranged in undefined rows. The fins are bright red.

Distribution   All seas, world-wide.

Habitat   Usually found at depths of several hundred feet.

Behavior   It swims by unudulating the whole body, like a snake. The eggs, 2.5 mm in diameter, contain small oily droplets which allow them to float. Before reaching a length of 2 in (5 cm), the larva has already changed into a miniature oarfish, similar to the adult. The strange alternative vernacular name, used in some countries in the northern hemisphere, stems from the belief that the fish accompanies shoals of herring in their migration.

GULPER
Eurypharynx pelecanoides

Classification   Class: Osteichthyes; Order: Anguilliformes; Family: Eurypharyngidae.

Description   Length about 3 ft (1 m). Soft eel-like body with a strangely shaped head and enormous mouth; the jaws, furnished with tiny and extraordinarily dilatable teeth, may measure up to one-third of the total length of the fish. The body is blackish, with a white line along the sides of the dorsal fin.

Distribution   Almost all tropical and subtropical seas.

Habitat   Abyssal waters, up to a depth of about 26,000 ft (8,000 m).

Behavior   Little known. The diet probably consists of plankton and small fish.

HATCHETFISH
Argyropelecus hemigymnus

Classification   Class: Osteichthyes; Order: Salmoniformes; Family: Sternoptichidae.

Description   Length 2½ in (6 cm). Body very laterally compressed, broad in front and much smaller toward the tail, shiny silver in color, with black spots on the back, at the base of the tail and around the pink photophores, from which the fish emits light.

Distribution   Mediterranean Sea and Atlantic Ocean to a depth of about 13,000 ft (4,000 m).

Habitat   It is a typical abyssal fish. Only very occasionally – for example, near the Strait of Messina – will the movement of the water carry it to the surface where it may rarely be seen stranded on beaches.

Behavior   It spawns throughout the year, but especially in spring. The eggs, 1 mm in diameter, are lightweight, oily and floating. After two days a larva is hatched, 2.5 mm long.

JOHNSON'S BLACK ANGLERFISH
Melanocetus johnstoni

Classification   Class: Osteichthyes; Order: Lophiiformes; Suborder: Ceratioidea; Family: Melanocetidae.

Description   Length 2 in (5 cm). Blackish color. Body very short, with highly extensible teguments. The jaws, too, with their long pointed teeth, can also be enormously expanded. There is a bait-filament on the head, terminating in a mass that contains the light-producing batteries.

Distribution   Atlantic Ocean.

Habitat   Deep abyssal waters.

Behavior   A predator of fish, it can swallow animals twice its own size. Young males can feed independently, but soon they attach themselves to the body of a female, becoming parasites.

SEA PEN
Pennatula sp.

Classification   Phylum: Coelenterata; Class: Anthozoa; Order: Pennatulacea; Family: Pennatulidae.

Description   Length up to 12 in (30 cm). It is a colonial animal, in which two different types are identifiable: The founding polyp, much bigger than the others, constitutes the main axis of the pen and lives on the seabed, its lower part buried in the substratum; the secondary polyps, which form by budding from the founding polyp, remain attached to the latter. These secondary polyps have the characteristic form of small flowers, with the mouth surrounded by tentacles. The colony can emit a beautiful blue-green luminescence.

Distribution   The genus is widely found in all seas.

Habitat   At medium depths.

Behavior   Although it generally leads a sedentary existence, the Sea Pen can move about on the seabed.

Note Among other coelenterates found in the abyss are the branching madrepores (stone corals) of the genus *Dendrophylla*.

TRIPODFISH
Bathypterois sp.

Classification   Class: Osteichthyes; Order: Myctophiformes; Family: Bathypteroidae.

Description   Length 8-12 in (20-30 cm). Elongated body with pointed head and very small eyes. The fins, especially the ventral (pelvic) fins, are very big, and each furnished with a stiff ray capable of supporting the fish's weight; in addition to these two supports there is another, represented by the lower lobe of the caudal fin. They thus form a tripod, from which the vernacular name is derived.

Distribution   Atlantic and Indian Oceans.

Habitat   Muddy beds at medium depths.

Behavior   Feeds on small crustaceans, but it is not known how it catches them.

VIPERFISH
Chauliodus sp.

Classification   Class: Osteichthyes; Order: Salmoniformes; Family: Chauliodontidae.

Description   Length up to 12 in (30 cm). Color gray or blackish, darker on lower side, with some metallic reflections. Body very long, almost straight, with a big head and a large mouth equipped with long teeth; the forward dorsal fin has a very long spinelike ray. Photophores, the luminescent organs, are scattered over the abdomen.

Distribution   It is found, although not in a continuous manner, in most temperate and tropical seas.

Habitat   At depths of about 1,650-3,300 ft (500-1,000 m), but has been caught at about 9,000 ft (2,800 m).

Behavior   A voracious predator, it feeds on other abyssal fish. The long ray on the dorsal fin has at the tip a small luminescent bait for attracting prey. The eggs float, although they lack the oily droplets found in the eggs of other fish. The larvae are about 1½ in (4 cm) long.

WINTERIA
Winteria telescopus

Classification   Class: Osteichthyes; Order: Salmoniformes; Family: Opisthoproctidae.

Description   Length about 6 in (15 cm). Body covered with large scales which fall off easily. Big tubular eyes, rather like those of the Barreleye. Mouth with weak jaws.

Distribution   Eastern tropical part of Atlantic Ocean.

Habitat   Abyssal waters.

Behavior   Not known; only a very few specimens have so far been caught.

Coral reefs

ANEMONE FISH
Amphiprion percula

Classification Class: Osteichthyes; Order: Perciformes; Family: Pomacentridae.

Description Length 3 in (8 cm). Color orange, with three vertical black-bordered white bands.

Distribution Seas around Australia and Melanesia; many other related species in Indopacific waters.

Habitat Coral reefs.

Behavior It lives in symbiosis with the sea anemones of the genus *Stichodactyla*, being unaffected by the poison from their sting cells. Settling near an anemone, the male fish cleans a small area of seabed, where the female later lays her eggs. Both parents incubate them together.

BLUE CORAL
Heliopora coerulea

Classification Phylum: Coelenterata; Class: Anthozoa; Order: Helioporaceae; Family: Hellioporidae.

Distribution Colonial organism. It forms branched skeletal structures, shaped like a hand; when alive it takes on a beautiful blue color, hence its common name.

Distribution Indian Ocean and western coasts of the Pacific Ocean.

Habitat Coral reefs.

Behavior The small polyps, brown in color, form a symbiotic relationship with tiny algae which lodge in their tissues. Details of reproduction and growth are unknown.

FUNGUS CORAL
Fungia sp.

Classification Phylum: Coelenterata; Class: Anthozoa; Order: Sclerotinia; Family: Fungiidae.

Description Large solitary polyps (unlike other madrepores, which are colonial), constructing skeletons similar to the cap of a fungus, with numerous plates, 4 in (10 cm), or more in diameter. Coloration very variable.

Distribution Indopacific waters.

Habitat Coral reefs.

Behavior In its cycle of growth it displays a characteristic alternation of sexual and asexual reproduction.

GIANT CLAM
Tridacna gigas

Classification Phylum: Mollusca; Class: Bivalves; Order: Eulamellibranchia; Family: Tridacnidae.

Description Giant mollusc, the shell of which may be up to 5 ft (1.5 m) wide, weighing over 440 lb (200 kg).

Distribution Indopacific waters.

Habitat Coral reefs.

Behavior The giant shell may be partially submerged among corals or jut out completely in the water, in which case it is anchored to the reef by the byssus. The half-closed valves let in water, which contains food in the form of plankton, as well as the light necessary to the algae that live in symbiosis within the clam's shell.

GORGONID
Gorgonia sp.

Classification Phylum: Coelenterata; Class: Anthozoa; Order: Gorgonaria; Family: Gorgonidae.

Description A colonial animal whose polyps build horn-like fan-shaped skeletons, up to 3 ft (1 m) high; the color is yellow or violet.

Distribution Indian Ocean.

Habitat Shallow waters in the sublittoral zone.

Behavior Sedentary organisms, with very restricted relationships, gorgonids feed on tiny planktonic animals borne on the currents.

HORNED BOXFISH
Lactoria cornuta

Classification Class: Osteichthyes; Order: Tetraodontiformes; Family: Ostracionidae.

Description Also known as the Trunkfish. Length up to 20 in (50 cm). Body reddish-brown with darker spots, very stiff because covered with bony plates. Two distinctive protuberances jut out above the eyes.

Distribution Indian and Pacific Oceans.

Habitat Coral reefs.

Behavior Because of its rigid structure, it swims slowly, feeding on tiny planktonic invertebrates. It possesses many poisonous skin glands which pour out a toxic substance into the surrounding water, providing defense against aggressors. However, the Boxfish is sensitive to its own poison.

LIONFISH
Pterois volitans

Classification Class: Osteichthyes; Order: Scorpaeniformes; Family: Scorpaenidae.

Description Length 14 in (35 cm). Large fins, especially the pectorals, which are broadly fringed. Very big mouth. Ventral, dorsal and anal fins bear poisonous rays. Color reddish-brown with transverse stripes.

Distribution Entire Indopacific region.

Habitat Coral reefs, especially tracts with abundant vegetation.

Behavior It is active mainly at night and feeds on crustaceans and fish. Fertilization is internal; the eggs deposited form a floating mass. Little is known about development.

MOORISH IDOL
Zanclus canescens

Classification Class: Osteichthyes; Order: Perciformes; Family: Acanthuridae.

Description Length up to 10 in (25 cm). Body fairly compressed, almost diskshaped; the adult has a spine above the eyes.

Distribution Indian Ocean; eastern and western basins of Pacific Ocean.

Habitat Along coasts, at no great depth.

Behavior Aggressive and territorial, it is a vegetarian.

ORGANPIPE CORAL
Tubipora musica

Classification Phylum: Coelenterata; Class: Anthozoa; Order: Alcyonaria; Family: Tubiporidae.

Description Colonial animal, shaped like a huge mass of parallel calcareous tubes, joined together by overlapping plates, perpendicular to them. The entire coral appears red, because of the iron salts present in the calcium carbonate of which the skeleton is formed. The tiny polyps which sprout from the ends of the tubes are greenish.

Distribution Tropical coasts of Indopacific area.

Habitat Coral reefs.

Behavior Feeds on small planktonic organisms.

PARROTFISH
Scarus coeruleus
Pseudoscarus guacamaia

Classification Class: Osteichthyes; Order: Perciformes; Family: Scaridae.

Description Length 12-16 in (30-40 cm). Very bright colors, blue-green in the Blue Parrotfish (*Scarus coeruleus*), golden yellow in the Rainbow Parrotfish (*Pseudoscarus guacamaia*). The teeth are welded together to form sturdy plates which have the appearance of a beak. Body covered with fairly large scales.

Distribution Both species inhabit the east coasts of America, from Florida to Brazil, and the Caribbean region.

Habitat Coastal zones near coral reefs.

Behavior Parrotfish feed literally on the thinnest branches of madrepores; in this way they are responsible for the continuous large-scale erosion of coral structures. They spend the night in a sort of cocoon, made of mucous material, which is secreted every evening by numerous cutaneous glands.

Coral reefs

The great builders of the coral reefs are the colonial corals known as madrepores, whose enormous skeletons are constituted of limestone. But many algae, particularly the red species, also have skeletal structures which play a part in enlarging and extending reefs: one group of such algae is known by the name coralline. The coral reefs are also inhabited, of course, by all kinds of other soft algae.

1 tropical sea anemone
2 anemone fish
3 striped surgeonfish
4 sea catfish
5 *Platygyra*
6 staghorn coral
7 cerianthid
8 triggerfish
9 organpipe coral
10 *Acropora dichotoma*
11 *Madrepora stellata*
12 *Stenopus* shrimp
13 horned boxfish
14 blue coral

15 zebra surgeonfish
16 sergeantmajor
17 blue parrotfish
18 Moorish idol
19 giant clam
20 fungus coral
21 lionfish
22 slate pencil
      sea urchin
23 rainbow parrotfish
24 gorgonid
25 unicorn surgeonfish
26 *Madrepora oculata*
27 *Acropora palmata*

SEA CATFISH
Plotosus lineatus
Classification Class: Osteichthyes; Order: Siluriformes; Family: Plotosidae.
Description Length 8-12 in (20-30 cm). Color brownish, with four whitish longitudinal lines. As in all catfish, there are numerous pairs of barbels. The paired fins have sharp rays, connected to poison glands.
Distribution Indopacific region.
Habitat Coral reefs.
Behavior A gregarious, predatory animal.

SERGEANTMAJOR
Abudefduf saxatilis
Classification Class: Osteichthyes; Order: Perciformes; Family: Pomacentridae.
Description Length 3-4 in (8-10 cm). Body relatively short and compressed; small mouth; large dorsal fin; ventral fins prolonged into a spine. Color blue-green with darker vertical stripes.
Distribution Waters of Indopacific region.
Habitat Coral reefs.
Behavior Lives in shoals but each fish is markedly independent. The males are strongly territorial and in the spawning season fiercely defend their nest and look after the eggs.

SLATE PENCIL SEA URCHIN
Heterocentrotus mammillatus
Classification Phylum: Echinodermata; Class: Echinoidea; Order: Echinoidea; Family: Echinometridae.
Description Large sea urchin with bright red, pencil-like spines; its diameter is almost 12 in (30 cm).
Distribution Warm waters of Indopacific region.
Habitat Coral reefs.
Behavior It moves slowly on the seabed, using the many pedicels which sprout from the lower side of the body. It feeds on small organisms, scraping them from rock surfaces.

STAGHORN CORAL
Acropora palmata
Classification Phylum: Coelenterata; Class: Anthozoa; Order: Sclerotinia; Family: Acroporidae.
Description One of the many stony reef-building corals or madrepores, the skeletons of which constitute the bony framework of coral reefs. A colonial animal, it forms branching structures, their color varying from yellow to green or brown.
Distribution Waters of Indopacific region.
Habitat Coral reefs.

Behavior It feeds on tiny planktonic organisms.

STENOPUS SHRIMP
Stenopus hispidus
Classification Phylum: Arthropoda; Class: Crustacea; Order: Decapoda; Family: Stenopodidae.
Description Length about 2 in (5 cm). Head and thorax covered with a spiny carapace, with transverse red and white stripes. Very long antennae. The first three pairs of feet are furnished with tiny chelae.
Distribution Indopacific waters.
Habitat Seabeds, coral reefs.
Behavior The female carries the eggs between her abdominal appendages, which form a kind of incubating pouch.

STONY CORALS
Acropora dichotoma
Madrepora oculata
Classification Phylum: Coelenterata; Class: Anthozoa; Order: Sclerotinia; Family: Acroporidae (for *Acropora*), Oculinidae (for *Madrepora*).
Description The stony corals or madrepores are colonial organisms which build remarkably complex calcareous skeletons, the shapes of which vary even within the same species, according to the conditions of the environment. The single individuals which form a colony are tiny polyps with a mouth surrounded by tentacles, in multiples of six.
Distribution Warm seas.
Habitat Warm, well-lit surface waters.
Behavior The relations between various madrepores is virtually irrelevant, for on the zoological scale these are very primitive sedentary organisms. The tiny one-celled algae that live in symbiosis within the cells of these stony corals need light to carry out chlorophyllous photosynthesis, and for this reason the madrepores cannot live in deep or turbid water. The subtracted carbon dioxide used by these algae in photosynthesis stimulates the deposition of the calcium carbonate which forms the skeletons of the madrepores.

SURGEONFISH
Acanthurus lineatus, A. velifer, Naso unicornis
Classification Class: Osteichthyes; Order: Perciformes; Family: Acanthuridae.
Description All surgeonfish possess two sharp caudal spines, which account for the common name. The livery is often multicolored, as in the case of *A. lineatus*, which can be up to 8 in (20 cm) long, with closely alternating blue, black and brown bands on the flanks. The colors of *N. unicornis* are less spectacular, but there is a distinctive appendage, up to 2 in (5 cm) in length, on the head. *A. velifer* is likewise quite big, about 16 in (40 cm) long.
Distribution Indian and Pacific Oceans.
Habitat Coral reefs.
Behavior These are aggressive fish, with territorial inclinations. Little is known of their reproductive biology.

TRIGGERFISH
Balistoides conspicillum
Classification Class: Osteichthyes; Order: Tetraodontiformes; Family: Balistidae.
Description Length up to 20 in (50 cm). Very gaudy livery, blackish with white spots on flanks and belly, and orange patterns around mouth, on forehead, back and fins; the fins also have blue bands and spots. Small mouth with a few conical teeth.
Distribution Indian and Pacific Oceans.
Habitat Coral reefs.
Behavior Solitary animal, fairly sedentary. Feeds on invertebrates caught on the seabed. It is capable of nibbling pieces of stony coral with its strong jaws.

TROPICAL SEA ANEMONE
Stichodactyla sp.
Classification Phylum: Coelenterata; Class: Anthozoa; Order: Actiniaria; Family: Stichodactylidae.
Description Typical sedentary polypoid form, with a tight crown of tentacles around the mouth. Dimensions vary according to species from very tiny up to a couple of inches; colors are also variable, usually yellow or pink.
Distribution Indian and Pacific Oceans.
Habitat Coral reefs.
Behavior Food consists of prey killed with the stinging tentacles.

Glossary

Amphibians Class of vertebrates capable of living both on land and in water. The latter environment is, with a few exceptions, indispensable for reproduction which, in the majority of cases, occurs by means of egglaying. As a rule the larvae are aquatic and provided with gills, while the adults, after metamorphosis, are terrestrial and furnished with lungs. The temperature of the body, covered by a particularly slippery skin, varies according to the surroundings. This class includes frogs, toads, salamanders and newts.

Arthropods Types of invertebrate with the body divided into segments, each furnished with a pair of legs. They include, among others, Crustacea (crabs, shrimp, lobsters, etc), Myriapoda (millipedes), Chilopoda (centipedes), Insecta and Arachnida (spiders, scorpions, etc).

Birds Class of vertebrates with a body covered by feathers; forelimbs transformed into wings; hind limbs adapted for walking on two feet (bipedal locomotion); hollow bones which, by lightening the overall weight of the animal, facilitate flying. All birds have a bill and lack teeth. The flying species – the vast majority – have well-developed pectoral (flight) muscles. The females lay eggs which have a calcareous shell. The body temperature remains constant, regardless of the outside temperature.

Breeding season Period in the year when an animal species is concerned with reproduction: As a rule this is the time when they form pairs or harems of varying numbers, and when they build nests or burrows for rearing their young. This period culminates either in the birth of fully formed young or in the laying of eggs which hatch after an incubation of varying duration.

Cells The structural and functional units of which living organisms are constituted. There are unicellular (one-celled) forms such as bacteria and protozoans, but the majority of living beings – animals and plants – are made up of many cells, often numbered in thousands of millions, individually invisible to the naked eye.

Colony Collection of animals of the same species, which, to a lesser or greater degree, live together in close association.

Courtship display A ceremony, often very complex and spectacular, performed by males of certain animal groups (especially birds) in order to attract the attention of the females. In the course of these displays they show off their livery, usually much more colorful than that of their partners, and also indulge in mimicry and song.

Cyclostomes Superclass of aquatic vertebrates, similar in form to eels. They are commonly known as lampreys and attack fish with their circular jawless mouth, sucking their blood.

Embryo Animal or plant organism in the first phase of development after fertilization.

Fish Superclass of aquatic vertebrates with a body covered by scales. They breathe with gills and swim with the aid of appendages called fins. The skeleton may be cartilaginous (sharks and rays) or bony (all others). The body temperature varies with that of the water. With a few exceptions, they are oviparous.

Gestation The period in which the embryo is growing in the mother's body.

Gregarious Any animal that lives in groups.

Habitat Environment in which a species lives, at least for some part of its existence.

Hibernation A more or less deep sleep in which all vital functions (heartbeat, breathing rate, etc) are slowed down, and during which all accumulated stores of fat are consumed.

Incubation Care of the eggs by mother, father or both parents by placing themselves over them or by enveloping them with their body, thus providing warmth and protection. Not all oviparous animals practice incubation: Many (especially invertebrates but also some fish, amphibians and reptiles) abandon the eggs to their fate.

Insects Class of arthropods which displays a richer variety of forms and adaptations than any other group in the animal kingdom. They are covered with a strong but elastic cuticle which supports them and prevents them from drying out. The body is divided into head, thorax and abdomen. The head is furnished with a pair of antennae, two compound eyes and mouthparts. The thorax comprises three segments to which are attached three pairs of legs and, in flying species, one or two pairs of wings. The abdomen is formed of a variable number of segments, with or without appendages. With some exceptions, insects reproduce by laying eggs. When they hatch, the larvae are, to a varying extent, dissimilar to the adults. The adult stage is attained either by straightforward growth (in more primitive groups) or after spectacular metamorphosis. The mature insect has a short life, exclusively devoted to reproduction.

Invertebrates All animals which do not have a vertebral column. They include unicellular organisms, sponges, jellyfish, corals, worms, insects, spiders, scorpions, centipedes, starfish, etc.

Larva Animal just emerged from the egg with appearance and behavior very different from those of the adult; it attains the latter stage after metamorphosis.

Livery The overall coloration of various animals, especially the plumage of birds.

Mammals Class of vertebrates comprising the subclasses Monotremata, Marsupialia and Placentalia, which have in common a constant body temperature independent of outside temperature fluctuations, and the presence of hair and nipples. The latter, in the females, secrete milk on which the young feed.

Marsupials Subclass of land mammals. The young are born very early and complete their development in a pouch of skin, known as the marsupium, situated on the mother's abdomen. Inside are the nipples, to which the young remain attached for some time.

Metamorphosis The transformation undergone during the course of growth, when an animal develops from larva to adult, for example from a caterpillar to a butterfly or from a tadpole to a frog.

Migration A journey, usually seasonal, undertaken by an animal, as winter approaches, in order to reach warmer areas. Certain animals migrate solely for the purpose of breeding, such as the eel or salmon.

Monotremes Fairly primitive subclass of land mammals. Although they are covered in hair and produce milk, they have many distinctive features of reptiles and birds. They lay eggs, lack teeth and have only one opening for expelling feces, urine, sperm and eggs. Their body temperature fluctuates by a few degrees, according to variations in outside temperature.

Oviparous Animal which lays eggs, inside which the embryo completes its development.

Ovoviviparous Animal which reproduces by laying eggs which are retained in the mother's body until they hatch, so that the young are born already fully formed.

Placentals Subclass which comprises the majority of present-day mammals. The embryo develops in the mother's womb and is linked to her by the placenta, a specialized organ through which it receives food and oxygen, at the same time getting rid of carbon dioxide and other waste substances.

Reptiles Class of land vertebrates (very few species lead an aquatic life) with the body covered by horn-like or bony scales which protect it from drying out. With the exception of a few lizards and almost all snakes, they have four legs suitable for walking on land, for swimming or for both functions. Apart from some ovoviviparous species, they lay eggs with a shell, inside which the embryo is immersed in a protective liquid. The body temperature depends on that of the environment. They include turtles, lizards, snakes and crocodiles.

Social Animals which live together in communities, in which each individual has a defined role and is either dominant or subordinate in relation to others, for example bees or ants.

Territory Area defended by an individual or by a group of individuals of the same species, to prevent it being occupied by intruders. It may be a hunting territory or a breeding territory; in the latter males will accept the presence of females of their own species, but not other males. The bounds of a territory are often marked with scent (urine or substances produced by various glands) or proclaimed vocally: the twittering of many birds in spring is essentially a call to the female and a warning to other males.

Tetrapod Superclass of vertebrates with four limbs.

Vertebrates Animals with a vertebral column and a skull which protects the brain, usually highly developed. They include the superclasses Cyclostomata, Fish and Tetrapoda. The last are subdivided into the classes Amphibia, Reptilia, Aves and Mammalia.

Viviparous Animal which does not lay eggs but gives birth to young that are already fully formed, although considerably smaller than the adults.

Index

Figures in italics refer to captions.
The word *in* indicates that the animal is referred to in the entry in the end **Note**.

188

Illustrations by:

Lorenzo Orlandi: 3, 30-31, 34-35, 38-39, 42-43, 46-47, 50-51, 126-127, 130-131, 134-135, 138-139, 142-143, 146-147. Alexis Oussenko: 54-55, 58-59, 62-63, 66-67, 70-71, 74-75. Gabriele Pozzi: 6-7, 10-11, 14-15, 18-19, 22-23, 26-27, 154-155, 162-163, 166-167, 170-171, 174-175, 178-179, 182-183. Giorgio Scarato: 150-151 Giorgio Scarato – Franco Spaliviero: 78-79, 82-83, 86-87, 90-91, 94-95, 98-99, 102-103, 106-107, 110-111, 114-115, 118-119, 122-123. Cover by Franco Spaliviero.